EEC ENVIRONMENTAL POLICY AND BRITAIN

Second edition 1987
Second revised edition 1989, 1990

Published by Longman Group UK Limited, Longman Industry and Public
Service Management Publishing Division, Longman House, Burnt Mill,
Harlow, Essex CM20 2JE, UK

First edition 1984 published by Environmental Data Services Ltd (ENDS).

British Library Cataloguing in Publication Data

Haigh, Nigel
  EEC environmental policy and Britain. — 2nd revised ed.
  1. Great Britain. Environment. Conservation Law.
  Effects of European Community Law
  I. Title
  344.104'46

ISBN 0-582-05959-3

The Institute for European Environmental Policy is an independent body for
the analysis of environmental policies in Europe. It seeks to increase the
awareness of the European dimension of environmental protection and to
advance European policy-making.

The Institute is characterised by a close involvement with parliaments, by a
wide network of contacts and by an ability to operate in several countries
simultaneously. The Institute is an integral part of the European Cultural
Foundation but has its own Board responsible for priorities and programmes.

Printed in Great Britain by Bell and Bain Ltd., Glasgow

EEC
ENVIRONMENTAL
POLICY
AND BRITAIN

2nd Revised Edition

Nigel Haigh

To Carola, Emily and Anna

Foreword

1987 has been an historic year for the European Community's environmental policy. The Single European Act which came into force on 1 July has given the EEC Treaty a chapter on the environment for the first time. After 15 years of making policy – some very important – we have come of age! And the European Year of the Environment (EYE) was launched on 21 March with the aim of promoting public awareness of environmental issues. Interest in the environment has never been greater, and the tremendous enthusiasm and hard work of those active in non-governmental organisations and in the voluntary sector are an inspiration to us all. The Institute for European Environmental Policy has been educating us about the European dimension for many years and this new publication is a major contribution to that work.

When Nigel Haigh's essay and handbook 'EEC Environmental Policy and Britain' was published in 1984 it was the first systematic attempt to analyse the practical effects of Community environmental legislation in a member state. Since then, as the number of environmental measures has steadily increased, greater attention has necessarily been focussed on their implementation, now the subject of an important chapter in the Community's Fourth Environmental Action Programme for 1987–92. The United Kingdom has encouraged this development. It is crucial that our efforts in Brussels, including the long nights of negotiation in the Council of Ministers that I experienced during my tenure as Minister for Environmental Protection, should lead to a real improvement in the state of our environment.

The original handbook has become a standard work of reference for those working on environmental protection. I readily agreed to commission Nigel Haigh to update it as a worthy contribution to EYE. I have no doubt that it will become an indispensable tool for everyone with an interest in the European Community's environmental policy.

William Waldegrave
Department of the Environment
August 1987

Preface to reprinted edition of 1990

In the three years since this second edition was published, EC environmental policy has continued its advance and British environmental legislation has been undergoing a long needed reform. When the book was reprinted in 1989 I added a postscript, and that is now replaced by a new and longer postscript. Anyone seeking information in any section of this book should turn to the postscript to see whether any developments are noted. But the postscript, when read as a whole, will also serve to give an impression of the range of recent achievements, even if no comment is made on what is still needed.

The extended appendix now provides a complete chronological list of over 270 items of EC environmental legislation published by the end of August 1990.

I would not have been able to prepare this postscript without the help of Jonathan Hewett. The material was gathered under a consultancy agreement with the Department of the Environment.

Institute for European Environmental Policy   Nigel Haigh
Endsleigh Street, London
August 1990

Preface to the second edition

The Institutions of the European Community (EC) continue to adopt environmental legislation at an astonishing pace. While some is of only limited interest, some is important by any standard and much of it acts as a stimulant to Britain as it attempts to modernize its own policy in this field.

The first edition of this book had two main purposes suggested by its subtitle: 'An Essay and a Handbook'. First, it set out in an easily comprehensible form the full corpus of EC environmental legislation that existed at the end of 1982, together with a discussion of the controversies surrounding each item and its impact in Britain. Second, from this extensive material I was able to draw conclusions on the nature of this entirely new development in environmental policy making and to show how EC policy was providing a yardstick against which Britain's own long established policies now had to be measured.

The adoption of so much new EC legislation in the last four years has rendered the handbook increasingly out of date, as indeed have certain developments in British policy. Accordingly the present book entirely replaces the 'handbook'. While some old material has been retained intact, most has been updated and many sections are entirely new. These include the important Directive on environmental impact assessment which is the first incursion by the EC into the field that in Britain is called town and country planning, and the Regulation introducing the concept of environmentally sensitive areas which is the beginning of a sea change in the Common Agricultural Policy.

Significant changes to British pollution policy are in prospect now that air and water legislation is under review and a unified pollution inspectorate is being established. Some of these changes are at least partly the result of EC legislation so that any new assessment of the overall impact of EC policy on British policy had best await the working out of these developments. In the meanwhile, the original essay still provides the only full discussion of the differences in character between British and EC environmental policy making and an account of that strange episode in nationalism when, to defend a negotiating position, the affected parties in Britain invented a policy for water pollution and claimed it as long established. That particular saga and the related dispute between Britain and other Member States are not yet over.

The 'essay' as a whole has therefore not been updated, nor included in this second edition. The only part that reappears here substantially intact is that discussing different approaches to pollution control. It is important for an understanding of the material that follows and of the dispute referred to above.

Institute for European Environmental Policy   Nigel Haigh
Endsleigh Street, London
July 1987

Acknowledgements

This book is the product of two periods of research undertaken, in its London office, by the Institute for European Environmental Policy. The first, from 1980 to 1983, was financed by the European Cultural Foundation and the Nuffield Foundation and led to the publication of the first edition. The second period of one year, from 1986 to 1987, was financed by the Department of the Environment who had asked me to update the book as a contribution to European Year of the Environment. The Institute and I are grateful for this financial support.

During the first period of research I was assisted for a time by Gertrud Weber (now Mrs Weber-Cooke), and during the second period by Eric Lummis in what should have been his retirement. Eric Lummis had already helped me in many ways during the first period when he was the official at the Department of the Environment responsible for coordinating the Department's dealings with the Community.

So many other people have helped with their time, with documents and information, and by commenting on drafts, that it would be impossible to thank them all by name. The majority, being officials, might prefer not to be identified. Collectively, therefore, I extend my thanks to many officials from central government departments (Department of the Environment particularly, but also of Transport and of Trade); from the Health and Safety Executive and the Nature Conservancy Council; from the Commission in Brussels, and its London office; from local authorities and water authorities; from the select committees of the House of Commons and House of Lords; and from the London office of the European Parliament.

Many industrialists, representatives from trade associations, the Confederation of British Industry and the Chemical Industries Association have been helpful in answering questions.

The following helped with various sections of the first edition: Konrad von Moltke and Cynthia Whitehead with that most complicated but fascinating of all Directives, the 'sixth amendment'; Hubert Meiners with some air Directives; John Parslow, Alistair Gammell and Stuart Housden with the birds Directive; David Gilbert with pesticides; David Baldock with the less favoured areas Directive, and Annie Roncerel with documentation.

For the second edition the following people have contributed substantially: Jilyan Kelly with the drinking water Directive; Alastair Baillie with the 'Seveso' Directive; Bill Sheate and Tony Long with the environmental impact assessment Directive; Simon Lyster with trade in endangered species; Stuart Housden with the birds Directive; and David Baldock with pesticides, less favoured areas, and environmentally sensitive areas.

I have discussed many legal questions with Richard Macrory, barrister, and with my colleague Pascale Kromarek from the Bonn office of the Institute, as well as with other lawyers from inside and outside government and the Commission. The opinions expressed on implementation of Directives nevertheless remain my own.

It is impossible for anyone who wants to follow environmental policy in Britain to do without the monthly *Environmental Data Services (ENDS) Report*, and although I have acknowledged ENDS as a source in some places, I am conscious that I have absorbed much information that appears here unacknowledged from ENDS and from conversations with its editor, Marek Mayer. Perhaps there is a certain symmetry in our relations in this respect.

I wish to thank Dr M W Holdgate and the Cambridge University Press for permission to quote from, and to reproduce a figure from, *A Perspective of Environmental Pollution*. The section on the environmental assessment Directive is based on an article that first appeared in the *Journal of Planning and Environment Law*.

Many ideas in this book have developed in discussions with colleagues at the Bonn and Paris offices of the Institute. Some I know I have taken wholesale and others my colleagues may not share. Pascale Kromarek, Graham Bennett and Thierry Lavoux have taught me much about the impact of EC policy in other countries. Konrad von Moltke, the Institute's founder director, set me on the path that led to this book. Under its new director, Ernst von Weizsäcker, our small Institute remains that rare thing in Europe, an organization where developments in European policy are followed closely but from the point of view neither of a Member State and the interest groups within it nor yet of one of the Community institutions.

Finally, I wish to thank my secretary Kate Partridge for coming temporarily to type drafts of the first edition and – this is the important point – for staying nearly seven years and so finding herself typing the second.

Contents

CHAPTER 1

Scope and structure

The nature of Community policy

The European Community's environmental policy is effectively embodied in items of Community legislation which then have to be implemented in the Member States.

This simple-sounding statement provides a convenient frame for this book which sets out all items of Community legislation together with an account of what has been done in Britain to implement them. Behind the simple statement there nevertheless lies a considerable area of uncertainty about what is meant by 'policy' generally and Community policy in particular.

It is clear that national policy is very much more than just national legislation. No one, for example, would regard British air pollution policy as being confined to what is written down in the national legislation since it gives so much discretion to the Air Pollution Inspectorate and to local authorities that, without an account of how these agents of government interpret and implement the broad duties placed upon them, a very dim picture of British policy would emerge. By contrast, the Community has no agents of its own able to carry out its policies.

The Community is therefore driven to producing legislation that places obligations on the Member States if the desired results are to be achieved. This means that Community policy, unlike national policy, is made explicit in items of legislation which is often very detailed, but which inevitably also leaves some measure of discretion to the Member States. A consideration of these items of legislation cannot therefore give a complete picture of Community policy since all they can do is to set out the intentions of policy. To discover whether these policy goals are being achieved it is necessary to examine how they are being implemented within the Member States. Community policy cannot therefore be regarded as some abstract concept existing on its own and separate from national policies. Community policy only comes to life when it is implemented in the Member States and has thereby become inseparably intertwined with national policies and practices. Since there are now twelve Member States it is an immense task to provide a complete account of how Community policy is being implemented, and to assess its effectiveness.

This book, while founded on the idea that Community policy is very much more than a collection of written texts, considers the effects of those texts in only one country: quite different effects can be expected in others[1].

The types of Community legislation

There are several types of Community 'legislation' set out in Article 189 of the Treaty of Rome, and these have not been changed by the amendments introduced by the Single European Act. They are:

Regulations
Directives

Decisions
Recommendations
Opinions.

The last two have no binding force and should not properly be regarded as legislative instruments. Indeed the Treaty does not use the word legislation.

A **Regulation** is directly applicable law in the Member States and is mostly used for rather precise purposes such as financial matters and the day to day management of the Common Agricultural Policy. It has so far been used only rarely for environmental matters. A **Directive** is binding as to the results to be achieved, but leaves to the Member States the choice of form and methods. It is therefore the most appropriate instrument for more general purposes particularly where some flexibility is required to accommodate existing national procedures and, for this reason, is the instrument most commonly used for environmental matters[2]. A **Decision** is binding in its entirety upon those to whom it is addressed. It has been used in the environmental field in connection with international conventions and with certain procedural matters.

The institutions of the Community

Community legislation is elaborated, discussed, adopted and interpreted by the Institutions of the Community. These Institutions and their powers are set out in Part 5 of the Treaty. They are the:

European Parliament
Council
Commission
Court of Justice.

There is also an Economic and Social Committee with a rather lesser status.

The **Parliament** is directly elected with a given number of seats for each Member State. The **Commission** consists formally of seventeen individuals appointed by national governments (two each from the five larger countries, one each from the others) who swear not to take instructions from their national governments. The Commission is assisted by officials who perform some functions similar to those of a civil service. The **Council** is composed of one Minister from each Member State who meet as required. The **Court of Justice** consists of judges appointed by national governments.

The legislature for Community legislation is effectively provided by the Commission and Council acting together. The power to propose legislation lies solely in the hands of the Commission, but only the Council may adopt the legislation (except for certain limited matters when the Commission is expressly empowered by the Council to act). It is important to recognize that the Parliament is therefore not a legislative body, but since it has to give an opinion on proposed legislation before the Council can adopt it, its voice must be heard and on several occasions in the environmental field it has influenced events. The **Economic and Social Committee** also expresses opinions on proposed legislation. The Court of Justice plays no role in the formulation of legislation but interprets it when cases are brought before it.

Matter included

All Community Directives, Regulations and Decisions which can reasonably be described as forming part of the Community's environmental policy and are capable of having an effect on Britain are included in this book and their effects in Britain discussed. A chronological list is provided in Appendix I. Nonbinding items such as Recommendations and Opinions encouraging the recycling of paper and the protection of the architectural heritage are not included here since any effect they have had in Britain is not noticeable.

To be useful a book of this kind should be complete, but there are always difficulties in deciding what constitutes completeness. The guiding principle adopted here has been to include everything listed by the Commission as part of its environmental policy as well as other items that are clearly environmental in their purpose and which can affect British environmental policy.

The report *Ten years of Community environmental policy* published by the Commission in March 1984 did not, for example, list the Directives controlling the use of pesticides which are included here. Nor did it list any legislation forming part of the Common Agricultural Policy even though some agricultural legislation has had environmental purposes since 1975. Relevant items are included here in Chapter 8.

Legislation concerned with radiation is not included. Nor is that concerned with food, animal feedingstuffs, fertilizers and materials and articles intended to come into contact with foodstuffs. In general legislation dealing with purely administrative matters such as appointing advisory committees or authorizing research programmes is also excluded.

All relevant items published in the *Official Journal* by 30 June 1987 have been included.

Structure

Community environmental legislation can be conveniently divided into six subject matter headings (water, waste, air, chemicals, wildlife and countryside, noise) and another heading covering items that cut across subject matter areas. Each of these seven headings is the subject of a separate chapter in this book. Another chapter briefly describes international conventions to which the Community is a party.

Each chapter is in turn divided into sections dealing with each item, or group of items, of Community legislation, and is preceded by a section outlining any relevant British legislation or policy. The section on British legislation is not intended to be complete but to cover the same ground covered by the Community legislation that follows, its purpose being to position the Community legislation in a British context. Each section is usually divided into the following parts:

Purpose of the legislation
The purpose is not always easy to understand from the text itself, and is therefore set out in a few lines.

Summary of the legislation
A summary of the legislation then follows. Comprehensibility has sometimes had to be sacrificed for completeness where a passage proves to be contentious or particularly significant for the subsequent discussion. As any summary of legislation is bound to do some violence to its intended meaning, the reader wishing to see the full text of the legislation should always refer to the *Official Journal* of the European Communities.

Development of the legislation
The development of each item is then described to the extent that this is possible. This has been done by reference to the public record, including:

1. the original typescript proposal from the Commission accompanied by an explanatory memorandum and bearing a 'COM' number, eg COM(79)834. The same proposal is subsequently published in the *Official Journal* but without the benefit of the important explanatory memorandum;
2. the report of the relevant Committee of the European Parliament;
3. the debate in the European Parliament and its formal opinion;
4. the opinion of the Economic and Social Committee;
5. the report of the House of Commons' Select Committee and debate in the House (if any);
6. the report of the House of Lords' Select Committee and debate in the House (if any).

The elaboration by the Commission of its original proposal is likely to have been known only to a limited circle, and the subsequent negotiations in the Council, and in the Council working groups that prepare material for decision by the Council, are confidential. Parliamentary discussion may nevertheless provide some reflection of the discussions taking place in the Council machinery and of the amendments being made, and may also point to difficulties that are being foreseen for the future. The Minister, for example, in reply to a debate in the House of Commons or House of Lords will often describe the current position on a proposed Directive including the amendments already agreed. Particularly useful is the evidence that is usually published with the House of Lords' reports recording the views of the major interested parties at a particular date, including that of government officials. The government also makes a practice of submitting explanatory memoranda to Parliament, and these too shed light on the process and the government's opinion at a particular time.

The parliamentary record in other countries has not been examined and such an examination could well reveal more about the development of various Directives than is recorded here. The Federal Republic of Germany and Denmark have parliamentary procedures for the systematic review of Community proposals, but it is widely recognized that in no other country are such proposals so systematically scrutinized publicly in Parliament as in Britain so that the material examined here is likely to have covered a considerable portion of the material publicly available.

Many officials have been consulted and occasionally reliance has been placed on information supplied by them which appears nowhere in the public record. In general, however, this approach has been avoided. Where the point is of import-ance, information given by a national official which cannot be confirmed from the public record has been checked with an official in another country or in the Commission.

It sometimes happens that points of difficulty in negotiating a Directive are resolved by the Council inserting general wording in the Directive and simul-taneously recording a statement in the minutes of the Council meeting by way of elaboration. These statements are sometimes published with the Directive or made public in other ways, but are otherwise confidential. For example, as appears in Section 4.8 (Dangerous substances in water), some statements have become known by appearing in a book published by a Commission official. To the extent that these statements affect the interpretation of a Directive and are not made public they amount to secret legislation and so cannot have been noted here. This secrecy has been criticized by the European Parliament – see their Resolu-tion of 24 May 1984 (OJ C172 2.7.84).

Formal compliance with the legislation

Directives usually require the Member States to transmit to the Commission within a given period a statement of the national legislation, regulations or administrative measures that give formal effect to the Directive. These 'com-pliance letters', as they are sometimes referred to, together with departmental circulars to the relevant administrative bodies (eg local authorities, water authorities) provide the basic raw material for an asssessment of the effect of the Directives on British legislation. An additional source of information are 'Rea-soned Opinions' sent by the Commission to the government when it believes that particular Directives are not being fully complied with. Whereas the Depart-ment of the Environment has made compliance letters available to those needing to see them, the 'Reasoned Opinions' from the Commission are not generally available, although some have become available to the author.

In some cases secondary legislation has had to be introduced in Britain to comply with certain Directives. In other cases the government has relied on existing primary and/or secondary legislation and has achieved compliance by taking certain administrative steps. The adequacy of these measures has been critically assessed and the conclusions reached do not always coincide with those of the government.

Effect on UK practice

A Directive is binding as to certain ends to be achieved, for example that certain standards are to be met by certain dates, while leaving to the Member State the choice of methods for doing so. For a Directive to be fully implemented, not only must the Member State have introduced the necessary laws, regulations or administrative provisions to enable these ends to be achieved, but it must also ensure that the ends specified in the Directive are also achieved in practice. A distinction may therefore in theory be drawn between **formal** and **practical** compliance, although the two will sometimes overlap.

Thus the designation of an existing body such as a water authority as the 'competent authority' for fulfilling certain functions under a Directive can be regarded as a mere formal step, but if a new body has had to be specifically created and given staff and money its creation would be a practical step as well.

It is in fact possible to have formal compliance without practical compliance and vice versa. Thus Luxembourg has ensured that there is formal compliance with a Directive concerned with titanium dioxide wastes (Section 4.15 Titanium dioxide) by issuing a Decree largely repeating the Directive, but there can be no practical compliance in Luxembourg since there is no titanium dioxide production there. Conversely there was for a time a failure of formal compliance by Britain of Directives concerned with the composition of detergents (Section 4.1 Detergents) and the sulphur content of fuels (Section 6.1 Sulphur content of gas oil) since the necessary British Regulations were late in being made, but the British government argued that the failure was only one of form since in both cases the relevant industries had voluntarily taken the required practical steps to achieve the standards before the British Regulations came into force.

Although the Member States are usually obliged by Directives to inform the Commission by means of the 'compliance letters' of the steps they have taken for formal compliance, and the Commission has a duty to see that the measures adopted are adequate, there is usually no obligation to inform the Commission of the practical steps taken, nor does the Commission have an inspectorate able to monitor what happens. The Community's interest must, however, extend beyond formal compliance alone and the Commission has made it a practice to investigate lapses in practical compliance when these are drawn to its attention. Sometimes Directives require 'situation reports' to be submitted to the Commission, and examination of these will disclose some practical effects of a Directive. Otherwise the principal way of finding out the effects of a Directive is to consult people on whom duties are placed or whose behaviour may have been influenced. This has been done largely by interviews or by correspondence.

The ultimate purpose of Community environmental legislation is of course to protect or improve the environment and not just to affect the behaviour of officials, industrialists and the public. It is however notoriously difficult quantitatively to attribute an environmental effect to a particular item of legislation even when intended to produce such an effect. For example, the smoke control orders made in Britain under the Clean Air Act 1956 will certainly have discouraged some people from burning raw coal in open fires, but since the public were anyway switching to other forms of heating it remains uncertain what proportion of the reduction in smoke is attributable to the Act. The same general point applies to Community legislation and the assessment is even harder given that the legislation is so new. The fact that there must be an effect on the environment is noted where it is possible to be confident of the fact, but no quantitative assessment of the extent of those effects has been attempted. Similarly, financial effects are sometimes noted, but no systematic attempt has been made to assess the cost of the Community's environmental policy either to the nation as a whole or to individual authorities or enterprises.

References
1   Haigh N, Bennett G, Kromarek P, Lavoux, T, 1986 *European Community environmental policy in practice, Volume I comparative report: water and waste in four countries*. Graham and Trotman, London.

2   House of Lords' Select Committee on the European Communities, *Trans-frontier shipment of hazardous wastes*, 9th Report Session 1983–84. HMSO.

CHAPTER 2

The action programmes on the environment

Every few years the Commission drafts an Action Programme on the Environment to outline its intentions for legislation and other activities in the years ahead. There is no obligation in the Treaty of Rome to do this, and in some other policy fields programmes are either not produced at all or not so consistently. The dates of approval by the Council of the action programmes so far produced, together with reports on progress from the Commission, are set out in the table below.

The first programme of 1973 had been called for by a declaration made by the Heads of State and government in October 1972. Before then the Community had no environmental policy although some items of legislation concerned with the environment (eg vehicle noise, labelling of chemicals) had already been adopted. Indeed there was then no mention of the environment in the Treaty. The first action programme was therefore necessary to chart a wholly new course. It was accordingly a long and comprehensive document. It started with a general statement of the objectives and principles of a Community environmental policy and then went on to spell out action that the Commission would propose:

1. to reduce pollution and nuisances;
2. to improve the natural and urban environments;
3. to deal with environmental problems caused by the depletion of certain natural resources;
4. to promote awareness of environmental problems and education.

This was to be done largely by proposing items of legislation.

Table 1 Action programmes on the environment

	Period covered	Date approved	OJ Reference
1st	1973–76	22.11.73	C112 20.12.73
2nd	1977–81	17.05.77	C139 13.06.77
3rd	1982–86	7.02.83	C 46 17.02.83
4th	1987–92	19.10.87	C328 7.12.87

Reports on progress

1st *Progress made in connection with the Environment Action Programme and assessment of the work done to implement it.* Communication from the Commission to the Council, COM(80)222, May 1980

2nd *Ten years of Community environment policy.* Commission of the European Communities, March 1984

Principles of Community environmental policy

The eleven principles listed in the first, and repeated in subsequent programmes, can be summarized as follows:

1. The principle of prevention: it is better than cure.
2. Environmental effects should be taken into account at the earliest possible stage in decision making.
3. Exploitation of nature or natural resources which causes significant damage to the ecological balance must be avoided. The natural environment can only absorb pollution to a limited extent. It is an asset which may be used, but not abused.
4. Scientific knowledge should be improved to enable action to be taken.
5. The polluter pays principle: the cost of preventing and eliminating nuisances must be borne by the polluter, although some exceptions are allowed.
6. Activities carried out in one Member State should not cause deterioration of the environment in another.
7. The effects of environmental policy in the Member States must take account of the interests of the developing countries.
8. The Community and the Member States should act together in international organizations and in promoting international and worldwide environmental policy.
9. The protection of the environment is a matter for everyone. Education is therefore necessary.
10. The principle of the appropriate level. In each category of pollution, it is necessary to establish the level of action (local, regional, national, Community, international) best suited to the type of pollution and to the geographical zone to be protected.
11. National environmental policies must be coordinated within the Community, without hampering progress at the national level. This is to be achieved by the implementation of the action programme and of the 'environment information agreement'.

The information agreement

The 'environment information agreement' is set out in the *Official Journal* (OJ C9 15.3.73 and OJ C86 20.7.74). It requires Member States to transmit relevant proposals for national legislation and administrative measures to the Commission, whereupon the Commission may within two months decide that the matter is appropriate for action at Community level. The Member State must then suspend its own proposal for five months while the Commission drafts Community legislation. If the system works effectively the Commission should always be aware of developments in national environmental policy, and simultaneously the Member States are provided with a mechanism for initiating Community policy. As will emerge from subsequent chapters, many items of Community legislation have been initiated in this way. The 'information agreement' has so far only been a gentleman's agreement (these English words appear also in the French and German texts published in the *Official Journal*) but in the fourth action programme the Commission has proposed that it should become a legally binding instrument.

Purpose and evolution of the Action Programmes

The action programmes effectively have two main purposes. They suggest specific proposals for legislation that the Commission intends to put forward over the next few years, and they provide an occasion to discuss some broad ideas in environmental policy and suggest new directions for the future. Rather few national ministries responsible for the environment produce comparable documents. The action programmes can be said to provide a policy framework, but unlike items of Community legislation, they cannot strictly be regarded as constituting Community policy. This is because, although the Council of Ministers will adopt a resolution on the action programme, what it usually does is to approve its 'general approach' and therefore does not commit itself to every point of detail. Each item will subsequently be decided on its merits after the Commission has made a formal proposal to the Council.

It is often said by Commission officials, and the point is repeated in the introduction to the fourth action programme, that the third action programme contained a major shift of emphasis. The two earlier programmes are said to have focused on curing acute pollution problems while the third programme emphasized the preventative approach. While Community policy has certainly evolved, in point of fact the two most important Directives to embody the preventative approach were foreshadowed in the earlier programmes and indeed the principle itself had been enunciated. Directive 79/831 on the notification of new chemicals before marketing (known as the 'sixth amendment' – see Section 7.1 Preventing risks) and Directive 85/337 on the environmental assessment of development projects (Section 10.1 Environmental impact assessment) were both proposed in the earlier programmes. The third programme did however introduce a section called 'developing an overall strategy' inspired to some extent by the World Conservation Strategy. However, this heading did not reappear in the fourth action programme.

In October 1986 the Commission submitted a draft fourth action programme to the Council. This programme, as well as outlining specific proposals for new legislation in the particular fields covered by later chapters in this book, includes a discussion of some 'general policy orientations'. These include the consequences of amendments to the Treaty of Rome. There is also a chapter consisting of reflections on pollution control.

Treaty amendments

The Treaty of Rome, as amended on 1 July 1987 by the Single European Act, now includes a new Title headed 'Environment' providing a clear legal base for actions by the Community relating to the environment. Previously there had frequently been arguments as to whether environmental legislation was properly founded on other provisions of the Treaty[1,2,3]. Potentially the most important new provision is the statement in Article 130R(2) that 'environmental protection requirements shall be a component of the Community's other policies'. However, the Treaty amendments, while removing some uncertainties, will introduce others. Hitherto all environmental legislation had to be agreed unanimously in the Council (since they were made under Articles 100 or 235, both of which require unanimous voting). Unanimity is still required under the new environmental Title, but under a new Article 100A dealing with the approximation of laws concerned with the functioning of the common market it is foreseen that legislation concerning environmental protection can be agreed by a qualified majority. The rules for qualified majority voting are laid down in the Treaty, and give the votes of the more populous countries a greater weight than those of the smaller. Some environmental legislation – such as that dealing with vehicle emissions and other standards for products – could arguably fall under either heading and it is not yet clear how a choice will be made. The Single Act also increases the powers of the Parliament.

'Implementation' and 'integration'

Two other headings under 'general policy orientations' are of great importance. One asserts that the effective **implementation** of Community environmental legislation by all Member States will be of primary importance. This book which discusses implementation in one country can be regarded as a contribution to the subject, and indeed the earlier edition was the first systematic attempt to consider implementation. The other heading emphasizes the need to integrate the environmental dimension into other policies. Although this **integration** had been listed as the first priority in the Council Resolution adopting the third action programme in 1983 rather little had been achieved except in the field of agriculture (see Section 8.5 Environmentally sensitive areas).

Reflections on pollution control

The passage with reflections on pollution control is something of a surprise for an action programme since it is long and tentative and its only conclusion is that the Commission should, together with the Member States, conduct a review of the different approaches to pollution control. Some of these approaches are discussed here in the next chapter. Nevertheless, the Commission is now committed to participating in a debate taking place in several countries and in other international organizations (eg OECD) on what is coming to be known as the cross-media approach to pollution control. This entails an approach which does not regard water pollution control as in a separate category from air pollution control or waste disposal, but recognizes that pollutants can move between the environmental media. Though tentative, this passage of the action programme suggests that there may well be changes in the way the Community deals with these problems in the coming years.

References

1   Von Moltke K 1977 *European Communities: the legal basis for environmental policy, Environmental policy and law* (3).

2   House of Lords' Select Committee on the European Communities, *Approximation of laws under Article 100 of the EEC Treaty*, 22nd Report Session 1977–78.

3   House of Lords' Select Committee on the European Communities, *Environmental problems and the Treaty of Rome*, Session 1979–80.

CHAPTER 3

Approaches to pollution control

> A chemical standard can be applied in any one of two ways –
> either to the contaminating discharge by itself or to the stream
> which has received the discharge. (Royal Commission on
> Sewage Disposal, Eighth Report, 1912)

The choice between the two types of standard quoted above has been the cause of a long running and still unresolved dispute between Britain and other Member States over water pollution. The way in which, sixty-five years ago, the Royal Commission attempted to reconcile the two approaches is still relevant today and is described in Section 4.0. These two types of standard – now usually called emission standards and environmental quality standards – are not the only ones available for pollution control and several others have been used in Community legislation.

One result of the dispute is that the idea has gained currency that the Commission and other Member States have a particular preference for uniform emission standards as the principal tool for pollution control, while only Britain has insisted on setting emission standards individually by reference to environmental quality. While this may fairly describe the positions adopted by the various parties over the disputed part of Directive 76/464 dealing with particularly dangerous substances (see Section 4.8 Dangerous substances in water), it does not fairly describe the positions taken over the rest of the Directive, and it becomes an oversimplification and positively misleading once it is extended to pollution generally or even generally to water pollution. To argue that there are two approaches which are in some sense opposed, and that Britain has long been committed to one and the other Member States to another, is both to misrepresent British practice as well as to misrepresent the complexity and variety of Community pollution legislation that has been agreed by all Member States. This chapter therefore outlines the range of pollution control tools that have been used in Community legislation so as to provide a context for the discussion of the Directives in the chapters that follow.

Pollutants have been defined by Holdgate[1] as substances causing damage to targets in the environment. The pollutant may be emitted from a source into the environment, through which it travels along a pathway till it reaches a target or receptor. The target may be man, or animal or plant life, or an inanimate structure (eg the stonework of a cathedral). It follows from this definition that if the pollutant reaches no target in damaging quantities because it has been rendered harmless either by being transformed into another substance or into a form where it cannot affect the target or because it has been diluted to harmless levels, then there has been no pollution.

It also follows that the mere emission of a potential pollutant to the environment does not necessarily constitute pollution and that to eliminate pollution one does not have to restrict emissions to zero.

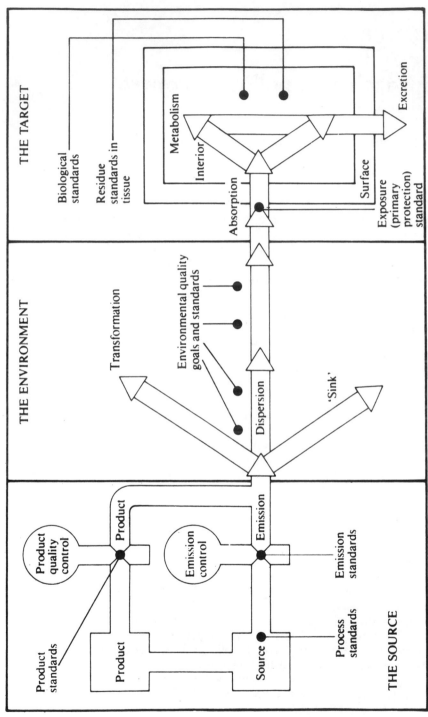

Figure 1: Possible points on the pollutant pathway at which standards or objectives may be set (Reproduced, with permission, from M W Holdgate, 'A Perspective of Environmental Pollution', CUP 1979)

Figure 1 illustrates the journey of a pollutant from source to target diagrammatically. To quote Holdgate:

> . . .the concentration a pollutant attains at a point is the resultant of the quantity of the input to the environment (from whatever pattern of sources, at whatever distance), the dispersion characteristics determined by the properties of the pollutant (density, solubility, diffusion coefficient) and those of the medium (current direction, rate of flow, rater of intermingling, absorption properties) and the rate of removal from the environment at all points along the pathway, whether caused by physical or biological agencies. . .Where emissions of a substance to the environment are tolerated, controls need to be adjusted so that targets are not unduly hazarded (just what constitutes undue hazard depends on the nature of the target and the value set upon it).

Figure 1 shows possible points along the pollutant pathway at which standards or objectives may be set as tools for control. The points may be at the source, in the environment, at or in the target itself. For the purposes of the present discussion it is immaterial whether the standards are set with legally binding force or are merely guidelines, and the words 'standards' and 'objectives' are used in this Chapter rather loosely and interchangeably. When it comes to controlling pollution in the real world there is a vast difference between what is legally enforceable and what is only a guide, but these differences need not concern us in this Chapter.

Let us take by way of example a fairly common pollutant which is known to present a hazard to human health and examine the possible tools for controlling it.

Lead can reach human beings from a number of sources. Lead occurs naturally in soil and is taken up by food plants; lead is washed from the soil into river water, from where it enters into water supply and so reaches the household tap; lead is discharged to rivers from sewage works and factories; some houses have lead plumbing which may dissolve if the water has certain properties; lead is found in paint which can be chewed by children or it can flake and be picked up and swallowed; lead is emitted into the air from lead works and can be inhaled or it can settle as dust on food or on the soil where it is taken up in food plants; lead is put into petrol and is dispersed with vehicle exhausts throughout centres of population.

Some of these sources are natural and so difficult or impossible to do anything about, while others are clearly within the power of man to control. The pathways from the sources to the target include air, water and soil, sometimes in combination.

As part of its environmental policy the Community has agreed Directives which seek to control lead at a number of points along its pathways to man or other targets. Let us consider these under the headings of the different tools for control shown in Figure 1 starting at the target and working backwards along the pathways:

Biological standards·
The Commission in 1975 proposed a Directive setting lead levels not to be exceeded in the human bloodstream. In the event this proposal was modified into a Directive designed to gather information about blood lead levels in the population at large and in critical groups (see Section 6.6 Screening for lead). The Directive no longer sets a biological standard in a legally binding way but does set certain reference levels which indicate that too much lead is present.

The advantage of a biological standard as a tool for control is that it covers the combined effect from all sources at the point where it matters, that is at the target to be protected. It suffers the disadvantage that it provides a signal only when the pollutant has already reached the target – possibly in excessive amounts. The Directive deals with this problem in these words:

> When the results of the analyses indicate that the reference levels have been exceeded in one or more cases, Member States shall take action to trace the exposure sources responsible for the levels being exceeded (and shall) take all appropriate measures. . .

Whatever remedial measures are appropriate must be taken somewhere further back along the pathway, since it is not possible to take control measures at the target itself except by removing the target from the pathway – such as by moving children away from homes near lead smelters.

Exposure standards
One control point further back along the pathway is the point of entry to the target. The standard here is called an 'exposure standard' or, in some circumstances, a 'primary protection standard'. By agreeing a Directive setting standards for the quality of drinking water (see Section 4.4 Drinking water), including the maximum concentration of lead permitted, the Community has sought to ensure that the amount of lead swallowed with water is limited. Water supply can be tested and the water treatment or supply system adjusted to ensure that the standard is met. A standard where the exposure is by breathing is set in a Directive on air quality standards for lead (see Section 6.4 Air quality – lead). Yet another Directive limits the quantity of lead, among other substances, in animal feedingstuffs (Directive 74/63 OJ L38 11.2.74).

Environmental quality standards
Going yet further back, standards can be set at a number of points in the pathway through the environment. One Directive sets a quality standard for surface water from which drinking water is to be abstracted (see Section 4.2 Surface water for drinking). If the constituents of river water, including lead, exceed a given concentration, then that point in the river must either not be used at all for abstracting drinking water or the treatment given to it must be of a specified kind. Other environmental quality standards for water have been set by Directives, including ones for bathing water (Section 4.7) and water supporting freshwater fish and shellfish (Sections 4.5 and 4.6) and although these could have included

standards for lead they have not done so. In the case of the freshwater fish and shellfish Directives, the targets could have been regarded as either the fish and shellfish themselves or the humans that consume them, although it emerges that the Directives are not intended primarily to protect man. The Directive on air quality standards for lead (Section 6.4), classed above as an exposure standard, can also be classed as an environmental quality standard.

As with biological and exposure standards, the breaching of an environmental quality standard does not provide an immediate indication of the action to be taken, but serves only as a signal that the pathway to the target contains too much of the pollutant.

Environmental quality standards may be expressed numerically as concentrations of substances, for example, in water or sediments, or in air, but it is also possible to have generalized quality objectives expressed in words relating to the use of the environment. These might be that the water should be suitable for the passage of migratory fish at all times, or suitable for the abstraction of drinking water.

Emission standards

A pollutant may be emitted to the environment at point sources such as from an outlet pipe to a river or from a chimney stack to air, or alternatively in a diffused way through the ventilation system of a factory, or from the exhausts of innumerable motor cars, or again by the diffused application of a pesticide or fertilizer to land. Only where the pollutant comes from a point source is it possible to set an emission standard at that point.

Emission standards may be set individually for each discharge, or uniform standards for a particular class of discharge may be applied across a whole area or country or even the Community. Directive 76/464 (see Section 4.8 Dangerous substances in water) requires all discharges to water of certain listed dangerous substances to be subject to emission standards but does not specify numerically what the emission standards are to be. Instead, limit values (upper limits) for these emission standards are to be laid down in subsequent (or daughter) Directives for certain particularly dangerous substances set out in a List I. For possibly less dangerous substances, set out in a List II, emission standards are the responsibility of the Member States and are to be set by reference to quality objectives. Since lead appears on List II and not on List I, the Community has no plans for setting emission standards for lead discharged to water, but this does not mean that Member States are not circumscribed by Community legislation. As we have seen, the Community has already laid down an environmental quality standard for surface water that is to be abstracted for drinking, and any emission standards laid down in Member States must be such that those quality standards are met at the abstraction points.

It is only for the List I substances that the Commission is to propose limit values which emission standards are not to exceed, but even here the Directive allows Member States the alternative of setting emission standards locally so long as environmental quality standards set by the Community are met. It is this alternative that Britain insisted upon and has chosen to follow (see Section 4.8 Dangerous substances in water). By following the alternative, the emission standard will depend on a number of factors including the capacity of the receiving environment to dilute the discharge, the environmental quality that will have been prescribed for it, and the quantity and quality of other emissions to it.

Emission standards may be set numerically (either in legislaton or administratively) as so many parts of a substance per million of effluent or per unit of productive output. Alternatively an obligation may be placed on the discharger to use the 'best practicable means' or 'best technical means available' for reducing emissions. As described in Section 6.0 this approach is used in Britain for air pollution, and as technology improves the emission standard will be progressively tightened. To make this sytem workable the Industrial Air Pollution Inspectorate sets numerical emission standards (called 'presumptive limits') which certain emissions to air are not to exceed, and these are revised from time to time. A Directive (see Section 6.8 Emissions from industrial plant) foresees the Community laying down emission standards for certain industrial plants including lead works.

Process or operating standards
Within a factory emitting a pollutant to the environment standards may be set relating to production methods, either to protect workers or to ensure that the minimum amount of pollutant is eventually discharged to the environment. In Britain, the Industrial Air Pollution Inspectorate prescribes methods of operating plants to minimize emissions to the environment and the Health and Safety Executive sets standards to protect workers. Standards to protect workers from lead have also been set in a Directive (see Section 7.7).

Product standards
The product of a manufacturing process may itself give rise to pollution when in use, or upon disposal, in addition to any pollution that may have been caused during its manufacture. Accordingly product standards may be set to control the composition or construction of the product. One example is the Directive setting standards for the lead content of petrol (Section 6.5). Other examples are the Directives concerned with the composition of detergents (Section 4.1) and with the construction of vehicles so as to limit emissions (Section 6.7). If drinking water is regarded as a product then the Directive on the quality of drinking water (Section 4.4) – classed above as an exposure standard – could also be regarded as a product standard.

A special case of a product standard is a total prohibition on the use of a substance for specified purposes such as that contained in the Directive restricting the use of polychlorinated biphenyls (see Section 7.2 Restrictions on marketing and use) to closed circuit electrical systems and some other limited applications. The requirement in a Directive that unleaded petrol must be made available can also be regarded as an example of a product standard (Section 6.5).

Although not strictly setting product standards, a number of Directives require certain products to be packaged and labelled in specified ways so as to minimize risks to the environment (see Sections 7.1 and 7.6). One such Directive requires paints containing more than a certain quantity of lead to be appropriately labelled.

In addition to the six standards applied at the control points shown in Figure 1, other approaches to pollution control are also possible such as the two described below.

Standards for total emissions or the 'bubble'
Rather than setting emission standards for each source of pollutant from a plant it is possible to set an upper limit for all emissions irrespective of origin. In the USA this is known as the 'bubble' concept: a notional bubble is drawn around a plant or area and an upper limit is put on the total amount of a pollutant allowed to pass into the bubble. Thus if a manufacturer succeeds in reducing his diffuse discharges he may emit more through a chimney stack and vice versa. The concept can be extended to an area covering several manufacturers in which case market forces may lead them to sell and buy among themselves the right to emit pollutants so long as the total does not exceed that prescribed. Thus a new manufacturer may have to pay existing polluters to reduce their emissions in order to create the 'space' for himself. This is also known as the 'emission offset policy'. The concept can be extended to a whole country or even to the whole Community or indeed globally. An upper limit has been proposed for the emission of sulphur dioxide from large combustion plants in each Member State (see Section 6.8 Emissions from industrial plants) and the Community has set an upper limit on the total production and thus effectively the emission, of chlorfluorocarbons (see Section 7.4). A total emission limit for such a useful and versatile material as lead has not so far been suggested.

Preventative controls
The approaches described above are mostly attempts to control pollution rather than to anticipate and so prevent it. Community preventative controls include one Directive, known as the 'sixth amendment' (see Section 7.1 Preventing risks by testing), which requires the potentially toxic effects of chemicals to be identified before they are marketed so that if necesary restrictions can be placed on their use under another Directive (Section 7.2 Restrictions on marketing and use). Another, known as the 'Seveso' Directive (Section 7.3), requires manufacturers to identify and take steps to forestall the risks to the environment from a major accident. A Directive on the environmental assessment of development projects (see Section 10.1) requires systematic identification of the environmental effects from a planned development, including pollution, before consent for the development is given.

This catalogue of available tools for controlling pollution shows that the Community has used them all – though not necessarily all of them for the example of lead that we have chosen. The use of one tool does not exclude the use of others and they are usually used in combination with one another to provide a network of protection.

This division into eight different categories of controls over pollution is not exhaustive and others can be devized. The following three are discussed in the fourth action programme on the environment.

The 'substance-oriented' approach
This approach involves taking a particular substance and considering how it may affect vulnerable targets or receptors by any environmental pathway and setting controls in these pathways as appropriate. The first attempt by the Community to follow this approach in a single Directive concerns asbestos (see Section 7.9).

The 'source-oriented' approach
This approach involves taking a particular industry or industrial sector and considering all the pollutants it emits and setting appropriate controls over these. This is also sometimes called the 'sectoral approach'. The first action programme proposed that this approach should be used but the only Directive that has so far been based on it concerns the titanium dioxide industry (see Section 4.15).

The 'cross-media' or 'multi-media' approach
This approach is based on the recognition that pollutants can move between different environmental media, and also that stringent controls over discharges to one medium can result in increased discharges to another medium. The cross-media approach in theory involves coordinating standards from all sources and in all media so as to consider the effects on all targets. While the objective is unassailable the difficulties lie in devising a workable approach. In Britain in 1976 the Royal Commission on Environmental Pollution put forward a concept based on the 'cross-media' approach that they called the 'best practicable environmental option'. They had proposed a unified pollution inspectorate to be responsible for discharges to air, water and to land and they had in mind that 'where choices exist as to the sector of the environment to which wastes should be discharged [the unified inspectorate] would be instrumental in deciding how different sectors should be used to minimize environmental damage overall'. The 'cross-media' approach has hardly begun to be adopted by the Community although the Directive on asbestos (see Section 7.9) can be regarded as related to it.

The dispute between the use of uniform emission standards and quality standards

The dispute between Britain and the other Member States is usually and rightly seen as concerned with the most practical and economic means to achieve an end on which all are agreed, but underlying it there are also differences in pollution theory. For those who believe that the purpose of pollution control is to prevent targets from being unduly put at risk, then the best points for controls are those nearest to the target. The reasons for exercising controls further back along the pathway are then practical: it simply may not be possible to exercise controls anywhere else. Viewed in this way emission standards are merely a means to achieving quality objectives/standards which in turn are set to protect identified targets, and these emission standards need be no more stringent than required to meet those quality objectives. The emission standards will therefore quite logically vary from place to place.

For those who believe that man should emit the least possible quantity of pollutant, even if it is having no known effect – an approach being developed in the Federal Republic of Germany under the name of the *vorsorgeprinzip* (the principle of anticipation or foresight) – then the point of emission is the logical point to set the controls and they should be as stringent as available technology permits: controls further down the pathway then serve only as checks that pollutants are not in fact reaching vulnerable targets, possibly from diffuse sources that are not controlled by emission standards. According to this view of pollution control there is no objection to uniformly fixed emission standards – although there may well be objections in economic theory since 'as stringent as available technology permits' begs a number of questions and uniform standards may not result in the best use of financial resources.

These alternative views are not always made explicit and are not always held consistently even in one country. In Britain, air pollution control has if anything been founded on the second view, since there is a duty to use the best practicable means (bpm) to prevent the escape of 'noxious or offensive gases' whether damage is being done or not, and the emission standards that form part of bpm are set nationally and applied with some consistency throughout the country (see Section 6.0 Relevant British legislation). In contrast, water pollution control in Britain has evolved so that it is now firmly founded on the first view with an emphasis on achieving defined quality objectives by setting emission standards locally (see Section 4.0 Relevant British legislation).

Although differences in pollution theory are important, the dispute between Britain and the other Member States over water pollution has in practice been much more concerned with administrative convenience and economic competition, both of which need a word of explanation.

The advantages of the uniform emission standards approach

The administration of centrally **fixed limit values** may well be easier than emission standards set by reference to quality objectives, firstly when granting authorizations and, secondly, when monitoring to ensure compliance. When authorizing a discharge to water using the limit value approach the presumption will be that the emission standard will equal the limit value – unless there is an obvious reason for it to be more stringent – and so the authority is spared the difficulty of calculating the emission standard by first defining a quality objective (if none already exists) and then taking into account the existing quality of the river, volume of flow, and the number, quantity and quality of other discharges. Indeed, one of the arguments against variable emission standards is that quality objectives do not provide a complete guide for allocating the total acceptable pollutant load between dischargers. When a river crosses a frontier between authorities – which may be within a Member State or may be a national frontier – the administrative advantages of uniform emission standards become greater since the tricky problem of allocating the permitted pollutant load is eliminated. When monitoring to ensure compliance it may also be easier simply to sample the actual discharge to ensure that the emission standard has not been exceeded, than to sample the environment and then try to determine which of a number of discharges was responsible for any breach. Furthermore, the concentration of the pollutant will be higher in the discharge than in the environment and so easier to measure – indeed in the environment it may be below the limit of detection.

These are the practical advantages of limit values. The economic arguments in favour are not that the approach results in the best use of economic resources but that all manufacturers are treated equally and that therefore the conditions of competition are not distorted.

The advantages of the quality standard approach

The advantages of setting emission standards individually by reference to **quality objectives** are threefold. First, controls will be most stringent where the environment is most vulnerable. This not only ensures protection of the environment but also provides economic incentives to industrialists to locate where the environment is best able to cope with the discharge. In theory industrialists will consequently choose of their own volition, other things being equal, to locate on a large river or an estuary rather than a small tributary. (If the limit value approach is pursued singlemindedly without regard for the receiving environment it would be possible to discharge into a small stream and to destroy all life in it while remaining within the limit value). Secondly, the monitoring of the environment which is essential to ensure that the quality objectives are being maintained, ensures that diffuse or non-point source discharges are taken into account and not just direct discharges. Thirdly, abatement will not be more burdensome than is necessary and limited financial resources can then be applied where they produce the maximum benefit.

Since Britain has short fast rivers and is washed by a turbulent and tidal sea, there has been an obvious argument of economic self-interest for Britain not to accept emission standards for water set by reference to what is necessary to protect, say, the Rhine, which drains many industrial areas and which is used as an important source of drinking water by Germans and Dutch. Since many of Britain's most polluting industries have chosen to locate on estuaries and drinking water is abstracted upstream, it can plausibly be argued that to set emission standards as stringent as those needed for a river that is to be used for drinking water is to fly in the face of the economic principle of comparative advantage: Britain for pollution purposes, it can be argued, is well favoured by geography just as for transport purposes or, more facetiously, for the purposes of growing lemons, it is disadvantaged by geography. Since Italian lemon growers take advantage of the sun that geography brings them, and grow lemons rather than engage in some other activity for that very reason, and since German industrialists benefit from proximity to continental markets as a result of geography, so also it is argued that Britain should quite properly profit from the ability to locate industries on estuaries or on the coast where acute pollution problems are less likely to arise and where the sea water can assimilate or destroy the pollutants.

Where toxic substances are persistent and bioaccumulable the arguments for allowing less than the best discharge abatement technology are harder to sustain and it is over these substances that the dispute has centred. Not least of the difficulties has been agreeing which are the truly persistent toxic substances.

The opposing arguments for emission limit values and for quality objectives that came to a head with Directive 76/464 have had the effect of forcing Member States into camps, with Britain often alone in one. But it would be a mistake to suppose that the two approaches are totally incompatible and that Britain and the other Member States have pursued one to the exclusion of the other. In Britain, as in other countries, policy has not always been singleminded and elements of both approaches have been used for both water and air pollution. In developing national positions for the purposes of the debate in the Community there has been a tendency – not entirely excusable, it must be said – to play down the elements that do not fit the negotiating position adopted so that a distorted picture emerges. Nationalism, even of a benign kind, and regard for the facts have never been easy bedfellows.

The need to reconsider the two approaches is being increasingly accepted both in Britain and elsewhere, and featured in the fourth action programme on the environment. In Britain the House of Lords has taken up the proposal put forward in the first edition of this book (in Appendix 4) for a change in British policy away from a refusal to accept uniform emission standards even for the most dangerous substances and the matter is under consideration by the government[2].

References

1   Holdgate, M W 1979 *A perspective of environmental pollution*, Cambridge University Press.

2   House of Lords' Select Committee on the European Communities *Dangerous Substances*, 15th Report Session 1984–85. HMSO.

CHAPTER 4

Water

4.0 Relevant British legislation

Early legislation

Long before legislators and administrators intervened, private individuals relied upon the English common law – that is to say the legal principles developed through case law and not expressed in a code or statutes – to protect water against pollution. The owner of a river bank can bring an action in the civil courts, technically for nuisance, and claim damages and an injunction if there is an infringement of his right to have the water of the river reach him in its natural flow, that is unaltered from its accustomed quality and quantity. Following a successful common law action in 1948 against Luton Corporation for polluting the River Lea, the Anglers' Cooperative Association was formed with the sole purpose of fighting pollution by making use of the common law and thus keeping it alive. The Association encourages angling clubs to become leaseholders and thus to acquire riparian rights. As a result, anglers bring a number of cases before the courts each year. The fact that riparian owners have not always defended their rights is easy to show since a 'natural flow' has not everywhere been maintained. Indeed, as the right is a private one and the riparian owner can be bought off by a polluter it has provided no basis for public policy. As a result, from the middle of the last century, a number of Acts of Parliament were passed applying to particular local authority areas or rivers and making it a criminal offence to discharge polluting matter.

The first Act making it a criminal offence to pollute any British river was the Rivers Pollution Prevention Act 1876 which remained in force until 1951. This Act dealt with sewage and industrial effluents separately. Sewage could only be discharged if the 'best practicable and available means to render harmless the sewage matter' had been used. Industrial effluents were virtually prohibited, since it became an offence to allow 'any poisonous, noxious or polluting liquid proceeding from any factory or manufacturing process' to flow into any stream, but the Act then severely limited the circumstances under which the law could be enforced in the 'seat of any manufacturing industry'.

Modern legislation starts with the Rivers (Prevention of Pollution) Act 1951 which placed a general duty on River Boards to maintain or restore the wholesomeness of rivers and gave them two novel powers: they could grant consent for discharges, subject to conditions; and they could make byelaws prescribing emission standards (which could be incorporated in the consents) which would have to be complied with for a whole river or stretches of it. This last power, which effectively allowed uniform emission standards to be laid down, was hardly used and was repealed in 1961. The 1951 Act applied only to inland waters, but it was extended to some estuaries and tidal waters by the Clean Rivers (Estuaries and Tidal Waters) Act 1960 and was further amended in 1961.

Apart from the broad duty to maintain or restore the wholesomeness of rivers, the 1951 to 1961 Acts gave no guidance on how the conditions to be attached to discharge consents were to be arrived at, but as an official report explained[1], the practice developed of placing conditions on discharge consents which took account of the condition and uses of the river. For example, rivers used for public water supply would in general require effluents of a higher quality than those not so used.

The subject had been considered at length for discharges of sewage in the eighth report of 1912 of the Royal Commission on Sewage disposal 1896–1915[2]. They showed that the 'nuisance-producing power of a normal sewage or effluent is broadly proportional to its powers of deoxygenating the water' and proposed as a test of the quality of rivers and sewage effluent the amount of dissolved oxygen taken up in five days (now called the Biochemical Oxygen Demand and abbreviated as BOD_5). They also classified rivers according to the appearance they presented to observers and found they corresponded to average BOD_5 values as follows:

Quality	BOD_5 values (mg/l)
Very clean	1.0
Clean	2.0
Fairly clean	3.0
Doubtful	5.0
Bad	10.0

A BOD_5 of 4.0 was regarded as being just free of signs of pollution, and the Royal Commission accordingly concluded that sewage discharged to any river should always be treated sufficiently to ensure that the river quality did not fall below this limiting figure of 4.0. They set out a method for making the calculation to achieve the standard of 4.0 in the river and gave some worked examples: if the river was itself of quality 1.0 and provided a tenfold dilution of the effluent, then the quality of the effluent would have to be no worse than 34; if the river was itself of quality 2.0 and provided an eightfold dilution, then the quality of the effluent would have to be no worse than 20.

Here, then, is a concise exposition of how to set emission standards by reference to the condition of the river and a desired quality objective. The Royal Commission is accordingly frequently relied upon in support of a policy of setting emission standards locally by reference to a river quality objective.

However, the Royal Commission also went on to argue that such an approach would be difficult to administer and would put unequal burdens on different authorities and they therefore recommended a uniform emission standard, which they called a 'normal standard' which was to be applied to all sewage discharges unless specified circumstances justified a different standard. They thus effectively tried to reconcile the two approaches. The normal standard was never enshrined in legislation – as intended – but was widely used in Britain. The arguments used by the Royal Commission in favour of a normal standard turn out to be very similar to those used today by some countries in favour of uniform emission standards for discharges of dangerous substances to rivers crossing national frontiers (see Section 4.8 Dangerous substances in water).

The Water Act 1973 and Control of Pollution Act 1974

By the Water Act 1973 the whole water industry was reorganized in England and Wales into ten water authorities. These were based on river basins on the grounds that it was most efficient to manage the water cycle as a whole. The new water authorities took over the responsibilities previously exercized by over 1600 separate local authorities, water undertakings and river authorities and their responsibilities include water supply, sewerage, sewage treatment, the management of rivers and aquifers including pollution control, land drainage, flood prevention and fisheries. In Scotland it is the River Purification Boards that are responsible for controlling the quality of rivers.

The principle Act concerned with water pollution is now the Control of Pollution Act 1974 (COPA), which covers Scotland too. Although enacted in 1974 it was only in 1986 that most of it had been brought fully into force. Unlike Part I of COPA dealing with waste (see Section 5.0 Relevant British legislation) which was innovative and made major changes to British legislation, Part II dealing with water is a logical extension of existing powers and its only really original feature is the provision for public access to information about discharges. Otherwise it effectively consolidates the matter in the earlier Acts and extends it to cover discharges to waters not previously controlled.

Consents for discharges

The 1974 Act requires discharges to rivers, the sea, specified underground waters or land to have the consent of the water authority which may be given subject to conditions. Since sewage works are the responsibility of water authorities, consents for these are granted by the Secretary of State. Until Part II came into force discharges to coastal waters were not controlled nor were all discharges to estuaries or to groundwater. There is no power in the Act for the Secretary of State to set emission standards to be applied uniformly throughout the country.

Quality objectives

Neither the water authorities nor the Secretary of State has any duty to set water quality standards or objectives. However, these have been set administratively, and without legally binding force, following a review of discharge consent conditions by the now defunct National Water Council[3]. Once quality objectives have been set, the authorities can endeavour to achieve them by controlling the discharges from their own sewage works and by setting appropriate conditions on the consents they grant to discharges from trade premises.

The only statutory obligations as to river quality are, perhaps surprisingly, not to be found in COPA but in the Water Act 1973 which places a general duty on the Secretary of State to secure the execution of a national policy for water including the restoration and maintenance of the wholesomeness of rivers and other inland waters (Section 1) and the duty on water authorities (Section 24) to prepare plans for 'the meeting of future demands for water and the use of water and restoring or maintaining the wholesomeness of rivers and other inland or coastal waters in their area'.

To implement the various Directives that set quality standards or objectives for certain waters, reliance has had to be placed almost exclusively on the powers to set conditions on discharge consents coupled with the powers of water authorities to make plans for the management of rivers.

Groundwater

Comprehensive powers to control most discharges to groundwater are contained in COPA but some powers existed previously in other legislation mentioned in connection with the groundwater Directive 80/68 (Section 4.9 Groundwater). The legislation concerning waste disposal, which is a potential major source of groundwater pollution is described in Chapter 5.

Drinking water

The Water Act 1945 places a duty on the water undertakers to supply 'wholesome' water and the Water Acts 1945 and 1973 place a duty on the local authority to ascertain the wholesomeness of public and private supplies within their area. Any dispute between water authorities and local authorities is determined by the Secretary of State. Before the drinking water Directive 80/778 came into force (Section 4.4 Drinking water) there were no mandatory standards in Britain defining what was to be regarded as wholesome, although the World Health Organization's European Standards were generally used as guidelines.

Detergents

There is no primary legislation controlling the composition or biodegradability of detergents for the purpose of preventing water pollution, and for many years standards were agreed voluntarily between government and the manufacturers. Standards for detergents are now laid down in Regulations made under the European Communities Act 1972 in order to implement various Directives (see Section 4.1 Detergents).

Dumping at sea

All dumping at sea requires a licence from the Ministry of Agriculture, Fisheries and Food. The licences used to be granted under the Dumping at Sea Act 1974 but are now given under the Food and Environment Protection Act 1985 that repealed the 1974 Act. Before issuing a licence the Ministry has to have regard to the need to protect the marine environment and to the practical availability of any alternative for disposal.

Further developments

In early 1986 the government announced its intention of transferring to the private sector the ten water authorities in England and Wales and subsequently issued a consultation paper on proposals for environmental protection under a privatized water industry. One of the proposals was that the Secretary of State should be empowered to set quality objectives and standards and the consultation paper acknowledged that the need to give effect to the requirements of EC Directives was one reason for this. The question was raised, in the European Parliament and elsewhere, as to whether a privatized body can be a 'competent authority' for the purpose of granting authorizations to discharge dangerous substances to water (see written question No 669/86 OJ C19 26.1.87). At least partly in response to this point the Conservative Party announced in its manifesto for the General Election in June 1987 that it would establish a National Rivers' Authority to take over the regulatory functions of the existing water authorities leaving the water supply and sewage functions to be transferred to the private sector. The government is now proceeding to develop these plans.

References

1   The Jeger Report 1970 *Taken for granted* Report of the Working Party on Sewage Disposal. HMSO.

2   Newsom George and Graham Sherratt J 1972 *Water pollution*. John Sherratt and Son Ltd.

3   National Water Council, 1978 *River water quality, the next stage: review of discharge consent conditions*.

4.1 Detergents

Detergents are covered by five interrelated Directives:

1. 73/404/EEC (OJ L347 17.12.73) proposed 16.6.71 – COM(71)655	Directive on detergents.
2. 73/405/EEC (OJ L347 17.12.73) proposed 16.6.71 – COM(71)655	Directive relating to methods of testing the biodegradability of anionic surfactants.
3. 82/242/EEC (OJ L109 22.4.82) proposed 8.2.80 – COM(80)40	Directive relating to methods of testing the biodegradability of nonionic surfactants and amending Directive 73/404/EEC.
4. 82/243/EEC (OJ L109 22.4.82) proposed 24.3.81 – COM(81)128	Directive amending Directive 73/405/EEC relating to the methods of testing the biodegradability of anionic surfactants.
5. 86/94/EEC (OJ L80 25.3.86) proposed 22.5.85 – COM(85)217	Directive amending for the second time Directive 73/404/EEC on detergents.
Binding dates (73/404 and 73/405) Notification date Formal compliance Exemptions possible	27 November 1973 27 May 1975 until 31 March 1989
Binding dates (82/242 and 82/243) Notification date Formal compliance	8 April 1982 8 October 1983
Binding dates (86/94) Notification date	11 March 1986

The notification date is the date when the Member States are notified of the existence of the Directive. Time limits normally run from the notification date. It is usually a few days after the date of the Directive, ie the date when it was signed by the President of the Council. The notification date used not to be printed in the *Official Journal* but there has been a recent and welcome change in practice.

Purpose of the Directives
In the 1950s widespread foaming of rivers resulted from the growing domestic use of 'hard' detergents which are difficult to break down by sewage treatment. This foam is unpleasant to look at, impairs photosynthesis and oxygenation of water and interferes with the sewage treatment process. 'Soft' or more bio-degradable detergents were subsequently developed, and one purpose of the Directives is to prevent the sale of 'hard' detergents. The other purpose is to ensure free trade in detergents within the Community.

Summary of the Directives

Directive 73/404 covers many types of detergent: anionic, cationic, nonionic and ampholytic. It prohibits the marketing of any of these detergents where the average level of biodegradability of the surfactants is less than 90 per cent ('surfactants' or 'surface active agents' are the essential constituents of detergents to which other constituents may be added. The Directive is not concerned with other constituents such as phosphates). Moreover, the use of those surfactants with an average level of biodegradability of not less than 90 per cent must not be harmful to human or animal health. The Directive can be called a 'framework' Directive because by itself it is largely unenforceable since it specifies no methods by which testing is to be carried out. These, being specific to the different types of detergents, are promised in subsequent 'daughter' Directives.

If a Member State decides that an imported detergent does not comply with the requirements of the Directive it can prohibit the marketing and use of the detergent and must inform the country of origin and the Commission accordingly. If the exporting country objects and agreement cannot be reached the Commission must obtain an opinion from an authorized laboratory in another Member State using the reference methods laid down in daughter Directives.

Directive 73/404 has been amended by Directives 82/242 and 86/94 to provide for exemptions for certain types of detergents and for certain uses until 31st March 1989 (the second deferment); the exemptions apply to those detergents which came on the market after 30 September 1980 only if they have a higher level of biodegradability than existing products for those uses. Another amendment is made by Directive 82/242 under which a committee is established for adapting the detergent Directives to technical progress.

Directive 73/405, the first of the daughter Directives, is concerned only with anionic detergents – the kind most commonly used. It originally laid down three methods of testing: a French method, a German method, and an OECD method but an amendment made by Directive 82/243 has added a British method called the 'porous pot test'. The biodegradability is to be no less than 80 per cent, the assumption apparently being that if this level is obtained on every test then the average level of 90 per cent required by 73/404 would also be obtained. This point is not made clear but compatibility between the two Directives must be assumed. The British government pointed out to the Commission the apparent inconsistency between the 90 per cent of 73/404 and the 80 per cent of 73/405 without apparently ever receiving a satisfactory reply.

Directive 82/242 is concerned with nonionic detergents and lays down four methods of testing: an OECD method, a German method, a French method, and a British method called the 'porous pot test'. The biodegradability is to be no less than 80 per cent. The Directive also amends Directive 73/404 (see above).

Directive 82/243 amends Directive 73/405 by updating the approved testing methods and – as described above – by including the British 'porous pot test' as one of the methods. It also amends 73/405 by laying down in an Annex a reference testing method which is to be used during the procedure set out in Directive 73/404 in the event of a dispute between Member States.

Directive 86/94 only defers the period of exemption for certain detergents (see above).

Formal compliance in the UK

Directives 73/404 and 73/405, although formally adopted in November 1973, had been agreed in principle one year earlier, before Britain joined the Community. They therefore formed part of the *'acquis communautaire'* – a phrase for which there is no real English equivalent but which means those duties, powers and obligations that the Community has acquired and by inference will not lightly give up or change. ('What we have we hold' may be too strong but conveys the flavour of the phrase.) The lack of British influence may have been the cause of subsequent difficulties: although the Member States were to have put into force the legal and administrative measures necessary to comply with the two earlier Directives in May 1975, it was not until 1st January 1979 that Regulations made under the European Communities Act 1972 came into force in Britain. These are the Detergents (Composition) Regulations 1978 (SI 1978 No 564) (amended by SI 1978 No 1546) and they apply to Scotland and Northern Ireland as well as to England and Wales. In December 1977 the Commission had issued a 'Reasoned Opinion' to the effect that Britain was not complying with the Directives. The delay in compliance seems to have been caused at least in part by the difficulties in establishing laboratory facilities able to test by the methods specified in Directive 73/405 which did not include the method traditionally used in Britain.

Compliance, however, was not strictly complete though this may be as much a fault of the framework Directive as of the Regulations. Detergents other than those which are anionic and have a level of biodegradability less than 80 per cent are not mentioned, nor is there any reference to 90 per cent average bio-degradability. The Commission, in not following up their Reasoned Opinion by initiating proceedings before the European Court, has presumably accepted that 73/404 is effectively not capable of being complied with where it deals with detergents not separately covered by a daughter Directive. The confusion concerning the 90 per cent requirement of 73/404 and the 80 per cent of 73/405 and the failure of the Commission to explain this seems to have been another reason for the delay over compliance.

Compliance was made complete in respect of Directives 82/242 and 243 by the Detergents (Composition) (Amendment) Regulations 1984 (SI 1984 No 1369) which came into force on 26 September 1984 and therefore covers nonionic detergents. Controls on the ampholytic and cationic detergents await further daughter Directives setting down appropriate test methods for biodegradability.

Effect on UK practice

The official response in Britain to the foaming of rivers had been the appointment of a committee in 1953, by the Minister of Housing and Local Government, to examine the effects of the increasing use of synthetic detergents.

The committee published a report in 1956 (the Jephcott Report)[1] which, among other matters, recommended the government to consider introducing legislation to be held in reserve to control detergents. This was never done so that the present Detergents (Composition) Regulations have had to be made under the broad powers provided by the European Communities Act 1972 which enable the government to implement any Community obligation.

The main recommendations of the Jephcott Report were that sewage authorities and detergent manufacturers should cooperate closely and find technical solutions to the problems of foaming and that a central coordinating body, to include government representatives, should keep progress under review. This resulted in the setting up of the Standing Technical Committee on Synthetic Detergents. The Committee issued a total of twenty annual reports before being wound up in 1980 and these tell a story of voluntary agreement and gradual technical progress. By 1964 the Confederation of British Industry felt able to give an undertaking to the Minister that after the end of 1964 no detergents based on propylene tetramer (the old 'hard' material) would be supplied to the British market. This agreement specified no set standards of 'hardness'. The Standing Committee continued to stress the need for improvement and by the time of the first two Directives British detergents already met the standards specified: indeed the Directives were criticized in Britain for being too lax. However, British industry apparently does not intend to reduce its standards because it is now as cheap or even cheaper to manufacture the softer detergents.

The Directives have therefore had no practical effect upon the quality of detergents manufactured in Britain. This does not mean that the Directives are useless as far as Britain is concerned since, without them, there would have been no Detergents (Composition) Regulations 1978 and without these Regulations, imports in Britain of 'hard' detergents could not be controlled without going through the rather elaborate procedure of Section 100 of the Control of Pollution Act 1974. The Standing Committee was abolished in 1980 in the government purge of 'quangos' and without anyone to monitor the voluntary undertakings given by industry, it is now the Regulations and the Directives that prevent backsliding.

Further developments
A European Agreement limiting the use of detergents by Members of the Council of Europe was signed or ratified by various members of the European Community between 1970 and 1980. A Protocol to this Agreement taking account of changes in Community legislation on this subject was presented for signature in October 1983. It was signed by the United Kingdom and other Community members and entered into force on 1 November 1984. The Commission in March 1985 put forward a recommendation for a Council Decision authorizing the Commission to conduct negotiations enabling the Community to become a contracting party to the Agreement.

References
1   Jephcott Sir Henry (chairman) 1956 *Report of the Committee on synthetic detergents*. HMSO.

4.2 Surface water for drinking

75/440/EEC (OJ L194 25.7.75) proposed 15.1.74 – COM(74)11	Directive concerning the quality required of surface water intended for the abstraction of drinking water in the Member States.

Binding dates
Notification date	18 June 1975
Formal compliance	18 June 1977
Standards to be set and met	no set date, therefore presumably by 18 June 1977
Improvements to be achieved	'over the next ten years', ie by 18 June 1985.

Purpose of the Directive

The Directive has two purposes: to ensure that surface water abstracted for use as drinking water reaches certain standards and is given adequate treatment before being put into public supply; and thereby to improve rivers or other surface waters used as sources of drinking water.

Summary of the Directive

Sources of surface water for the abstraction of drinking water (referred to as 'surface water') are to be classified by their existing quality into three categories: A1, A2 and A3 corresponding to the three standard methods of treatment required to transform the 'surface water' into drinking water. Annex I defines the three methods of treatment that must be used for A1, A2 and A3 waters respectively. In summary, A1 water requires only simple physical treatment (filtration) and disinfection, A2 requires normal physical treatment, chemical treatment and disinfection, while A3 water requires intensive physical and chemical treatment and disinfection.

The physical, chemical and microbiological characteristics which define the quality of A1, A2 and A3 water are set out in Annex II. Forty-six 'parameters' are listed against which numerical values are given under six columns: an I (or imperative) value and a G (or guide) value for each category A1, A2, A3. The parameters include temperature, BOD_5, nitrates, lead and faecal coliforms. For some parameters no I or G values are yet given but the Directive provides for these to be added later.

The Member States are required to lay down values for sampling points where water is abstracted whenever an I or G value is given. The values set must be no less stringent than the I values and the G values are to be respected as guidelines. Sometimes no I value is given in Annex II and the G value then provides guidance. Once values are set, Member States must then ensure that 95 per cent of the samples of 'surface water' meet the values laid down for the I values and that 90 per cent of the samples do so for the other values laid down.

Article 8 provides for waivers in the case of floods or natural disasters and in the case of certain parameters because of exceptional conditions. The Commission must be notified of these.

Article 4 prohibits the use of 'surface water' worse than A3 from being used for the abstraction of drinking water. In exceptional circumstances, such water may be used provided suitable processes such as blending raise the quality but the Commission must be notified of the exceptions – in advance in the case of new installations.

Article 4 also requires a plan of action, including a timetable, for the improvement of 'surface water' and especially A3 water. This timetable is to be drawn up in the light of the need to improve the surface water and of economic and technical constraints. Considerable improvements of low quality sources are to be achieved within ten years. The Commission is to examine the plans and timetables and will, if necessary, submit appropriate proposals to the Council. There is no obligation on the Commission to publish a report comparing these plans. There is also no obligation on Member States to send a report to the Commission on the improvements achieved within the ten year period.

Development of the Directive

This was the first proposal for a Directive concerning water following adoption of the first action programme on the environment of 1973 and was inspired by a draft French decree setting out a legally binding technical specification for 'surface water'. Discussion on the proposal had in fact started before Britain joined the Community on 1 January 1973.

The Environment Committee of the European Parliament wanted the proposed Directive strengthened by prohibiting absolutely – without any temporary derogation – the use of surface water falling below a minimum standard, but Commissioner Scarascia Mugnozza, replying to the debate in the European Parliament (13 May 1974), discussed the conflict – which was to occur with subsequent Directives – between perfection and practicality:

> We believe that if this reservation were omitted, we should encounter difficulties in implementation, in that where there were no alternative water resources, use of this type of water would of necessity become unavoidable; it is better, therefore, to provide in advance for possible exceptions (though only on a temporary basis), but have at our disposal a generally applicable piece of legislation, than to lay down a restriction which we know cannot be observed.

Since the House of Commons and the House of Lords had not yet established Scrutiny Committees when the Directive was proposed, it escaped parliamentary discussion in Britain. British officials despite feeling disadvantaged by their unfamiliarity with the procedures for influence and negotiation have nevertheless claimed responsibility for several practical provisions now in the Directive[1]. Notable among these is the provision that only 95 per cent of the samples need comply with the values set, and the vague description of 'sampling point' which enables it to mean the point at which water leaves a reservoir for treatment rather than the point in the river from which it is abstracted to be stored in a reservoir.

Formal compliance in the UK

There is no legislation setting standards for 'surface water' in Britain but the water authorities in England and Wales and other authorities in Scotland and Northern Ireland have a statutory duty to supply 'wholesome' water and have the powers to do so. They also have powers to grant consents for dischargess to water and powers to produce improvement plans. The Directive has therefore not been implemented by any new legislation or regulations made under existing legislation, but by administrative action, that is to say by the central government informing the authorities of the Directive and advising them of the steps that they should take. The assumption is that the authorities responsible will interpret their statutory duties in the light of the Directive. The existing legislation in England and Wales enabling this to be done consists of the Water Acts 1945 and 1973, and the Control of Pollution Act 1974. There is equivalent legislation in Scotland and Northern Ireland.

On 17 June 1977, one day before the date for complying with the Directive, the Department of the Environment (DoE) wrote formally to all the water authorities in England sending them a copy of the Directive and advising them of the steps they had to take. This followed discussion with water authorities over the previous year. A copy of the letter was sent to the Commission as evidence of this administrative action.

The Commission was not convinced that this constituted compliance and after letters and a meeting, the DoE on 19 October 1979 sent a memorandum to the Commission explaining the relationship between the DoE and the water authorities and the comparable arrangements in Scotland and Northern Ireland. The memorandum stated that:

> obligations which are clear from the Directive itself are not the subject of instructions from the government to the water authorities. As with domestic legislation, the authorities apply the Directive using their own resources and legal advice. The government is responsible to the Community for seeing that the aims of the Directive are met, and in the event of a water authority's failing to ensure that a Directive was implemented the government could take action to ensure that it did so. However, this is a safety net procedure which is not likely to be required in practice.

Notwithstanding this memorandum, the Commission issued a Reasoned Opinion on 18 July 1980 to the effect that the UK had not adopted all the necessary provisions for compliance with the Directive and published this fact in the *Bulletin of the European Communities*. The Reasoned Opinion mentioned in particular that the measures for implementing the Directive in Scotland and Northern Ireland had not been communicated to the Commission.

The government replied to the Reasoned Opinion by letter dated 18 September 1980 and referred to further existing legislation covering Scotland and Northern Ireland. It expressed the view that the Directive had indeed been properly complied with all along and, in effect, asked the Commission to withdraw its Reasoned Opinion. Though the Reasoned Opinion has not been withdrawn (a course of action not followed by the Commission) the replies from the UK government appear to have satisfied the Commission and no further action has been taken. The issue of compliance by administrative action which so troubles the Commission is discussed further in Appendix 3 of the first edition of this book.

Effect on UK practice

Fears expressed when the Directive was initially proposed that many drinking water sources might have to be abandoned and large sums of money spent on improvement schemes have not turned out to be justified[1]. Lists of 'surface waters' submitted to the Commission by the DoE in September 1981 covering England and Wales and in February 1982 covering Scotland included no source worse than A3 and no such British sources have otherwise been notified to the Commission under Article 4. Of the 679 sources listed in England and Wales, 207 were A1, 408 were A2 and 10 were A3: 54 sources were not classified but were understood to be A1 or A2. Of the 29 sources listed in Northern Ireland, one was A1 and 28 were A2. All sources in Scotland are unpolluted upland rivers of A1 or A2 quality. Some of the A3 sources only achieved their A3 status by virtue of waivers under Article 8. One source is on a river which receives an intermittent discharge from a mine. During discharge the river is below A3 quality but the rest of the time it is A2 quality with a waiver. Abstraction only takes place when the river is of A2 quality. The fact that a particular source received a waiver for a particular parameter was notified to the Commission but the exact extent of the waivers has not been made public. The waivers usually concerned colour, nitrates, iron, ammonium and sulphates.

Waivers for lead were given in three instances when the sources are in areas where lead exists in the soil and lead compounds are found in surface waters after heavy rainfall. The DoE said that public health was not at risk in these cases because the lead is removed during treatment processes.

In four cases the treatment given to the 'surface water' was lower than specified in the Directive. Since there is no specific provision in British law that treatment must match the quality of the source – though clearly this is normal practice – the Directive may well have highlighted these deficiencies. All water authorities in England and Wales had set values for the sampling points. All had followed DoE advice and set values equal to the I values in the Directive.

Where only G values appear in the Directive, the practices differed and five water authorities used their own initiative in setting G values – sometimes more stringent than the G values in the Directive. The rest of the water authorities set G values given in the Directive. The actual values set have not been transmitted to the Commission, nor are they necessarily to be published.

In England and Wales the plans, with timetable, for improving 'surface waters' required under Article 4 now form part of the plans for 'the use of water and restoring or maintaining the wholesomeness of rivers' that water authorities have a duty to prepare under Section 24 of the Water Act 1973. By 1986 substantial improvements had been made in the quality of surface waters abstracted and, for example, the number of A3 sources had been reduced from ten to two. It would be easy to say that all upgrading of treatment plants to match the quality of the source was a result of the Directive, but many of these improvements would have been programmed anyway. The most that can be said is that the Directive has drawn attention to some deficiencies and may have hastened improvements.

Sampling and analysis of the parameters are the subject of a separate Directive 79/869 (see Section 4.3) and during a debate in the House of Commons (18 June 1979) on the proposal for that Directive the Minister, Marcus Fox, referred to the surface water Directive and summed up the official view:

> Its application in the United Kingdom has caused no concern or difficulty, since the standards of water that we abstract for drinking are at least as good as and often better than those laid down.

The Commission, somewhat belatedly, wrote in 1986 to all Member States referring to the ten-year review and asking a number of questions about progress in implementing the Directive and that on sampling (see Section 4.3). The DoE is using this request to make their own review of progress.

References
1   Goodman A H 1979 EEC Directive on the quality of surface water intended for the abstraction of drinking water, *Journal of the Institute of Water Pollution Control* **78** (2).

4.3 Sampling surface water for drinking

79/869/EEC (OJ L271 29.10.79) proposed 26.7.78 – COM(78)363	Directive concerning the methods of measurement and frequency of sampling and analysis of surface water intended for the abstraction of drinking water in the Member States.
Binding dates	
Notification date	11 October 1979
Formal compliance	11 October 1981

Purpose of the Directive

The Directive supplements Directive 75/440 (see Section 4.2) by recommending methods of measuring the parameters for surface water quality and setting the frequencies for such measurements.

Summary of the Directive

The parameters listed in Directive 75/440 must be measured with the 'precision' and 'accuracy' (as defined) set out in Annex I. The 'reference methods' of measurement also set out in Annex I must be used 'as far as possible' but are not mandatory. The frequency of sampling is to be set by Member States and is to be no less than the frequencies set out in Annex II. These frequencies increase as the quality category of 'surface water' decreases and as the population served increases, in other words A3 water has to be sampled more frequently than A2 water, and an A2 source for a population over 100 000 has to be sampled more frequently than for a smaller population. The Member States may reduce the frequency of sampling for certain parameters if a survey shows that the values obtained are much better than the values set. If the water is of better than A1 quality no regular analysis may be necessary. Member States may also determine the frequencies themselves for 'surface water' serving very small populations.

Member States are to provide the Commission, at its request, with information on the frequency and methods of analysis used. The Commission is at regular intervals to draw up a consolidated report but does not have to publish it.

Development of the Directive

The government submitted two memoranda on this Directive to the House of Commons, one in January 1979 and one in June 1979. Between these dates the proposal for the Directive was substantially modified and the government's attitude changed. The first memorandum listed a number of unsatisfactory features and said:

> It is difficult to see what justification there is for using a

Directive to impose a Community policy on such highly complex, detailed and technical matters.

The second memorandum explained that the analytical methods were no longer to be mandatory but were now merely 'reference methods' and that the provision for reducing the sampling frequencies could be used without having to seek the consent of the Commission. Accordingly the Minister, Marcus Fox, said in the House of Commons' debate (18 June 1979) that the proposed Directive was now more like a Recommendation and that:

It does not perhaps matter too much what title is given to a document which has so little effect on the United Kingdom.

The Minister also claimed that:

The United Kingdom managed to secure a number of major changes which meet some of the points of criticism . . in its present form, the Directive would not hinder the continuation of present United Kingdom practices, and would not force additional burdens upon us.

Formal compliance in the UK

The legal powers set out in the previous section describing Directive 75/440 also provide for monitoring water quality, so no new legislation has been required. As with that parent Directive, implementation has been by administrative action. A circular letter from the DoE, with the Directive reproduced as an Appendix, was sent to the water authorities on 31 March 1982 (nearly six months after the due date) appointing them as competent authorities for the purposes of the Directive. An identical circular letter was sent by the Welsh Office to the Welsh Water Authority, and a generally similar letter was sent by the Scottish Development Department to the Scottish water supply authorities. The circulars explained the Directive. On 5 July 1982, in reply to a letter from the Commission pointing out that the date for formal compliance had passed, copies of these letters were sent as evidence of the administrative action taken to comply with the Directive.

Effect on UK practice

The statement by the Minister that the Directive would not force additional burdens on Britain has been largely, but not entirely, confirmed by the water authorities.

The methods of measurement used already conformed in general with the 'precision' and 'accuracy' of the reference methods set out in the Directive. However, several water authorities had to include more parameters in their analytical programme. Any increase in expenditure due to more sophisticated analytical techniques has not resulted in any overall increase in expenditure since the frequency of sampling has, in general, been much greater than is required by the Directive.

The circular letters mentioned above and sent by central government departments to the water authorities (and water supply authorities in Scotland) asked the authorities to supply information in a prescribed form about frequency of sampling and the methods of analysis to enable the DoE to supply information to the Commission at its request. Therefore, one effect of the Directive is that central government now has more information than it would have had otherwise. The Commission in 1986 asked for further information (see Section 4.2). Apart from the information aspect, the general effect of the Directive was summed up by the Head of the Analytical Division of the Water Research Centre in an otherwise fairly critical paper:[1]

> In fact, the frequencies commonly applied at present for many waters are substantially greater than those in the Directive. The main impact on the UK seems, therefore, to be the need to obtain information on the concentrations of any parameters not previously measured. Depending on the extent of this need, a substantial amount of additional analysis may initially be involved but it will be of value to make good any gaps in knowledge of water quality.

A more jaundiced view of the Directive was expressed by a DoE official to the House of Lords in connection with their investigation into a rather similar proposed Directive (Section 4.15):

> In the end we dealt with the problem by negotiating in Brussels with our partners a directive which, whilst one may not think it is of any particular use, at least does not do any particular harm. It sits there, as it were, as a monument to precedent.[2]

References

1   Wilson A L 1980 EEC Directives: Requirements for sampling and analysis *Symposium on EEC Directives*. The Institution of Water Engineers and Scientists.

2   House of Lords' Select Committee on the European Communities 1981 *Monitoring of waste from the titanium dioxide industry*, 40th Report Session 1980–81. HMSO.

4.4 Drinking water[1]

80/778/EEC (OJ L229 30.8.80) proposed 22.7.75 – COM(75)394	Directive relating to the quality of water intended for human consumption.

Binding dates
Notification date	17 July 1980
Formal compliance	17 July 1982
Standards to be met	17 July 1985 (unless derogations made or delay granted).

Purpose of the Directive

Standards for the quality of water intended for drinking or for use in food and drink manufacture are laid down in order to protect human health. The Directive has the additional effect of protecting the environment, as drinking water sources must be sufficiently free from contamination to allow inexpensive water treatment. The Directive has indirect links with Directives 75/440 and 79/869 (see Sections 4.2 and 4.3) concerning surface water. Waters officially recognized as natural mineral waters are covered by a separate Directive 80/777 OJ L229 30.8.80.

Summary of the Directive

The Directive covers all water for human consumption including public and private water supplies, bottled water not recognized as mineral water or medicinal water by individual Member States, and water used in the food industry. In some instances, water used in the food industry may gain exemptions if its use does not affect the wholesomeness of the finished product. Regular water quality monitoring is to be carried out by Member States and samples must be taken at the point at which the water is made available to the user. The exact points of sampling are to be determined by the competent national authorities.

The Directive lays down some sixty-two water quality standards and guidelines for water quality monitoring. It contains three Annexes.

Annex 1 lists the water quality standards, some of which have accompanying comments. Three types of standard are used: the Guide Level (GL), the Maximum Admissible Concentration (MAC), and the Minimum Required Concentration (MRC). Member States must set values for all parameters with MAC or MRC values and must ensure that water meets them. These values must be as stringent as the MAC and MRC standards. When the Directive only gives a GL standard, a Member State may use its discretion as to whether it sets a standard or not. For some parameters no standard has been set: the parameter appears in the Directive only in order to draw the attention of Member States to its existence and to alert them to the possibility of its regulation in the future.

The parameters are divided into six categories:

1. organoleptic parameters, eg colour, odour, taste;
2. physiochemical parameters, eg pH, conductivity;

3.   parameters concerning substances undesirable in excessive amounts, eg nitrates, nitrites;
4.   parameters concerning toxic substances, eg mercury, lead, pesticides;
5.   microbiological parameters, eg coliforms, faecal steptococci;
6.   minimum required concentration for softened water intended for human consumption, eg hardness, alkalinity (there are no MACs in this table).

Annex II is concerned with water quality monitoring and the manner in which it should be conducted so as to ensure that the standards in Annex I are complied with. It contains two tables: one groups parameters together to form standard pattern analyses; and the other states the minimum frequencies at which these standard analyses are to be performed. The frequency of monitoring is greatest in systems that supply water to a large population, and for parameters such as residual chlorine and total coliforms. For supplies serving less than 5000 people, monitoring is at the discretion of the competent national authority. Member States are obliged to conform exactly with Annex II.

Annex III contains reference methods of analysis. Not all of the parameters have yet been given reference methods of analysis. Annex III must be adhered to as far as practicable. Laboratories using methods of analysis not found in Annex III are required 'to ensure that the results thus obtained are equivalent to or comparable with the results obtained by the methods indicated in Annex III'.

Member States may derogate from the standards set in Annex I in a number of circumstances. Article 9 makes provision for derogations arising from the nature and structure of the ground in the area in which the supply in question emanates, and also for situations arising from exceptional meteorological conditions. It does not apply to toxic and microbiological parameters, and derogations must not constitute a public health hazard. Derogations arising from the nature and structure of the ground may be permitted for long periods of time and are granted by the competent national authority of the Member State itself but the Commission must be informed if the derogation relates to a daily supply of 1000 m^3 or above, or to a population of more than 5000.

Article 10 covers derogations occurring in two circumstances: following emergencies, and when a poor quality water supply for which adequate treatment is not possible must be used constantly. In both cases derogations may only be granted for a limited period of time and neither may constitute an unacceptable risk to health. Derogations may be granted for all parameters in Annex I. The 'competent national authority' of the Member State concerned must determine the maximum value or values which the relevant parameters may reach. The Commission must be informed immediately that a derogation under Article 10 is needed and its duration and causal factors must be indicated.

Under Article 20 delays may be granted to Member States by the Commission if particular difficulties are being experienced with compliance with the Directive. Delay applications must be submitted with a time-limited plan of remedial work, and must relate to geographically defined population groups. Delays may be granted for any parameter in Annex I.

The Directive details two ways in which it will relate to the food industry. Firstly, it allows water used in the food industry to be excluded from meeting the requirements of Annex I (except for toxic and microbiological parameters) if its use does not affect the wholesomeness of the finished product. In order for an industry to be eligible for partial exemption it must pass on information proving that the wholesomeness of the product is not affected to the competent national authority, which then applies to the Commission. Secondly, it states that Member States may not act to prevent or inhibit the marketing of foodstuffs on grounds relating to the quality of the water if it reaches the standards laid down by the Directive.

One other area affected by the Directive is the packaging and labelling of water with information regarding its suitability for consumption by infants. Member States wishing to introduce special provisions relating to such information must inform the Commission and other Member States beforehand.

Development of the Directive

Although the Directive flows from the first action programme on the environment of 1973 it originated in the Health Protection Directorate. It was a response to the mounting concern about the increased reuse of waste water for potable supply and the rising number of new organic and other trace substances entering into the water supply. There was a need to confirm that waste water treatment processes could adequately protect public health. The standards in the Directive are based on the WHO 1970 Drinking Water Standards which were not legally binding[2].

The negotiations for the Directive were lengthy, the main difficulties concerning the standards for the large number of parameters. Many of these were contentious because of cost as well as health factors. The Netherlands wanted very stringent standards for sodium, chloride and conductivity so as to control the activities of countries of the upper Rhine that were polluting the river from potash mines. The final version of the Directive however, does not even contain a MAC for chlorides and conductivity.

Another particularly contentious parameter was lead. Britain campaigned for a more lenient standard than the 50 μg/l set in the draft Directive, which was controversial because it was then half the 1970 WHO European standard. It would have been impossible for Britain to meet this standard in a short period of time although the lead problem had already been acknowledged in Britain and remedial work begun. The House of Lords' Select Committee reported that 7–10 per cent of households in England and Wales, and a higher proportion in Scotland, would not be able to comply with the proposed lead standard and stated that:

> . . .because of the high proportion and the long standing
> nature of the problem, the Committee believe that the two
> years for compliance with the Directive is wholly unrealistic.

Partly in response to Britain's views the final version of the Directive contains a number of additions that make the lead parameter easier to comply with. Firstly, a 'comment' was added to the lead standard in Annex I which raises the MAC in certain circumstances. Imprecise language has been used to give a great amount of flexibility. Secondly, the period of time given to comply with all of the parameters in the Directive was extended from two to five years. Thirdly the possibility of delays was introduced.

Surprisingly the nitrate parameter was not widely regarded as a problem during the negotiations and only the UK government apparently foresaw difficulties in meeting it.

One reason for the frequent use of imprecise language in the Directive is the inadequate state of scientific knowledge of the chronic health effects of many substances now found in water. Another is the large number of parameters to be regulated and the complicating influence of such things as synergistic reactions. Scientific uncertainty and political compromise are probably responsible for the phrase found in Articles 9 and 10 relating to derogations: they are not to constitute a 'public health hazard'. No precise information is given as to the way this is to be interpreted. The Economic and Social Committee stated in relation to Article 10 derogations that it was:

> . . .absolutely essential that some guidelines should be given
> in order to meet with emergency situations and that these
> could not be left entirely to the discretion of local authorities.

Guidance on water quality monitoring is also lacking. For example, there is no guidance on sample collection and storage yet the way in which samples are handled can significantly affect the results of water quality analysis. Annex III contains reference methods of analysis but no performance criteria for use when methods other than those listed are used. A number of the problems have been highlighted in a report by EUREAU in which it is pointed out, for example, that for dissolved or emulsified carbons, and phenols, the detection limits are above the MAC[3].

Formal compliance in the UK

The Directive sets mandatory limits for water quality for the first time in the UK. For physical and chemical quality, water undertakers and local authorities had previously relied on the 1970 WHO European Standards for drinking water and its revision in 1984, and on a DoE report, 'The Bacterial Examination of Drinking Water Supplies'[4] for guidance on bacteriological quality. The statutory obligations on water undertakers under the Water Act 1945 are to supply 'wholesome' water and on local authorities under the Water Act 1945 and the Water Act 1973 to ascertain the 'wholesomeness' of public and private supplies within their area. 'Wholesome' is not defined in quantitative terms, but is generally understood to mean that water is to be clear, palatable and safe. Any dispute between water undertakers and the local authorities, who have to ascertain that a water undertaker is supplying wholesome water, is referred to the Secretary of State. Broadly similar provisions are contained in the Water (Scotland) Act 1980. In Northern Ireland public water supplies are the direct responsibility of the government.

A formal letter of compliance was sent to the Commission on 7 September 1982 stating that the Directive would be implemented by 'administrative provision which makes full use of the United Kingdom's legislation'. The letter included an apology for the delay in communicating the provisions and lists the relevant official documents for England and Wales. Those for Scotland and Northern Ireland were produced later. In fact Denmark was the only country to introduce legislation by the date stipulated. The chief document mentioned in the letter of compliance is DoE Circular 20/82 which gives guidance on the implementation of the Directive in England and Wales. More detailed procedural guidance to statutory water undertakers and guidance on matters which the

Directive specifically states are within the competence of the Member State are contained in DoE letters to the water industry reference numbers WI 7/1983, WI 7/1984 and WP 10/1986. Similar letters were issued in Scotland by the Scottish Development Department. DoE Circular 25/84 deals with the application of the Directive to private supplies and to water used in food businesses.

DoE Circular 20/82 includes the full text of the Directive in an annex. It places responsibility for administering the Directive on the statutory water undertakers and local authorities. Their previously existing statutory duties are linked to the new obligations created by the Directive by the following statement in the Circular:

> The Secretaries of State will regard compliance with the terms of the Directive as a necessary characteristic but not a complete definiton of any water that is to be considered wholesome; they will be guided accordingly in any dispute concerning wholesomeness referred to them under S.11 of the 1973 Act, or concering inadequate quality under S.13 of the 1945 Act, as substituted.

With regard to the parameters with a MAC, the Circular says that the government intends, in respect of those parameters, to adopt the levels shown in the Directive. The Circular itself is being regarded as authority for the 'adoption' of the MAC values since no other document appears to have done so, although Circular WI 7/1983 sets MAC values for a few parameters for which only a GL was given.

Some of the MAC values are being regarded as absolute and some as averages over time. The government's advice on this and on the sampling location has been summarized as follows[5]:

1. for microbiological parameters the MACs are limits for individual samples taken from the distribution system and at consumers' taps;
2. for copper, zinc and lead the MACs are limits for individual samples at consumers' taps subject to qualifying comments about the frequency and extent to which the limit may be exceeded in a water supply zone. All these parameters may be affected by the consumer's pipework and the time the water has been standing in it;
3. for sodium the MAC is expressed as a percentile calculated over a three-year period in a water supply zone;
4. for odour, taste, aluminium, nitrate, chlorine containing trihalomethanes, iron and manganese the MAC is an average over any three-month period in a supply zone because the concentration of these parameters can vary significantly seasonally;
5. for all other parameters the MAC or MRC is an annual average in a supply zone.

The Directive says nothing about allowing averages or about the MACs being absolute but a Commission official has stated that the MAC values are absolute.[6] It may be on this point that the Commission has decided to start infringement procedures against the UK.

DoE Circular 25/84 places responsibility for administering private supplies on local authorities since they already have the duty to ascertain wholesomeness of supplies in their area. However, the legislation was not designed to give local authorities power of entry onto premises and land to examine a private supply and there is uncertainty whether existing powers are adequate. A consultation paper issued by the DoE in January 1986 includes proposals to clarify and extend these powers and legislation is being prepared.

Effect on UK practice

The Directive has led to greater public scrutiny of water supplies. It has been necessary for water undertakers to apply for derogations and delays and this has clearly exposed problem areas.

By March 1987 derogations under Article 9 had been made for 197 specific water supply zones in England mostly relating to manganese (53), nitrate (48), iron (46) and aluminium (17). In addition the Commission has been requested for the following three sets of delays for England:

1. delays for 118 individual supply areas mainly for the following parameters: microbiological (84), aluminium (34), manganese (13) and iron (10) (nearly all of these are expected to comply by 1990);
2. a delay until 1989 for all zones where more than $2^1/_2$ per cent of properties on a random survey have exceeded the MAC for lead;
3. a delay until 1995 for all private supplies serving less than 500 people.

Although private supplies account for only 1 per cent of water supplied in the UK, they exist throughout the country and may number over 100 000; their location is often unknown to local authorities. The Directive could have an important impact on water quality in this sector and the problems of implementation are administrative, legal and financial as well as scientific. A consultation paper was issued in 1986 by the DoE in an effort to resolve the question of improvement but no final decisions have yet been taken.

The precise impact of the Directive on public health protection in Britain is difficult to assess because often it has not so much initiated new measures as given added impetus to remedial work already begun, particularly for lead. Aluminium, iron and manganese had also been recognized as problems, their adverse effects in general being unrelated to health. The large number of delay applications for total and faecal coliforms has highlighted an area which had not previously received much public attention, but which is fundamental to public health protection. British supplies seem to have been exposed as inadequate to some degree in this area.

It is also difficult to gauge the precise financial impact of the Directive. Many new schemes have more than one purpose so their costs can only be partly attributed to the Directive, such as water mains replacement and reservoir rehabilitation. Reaction to the Directive as a whole from water authorities has been mixed, with most showing antipathy towards the necessity to monitor and conform to some of the non-health related parameters without increases in their budget. However, the increased monitoring has had the positive effect of providing much more information than was previously available about drinking water quality.

Three problem parameters are discussed below.

Lead
In 1983 the government set a target date of December 1989 for compliance with the lead parameter and a delay under Article 20 was formally requested in 1985. No decision has yet been made by the Commission, which has asked for details of the geographical areas to which the delay is expected to apply. The causes of high lead levels in water are almost always the presence of lead pipes connecting the mains in the street to the consumer's taps and a supply of water which has a high capacity for dissolving lead compounds. Such water is usually soft and acidic, but recently it has been established that some hard waters can also give rise to high lead levels. Although water quality is a very important controlling factor, the lead concentrations in tap water also depend upon the length and quality of lead pipe, domestic water use patterns, rate of flow, ambient temperature and other factors. This produces variations within an individual house throughout the day, and therefore also between different houses and between different areas. It has been estimated that between 7 and 10.5 million out of a total of 18.5 million households in the UK have lead pipework at some point between the mains and tap. Of the five million households in areas where water is significantly plumbosolvent, about half will have lead in the connection pipe and many of these will also have lead pipework within the house[7].

The lead problem is complicated by a divided responsibility between householder and water undertaker. The duty of the water undertaker is to supply 'wholesome' water to the premises but it is still under a common law duty of care in respect of the quality of water within the premises of a consumer.[8] A water authority may be found negligent for not taking steps to reduce the plumbosolvency of water supplied through known lead pipes. However, if action has been taken by an authority to reduce water plumbosolvency, it is up to the consumer to replace the pipes on his property. To aid such replacement the government has made grants available. A local authority may be deterred from advertising these grants very widely because of the costs involved. The national cost of wholesale application for pipe replacement has been estimated as over £1000 million.[7] This figure excludes the cost of identification of problem areas.

The high cost of wholesale pipe replacement makes it a long-term solution. To comply with the Directive other measures need to be taken. Where appropriate, water suppliers are modifying water treatment by pH adjustment and by the addition of orthophosphate to reduce plumbosolvency.

Although it is plain that the government was taking steps to deal with the problem of lead in drinking water, the Directive has induced a greater sense of urgency.

Nitrate
It has been recognized for about forty years that excessive quantities of nitrate in drinking water can be harmful to health. High nitrate levels are known to cause methaemoglobinaemia, but of the 2000 cases worldwide since 1945 only 10 have occurred in Britain and there have been no cases since 1972. The other health effect that may be caused by high levels of nitrate is gastric cancer but, according to the Royal Commission on Environmental Pollution, the evidence for this has so far been judged to be 'weak and equivocal'.[9]

The Directive set a standard of 50 mg/l whereas the WHO recommended a level of less than 50 mg/l but considered 50 to 100 mg/l acceptable. The Directive has therefore had had the effect of focusing attention on supplies that had not previously been a cause of contention.

During the 1970s the British government had felt reassured about the nitrate problem particularly after the publication of the Royal Commission's report in 1979.[9] A turning point in the attitude of the government came after the publication of a report by the Standing Technical Advisory Committee on Water Quality in 1984.[10] The STACWQ report had a different tone. It predicted that if present trends in fertilizer application continued, mean nitrate concentrations in surface waters would rise by an average of 2–3 mg/l (as nitrogen) over the next ten to twenty years and this would considerably increase the proportion of abstractions exceeding the Directive limit of 11.3 mg/l (as nitrogen) which is equivalent to 50 mg/l (as nitrate). Predictions for groundwater were complicated by the relative shortage of long-term data and the uncertainties about controlling the movement of nitrates laden water through aquifers. A comprehensive picture of the present situation on nitrate in water is given in the report[11] of the Nitrate Coordination Group.

To comply with the Directive the government has decided to allow derogations in certain circumstances. Time-limited derogations are granted if the concentration of nitrate ion in supply does not exceed a three-monthly average of 80 mg/l and a maximum of 100 mg/l, except in exceptional and transitory circumstances.[12] Water undertakers are also expected to comply with advice given by the Joint Committee on the Medical Aspects of Water Quality on this matter.

In November 1985, fifty-seven applications for derogations had been made to the Department of the Environment and had been approved.[13] They are to be reviewed in July 1988. It is doubtful whether derogations for nitrate can be properly made under Article 9 because such derogations may only be granted for situations 'arising from the nature and structure of the ground' from which the water supplies are drawn. Although nitrates occur naturally in soil they are also applied by farmers.

The courses of remedial action open to water authorities when dealing with high nitrate supplies are nearly all costly. It is for this reason that control of nitrate has become a sensitive political issue.

The choice of remedial action includes blending different supplies to reduce the nitrate level of the water put into the distribution system; treating water to reduce nitrate levels; and exploiting new sources with lower nitrate levels. Denitrification technology has been a topic of research for some years now and treatment processes exist, but are expensive and produce a poorer quality water. Providing nursing mothers with bottled waters in areas of high nitrate concentrations may be a cheaper alternative, but is not favoured as a general solution. Water authorities also have powers to control farming activities in protection zones designated under Section 31(5) of COPA but these powers have not been used.

The Directive has certainly concentrated attention on the issue of nitrates. The decision of the Commission, and possibly ultimately the Court of Justice, on the validity of the derogations so far made will be crucial in determining action. It is clear that there are major problems in meeting the nitrate MAC in other countries too.

Pesticides
Parameter 55 in Annex I is entitled 'Pesticides and Related Products' and thus covers a large number of substances, some of which are more toxic to man than others. Since the Directive was agreed a significant amount of scientific progress has been made identifying the more dangerous substances and Britain has asked

for the standard to be reviewed. More efficient public health protection would be provided by regulating most stringently the substances with a greater health risk. According to DoE letter to the water industry WP 10/1986, the DoE does not seem to expect water suppliers to comply with the standard as now stated.

References

1   This section is based on a draft by Jilyan Kelly drawing on her MSc thesis for the Centre for Environmental Technology, Imperial College, London.

2   World Health Organization 1970 *European standards for drinking water* 2nd edn. WHO, Geneva.

3   EUREAU 1984 Directive of 15 July 1980 (80/77/EEC) *Remarks on its application*, p4.

4   Department of the Environment 1982 *The bacterial examination of drinking water supplies*. HMSO, London, no 71. (Reports on public health and medical subjects.)

5   Hydes O D 1986 *EC Directive relating to the quality of water intended for human consumption*. Paper to Institute of Environmental Health Officers, seminar on 'Water Leisure, Recreation and Consumption', Exeter, 22 July 1986.

6   *Water Bulletin*, 5 December 1986. Questions for Brussels on water quality, Report of a seminar of the European Institute for Water.

7   Water Research Centre 1983 *Lead in drinking water* R 187. Water Research Centre, p1.

8   Macrory R 1985 *Water Law*. Longman, London, p105.

9   Royal Commission on Environmental Pollution 1979 *Agriculture and pollution*, 7th Report. HMSO, London.

10   Standing Technical Advisory Committee on Water Quality 1984 *Fourth biennial report*. HMSO, London, no 37. (Standing technical committee reports.)

11   (Nitrate Coordination Group 1986) *Nitrate in water: a report of the Nitrate Coordination Group*. HMSO, no 26 (Pollution paper.)

12   Department of the Environment 1985 *New standards for drinking water quality*. Memorandum by the Department of the Environment, Press Notice 363, 23 July 1985.

13   Official Report, House of Commons' Written Answers, 4 December 1985.

4.5 Water standards for freshwater fish

78/659/EEC (OJ L.222 14.8.78) proposed 26.7.76 – COM(76)401	Directive on the quality of fresh waters needing protection or improvement in order to support fish life.

Binding dates
Notification date	20 July 1978
Formal compliance	20 July 1980
Designation of waters	20 July 1980
Standards to be met	20 July 1985

Purpose of the Directive

In order to allow fish to live in favourable conditions, quality objectives are to be set for designated stretches of river or other fresh waters.

Summary of the Directive

The Member States are themselves to designate fresh waters needing protection or improvement in order to support fish life. Two categories of water are to be designated: suitable for salmonids (salmon, trout) and suitable for cyprinids (coarse fish). An Annex sets out fourteen physical and chemical parameters against which are listed I (imperative) and G (guide) values for salmonid and cyprinid waters. Member States are to set values no less stringent than the I values and 'shall endeavour to respect the values in column G'.

Member States are to establish pollution reduction programmes and are to ensure that within five years of designation the waters conform to the values set. The Annex also sets out minimum sampling frequencies but where the water quality is high, sampling frequency may be reduced. Certain reference methods of analysis for the parameters are set out in the Annex but other methods may be used so long as comparable results are obtained. If sampling shows that a set value is not being met, appropriate measures are to be taken.

Derogations may be given by Member States for certain parameters because of exceptional weather or special geographical conditions or because of 'natural enrichment'. These are to be communicated to the Commission.

Member States are to supply the Commission with a list of designated waters and, five years later, with a detailed report on the designated waters.

Development of the Directive

Two difficulties were posed by the Directive as proposed. Who was to be responsible for designation, and were the parameters realistic? Both difficulties were eventually resolved by amendment but not before a considerable amount of heat had been generated. The two difficulties seem to have been universally noted because they were discussed in the European Parliament's debate (14 January 1977), in the report of the Economic and Social Committee (23 February 1977), in the House of Lords' debate (28 June 1977), and the House of Commons' debate (6 April 1978).

The first difficulty was created by ambiguous draftsmanship. Article 1 of the Directive as finally agreed is quite clear:

> This Directive concerns the quality of fresh waters and applies to those waters designated by the Member States as needing protection or improvement in order to support freshwater fish (Article 1).

The proposed Directive on the other hand had Articles 1 and 4 as follows:

> This Directive concerns the quality requirements for waters capable of supporting freshwater fish (Article 1).

> For the purposes of applying this Directive, the Member States shall specify those waters capable of supporting freshwater fish (Article 4).

The difficulty posed by the original wording was explained in a memorandum submitted on 29 March 1978 by the Minister, Denis Howell, to the House of Commons before it debated the proposed Directive:

> . . .the extent of a Member State's obligation to designate waters under the Directive was obscure. The original text of Articles 1 and 4 might have implied designation of all rivers which supported fish life or which were potentially capable of doing so, whether or not the Member State was willing or able to provide the resources necessary to bring them up to pre-scribed standards within the five years allowed under Article 5.

Although the original Article 4 laid on Member States the administrative task of designation, the Article was not clear whether their discretion was unfettered. Would the Commission, for example, be able to question why a certain stretch of river had not been designated, and in the extreme could the Commission have taken the Member State to the Court for failure to designate a stretch of river 'capable of supporting freshwater fish'? The very use of the word 'capable' must also cause confusion since almost any waters are capable of supporting fish if given adequate treatment.

Not everyone could see the ambiguity. In the European Parliament's debate, the rapporteur, Mrs Kruchow, argued against an amendment by a British MEP, James Spicer, which sought to draw attention to the ambiguity:

> . . .I cannot commend this proposed amendment. I fear it is based on a misunderstanding. The Directive we are dealing with today does not deal with the existence of fish in freshwa-ter areas capable of supporting them, but with the freshwater areas in which the individual governments have decided fish should be able to survive.

Lady White in the Lords' debate quoted Mrs Kruchow's words and commented that: 'This is an attitude of mind to which we. . . find it extraordinarily hard to adapt ourselves'. Lady White pointed out that Mrs Kruchow's interpretation could mean that Member States need designate nothing at all and that the Directive would then be inoperative. The same point was made by the Economic and Social Committee:

> The Committee feels that leaving it (designation) up to the Member State. . . could slow up or even rule out any action to improve quality standards for water in a large number of EEC rivers.

The then Director of the Commission's Environment and Consumer Protection Service (Mr Michel Carpentier) tried to answer these points in long letters to Lady White and Lord Ashby following the Lords' debate. Lord Ashby, having assumed little or no discretion on the part of Member States, had argued in the debate that if the Directive applied to all waters in Britain already supporting fish, then vast costs would be incurred. To Lord Ashby, Mr Carpentier wrote as follows, though without acknowledging that another interpretation was possible:

> It is quite inaccurate to say that the Directive will apply. . . to all rivers in which fish are currently found. This is not the case. It will apply to designated waters, and it is, in your case, the United Kingdom which will make the designation.

To Lady White, Mr Carpentier explained why the Directive would still be effective:

> I am shocked by your suggestion that Member States will simply select a few areas of pure waters as the designated area, and let the question rest there. I have more faith in the seriousness and commitment to the improvement of the environment of the government of our Member States. . . What will be the reaction of public opinion if it discovers that in the Member State where it resides, few or no areas have been designated under the Directives. . . there would be a clamorous protest.

In the event Lady White has been proved right and Mr Carpentier's faith is being put to the test. Several Member States have not designated any waters and in those countries the Directive is therefore effectively inoperative.

The difference between English and continental traditions of drafting and interpreting legal documents does not in this case seem to have led to different people giving a different meaning to the words of the Directive as proposed. With the benefit of hindsight, one can see that had the Commission and its critics both realized that the original Articles 1 and 4 could be read in two ways, the ambiguity would have been resolved without acrimony. It would then not have been necessary for Mr Carpentier to say 'Why did Lord Ashby presume that the Directive automatically applies to all fish-bearing waters in the UK?' and Lord Ashby would not have presumed that it did.

The second difficulty created by the Directive as proposed concerned the parameters. Lord Nugent, then the Chairman of the National Water Council, giving evidence to the Lords' Select Committee said:

> The fact is that the Commission are here proposing standards of perfection, which is what they have done before. I have had the pleasure of meeting the officials concerned and I know that this is their policy; they think that the right thing to do is to establish standards of perfection although, quite obviously, in practice it is simply impossible to conform to them. So we do make a stringent criticism of these standards as being higher than is normal in practice for rivers in which fish live and thrive'.

In the event, a number of parameters originally proposed were altered including temperature, dissolved oxygen, phosphates and phenols. The nitrate parameter was completely deleted. In the Commons' debate the Minister, Kenneth Marks, commented: 'All the changes were towards the United Kingdom point of view, quite a few to meet specific United Kingdom problems and in response to pressure from us.' Linked to the realism of the parameters was the issue of the scientific basis for them. The Lords' report had said: 'The reason why the draft Directive's standards are so unrealistic may be explained, in part, by the failure of the Commission to accept some of the advice submitted by a group of experts set up by the Commission for that purpose.' Lord Ashby in the Lords' debate emphasized the point which continues to be a live one. He urged the government to persuade the Commission to set out clearly the scientific evidence upon which they base their proposals for Directives, and to state their reasons when Directives differ from that advice.

Formal compliance in the UK

The water authorities in England and Wales and the appropriate bodies in Scotland and Northern Ireland already have the powers to control discharges to all inland waters and to take samples. No new legislation was therefore necessary to implement the Directive. The existing legislation is:

Rivers (Prevention of Pollution) Acts 1951 and 1961
Salmon and Freshwater Fisheries Act 1975
Rivers (Prevention of Pollution) (Scotland) Acts 1951 and 1965
Water Act (Northern Ireland) 1972
Pollution Control and Local Government (Northern Ireland) Order 1978

Implementation has accordingly been by the following administrative action. In October 1978 the DoE sent a copy of the Directive to the water authorities together with an eight-page circular letter explaining it and stating that many of the functions involved were being delegated to the water authorities. The Circular advised water authorities to consult local authorities and fishing and other environmental interests on the designation of waters and on other matters.

The Scottish Development Department sent a circular letter on 7 March 1979 to the Convention of Scottish Local authorities, the Scottish River Purification Boards' Association and the Association of Scottish District Salmon Fishery

Boards explaining the Directive and stating that the Secretary of State for Scotland would designate the waters although suggestions were invited.

The Department of the Environment for Northern Ireland is also the water authority and so no question of delegating the task of designation arose.

In July 1980, as required by Article 15, the DoE submitted to the Commission a list of designated waters and in August 1985 a report as required by Article 16 on the state of designated waters.

Effect on UK practice

The DoE Circular of October 1978 suggested the setting up of a working group with representatives of government departments and water authorities to prepare more detailed advice on the Directive. The result was an undated eighteen page advice note issued in the second half of 1979. This note stated that the aim should be to designate as many waters as possible without affecting existing capital expenditure plans, in other words to designate intially only those waters which already met the standards or would do so by July 1985 after improvements which were already programmed.

In July 1980 the DoE sent to the Commission a list of waters designated in England, Wales, Scotland and Northern Ireland. Further designations were notified in 1981 and 1985. The government's advice seems to have been followed and in England and Wales only two water authorities designated waters which did not then already comply with the standards. Designations are nevertheless extensive and some water authorities have designated 50 per cent of their total length of rivers. The total designated amounted to about 45000 km of salmonid waters and 5500 km of cyprinid. In Scotland almost all the designated waters already met the standards and all did in Northern Ireland. Some water authorities issued consultation papers setting out their intended designations and made changes as a result of representations received from fishing interests. Only those authorities which designated waters not yet up to the required standards are required by the Directive to have programmes for river improvement and these are covered by existing forward plans.

The water authorities reported no increase in manpower to carry out the monitoring required though several said that they had to redeploy staff. They had to monitor for substances that they had not monitored before. In Northern Ireland monitoring has involved some increase in expenditure. Most water authorities reported that their existing monitoring was more frequent than required by the Directive. One water authority hinted that the Directive had prevented a cutback in monitoring.

The values set for the parameters have not been published and the Directive is silent on the need to do so. The DoE did, however, in its circular of October 1978 say that it would expect information about the application of the Directive to be available to the public.

Overall it cannot be said that the Directive has yet had any significant effect on Britain. It does however provide a prop against backsliding which is particularly important at a time of financial cutbacks. The comment of one water authority that the Directive had prevented a cutback in monitoring is perhaps a pointer here. The Directive allows more designations in the future and fishery interests can, therefore, use the Directive in arguments about raising the standards of stretches not yet designated. One water authority remarked that an indirect effect of the Directive had been a refinement of its water quality classification system.

In August 1985 the DoE submitted a report, together with maps, to the Commission on the state of the designated waters. Some minor changes in designations were notified, the net effect on totals being almost negligible. Some further derogations were also notified: it was explained that as the reporting year 1984 was a year of drought, there was a rational basis for such further derogations.

The UK view was that the original designations were made on a rational basis and that subsequent failures to comply were either justifiably derogated or could be remedied by policies in respect of farm and industrial discharges or by new schemes of works to deal with sewage effluent.

The UK action is in contrast to many other Member States. It was reported in October 1985 in a reply to a question in the European Parliament that only four other Member States had made designations. These designations were mostly very much smaller proportionately than those of the UK.

4.6 Shellfish waters

79/923/EEC (OJ L281 10.11.79) proposed 3.11.76 – COM(76)570	Directive on the quality required for shellfish waters.

Binding dates
Notification date	5 November 1979
Formal compliance	5 November 1981
Designation of waters	5 November 1981
Standards to be met	5 November 1987

Purpose of the Directive

The Directive seeks to ensure a suitable environment for shellfish growth. It is not intended by itself to protect the quality of shellfish for consumption, which in Britain is usually achieved by cleansing the shellfish after harvesting.

Summary of the Directive

The Member States are themselves to designate coastal and brackish waters which need protection or improvement so as to support shellfish. Initial designations were to be made by 5 November 1981 but additional designations can be made subsequently. Member States are to establish pollution reduction programmes so that within six years of designation the waters conform with values set by Member States. These values must be set for twelve physical, chemical or bacteriological parameters listed in an Annex. The Annex sometimes specifies I (imperative) values and sometimes G (guide) values and sometimes both. The values set by the Member States must be at least as stringent as the I values. The waters must be sampled at frequencies given in the Annex but sampling frequency may be reduced when the quality of the water is known to be high.

Member States must provide the Commission with a list of designations, and six years following designation, with a detailed report on the designated waters.

Development of the Directive

The European Parliament pointed out that the proposed Directive would require an increase in the number of personnel carrying out sampling, but otherwise welcomed the proposal. The House of Lords' Scrutiny Committee expressed sharp criticisms but were not alone in doing so as is shown by the comment of the Minister, Kenneth Marks, in the House of Commons' debate (6 April 1978):

> The shellfish proposal has been so severely criticized on all sides in Brussels that if any new proposal does emerge it will have to be radically different from the original if it is to be acceptable either to the United Kingdom or to other Member States.

Replying to the debate in the House of Lords (28 June 1977) the Minister, Baroness Birk, agreed with the main criticisms of the Lords' report:

> . . .it is hard to see just what is the aim of the proposal. According to the Commission it is concerned with encouraging shellfish growth, not with protecting human health. But the bacterial levels proposed relate only to human health.

This point was obviously successfully pressed in negotiations because the faecal coliform count – an indicator of pollution by sewage – proposed initially as an I value appears only as a G value in the Directive. Thus if Member States want to use the Directive as a means of protecting human health they may do so but are not obliged to.

The proposal made in the Lords' report that the Commission should consider a strategy based on monitoring the shellfish directly rather than the water in which they grow was however not supported by the Government. Baroness Birk said:

> This is interesting but it does have limitations. Direct examination of shellfish can give us an immediate impression of their state of health. But I am told that shellfish are generally more sensitive to pollution in their early stages. While certain environmental conditions would allow the adults to survive and grow, they might not be good enough for the larvae. So, if the aim was to protect shellfish, we would set standards for the water quality and monitor that as well as the shellfish themselves.

The proposed Directive was also criticized on the same grounds as the freshwater fish Directive (see Section 4.5): who was to be responsible for designating waters? When this point was clarified, the other criticisms had less force since Member States were then at liberty not to designate any waters where they felt the provisions of the Directive to be excessively burdensome. Indeed by April 1982 only Denmark, Ireland and the United Kingdom had designated shellfish waters, and the Federal Republic of Germany has stated that it will not be making any designations for the time being (see European parliamentary question No 120/82 OJ C132 24.5.82). In the event, substantial changes to the proposed Directive were made before it was adopted.

Formal compliance in the UK

Control of pollution of tidal waters and the sea came later in Britain than control of inland waters and is still incomplete. When Part II of the Control of Pollution Act eventually came into force in 1986, there was control of all discharges to estuaries and coastal waters up to the three-mile limit, but until then, compliance with the Directive in England and Wales was based on the Clean Rivers (Estuaries and Tidal Waters) Act 1960 which only covers post-1961 discharges. So long as shellfish waters were not polluted by a discharge not controlled under that Act the existing legislation was held to be sufficient.

In Scotland, the Rivers (Prevention of Pollution) Scotland Act 1951 and 1965, and in Northern Ireland the Water Act (Northern Ireland) 1972 were relied upon.

Accordingly no new legislation has been introduced in Britain to comply with the Directive, nor have any Regulations been made under existing Acts. Compliance has been by the following administrative action.

In January 1980 the DoE sent a copy of the Directive together with a seven-page advice note to the water authorities. This note explained the Directive, explained that water authorities would be largely responsible for implementation, and concluded by suggesting the establishment of a working group with representatives of government departments and water authorities to prepare further advice to ensure consistency of implementation. This further advice followed in a note dated November 1980.

In March 1981 the Scottish Development Department issued a circular letter with an advice note not dissimilar to the DoE note of November 1980, except that it announced that it was the Scottish Office that would be responsible for designations. This Scottish letter suggested certain designations but, in inviting suggestions for further designations, pointed out that only waters already controlled by the Rivers (Prevention of Pollution) Scotland Act should be included.

In November 1981 the DoE sent to the Commission a list of twenty-seven shellfish waters which had been designated in England, and Scotland totalling some 314 square kilometres in area. No waters in Northern Ireland or Wales were included in that list but in January 1983 the DoE wrote to the Commission saying that Strangford Lough in Northern Ireland and Menai Strait in Wales had been designated.

The lists submitted were undoubtedly limited to those which already met standards or would do so under current plans (see next paragraph). One constraint may have been the lack of powers available then to control estuarial waters, which have since been brought under control by the bringing into force of the Control of Pollution Act.

Effect on UK practice

The advice given by the DoE in its note of November 1980 was that the initial round of designations should not put an extra burden on capital expenditure in the current economic circumstances and that, consequently, only a fairly small number of waters should be designated. These were to be those which either already met the standards or which were capable of doing so by October 1987 after improvements which were already programmed. This advice seems to have been followed. Some waters which have not been designated could be designated later when water quality improves.

Some extra expenditure on sampling and monitoring has been incurred, but most authorities have simply diverted resources from other areas.

One Scottish Board has said:

> Yes, implementation of the Directive is likely to cause changes in our practices, financial outlay and manpower. Because the designated waters will, for the most part, be of good quality the Board will have afforded them low priority for monitoring purposes in the past. Once they are desig-

nated, we are committed to providing a certain level of surveillance which means that, unless additional resources are granted to meet this, we will have to direct some of our existing resources away from investigations of areas which are more seriously polluted, and therefore of fundamentally greater concern to us.

The designation of waters in Northern Ireland must be resulting in a change in practice because no monitoring programme for shellfish waters was previously carried out.

The Directive must also have provided additional pressure for bringing Part II of the Control of Pollution Act 1974 into force. Water authorities can now concern themselves more with sea water than they had to at the time of designation. The mere fact of having to consider shellfish waters for designation (and bathing waters – see Section 4.7) forced the water authorities to involve themselves with sea water earlier than they would have otherwise. Action taken to improve bathing waters announced in 1987 will have consequent effects on improving shellfish waters and may therefore lead to further designations.

Work is currently in hand to produce a report on the results of the Directive and is expected to be published in July 1987.

4.7 Bathing water

76/160/EEC (OJ L31 5.2.76) proposed 3.2.75 – COM(74)2255	Directive concerning the quality of bathing water.

Binding dates

Notification date	10 December 1975
Formal compliance	10 December 1977
First regular report to be submitted to Commission	10 December 1979
Derogations to be communicated to Commission	10 December 1981
Standards to be met	10 December 1985 (unless derogations given)

Purpose of the Directive

The quality of bathing water is to be raised over time, or maintained, not just to protect public health but also for reasons of amenity. This is to be done largely by ensuring that sewage is not present or has been adequately diluted or destroyed.

Summary of the Directive

Bathing water is defined as fresh or sea water in which: bathing is explicitly authorized, or is not prohibited and is traditionally practiced by a large number of bathers.

An Annex lists nineteen physical, chemical and microbiological parameters against thirteen of which are indicated I (imperative) and/or G (guide) values. The most important of these values are the coliform counts. The Member States must set values which bathing water must meet, the values being no less stringent than the I values, with the G values being observed as guidelines. The values set have to be met by December 1985, but in exceptional circumstances, derogations from the time limit may be granted by the Member States. Derogations have to be justified by reference to a management plan and must be communicated to the Commission by December 1981. To conform with the Directive, 95 per cent of samples for parameters where an I value is given must meet the values set and 90 per cent of samples in other cases.

The Annex lays down minimum sampling frequencies (for several parameters this is fortnightly during the bathing season, about ten to twelve times a year) and the Directive specifies where and how samples are to be taken, but it does not specify how samples are to be handled before analysis. Some parameters, such as streptococci and salmonellae, only have to be checked when there is reason to suppose that the substance is present. The Directive does not specify methods of analysis but sets out 'reference methods' and any other methods used must be comparable.

Waivers may be granted for certain parameters because of exceptional weather or geographical conditions or because of 'natural enrichment'. Waivers must be notified to the Commission together with the reasons for them and the periods anticipated.

At regular intervals from December 1979 Member States are to submit a comprehensive report to the Commission on their bathing waters. The Commission may publish this information with the consent of the Member State concerned.

Development of the Directive

In addition to technical difficulties relating to the parameters and to the time allowed for meeting them, the main difficulty experienced during development of the Directive concerned the definition of bathing waters. A further difficulty was created by the European Parliament and exacerbated by a possibly inadvertent remark by a Commissioner.

In its formal opinion, the Parliament proposed that bathing should be prohibited in water that did not meet the values set in the Directive. During the debate preceeding the adoption of this opinion (13 May 1975) three British members objected to this proposal. Sir Derek Walker-Smith said prohibition would pose problems of acceptability by individual citizens; Lord Bethell said that large numbers of warning signs would have to be erected where water quality was not up to the standards required; and James Spicer said that prohibition would be bad law because it could not be enforced. James Spicer proposed an amendment to say that bathing should be discouraged rather than prohibited. In replying to the debate, Commissioner Scarascia Mugnozza could have said that the Commission's proposal did not contemplate any prohibition of bathing but, quite inexplicably, he spoke against James Spicer's amendment which was accordingly defeated. By doing so, the Commissioner created the idea that prohibition was to form a part of the Directive and thereby caused a needless reaction, at least in Britain.

Six weeks later the House of Commons' Scrutiny Committee in taking evidence from the Minister, Denis Howell, asked as its first question whether bathing would be forbidden. Despite the Minister's reply that he thought the short answer was 'no', the Committee's interim report on 8 July said that further information was being sought. The House of Lords' Scrutiny Committee also allowed itself to be misled. Its report of 29 July pointed to the possibility either of widespread prohibition of bathing or of the United Kingdom being in default of the Directive. The Committee added that prohibition would produce a very strong public reaction. Some assurance on this point must subsequently have been given because the Commons' Scrutiny Committee's final report on 16 September stated 'there would be no question of any restriction or prohibition of bathing as a result of the Directive'. Such an assurance at second hand could not have satisfied one of the law lords, Lord Diplock, who felt moved to say in the House of Lords' debate (13 October 1975) that any subordinate legislation made in Britain under the European Communities Act prohibiting bathing could be questioned by a person prosecuted for unlawful bathing for being ultra vires the Treaty of Rome. The Minister, Lady Birk, attempted to still these fears:

> The proposal at no point mentions prohibition of bathing. . .
> I can say quite categorically that the Government have no
> intention whatsoever of asking for powers to prohibit bathing

in this country where the standards in the Directive cannot be met. . .

Despite this firm assurance it took some time before the idea that the Community would prohibit bathing finally died in Britain.

The difficulty of finding a definition for bathing water arises from the fact that only a few countries have a system for authorizing bathing and no such authorization is known to take place in Britain. The Directive as proposed accordingly defined bathing waters as those where bathing was authorized *or tolerated*. Since bathing is tolerated almost everywhere in Britain, the whole of the British coastline, which was then the longest of any Member State (Greece was yet to join the Community), would have to be monitored at great expense, despite the fact that very little bathing takes place along much of it. This problem was overcome in the Directive as agreed by omitting 'tolerated' and referring instead to water 'in which bathing is not prohibited and is traditionally practised by a large number of bathers'. The Directive is therefore different from the freshwater fish and shellfish Directives (see Sections 4.5 and 4.6) in that bathing waters are not 'designated' by Member States. Waters either are, or are not, 'bathing waters' within the definition of the Directive.

Various other changes were made to the proposal before it was adopted, one being to give Member States the power to grant derogations from the ten-year time limit, a change which Britain had pressed for.

Technical issues

The values set out in the Directive have been the subject of much discussion and criticism with scientific questions becoming intertwined with policy matters. Was the Directive intended as a public health measure, or was it also concerned with ensuring that bathing was pleasurable? The British government's view[1] based on a 1959 report from the Medical Research Council[2] is that for all practical purposes there is no risk to health from bathing in British coastal waters unless the pollution is so gross as to be aesthetically revolting. If correct, this view must lead to the conclusion that the Directive goes much further than protecting public health and is intended to ensure minimum standards of amenity. The question then arises whether setting bacteriological values for sea water is a reasonable method of establishing amenity standards. The Chairman of the Committee that produced the Medical Research Council report believes it is not and has criticised the Directive for laying down limits for coliform organisms with no attempt to relate these to health or aesthetics.[3] This view is not shared by all in Britain and many water authorities have found it helpful to have the numerical values of the Directive as a yardstick. The Clyde River Purification Board found that waters which were visibly polluted and where noticeable amounts of sewage solids were present invariably had coliform concentrations greatly exceeding the values in the Directive while, conversely, waters which conformed to the values were almost invariably satisfactory from an aesthetic standpoint.[4]

Coliform counts have the merit of being easy to carry out. Coliforms grow in the human gut and, though they are not themselves all harmful to man, their presence in water indicates faecal contamination. A coliform count therefore provides a reasonable indicator of the extent to which sewage has been diluted or destroyed, but is not a good indicator of risk to health since the pathogens contained in the sewage depend on the health of the population giving rise to it. (Dilute sewage from a town infected by cholera is more dangerous than stronger sewage from a healthy town). This reinforces the view that the Directive is concerned more with amenity than with health, in which case the practice of chlorinating sewage to kill bacteria – a practice sometimes adopted to meet the values in the Directive – has little to commend it. If the Directive is concerned with health, then it has been argued that warm southern waters need a more stringent standard than do colder waters because the longer a bather stays in the water, the more water and pathogens will he swallow. In fact, the Directive as proposed made a distinction between waters warmer and colder than 20°C but this disappeared before the Directive was agreed. A factor pulling in the opposite direction is that the stronger sunlight in the Mediterranean kills bacteria more quickly.

The Directive gives no guidance on the manner in which samples are to be handled before being analysed but since exposure to bright summer sunshine for half an hour may reduce the coliform count by 90 per cent,[5] samples must be handled in similar ways by the different authorities if the results of analysis are to be comparable. It is all too easy to cheat since 'by the judicious choice of sampling time and place, method of transport to the laboratory and analytical technique, doubtful beaches could appear to comply with the mandatory limits'.[4] The comparative reports on water quality to be issued by the Commission will have to be treated with caution.

Formal compliance in the UK

When the Directive was being negotiated, it was expected that Part II of the Control of Polluton Act 1974 would be in force by the date for formal compliance in December 1977. In March 1977 the DoE sent a six-page advice note to the water authorities which described the Directive and said that there was doubt over how far compliance could be achieved without the Act being in force. Doubts concerned both the power to monitor coastal waters and the ability to control discharges.

Shortly after the date for formal compliance, the Government sent a letter to the Commission referring ιo the Control of Pollution Act as containing the necessary powers for compliance but omitting to say that the relevant sections of the Act were not yet in force. The letter also said that discussions were being held with the relevant authorities about identification of bathing waters. Curiously, in all the correspondence that was to follow between the Commission and the government, the Commission apparently never mentioned that the relevant sections of the Control of Pollution Act were not in force, although its officials were aware of this, nor did the government point out that it had subsequently satisfied itself that other powers existed which effectively enabled it to comply with the Directive without the benefit of the Control of Pollution Act. For England and Wales these powers are contained in the Water Resources Act 1963 and the Water Act 1973. Section 113(1)(b) of the 1963 Act provides water authorities with the power to take samples from the sea and tidal waters and the 1973 Act gives the water authorities control over their own sewage discharges. The relevant powers of the Control of Pollution Act were eventually brought into force in 1986.

The Commission's disquiet about British compliance with the Directive – which ultimately led to a 'Reasoned Opinion' being issued in 1980 – first concerned the administrative steps taken by the government. This disquiet was expressed in a letter from the Commission of 3 July 1979 and probably stemmed from the knowledge – the story is told by Ruth Levitt[6] – that the Secretary of State for the Environment, Peter Shore, had delayed advice from the Department to the water authorities while he considered the matter personally. But by the time the Commission had sent its letter, a new government was in power and the long awaited advice note to water authorities was ready to be issued and was simultaneously released to the press on 9 July 1979, only a few days after the Commission's letter. The advice note announced that the water authorities in England and Wales were being formally appointed as the competent authorities for the purposes of identifying bathing waters, for sampling, and for ensuring that the standards are met, and then set out guidelines to enable them to identify bathing waters – only just in time for the bathing season.

On 18 December 1979, thereby just missing the due date, the government sent a formal letter to the Commission enclosing a list of the waters which had been identified together with a technical report on their quality. The list, no doubt inadvertently, failed to indicate positively that no waters had been identified in Scotland and Northern Ireland, so that it was left to the Commission to guess whether the process of identification had or had not taken place in those countries.

On 3 July 1980 the Commission wrote inquiring, among other matters, why no waters had been identified in Scotland and Northern Ireland, but barely could a reply be sent before, on 16 July, the Commission issued a Reasoned Opinion to the effect that the UK had failed to take all the necessary steps to comply with the Directive. The government replied on 18 September 1980 to confirm that no waters in Scotland or Northern Ireland had been identified as bathing waters. The letter effectively asked for the Reasoned Opinion to be withdrawn.

The Commission made it clear in replies to questions in the European Parliament (Question No 399/84 OJ C268 8.10.84 and Question No 1959/84 OJ C168 8.7.85) that it was not satisfied with the way the definition of bathing waters had been interpreted in Britain and that it was discussing the matter with British officials. It threatened to start infringement procedures. As a result of these discussions the government announced on 3 February 1987 that an additional 362 bathing waters (bringing the total to 389) had been identified for the purposes of the Directive (see below). A circular on the implementation of the Directive is to be issued.

Identifying bathing waters

The British government has stated that it is not aware of any statutory provision enabling any public body explicitly to authorize bathing. The government's view is that to fall within the first limb of the definition of the Directive, there must be some authorization made in an open and declaratory form, but that in Britain entitlement to bathe derives from custom or prescription which is the very antithesis of explicit authorization, since one can only acquire something by custom or prescription if there has been no positive grant. The government argues that the making of byelaws under Section 231 of the Public Health Act 1936 regulating the areas in which public bathing is permitted merely allows local authorities to limit an existing entitlement and does not create one. Accordingly, Britain has relied entirely on the second limb of the definition of bathing waters, ie where it is traditionally practised by a large number of people, as indeed have most other countries.[7] However, most other countries have not used a numerical criterion for identification but have relied on other criteria, such as accessibility.

In its first advice note of March 1977 the DoE suggested the setting of guidelines to ensure consistency by the various water authorities in identifying bathing waters. The advice note went on to point out that Mediterranean beaches would be used much more by bathers who actually entered the water than northern ones, and that on that basis there were likely to be rather few places in Britain that fell within the definition. The advice note also pointed out that the financial implications were potentially significant.

It seems at that time to have been the government's policy – a policy consistent with its stance on the shellfish and freshwater fish Directives (see Sections 4.5 and 4.6) – that existing water authority priorities for spending money on water quality should not be excessively distorted by Community commitments and that, therefore, few waters should be identified. A DoE official has pointed out that 'evidence collected by water authorities for the purpose of this Directive has shown a tendency for the British holiday-maker to sit on the beach, but not to venture into the water',[8] and it has even been suggested that, seen in a European context, there are no British bathing waters used by a 'large number' of bathers. It was also assumed that district councils covering seaside resorts would want to see their bathing waters identified for promotional reasons but that water authorities could not be expected to undertake excessive financial burdens. A draft DoE advice note apparently circulated among water authorities late in 1977 suggested a lower density of bathers as a guide to the meaning of 'large' than was finally decided upon. The final guidelines published in the advice note of 9 July 1979 were that bathing waters with fewer than 500 people in the water at any time should not be identified; that any stretch where the number of bathers was more than 1500 per mile should be identified; while those with between 750 and 1500 per mile were open to negotiation between water authority and district council.

The water authorities and district councils conducted an identification exercise in August 1979 and, as a result, twenty-seven bathing waters were communicated to the Commission in December 1979. This must be contrasted with over 600 beaches in England and Wales from which bathing regularly takes place.[9]

There can be little doubt that the choice of guidelines in 1979 was influenced by the government's desire to do something to implement the Directive while not putting too great a financial burden on water authorities at a time of public expenditure restraint. Blackpool, assessed at between 750 and 1500 bathers per mile, and which, by agreement between the water authority and district council, has not been identified, would probably have fallen within guidelines suggested at an early stage resulting in an expenditure of between £10 and £50 million to bring the water up to standard. Similarly, there are bathing waters in Scotland which could possibly have been identified if the earlier suggested guidelines had been followed. At Brighton the numbers fell just within the range for identification, and although the water conforms with the Directive it was not identified despite the desire of the district council that it should be. The suspicion inevitably arises that it would have been difficult simultaneously to include Brighton but exclude Blackpool despite the fact that the formal decision to identify waters had been delegated to water authorities.

In 1984, in response to criticism by the Royal Commission on Environmental Pollution at the choice of only twenty-seven bathing waters, the government had announced that it would be monitoring many more bathing waters defined, for example by sites with lifeguards or at which changing huts, car parks or toilets are provided on a substantial scale for bathers.[10]

As mentioned above, the European Commission threatened infringement proceedings because it was not satisfied with the identification of only twenty-seven contrasted with many more in other countries,[7] and in 1987 the government announced that, following consultations with the water authorities and the Commission, a further 362 waters had been identified. The reasons for this change of heart were in part the fear of an advserse judgement by the European Court, which would have had to interpret a very vague definition, but also the amount of criticism within Britain. It was obvious to all that the intentions of the Directive were not being fulfilled. By identifiying many more bathing waters the government has now however faced itself with the problem that many of them do not meet the standards.

Effect on UK practice

Even before the Directive came into force its existence stimulated some water authorities to monitor coastal waters. Water authorities were expecting to have to do this anyway in fulfilment of their forthcoming duties under the Control of Pollution Act but, as the relevant parts of the Act were not brought into force for many years, it was the Directive that gave the sharper stimulus, particularly in providing a yardstick by which to measure water quality.

Despite the many criticisms of this Directive, several water authorities found it useful. The National Water Council in 1978 had called it '. . .the least satisfactory EEC Directive on water quality to emerge up to now. . It is not well judged scientifically and may well be costly to administer; it would also lead to a distortion of investment in environmental improvement'. Even for water authorities that had identified no bathing waters before 1987, the Directive provided a yardstick to be used in the design and location of new sewage outfalls. The Directive also resulted in research on water movement using modelling techniques and microbiological tracing methods.

The twenty-seven bathing waters originally identified in 1979 fell within five water authority areas:

South West WA	11	Torquay (Oddicombe, Meadfoot, Torre Abbey), Paignton (Paignton Beach, Goodrington, Broadsands), Penzance (Sennen), St Ives (Porthmeor, Porthminster), Newquay (Fistral, Towan)
Wessex WA	6	Christchurch, Bournemouth, Weston-super-Mare, Weymouth, Poole, Swanage
Yorkshire WA	4	Scarborough North Bay, Scarborough South Bay, Bridlington North Bay, Bridlington South Bay
Southern WA	4	Sandown Beach, Shanklin Beach, Ryde, Margate
Thames WA	2	Southend/Thorpe Bay, Southend/Westcliffe Beach

Annual reports on the quality of these bathing waters were submitted to the Commission by the DoE, and the results have been summarized in a DoE digest of statistics.[11] For the years 1980 to 1984 between 70 and 78 per cent of the twenty-seven waters complied with the limits for faecal coliforms. Although some bathing waters improved over the period and some deteriorated, there was no significant trend for the twenty-seven waters taken as a whole.

In December 1981 the DoE informed the Commission that it had granted derogations from the ten-year time limit in respect of four of the identified bathing waters on the assumption that compliance for these waters would not be guaranteed: Scarborough North and South Bays, Ryde, Margate. As required by the Directive, these derogations were justified by management plans. These plans have involved expenditure and although the Directive will have applied pressure, these expenditures cannot be attributed entirely to the Directive since several of them were under discussion before the Directive.

The decision to identify 362 more bathing waters in January 1987 will transform the effects of the Directive in Britain by applying much greater pressure for investments. When announcing the decision the Minister (William Waldegrave) said that of those waters that had already been surveyed (in fact the great majority of the total of 389) more than half met the standards of the Directive and that remedial works were in hand or planned for many of the others. In · eply to a parliamentary question on 4 February 1987 the Minister said that some £70 million was being spent annually on schemes related to the improvement of bathing water quality. He referred particularly to a scheme at Blackpool where some £35 million would be spent on a scheme to be operational by 1993.

In reply to a further parliamentary question on 4 March 1987, the Minister admitted that, at the present rate of spending, it would not be till the end of the century before nearly all the bathing waters would comply with the standards. Whereas the Commission may now be satisfied with the identification of bathing waters, the fact remains that Britain is in breach of the Directive in that the standards are not met at a large number of waters. In this respect it is no different from some other countries, such as France.

Obviously this deficiency cannot be cured overnight and it remains to be seen whether the Commission, and the public, will be satisfied with the rate of progress. The expenditure of £70 million per annum is not a commitment of new money but represents the sums allocated in the forward plans of water authorities whose responsibility it now is to meet the standards. However, expenditure by the water authorities is limited by the policies of central government. If the Commission is not satisfied that progress is fast enough it is the central government and not the water authorities who would be taken to the European Court, and this possibility must now be a factor weighing on the government when it decides on expenditure limits for the water authorities.

References
1.   Reply to a parliamentary question, House of commons 28 July 1981.

2.   Medical Research Council 1959 *Sewage contamination of bathing beaches in England and Wales* Memorandum No 37. HMSO, London.

3. Moore B 1977 The EEC Bathing Water Directive, *Marine Pollution Bulletin* 8 (12).

4. Hammerton D 1978 *EEC Directives on the quality of bathing water and on water pollution caused by the discharge of dangerous substances – The River Purification Board viewpoint.* Institute of Water Pollution Control (Scottish Branch), Symposium on River Pollution Prevention, March 1978.

5. Gameson A L H 1979 EEC Directive on quality of bathing water, *Journal of the Institute of Water Pollution Control* 78 (2).

6. Levitt Ruth 1980 *Implementing public policy.* Croom Helm, London (Chapter 5 takes the Bathing Water Directive as a case study).

7. *Implementing EC Directive 76/160 concerning the quality of bathing water.* Conclusions of a seminar held in Montpellier (12–15 October 1986) by the Institute for European Environmental Policy.

8. Renshaw D C 1980 *The EEC Directives and water quality.* The Institution of Water Engineers and Scientists, Symposium on EEC Directives, London.

9. *The golden list of clean beaches in England and Wales.* The Coastal Anti-Pollution League Ltd.

10. Department of the Environment 1984 *Controlling pollution: principles and prospects. The government's response to the Tenth Report of the Royal Commission on Environmental Pollution.* HMSO, No 22 (Pollution paper).

11. Department of the Environment 1986 *Digest of Environmental protection and water statistics No 8 1985.* HMSO.

4.8 Dangerous substances in water

76/464/EEC (OJ L129 18.5.76) proposed 21.10.74 – COM(74)1706	Directive on pollution caused by certain dangerous substances discharged into the aquatic environment of the Community.

Binding dates
    Notification date   5 May 1976

As no dates are set in the Directive, the Commission suggested the following deadlines in a letter dated 3 November 1976:

System of authorizations	15 September 1978
Pollution reduction programmes for List II substances	15 September 1981
Programmes to be implemented	15 September 1986

This Directive is still often incorrectly referred to as ENV 131, a designation referring to an unpublished draft which differed substantially from the Directive.

Purpose of the Directive
The Directive sets a framework for the elimination or reduction of pollution of inland, coastal and territorial waters by particularly dangerous substances. Subsequent daughter Directives are to set standards for particular substances. The Directive is also intended to ensure consistency in implementing various international Conventions and to reduce distortion to conditions of competition.

Summary of the Directive
An Annex has a List I and a List II of families and groups of dangerous substances. List I includes substances selected on the basis of their toxicity, persistence and bioaccumulation, eg organohalogen and organophosphorus compounds, carcinogenic substances, and mercury and cadmium compounds. List II includes possibly less dangerous substances such as zinc, copper and lead compounds, cyanide and ammonia. For the purposes of the Directive any List I substance is to be treated as a List II substance until a 'daughter' Directive sets limit values for it.

Member States are to take appropriate steps to eliminate pollution by List I substances and to reduce pollution by List II substances. 'Elimination' of pollution does not necessarily mean a zero-emission since pollution is defined not by reference to the presence of a substance but to its effects.

Discharges of both List I and List II substances are to be subject to prior authorization by a competent authority, but these authorizations are arrived at in different ways.

For controlling **List II** substances, Member States are to establish pollution reduction programmes with deadlines for implementation. All discharges liable to contain a List II substance require prior authorization with emission standards being laid down. These emission standards are to be based on quality objectives. These quality objectives must be laid down in accordance with any existing Directives. Summaries of the programmes and the results of implementation are to be communicated to the Commission which is to arrange for regular comparisons. The Commission may make proposals to ensure sufficient coordination of national programmes.

For controlling **List I** substances, Member States may choose between two alternative regimes. The preferred regime entails limit values which emission standards are not to exceed. (It is often said in Britain that the Directive requires 'uniform emission standards' to be laid down. This is incorrect and the words 'uniform emission standards' do not appear in the Directive. What the Directive requires is the laying down of *limit values* at Community level and the authorities in the Member States may impose emission standards more stringent than the limit values but not less stringent.) These emission limits are to be fixed uniformly throughout the Community in daughter Directives. The alternative regime entails emission standards set by reference to quality objectives. The quality objectives are also to be laid down in daughter Directives. Use of the alternative regime is conditional on the Member State proving to the Commission that the quality objectives are being met in accordance with a monitoring procedure set up by the Council.

At the Council meeting of 4 May 1976 all Member States except Britain declared that they would adopt the preferred regime[1].

The emission limits are to be laid down mainly on the basis of toxicity, persistence and bioaccumulation taking into account the best technical means available, though this latter point was qualified in a statement made at the Council meeting of 4 May 1976 to the effect that 'best technical means available' is to take into account the economic availability of those means.

Member States are to draw up inventories of all discharges which may contain List I substances, and supply them to the Commission at its request. The Commission may also ask for information about authorizations and the results of monitoring.

Two points need to be emphasized. First, programmes for the reduction of pollution are required for List II but not for List I substances. But, secondly, since all substances are to be treated in law as List II substances until a daughter Directive converts a substance into a List I substance, all substances, at least initially, should in theory be made the subject of pollution reduction programmes, based on quality objectives. By the end of 1986 only a few substances had been put into List I (see 'Further developments' below). All other potential List I substances remain, in law, List II substances.

Development of the Directive

The day before the Council was due to consider this Directive on 16 October 1975 a leading article in *The Times* under the headline 'The Rhine and the Thames' explained the differences between the British government and the Commission concerning this Directive in terms highly critical of the Commission. No other water Directive has been the focus of so much attention in Britain. As well as being the most contentious, it is also potentially one of the most important and certainly implies the largest programme of work for the future. It also has a number of other distinctive features: unlike all other water Directives, no date is set for compliance; the proposal submitted by the Commission to the Council was a proposal for a Decision and not a Directive; and there is no foundation for that part of the Directive dealing with limit values in the first action programme.

The preamble to the Directive explains its origins by referring to the need to coordinate the implementation of several international conventions concerned with river pollution that were under discussion when the Directive was proposed in October 1974:

the Paris Convention for the prevention of marine pollution from land based sources – adopted 4 June 1974;
the Convention for the Protection of the Rhine against chemical pollution – adopted 3 December 1976;
the draft Strasbourg Convention for the protection of international watercourses against pollution – not yet adopted.

The three Conventions (see Chapter 11) affect, or will affect, different Member States to different extents. The Paris Convention is concerned only with discharges, including those from rivers, into the North Sea and north east Atlantic. The parties to the Rhine Convention are its riparian States plus the European Community. The Strasbourg Convention, being negotiated under the auspices of the Council of Europe, will deal only with rivers crossing national frontiers and so will not affect, for example, the Seine or the Thames. All three Conventions have two lists inspired by the generally similar lists in the Oslo and London Conventions concerned with dumping at sea.

The **Paris Convention** has two lists which are similar but not identical to the lists in the Directive. Unlike the Directive, pollution reduction programmes with time limits are to be implemented for both lists but for neither list, again unlike the Directive, do emission limits have to be laid down.

The **Rhine Convention** similarly has two lists. An International Commission is to lay down emission limits which discharges of List I substances are not to exceed, but List II substances are to be subject to emission standards set by national authorities by reference to quality objectives and national programmes. The Rhine Convention is therefore rather similar to the preferred regime of the Directive.

The **Strasbourg Convention** has not been agreed, and officially no draft is public, but the Commission's explanatory memorandum accompanying the proposal for the Directive (or Decision as it then was) – COM(74)1706 – suggested that the Convention might include quite stringent standards for the international rivers that would be covered by it.

The Belgian government is given the credit for initiating the Directive by the report of the Environment Committee of the European Parliament. The Belgian government appears to have believed that Antwerp, lying on the Scheldt, and hence subject to the possibly stringent standards of the Strasbourg Convention, would be at a disadvantage in comparison with, say, London or Le Havre which do not lie on international rivers. The Belgian government appears to have persuaded the Commission that there was a need to ensure that all Member States should be subject to similar provisions. Seen thus, the origin of the Directive was economic, and the economic self-interest of Britain, where many discharges are made to estuaries or short fast rivers, lay in resisting centrally fixed emission limits. The discussions that followed were clearly coloured by this as emerges from the deliberations in Parliament.

The Directive/Decision as proposed involved emission limits for both List I and List II substances set by a qualified majority vote in the Council. On 15 January 1975 DoE officials giving evidence to the House of Lords' Scrutiny Committee were asked whether this was something that appealed to the British government or whether it was something that had 'at the very least, a germ of controversy and difference about it'. They were also asked whether behind the technicalities 'there might lurk a controversial political problem of inequality in competitive trading relations between ourselves and our continental partners?'. The replies indicated clearly the government's concern but curiously the Scrutiny Committee's report did not make much of the issue – certainly in comparison to reports that were to follow. Indeed the House of Lords never formally debated the proposal though they often referred to it in debates on other Directives.

Two months later when the Minister, Denis Howell, and DoE officials gave evidence before the House of Commons' Scrutiny Committee, the proposal had already been modified. An official explained that 'there is general agreement among the delegations that the right approach for dealing with the substances in List II would be to set environmental quality objectives'. The Rhine Convention, to which Britain is not a party, also shows that the use of variable emission standards set nationally according to quality objectives was a concept accepted by other countries even for dangerous substances. It was only over the List I substances that Britain was eventually to differ from the other Member States.

The Chairman of the Commons' Scrutiny Committee asked whether the government would be pressing strongly for the retention of the delegated authority to set emission standards in accordance with current British practice 'or whether you will be tending to assent to a more centralized Directive of the kind which the instrument predicts'. The official's reply was ambivalent implying that Britain might be prepared to accept centrally fixed emission limits for List I substances: 'I think it worth stressing that List I substances are, in fact, a very small and special group, and there are reasons why a particular approach might be appropriate for them.' When pressed further, he explained that List I substances were already closely controlled in Britain and said: '. . .these are, of course, very toxic substances, and the differences would not be great between a uniform emission standards' approach and a flexible approach such as we adopt in this country.' In the event, the British government finally decided to resist centrally fixed emission limits for List I substances and no agreement was reached at the Council meeting of 16 October 1975. A compromise allowing two regimes for List I was then agreed in principle at the Council meeting in December.

The replies by DoE officials to the Commons' Scrutiny Committee show that there was the possibility of Britain agreeing to centrally fixed limit values for List I substances, a possibility known to Commission officials. The confusion that finally culminated in the failure of the October 1975 Council meeting and the subsequent recriminations was exacerbated by the difficulty that British officials had in obtaining a decision from Ministers at a time when a referendum was being held in Britain on the question of Britain's continuing membership of the Community. British industry was strongly opposed to centrally fixed emission limits for reasons of self-interest and this view finally prevailed in the government. The fullest statement of the British government's position is the 3700 word speech made by the Minister, Denis Howell, at the October Council meeting.

The Minister emphasized the environmental, administrative and economic soundness of the British government's traditionally decentralized approach, and while accepting that other reasons applied in other countries, ignored the counterarguments that had been rehearsed even in the British context. The Commission and the other Member States for their part emphasized the competition argument and the administrative convenience of fixed emission limits while overlooking the lack of logic inherent in holding such a position for List I but not List II substances. Whatever arguments about competition and administrative convenience apply to List I must also apply to List II, and everyone had agreed that List II substances should not be subject to emission limits. The protagonists thus found themselves in curious positions: the British who so frequently like to describe themselves as being pragmatic found themselves wedded to a doctrine, and other countries who pride themselves on being logical found themselves advocating a Directive with a fundamental illogicality which can only be justified on grounds of expediency. The British insistence on the doctrine of environmental quality objectives is all the more curious given that it was not a doctrine that had been practised in Britain in the explicit way required by the Directive.

In addition to the major changes concerning Lists I and II, the proposal was also changed in a way which renders the inventory of much less value. Whereas the proposal required an inventory for discharges of both List I and List II substances, the Directive only requires an inventory of List I substances. Since all substances are to be treated in law as List II until effectively put into List I by a daughter Directive and since daughter Directives relating to only six substances had been agreed by the end of 1986, the inventory is of very limited value.

Formal compliance in the UK

Being a framework Directive few obligations are immediately placed on Member States, and since the Directive differs from most in not specifying dates by which Member States are to bring in the laws, regulations and administrative provisions necessary for compliance, the government has never formally written to the Commission about them nor has the Commission asked for details. Why no dates were set remains a mystery. The Commission realized, after the Directive was adopted, that dates were desirable and accordingly wrote to Member States on 3 November 1976 suggesting that a system for the authorization of List I and List II substances should be introduced by 15 September 1978 and that programmes for reducing pollution by List II substances should be introduced by 15 September 1981 and implemented by 15 September 1986.

Under the Control of Pollution Act all discharges of List I and List II substances can be subject to an authorization procedure except those produced by the Crown which includes the Royal Naval Dockyards. However, until the relevant parts of the Act were brought into force finally in 1985 some discharges to estuaries and coastal waters were not subject to authorizations so that formal compliance was incomplete. Most discharges were however controlled under the previously existing legislation. The Royal Naval Dockyards pose a problem: although significant sources of pollution they are not covered by existing legislation nor does the Directive provide exemption for them, although they could possibly be exempted by the provisions of Article 223 of the Treaty of Rome dealing with security matters.

The requirement for Member States to establish programmes with deadlines for the reduction of pollution is covered by existing legislation. The DoE can ask water authorities to include these in their plans prepared under Section 24(1) (c) of the Water Act 1973:

> It shall be the duty of each water authority . . . to prepare a
> plan as to action to be taken during the period . . . for the
> purpose of . . . restoring or maintaining the wholesomeness
> of rivers and other inland or coastal waters. . .

There is, however, not yet any legislation requiring the authorities to lay down environmental quality objectives by reference to which the Directive says that some emission standards must be set, although they are free to do so as part of their forward plans.

Circular 18/85 was issued by the Department of the Environment on 2 September 1985 covering implementation of Directive 76/464 as well as certain daughter Directives. It states that in the United Kingdom it is the intention to use the quality objective approach wherever and whenever possible. It directs water authorities to select the quality objective (quality standard in UK terminology) which they consider appropriate from those set out in Annex II of each daughter Directive and repeated in Appendix I to the Circular. Quoting from the daughter Directives the selection must be made 'having regard to the intended use of the area affected, while taking account of the fact that the purpose of this Directive is to eliminate all pollution'. It is for water authorities to select the appropriate quality standard for each stretch of water affected. They are also responsible for determining the area to which the standards will be applied. In so doing they have to allow a reasonable zone for a discharge to mix with the receiving water. Where there are multiple discharges these zones may well overlap.

Exceptionally, where quality standards cannot initially be met, provision is made for limit values to be used until quality objectives can be achieved. DoE's agreement is needed in such cases. Since the government in its negotiations in the Council argued forcibly in favour of the quality standards approach it must be an embarrassment to have to rely on the limit value approach even if only rarely.

The Circular says that 'authorizations' in the terms of the Directives will generally be the normal discharge consents under powers in the Control of Pollution Act 1974. These have to specify emission standards in terms of maximum concentrations and maximum quantity over a period of time. They may be expressed in a manner appropriate to the water authority's system of control.

The Circular provides an interpretation of 'substantially' in relation to an increase in capacity to process the substance in question by an existing plant to decide whether a plant is required to be treated as a new plant and thus have to employ the 'best technical means available' (btma) as required by the daughter Directives. A 20 per cent or more increase in handling capacity of the particular substance is given as making an existing plant a new one for the purposes of the daughter Directives. However, it is pointed out that the government holds the view that setting different emission standards to reflect different environmental conditions does not normally lead to distortion of competition; the main concern should be elimination of pollution. Except in the case of chloralkali plants, no guidance on 'btma' is given beyond that of requiring water authorities to discuss how 'btma' is to be interpreted with DoE on a case by case basis.

Other parts of the Circular lay down requirements for monitoring and submission of returns which will enable the requirements of the 'daughter' Directives to be met.

Effect on UK practice

The major effect of this Directive has been less of a change in practice than a refinement of thought: the British have been stimulated into developing their previously imprecise ideas on the use of environmental quality objectives since the Directive makes these mandatory for the first time. The River Quality Objectives (RQOs) that water authorities began laying down in 1978 for each stretch of inland river can therefore be attributed to the Directive even though the Directive does not require RQOs in quite that form. Having said this, it must be emphasized that some people in the water industry do not attribute the introduction of RQOs at that period to the Directive but to the impending introduction of Part II of the Control of Pollution Act which has now resulted in publication of authorizations and the possibility of prosecution if discharges do not comply with them. According to this account, the introduction of RQOs was to enable a logical revision of emission standards before their publication. It is perfectly possible that both explanations are correct and simply happened to coincide. Whatever explanation is given by the water Authorities for the introduction of RQOs, government officials were aware that the Directive made quality objectives mandatory and would therefore have encouraged their introduction.

The precise requirement of the Directive is that quality objectives (the term 'quality standards' would have been more appropriate) should be laid down specifically for the purposes of programmes for the reduction of pollution by List II substances. Unlike the generalized RQOs these quality objectives will, in practice, have to specify concentrations of each List II substance for different stretches of rivers, estuaries and coastal waters. The response of the DoE to this requirement was to place a research contract with the Water Research Centre to propose appropriate quality objectives for different waters initially for six non-ferrous metals: copper, lead, nickel, zinc, chromium and arsenic. This research and the greater emphasis on toxic substances that it implies can be attributed directly to the Directive. The results of this research have been published[2] and the standards proposed in it were recommended to the water authorities in DoE Circular 18/85. Other Member States are even less far advanced so that the 1981 deadline suggested by the Commission was clearly unrealistic.

Even the requirement for authorization for List I and List II substances has yet to be fully implemented in practice since not all List I and List II substances have been individually authorized. For example, every sewage work discharges zinc, but it is very unusual for a specific authorization for zinc to be given to a sewage works' discharge. The form of the authorization – British legislation uses the word 'consent' – has usually been for consent to be given in a generalized form to all effluent from a sewage works subject to biochemical oxygen demand (BOD_5) not exceeding X and suspended solids (SS) not exceeding Y. Zinc, being a constituent of sewage works' effluent, is therefore 'consented' or 'authorized' but not with a specific emission standard laid down for it as required by the Directive. Even when a sewage works is receiving industrial discharges it is quite usual for toxic metals not to be individually authorized. Major industrial dischargers of toxic substances may also well have emission standards laid down for a group of toxic substances taken together. The manner of drafting consent conditions is in some cases being changed as a result of the Directive.

The inventory of List I substances is something for the future. Since only a few substances have so far been effectively put into List I, the Commission can only formally ask for an inventory of discharges of these substances. Nevertheless, the requirements for an inventory have stimulated the DoE and the water authorities to consider how this information could be gathered and some extra monitoring work can be attributed to the Directive.

One other effect of this Directive is that water authorities have had to provide information to the DoE about List I substances in order to help the DoE in its negotiations over the various daughter Directives. Despite complaints about the time involved, this process has concentrated thinking on the control of toxic substances.

Further developments

List I substances
In June 1982 the Commission submitted a Communication to the Council (OJ C176 14.7.82) concerning List I substances. This explained that studies had identified 1500 substances used for technical purposes belonging to the families and groups of List I and that of these 1000 are produced or used in quantities of less than 100 tonnes per year, 186 more than 1000 t/yr, 44 more than 10 000 t/yr and only 25 in excess of 100 000 t/yr.

Five hundred of the substances had been examined to evaluate risks to water and pared down to a priority list of 108 substances for further study. Fifteen were selected to be studied first. In addition to these 108 substances, 21 substances had already been studied, making a total of 129 substances. They are listed in the Communication with the caveat that the list is not final. The list includes the following for which proposals have already been made or a decision taken not to make one:

1. Mercury and its compounds: the subject of Directives 82/176 and 84/156 (see Sections 4.10 and 4.11).
2. Cadmium and its compounds: the subject of Directive 83/513 (see Section 4.12).
3. Hexachlorocyclohexane (lindane): the subject of Directive 84/491 (see Section 4.13).
4. Aldrin, dieldrin and endrin: the subject of a proposed Directive (COM(86)534 OJ C146 12.6.79; COM(79)243 and COM(86)534 OJ C309 3.12.86.
5. Carbon tetrachloride, chloroform, DDT and pentachlorophenol: Directive 86/280 (see Section 4.14) covers three of these substances but not chloroform.
6. Chlordane and heptachlor: no Directive to be proposed – use already restricted by Directive 79/117 (see Section 7.6).

In February 1983 the Council adopted a Resolution (OJ C46 17.2.83) noting the Commission's Communication described above and stating that the list of 129 substances would serve as a basis for further work. Member States were to provide the Commission within three years, and some have done so, with all readily available data concerning the list including data on:

production, use and discharges by industries;
diffuse sources;
concentration in water, sediments and organisms;
remedial measures taken or envisaged and their effect.

Initial attention was to be focused on eleven listed substances. This Resolution in effect supersedes the ineffective provision for an inventory in Directive 76/464.

List II substances
The Commission called a meeting of experts from Member States in 1981 (see European parliamentary question C305 22.11.82) at which priorities were set for comparing national programmes for List II substances. Six substances have been selected for priority attention: chromium, lead, zinc, copper, nickel and arsenic (the same list studied by the Water Research Centre[2] – see above) and Member States were asked about their programmes for chromium. As a result of information supplied by some Member States, including the United Kingdom, the Commission has proposed a Directive on quality standards for chromium (COM(85)737 OJ C351 31.12.85).

References

1   Johnson Stanley P 1979 *The pollution control policy of the European Communities*. Graham and Trotman Ltd, London.

2   Gardiner J and Mance G 1984 *Environmental standards for List II Substances*. Water Research Centre (WRC Reports TR 206–212).

4.9 Groundwater

80/68/EEC (OJ L20 26.1.80) proposed 24.1.78 – COM(78)3	Directive on the protection of groundwater against pollution caused by certain dangerous substances.

Binding dates

Notification date	19 December 1979
Formal compliance	19 December 1981
New discharges to be controlled	19 December 1981
Existing discharges to be controlled	19 December 1985

Purpose of the Directive

Seventy per cent of the Community's drinking water and 25–30 per cent of the United Kingdom's is extracted from underground sources. In order to protect exploitable groundwater sources, which are very difficult to restore once polluted, both direct and indirect discharges of dangerous substances are to be prohibited or regulated.

Summary of the Directive

A List I and List II of families and groups of dangerous substances are given in an Annex, those on List I being generally more dangerous than those on List II. The Annex makes it clear that only those substances within the limited groups and families which exhibit certain specified characteristics are to be classed in the appropriate list. (The lists are not quite identical to Lists I and II of Directive 76/464 – see Section 4.8.)

Member States are to 'prevent' the introduction into groundwater of List I substances and to 'limit' the introduction of List II substances so as to avoid pollution. 'Pollution' is defined by reference to the effect of a substance rather than by its presence. 'Groundwater' is also defined.

The Directive does not apply to radioactive substances nor to discharges of domestic effluents from isolated dwellings situated outside areas protected for the abstraction of drinking water. Nor does it apply to discharges containing List I or List II substances in a quantity and concentration so small as to obviate any present or future danger.

All direct discharges (ie without percolation through the ground) of **List I** substances are to be prohibited (except in trace quantities) though if after investigation the groundwater is found unsuitable for other uses such discharges may be authorized. Reinjection into the same aquifer of water used for geothermal purposes, water pumped out of mines and quarries or water pumped out for civil engineering works may be authorized after investigation.

All direct discharges of **List II** substances are to be subjected to investigation before being authorized.

Any disposal on land of either List I or List II substances which might lead to indirect discharges is to be subject to investigation before being authorized.

(Authorizations are also required under the waste Directives, see Sections 5.1 and 5.2.) Any other activity likely to lead to indirect discharges of List I substances is also to be controlled and the control measures in respect of List I substances are to be notified to the Commission. Artificial discharges for the purpose of groundwater management are to be specially authorized on a case by case basis, and only when there is no risk of polluting the groundwater. All the authorizations mentioned above may only be issued if the groundwater quality is undergoing the requisite surveillance.

The nature of the above mentioned prior investigations is explained, and the particulars of the above mentioned authorizations are set out. All authorizations may be granted only for a limited period and must be reviewed every four years. The competent authorities are to monitor compliance with authorizations and the effects of discharges on groundwater.

Existing discharges of List I and II substances must be brought within the provisions of the Directive by 19 December 1985.

An inventory of authorizations is to be kept. The Commission may ask for information, on a case by case basis, about:

authorizations;
the inventory;
the prior investigations mentioned above;
the results of monitoring.

The information acquired by the Commission must only be used for the purpose for which it was requested. This is not to prevent publication of general information or surveys which do not contain information relating to particular undertakings.

Where transfrontier groundwater is concerned, the competent authority of a Member State which intends to grant authorization for a discharge must first inform other Member States concerned. At the request of one of the Member States consultation must be held before an authorization is issued, and the Commission may participate.

Development of the Directive

Although the Directive was agreed within two years of being proposed – which is quite rapid for Community legislation – it underwent quite significant modification in the process. The European Parliament's Environment Committee proposed many amendments in some respects making the Directive more stringent. The most important of these was that List I substances should not be indirectly discharged to groundwater even when subject to authorization, and a ban on all direct and indirect discharges in areas where the groundwater is used, or could be used, for drinking. In the debate in the European Parliament (14 November 1978) Commissioner Natali welcomed the amendments but noted that the Commission 'must expect serious objections from some Member States during the discussion at the Council of Ministers'. He was probably right because on the very same day the House of Commons debated the proposal and amended the government's motion for a resolution to read 'this House. . . cannot accept proposals that require a ban on all types of direct discharge, particularly those found acceptable in the United Kingdom'. This resolution, although apparently tying the Government's hands by forcing it to resist the proposed Directive as amended by the European Parliament, in practice did not really do so since the European Parliament had already proposed significant exceptions to allow traces of List I substances and to allow the practice of recharging aquifers from rivers which inevitably contain some List I substances. The Minister, Ken Marks, expressed the government's preference for the freedom to examine each case on its merits, and opposition to the idea of generalized bans:

> this kind of case by case approach which we have adopted is a
> very different matter from an extended ban plus exemptions.
> It is more flexible. . .

In the event, the European Parliament's proposed amendments were substantially modified and the Directive as agreed is in effect an 'extended ban' with enough exemptions to overcome what the British Minister called 'our basic dislike of outright banning'.

Formal compliance in the UK

The government's formal 'compliance letter' sent to the Commission in December 1981 stated that the statutory powers necessary to secure compliance were contained primarily in the Control of Pollution Act 1974, and referred to the powers of the water authorities and waste disposal authorities to grant or withhold authorizations for the discharge of effluent and the disposal of waste respectively. (See Section 5.0 for a description of legislation on waste.)

The letter went on to explain that for the disposal of wastes from mines and quarries the necessary powers were available to planning authorities under the Town and Country Planning Act 1971 and the Town and Country Planning (General Development) Order 1977 and, in addition, that Section 18 of the Control of Pollution Act 1974 enabled regulations to be made to bring these wastes under the licensing controls in that Act, should it prove expedient to do so. The letter also listed the extra legislation covering Scotland and Northern Ireland.

In March 1982 the DoE published Circular 4/82 explaining the provisions of the Directive to the water authorities, waste disposal authorities, and mineral planning authorities and appointing them the competent authorities for the discharges under their control. A similar circular was issued in Scotland. A copy of the circulars was sent to the Commission.

The 'compliance letter' did not, however, say that the relevant parts of Part II of the Control of Pollution Act dealing with water were not yet in force, nor did the Circular do so explicitly (although the fact could be deduced by the careful reader noting the choice of tense, eg 'the necessary authorization of discharges or discharge producing activities *will* be provided under the consent procedures in Sections 34 et seq. . .').

Even though existing discharges did not have to be brought within the provisions of the Directive until December 1985 there must have been a formal failure to comply with the Directive, since it required the Member States to have brought into force the 'laws, regulations and administrative provisions necessary to comply with this Directive within two years of its notification' (by December 1981) and consent for discharges under the Control of Pollution Act only came into operation from July 1984 under SI No 865 1984. For existing discharges this failure may be merely one of form. The Directive applied to new discharges from December 1981 and, to the extent that there have been such discharges that cannot have been controlled by existing legislation, the failure will have been more than merely a matter of form.

In addition to the existing powers to control waste disposal in Part I of the Control of Pollution Act, there were some other controls over groundwater pollution even without Part II being in force. These included powers under the Water Act 1945 for water authorities to make byelaws preventing discharges where water supplies might be contaminated whether on the surface or under-ground, and powers under the Water Resources Act 1963 to prevent pollution of underground water by discharges into wells, boreholes and pipes. However, these provisions were not adequate for complete compliance and were not mentioned in the compliance letter presumably because they would effectively be superseded when Part II of the Control of Pollution Act came into force.

Since the Directive requires direct discharges to *any* groundwater of both List I and List II substances to be controlled, and since Sections 31 and 56 of the Control of Pollution Act only give powers of control to 'specified' underground waters, the Circular explained that it would be necessary for water authorities to 'specify' *all* underground waters. Interestingly, the Act only empowers underground waters to be 'specified' if they are capable of being used for any purpose, but the DoE's advice is that all groundwaters must be capable of some use and can therefore be 'specified'. SI 582 1984 made operational the concept of specification referrred to in the Act – The Control of Pollution (Underground Water) (Specification) Regulations 1984. This Regulation laid down the document to be used in specifying underground waters for the purpose of controlling discharges to them and the particulars to be included in it.

Effect on UK practice

Circular 4/82 asserted that the Directive 'will serve in the main to underline and reinforce, rather than alter, current policy and procedures on (the protection of groundwater against pollution by certain substances) insofar as the United King-dom is concerned', and this is a fair summary of the attitude of the water authorities. Since then all water authorities have specified underground waters in their regions according to the requirements of SI 582. As far as is known all existing discharges have also been controlled as required by the Directive by the due date of December 1985.

The major advance in control of groundwater in Britain came with the establishment of the water authorities in 1974 and, given that waste disposal is a potential major source of groundwater pollution, with the bringing into force in 1976 of Part I of the Control of Pollution Act which placed an obligation on waste disposal authorities to refer any applications for a site licence for the disposal of waste to the water authority (see Section 5.0). Any unresolved dispute between the authorities has to be referred to the Secretary of State. Partly in order to provide guidance to the waste disposal authorities some water authorities have drawn up aquifer protection policies[1] which among other matters have indicated zones where waste disposal is not acceptable, and this policy development cannot be attributed to the Directive. By and large, a good working relationship has developed between water authorities and waste disposal authorities with rather few disputes being referred to the Secretary of State – although a survey of waste disposal authorities in 1980 showed that there are some exceptions to this[2].

What the Directive should do is to concentrate attention on the possibility of the listed substances reaching groundwater both when consenting direct discharges, either from waste disposal sites or elsewhere, and when authorizing indirect discharges from waste disposal sites under the site licensing provisons of Part I of the Control of Pollution Act. Circular 4/82 explained, however, (paraphrasing the Directive) that

> waste disposal operations will not come within the terms of the Directive unless they might result in listed substances reaching groundwater, and in a quantity and concentration likely to cause deterioration in the quality of usable groundwater. . . this will limit the number of sites likely to be affected.

There remains suspicion that some waste disposal operations may be resulting in deterioration in the quality of usable groundwaters but the extent and degree is unknown.

One consequence of the Directive is that DoE Circular 39/76 which gave advice on the balancing of interests between water protection and waste disposal has had to be modified. The volume of an aquifer is no longer to be a factor for consideration in reaching a decision since the Directive requires *all* usable groundwater to be protected.

One query has been posed concerning those cases where site licenses authorize the dilution and dispersal of liquid wastes within the site to underground waters and the authorities concerned have thus accepted that such waters have been designated for disposal of List I and List II substances. As the specification of underground water applies to water used for any purpose, the question arises whether the use for disposal of such substances should be specified and approved for deliberate pollution. It has been suggested that such waters should cease to be specified and therefore effectively decontrolled.

The discharges from the disposal of mining and quarrying waste can also give rise to groundwater pollution, although Circular 4/82 claimed that the number of cases where discharges would come within the terms of the Directive is likely to be minimal. The circular nevertheless advised the mineral planning authorities, in consultation with the water authorities, to consider whether conditions imposed on existing permissions at sites in active use are sufficient to ensure the protection of groundwater, and this must result in extra work. The Circular explained that changes were envisaged in the legislation (The Town and Country Planning General Development Order 1977) requiring water authorities to be consulted on all applications for the winning and working of minerals, and requiring the submission for approval of schemes for tipping on an existing tip on which water authorities will also have to be consulted.

References
1   Selby K H and Skinner A C 1979 Aquifer protection in the Severn-Trent region: policy and practice *Journal of the Institute of Water Pollution Control* **78** (22).

2   Nash J M and Kahn A Q (South Yorkshire County Council) 1980 *Waste disposal by landfill and groundwater pollution: a survey of waste disposal authorities in England by questionnaire* (typescript provided by authors).

4.10 Mercury from chloralkali industry

82/176/EEC (OJ L81 27.3.82) proposed 14.6.79 – COM(79)296	Directive on limit values and quality objectives for mercury discharges by the chloralkali electrolysis industry.

Binding dates

Notification date	25 March 1982
Formal compliance	1 July 1983
Standards to be met	1 July 1983 and 1 July 1986
Commission's comparative assessment	every five years, ie first report presumably due 25 March 1987.

Purpose of the Directive

This is the first of the daughter Directives flowing from Directive 76/464 on pollution of water (see Section 4.8). The present Directive is concerned with only one substance – mercury – discharged by only one manufacturing process. The production of chlorine by plants in which alkali chlorides are electrolysed by means of mercury cells (known as chloralkali electrolysis) was selected for early attention because of the large quantity of mercury discharged. A separate Directive – covers mercury discharged from other sources (see Section 4.11).

Summary of the Directive

In accordance with the compromise enshrined in the parent Directive 76/464 (Section 4.8) Member States may authorize discharges of mercury and its compounds from chloralkali electrolysis plants following either of the two regimes described in Directive 76/464, that is authorizations are to conform either to limit values or to quality objectives specified below (although a special provision not foreshadowed in the parent Directive has been introduced for new plants).

Limit values

The limit values are summarized in Table 2. The authorizations issued by the Member States must be at least as stringent as these limit values and must be reviewed at least every four years.

Different limit values are laid down for plants using the 'lost brine' and 'recycled brine' processes. The limit values are expressed in two ways: (a) in terms of concentration, ie micrograms of mercury per litre discharged and (b) in terms of quantity in relation to capacity, ie grams of mercury per tonne of installed chlorine production capacity. The limit values in terms of quantity *must* be observed, while those given in terms of concentration should *in principle* not be exceeded.

The limit values set out in Table 2 are monthly average limit values, and daily average limit values are four times these. Sampling is to be done daily.

Table 2   Limit values of mercury from chloralkali industry

		1 July 1983	1 July 1986
1.	*In terms of concentration* (micrograms per litre of all mercury-containing water discharged)	75	50
2.	*In terms of quantity* (grams per tonne installed chlorine capacity)		
	Recycle brine (mercury in discharges from chlorine production unit)	0.5	0.5
	Recycle brine (total mercury in all mercury-containing waters discharged from site)	1.5	1.0
	Lost brine (total mercury in all mercury-containing waters discharged from site)	8.0	5.0

Quality objectives
The following four quality objectives for mercury concentrations are laid down and in addition the quality objective laid down in any other Directive must also be observed. The concentrations in affected areas of water (the arithmetic mean of the results obtained over a year) may be multiplied by 1.5 until 30 June 1986 provided the Commission is notified beforehand.

1. Fish flesh — 0.3 mg/kg wet flesh
2. Inland surface waters — 1.0 μg/l
3. Estuary waters — 0.5 μg/l
4. Sea and coastal waters — 0.3 μg/l

It is for the competent authority to determine the area affected by discharges in each case and to select from among the above quality objectives those that it deems appropriate. It should have regard to the intended use of the area affected and bear in mind that the purpose of the Directive is to eliminate all pollution. Emission standards are to be set by the Member States so that the appropriate quality objective(s) is or are complied with in the area affected. In addition, the concentration of mercury in sediments or in shellfish must not increase significantly with time.

New plant
Member States may grant authorizations for new plant only if such authorizations *contain a reference* to the standards corresponding to the best technical means available for preventing discharges of mercury. In a Statement printed with the Directive but not legally forming part of the Directive, the Council and Commission stated that:

> the application of the best technical means available makes it possible to limit discharges of mercury from the site of a new industrial plant using the recycled brine process to less than 0.5 g/tonne of installed chlorine production capacity.

A Member State wishing to grant an authorization for a new plant when for technical reasons the best technical means available are not to be used, must first justify this to the Commission. Within three months the Commission is to send a report to the Member States with its opinion on the proposed derogation.

The purpose of this provision is apparently to shame any Member State into insisting on the best technical means available for new plant even if the limit values or the quality objectives would be met by cheaper but less than the best technically available means. However, in this connection it is necessary to bear in mind that when Directive 76/464 was agreed a Statement was recorded in the Council minutes to the effect that 'best technical means available' is to take into account the economic availability of those means (see Section 4.8).

Monitoring and analysis
A reference method of analysis for determining the presence of mercury is given, but other methods may be used provided the limits of detection, precision and accuracy are as good. Member States are to be responsible for monitoring waters affected. When the waters of several Member States are affected, the Member States are to cooperate with a view to harmonizing monitoring procedures.

Comparative assessments
The Member States are to supply the Commission at its request with details of authorizations and the results of monitoring to determine mercury concentrations. The Commission is to prepare a comparative assessment of the implementation of the Directive by the Member States and every five years forward it to the Council. As it does not have to be sent to the Parliament it need not be published.

Development of the Directive
Though this was the first daughter Directive it was not the first proposal; that was for the 'drins' (the pesticides aldrin, dieldrin and endrin). Development of this Directive was bound up with consideration of the 'drins' proposal (COM(79)243) and the two need to be looked at together at least for the initial stages. Essentially the discussion of the daughter Directives was a re-run of all the

old problems which had so beset the parent Directive and the differences of view about the limit value and the quality objective approaches. Significantly it showed the suspicions held by the continental countries and a determined attempt by the Commission to make the quality objective approach one which would result in very much more stringent standards for emissions.

It is interesting to note the time taken, first, in making in the proposals and, second, in getting agreement. The parent Directive was agreed in 1975 (adoption was not until May 1976 because of lengthy discussions on the finer points of the text): the first proposal (on 'drins') took over three years to produce and dealt with discharges from only one plant in the Community. It has yet to be agreed. The second proposal (mercury from chloralkali plants) appeared a month later and was finally adopted in March 1982 – over six years from agreement of the parent Directive. Since then a further four daughter Directives have been adopted covering six substances in all out of 129 substances identified as possible List 1 substances (see Sections 4.11, 4.12 and 4.13).

The original proposals for both this Directive and the 'drins' consisted of two separate Directives: one dealing with limit values and the other quality objectives. The UK held that this method of implementing 76/464 was not in accordance with its terms, an opinion which was supported by the legal services of the Council of Ministers. The Economic and Social Committee also recommended one Directive. As a result of the arguments for a single text the proposals were amended accordingly in negotiation in the Council machinery. All subsequent proposals for further substances have appeared as single texts covering both limit values and quality objectives.

The UK, as the only country which had not declared its intention to use limit values, was concerned to ensure that the compromise reached on 76/464 permitting the use of quality objectives resulted in equality of treatment in the two approaches – hence its opposition to two separate Directives. The other main points of difficulty which the UK government raised, and which were supported by both Houses of Parliament, focused on apparent differences in treatment and a seeming failure to understand the basis on which quality objectives worked in practice. They covered:

the differences in time scales, since limit values were to be attained in three stages the last being July 1989, whereas quality objectives were to be applied from July 1983;
the need for more stringent controls over emissions where the quality objective approach is being followed than would be required of those using the limit value approach;
requirement to institute reduction programmes for indirect discharges where quality objectives were used when these in effect would take account of such discharges;
confusion in use of the term 'quality objectives' by equating them with 'quality standards' and setting standards unrelated to use;
complex monitoring procedures for quality objectives.

The Commission issued in December 1980 an amendment to its proposals which followed those recommended by the Economic and Social Committee. It dropped the requirement for a reduction programme for indirect discharges from both parts of its proposal, ie both for limit values and quality objectives.

The Directive as adopted reveals that most of the points raised by the UK were met. The quality objectives set were less stringent and provided for distinction between estuarial and other tidal waters. The time scales for both limit values and quality objectives were on the same basis. The monitoring requirements for quality objectives were modified to drop the concepts of various zones.

The greatest difficulty arose over the treatment of new plant. The original Commission proposal set limit values for new plant at the level to be achieved by recycled brine plants in July 1989; while the quality objectives proposal made, logically enough, no reference to them. The competition aspect was particularly important to the French and Italians and they argued that if a country applying quality objectives did not have to apply the limit values that would otherwise apply in the case of a new plant there would be distortion of competition. To the UK it was important to uphold the principle underlying the use of quality objectives: the emission standard to be applied to any plant new or otherwise should be related to the quality to be met in the receiving waters. The deadlock reached in the Council of Ministers was finally resolved by a complicated wording supported by statements in the Council minutes. Authorizations for new plants must contain a reference to best technical means, the standards corresponding to them and, where the measures do not conform to these standards, the reasons must be supplied to the Commission. The Commission is required to report to Member States with its opinion. The wording actually avoids requiring best technical means to be used so satisfying the British point of principle but in effect creating a climate in which it would be very difficult not to use them. Implicit in the agreement, though unstated, is the understanding that it wold be unrealistic to build a new plant which did not make use of processes based on the best technical means available. The publication of a Council minute to accompany a Directive set a precedent.

Formal compliance

The UK government formally notified the Commission in July 1983 of how it would comply with the requirements of the Directive. It explained that in England and Wales the necessary powers were contained in the Control of Pollution Act 1974 which empowered water authorities to grant or withhold authorizations for the discharge of effluent to the relevant waters. Though there were no discharges in Scotland or Northern Ireland, the necessary powers existed there too. Water authorities were given detailed guidance on the implementation of the Directive in an advice note issued in August 1982. In England and Wales water authorities were to be the competent authorities to issue authorizations which would generally be in the form of normal discharge consents. In amplification of the Council and Commission view published with the Directive, the Department stated that an interpretation of the term 'best technical means' would have to be evolved and further advice might have to be issued. It also made clear that the term 'substantial' in relation to an increase in production justifying classification as a new plant should refer to an increase of 20 per cent or more.

With the compliance letter the government sent the Commission a copy of the advice note to water authorities and also an inventory of discharges from the five plants listed below.

Subsequently the Department issued Circular 18/85 dated 18 September 1985, which covered the parent Directive 76/464 and all other daughter Directives adopted at that date. The contents of the Circular are summarized in Section 4.8 and do not materially differ from the advice to water authorities issued in August 1982.

Effect on UK practice
In July 1983 the DoE sent to the Commission the first annual return required by the Directive listing the five plants operating in Britain and setting out the details of the consent conditions. The five plants are:

1. Castner-Kellner Works, Runcorn (ICI) discharging into the Weston Canal and affecting the Mersey Estuary and Liverpool Bay (lost brine process);
2. Hillhouse Works (ICI) discharging into the Wyre Estuary and affecting Morecambe Bay and Liverpool Bay (lost brine process);
3. Ellesmere Port (Associated Octel) discharging into the Manchester Ship Canal and affecting the Mersey Estuary and Liverpool Bay (recycled brine process);
4. Sandbach Works (Hays Chemical – previously BP Chemicals) discharging into the Trent and Mersey Canal affecting the Mersey Estuary (recycled brine process);
5. Staveley Works, Chesterfield (Staveley Chemicals) discharging into the River Rother and affecting the River Don (recycled brine process).

In three cases the plants were to meet the environmental quality standards for fish flesh and estuarial waters; at the Sandbach Works, as the plant discharged to a canal with a limited flow, limit values were to be met; at the Staveley Works, discharging to a river, the environmental quality standards would not be met until 1986.

There are a number of clear conclusions to be drawn from the lengthy process between the drawing up of the proposal in 1979 until its adoption in 1982 and subsequent implementation. It is a demonstration of the effect of Community legislation on UK practice in a number of areas.

The first effect is that the UK had to establish what it actually meant by using quality objectives. It had to produce figures which would stand up to examination where none had existed before. It had to show the link between the mercury content in the environment and the effect on human health to establish what a safe level was and thus establish quality standards. As described in the evidence to the House of Lords' Scrutiny Committee, a trial was carried out on diets and concentrations of mercury in hair and blood in the Liverpool Bay area, in other words among those exposed to the highest concentrations of mercury in this country and most at risk. The consequent recommendation for a standard of 0.3 milligrammes per kilogramme of fish flesh was in fact adopted by the Commission in its proposal.

The second effect is that on industry. The major companies with chloralkali plants such as ICI were well aware from the time that Directive 76/464 was first proposed in 1974 that mercury from chloralkali plants was going to be high on the list of substances to be tackled. The question for these companies was what should they do about the likelihood of more rigorous controls on discharges from such plants. In the event ICI decided to clean up mercury discharges from its Castner-Kellner Works at Runcorn.

By 1983 it had spent some £25 million at 1982 prices with annual running costs estimated at £1.09 million. BP Chemicals had a similar problem with its Sandbach Works. In 1976 it was decided to modernize the works with a significant increase in its mercury cell capacity. The process engineers were faced with the task of anticipating legislation. Uncertain at that time of the objectives and related standards to be set for the receiving waters, the designer was forced to begin with a study of the technology available for the recovery of mercury. That led to the decision to install a resin bed absorption unit involving a capital investment of £1.3 million the benefits of which derived entirely from the reduced mercury discharged to the receiving waters. The quality objective expected to apply to the Sandbach Works was that the total mercury in the water should not exceed 1 μg/l as an annual average. In both cases doubts have been expressed as to whether the environmental benefits justified the very heavy costs incurred. Also stressed was the difficulties of taking decisions when uncertain of the future requirements that would be imposed.

The third effect worth noting is the way the Directive has been implemented in practice in the UK. As explained in Section 4.8 the implementing advice to water authorities provided for them to specify limit values where quality standards could not initially be met. This in fact is what has happened in the case of the BP Sandbach Works. Despite the earlier claims, the discharges into a canal cannot meet the Directive's environmental quality standards and the consent issued to the plant stipulates compliance with the limit value. This action at first sight may appear surprising given the UK's long campaign in support of the principle of tailoring limits on emissions to the quality standards needed to meet quality objectives set for different uses of water. However, the Directive clearly allows a choice, even if it might have been thought that either one or the other system would have been followed consistently within one country. On the other hand, it shows that the limit value approach can on occasion require less stringent controls than the quality objective approach.

4.11 Mercury from other sources

84/156/EEC (OJ L 74 17.3.84) proposed 15.12.82 – COM(82)838	Directive on limit values and quality objectives for mercury by sectors other than the chloralkali industry.

Binding dates

Notification date	18 March 1984
Formal compliance	12 March 1986
Standards to be met	1 July 1986 and 1 July 1989
Commission's report	12 March 1988 and every four years thereafter.

Purpose of the Directive

This is the third of the daughter Directives flowing from Directive 76/464 on pollution of water (see Section 4.8). The present Directive is concerned with mercury discharged from manufacturing processes other than the chloralkali process which was the subject of the first daughter Directive 82/176 (see Section 4.10).

Summary of the Directive

In accordance with the compromise enshrined in the parent Directive 76/464 Member States may authorize discharges of mercury and its compounds from plants in industrial sectors other than the chloralkali industry either by setting limit values or establishing emission standards enabling quality objectives to be complied with, in accordance with those laid down in the Directive. For multiple sources which are not industrial plants, and to which emission standards cannot be applied in practice, special programmes to avoid or eliminate pollution are to be drawn up by Member States. In the case of new plants, authorizations may normally only be granted if they apply the standards corresponding to the best technical means available but no specific guidance is given as to the standards achievable by the use of best technical means, as is the case for chloralkali plants.

Limit values

The limit values are summarized in Table 3. The authorizations issued by the Member States must be at least as stringent as these limit values and must be reviewed at least every four years.

Different values are laid down for different industrial sectors. For sectors not mentioned, the Council will, if necessary, fix limit values at a later stage. In four sectors values are expressed in two ways: (a) in terms of concentration, by milligrams of mercury per litre in effluent; and (b) in terms of quantity in relation to mercury processed, by grams per tonne of mercury processed or of production capacity of a particular process. In two sectors, only the first way is laid

Table 3 Limit values for mercury discharged from other sources

	1 July 1986	1 July 1989
1. *In terms of quantity* (grammes per tonne of vinyl chloride production capacity or mercury processed		
Chemical industries using mercury catalysts in:		
a) vinylchloride production	0.2	0.1
b) other processes	10.0	5.0
Manufacture of mercury catalysts	1.0	0.7
Manufacture of other mercury compounds	0.1	0.05
Manufacture of batteries	0.05	0.03
2. *In terms of concentration* (milligrams per litre of effluent) Sectors above plus non ferrous metal industry and toxic waste treatment plants	0.1	0.05

Notes: (i) Member States must themselves fix emission standards for mercury discharges from sectors not listed above, taking account of best available technical means, pending determination of limit values by the Council at a later stage.

(ii) The Commission will submit proposals for more stringent limit values to be introduced by March 1994.

down. The limit values correspond to a monthly average concentration or to a maximum monthly load. The daily average limits are twice the corresponding monthly average limit values. Limit values expressed as concentrations should not *in principle* be exceeded but those in terms of quantity *must* be observed because concentrations of mercury in effluents depend on the volume of water involved which differs for different processes and plants.

A sampling procedure must be set up based on taking a representative sample over a period of twenty-four hours. The quantity of mercury discharged over a month must be calculated on the basis of the daily quantities of mercury discharged.

Quality objectives
The quality objectives are those set for mercury discharged from chloralkali plants in Directive 82/176 (see Section 4.10). The same conditions apply except that the concentrations may be multiplied where necessary for technical reasons by 1.5 until 1 July 1989 provided that the Commission has been notified beforehand.

New plant
The same conditions apply to new plant as in the cadmium Directive 83/513 (see Section 4.12) ie authorizations may only be granted if they apply standards corresponding to the best technical means when necessary for the elimination of pollution or to prevent distortion of competition. In the same way, derogations must be notified to the Commission with reasons. In addition to passing on the evidence to other Member States the Commission will also send a report to all Member States as soon as possible with its opinion on the derogation.

Monitoring and analysis
The reference method of analysis to be used is the same as that specified in Directive 82/176 (see Section 4.10), but other methods may be used provided the limits of detection, precision and accuracy are as good.

Periodical report
The Member States are to supply the Commission at its request with details of authorizations and the results of monitoring to determine mercury concentrations. On the basis of this information the Commission is to prepare a report on the implementation of the Directive every four years. It is not stated what the Commission should do with it. The Commission is required to submit appropriate proposals to the Council in the event of a change in scientific knowledge relating principally to the toxicity and persistence of mercury in living organisms or sediments or of an improvement in the best technical means available.

Development of the Directive
The proposal for the Directive was submitted nine months after adoption of the Directive on mercury from the chloralkali industry and was therefore influenced very much by what had been agreed therein. Nevertheless, certain points received criticism in the United Kingdom, though the government's attitude was that it was acceptable in principle as the quality objectives proposed were identical with those in the earlier Directive. The main point of criticism related to the application of limit values to the point of entry into public sewers. Other fears expressed concerned the burden of sampling and monitoring requirements.

The European Parliament's amendments were confined to stressing that the quality objective approach should only be by way of exception and to requiring that such exceptions after acceptance by the Commission be reported to the Council and Parliament.

The House of Lords did not report on the proposal but it was considered by the Standing Committee of the House of Commons who raised similar objections to those already mentioned.

The cadmium proposal had raised the same issue about the application to the point of discharge to sewers. This point was settled on adoption of the cadmium Directive (Section 4.12) and a similar wording was adopted for this Directive which got over the difficulties of the United Kingdom. Other changes to the proposal covered the exclusion of Greenland and the dropping of the term 'comparative assessment'; instead the Commission is to make a report every four years. There are therefore differences here compared with the previous Directive on mercury. Other changes were made to Annex 1 dealing with limit values in addition to the later dates which became necessary because of the time taken since the original proposal. They included specific references to the vinylchloride industry and the dropping of the category of analytical laboratories; the latter will be covered in the specific programmes to be drawn up by Member States for mercury discharges from multiple sources.

Formal compliance in the UK

The legislation and administrative measures enabling the Directive to be complied with have been described in connection with the chloralkali industry Directive. The only difference concerns the programmes for discharges from multiple sources. The DoE Circular 18/85 instructs the water authorities that they need not take any action on drawing up such programmes (Article 4.1) at this stage as this would be a DoE responsibility. It is suggested that they may wish to advise that mercury be used as little as possible in analysis and that discharges should not be disposed to water.

Effect on UK practice

Since compliance was only effective from 1 March 1986, it is premature fully to evaluate the effects of the Directive. But some action has already been taken as described in Section 4.10 largely because the UK quality objective approach can make no distinction between sources of mercury. The quality objectives are likely to be everywhere met, but one problem has been identified in the River Yare within the area of the Anglian Water Authority where eels have been found with levels of mercury in their flesh above the limits in the Directive even though the water itself meets the quality objective. This is thought to be due to historic discharges resulting in mercury in sediment. It is thought that this problem will be cured in time as the mercury is steadily diluted.

4.12 Cadmium

83/513/EEC (OJ L291 24.10.83) proposed 17.2.81 – COM(81)56	Directive on limit values and quality objectives for cadmium discharges.
Binding dates	
Notification date	28 September 1983
Formal compliance	28 September 1985
Limit values to be met	1 January 1986 and 1 January 1989
Commission's comparative assessment	every five years, but first report four years after notification, ie 26 September 1987.

Purpose of the Directive

This is the second of the daughter Directives flowing from Directive 76/464 dealing with pollution of water (see Section 4.8). The present Directive is concerned with only one substance – cadmium – and applies to most industrial discharges of cadmium, a specific exception being those from the manufacture of phosphoric acid or fertilizer for which no limit values are set.

Summary of the Directive

In accordance with the compromise enshrined in the parent Directive 76/464 (see Section 4.8) Member States may authorize discharges of cadmium and its compounds either by setting limit values or establishing emission standards enabling quality objectives to be complied with, in accordance with those laid down in the Directive. In the case of new plant, authorizations may only be granted if they apply the standards corresponding to the best technical means available but in contrast to the Directive on discharges of mercury from chloralkali plants no guidance is given as to the standards achievable by the use of best technical means available.

Limit values

The limit values are summarized in Table 4. The authorizations issued by the Member States must be at least as stringent as these limit values and must be reviewed at least every four years.

Different values are laid down for different industrial sectors. The limit values are expressed in two ways: (a) in terms of concentration, by micrograms of cadmium per litre of discharge and (b) in terms of quantity in relation to load, by grams of cadmium discharged per kilogram of cadmium handled. In the first case the values are measured in relation to monthly flow-weighted average concentration of total cadmium; in the second case as a monthly average. The second value (limit in relation to load) must be complied with in all cases because different processes and plants vary in the quantity of water used which may affect the concentration of cadmium in the effluent. Limit values expressed as maximum concentrations may not be greater than those expressed as maximum quantities divided by water requirements per kilogram of cadmium handled. It is intended to set more stringent limits with a view to their coming into force by 1992.

The daily average limits are twice the monthly limit values. Sampling is to be carried out daily but a simplified procedure may be adopted where discharges do not exceed 10 kg of cadmium per year or in the case of electroplating plants the total volume of the electroplating tanks is less than 1.5 m³.

Though no limit values are set for manufacture of phosphoric acid or fertilizer from phosphatic rock, Member States are still bound by Directive 76/464/EEC to fix emission standards for such plants.

Quality objectives
The following quality objectives were laid down:

the total cadmium concentration in inland surface waters affected by discharges must not exceed 5 μg/litre;

Table 4   Limit values for cadmium discharge

	1 January 1986	1 January 1989
1. *In terms of concentration* (milligrams of cadmium per litre of discharge)		
Zinc mining, lead and zinc refining, cadmium metal and nonferrous metal industry	0.3	0.2
Manufacture of cadmium compounds	0.5	0.2
Manufacture of pigment	0.5	0.2
Manufacture of stabilizers	0.5	0.2
Manufacture of batteries	0.5	0.2
Electroplating	0.5	0.2
2. *In terms of quantity* (grams of cadmium discharged per kilogram handled)		
Manufacture of cadmium compounds	0.5	—
Manufacture of pigment	0.3	—
Manufacture of stabilizers	0.5	—
Manufacture of batteries	1.5	—
Electroplating	0.3	—

Notes: (i)   Member States will fix emission standards for sectors not mentioned taking account of best technical means available, pending determination of limit values by the Council at a later stage
  (ii) Where no quantity limits have been set, it has proved impossible to fix figures
  (iii) Limit values for plants discharging less than 10 kg of cadmium per year may be suspended until 1st January 1989 where absolutely necessary

the concentration of dissolved cadmium in estuary waters affected by discharges must not exceed 5 μg/litre;
the concentration of dissolved cadmium in territorial waters and in internal coastal waters other than estuary waters affected by discharges must not exceed 2.5 μg/litre;
in the case of waters used for the abstraction of drinking water, the cadmium content must conform to the requirements of Directive 75/440 (see Section 4.4).

It is for the competent authority to determine the area affected by discharges in each case and to select from among the above quality objectives those that it deems appropriate having regard to the area affected and bearing in mind that the purpose of the Directive is to eliminate pollution. Emission standards are to be set by the Member States so that the appropriate quality objective(s) is or are complied with in the area affected.

In addition cadmium concentrations must be determined by the national network set up for this purpose and the results compared with the following concentrations:

in the case of inland surface waters, a total cadmium concentration of 1 μg/litre;
in the case of estuary waters, a dissolved cadmium concentration of 1 μg/litre;
in the case of territorial and internal coastal waters, other than estuary waters, a dissolved cadmium concentration of 0.5 μg/litre.

If these concentrations are not complied with at any one of the points on the national network, the reasons must be reported to the Commission.

Furthermore, the concentration of cadmium in sediments or in shellfish must not increase significantly with time; and where several quality objectives are applied to waters in an area, the quality of the waters must be sufficient to comply with each of these objectives.

New plant
Member States may only grant authorizations for new plant if those plants apply the standards corresponding to the best technical means available when that is necessary for the elimination of pollution in accordance with Article 2 of Directive 76/464 (see Section 4.8) or for the prevention of distortion of competition. What standards can be achieved by best technical means is not specified either in the Directive or in any published supplementary statement.

A Member State wishing to grant an authorization for a new plant when for technical reasons the best technical means available are not to be used, must first justify this to the Commission. Within three months the Commission is to send a report to the Member States with its opinion on the proposed derogation.

The purpose of this provision is apparently the same as for mercury discharge from new chloralkali plant.

Monitoring and analysis
A reference method of analysis for determining the cadmium content of waters sediments and shellfish is given, but other methods may be used provided the limits of detection, precision and accuracy are as good. Member States are to be responsible for monitoring waters affected. When the waters of several Member States are affected, the Member States are to cooperate with a view to harmonizing monitoring procedures.

Comparative assessments
The Member States are to supply the Commission at its request with details of authorizations and the results of monitoring to determine cadmium concentrations. The Commission is to prepare a comparative assessment of the implementation of the Directive and forward it to the Council every five years except that the first report will be four years after notification of the Directive.

Development of the Directive
In the United Kingdom the proposal received a warmer welcome than usual since it was felt that it took account of a number of points which had caused difficulty in the past. In particular it provided within one proposal alternative approaches using either limit values for discharges or environmental quality objectives; it also covered all discharges (except one) of cadmium to the aquatic environment. Nevertheless there were a number of aspects thought to be unsatisfactory. They covered such items as the exclusion of the manufacture of phosphoric acid from phosphate rock from control by limit values; the application of 'best technical means' to all new plants; the application of limit values to the point of discharge from the plant even when discharged to a sewer and subsequent treatment at a purification plant; and the very much more stringent level which would result from the application of the quality standards (objectives) proposed in comparison with that from use of limit values. Changes were to be made in the course of negotiations in the Council machinery which would result in these difficulties being resolved.

Six months after the original proposal was issued the Council reached agreement on the first of the daughter Directives of Directive 76/464 – discharges of mercury from chloralkali industry (Section 4.10). As a consequence, changes were agreed so that the cadmium Directive closely followed the mercury one in structure and content.

Subsequently the Commission submitted some amendments to the original proposal to take into account a number of amendments proposed by the European Parliament, mainly relating to the quality objectives. In its Explanatory Memorandum the Commission added that the changes would align the wording in this proposal with that of the Directive on mercury discharges adopted earlier. The Department of the Environment in its Explanatory Memorandum to Parliament disputed this statement. The main difference appears to have been the amendment concerning using quality objectives set in other Directives.

The House of Lords in its report and debate pointed out that the omission of any control of direct discharges of cadmium from the manufacture of phosphoric acid from phosphate rock (because there was no technically and economically feasible method of treatment) was a serious weakness. A Member State applying the quality objective approach would, on the other hand, be controlling such discharges. It was acknowledged that Member States using the limit value approach were required under the parent Directive to apply national programmes based upon quality objectives where no specific provision was made elsewhere. Since discharges of cadmium from such plants constitute the main source of cadmium discharges, it was considered that measures to control pollution from this source should be taken throughout the Community. The European Parliament made the same point and recommended a limit value be set. The Directive as adopted made explicit the requirement for Member States to fix emission standards for these discharges.

The problem about new plants and the application of 'best technical means' was resolved by adopting a changed wording from that in the Directive on mercury discharges from chloralkali plants by requiring authorizations for new plants to apply 'the best technical means in order to prevent pollution or distortion of competition' (instead of 'to prevent discharges').

The question of where limit values should apply reflects a sharp division of views between the United Kingdom with a more extended system of sewers and that of the continental countries with fears of weakening the equality of competition principle by allowing limit values to be bypassed. The commonsense solution of permitting limit values to be applied at the point where waste waters leave a treatment plant where these treat effluents from plants using cadmium was adopted in this case and will presumably set a precedent for subsequent proposals.

The House of Lords was very critical of the disparity between the effects of the limit values set and those from quality objectives. As Lord Ashby pointed out in the debate on the proposal in the House of Lords on 14 December 1981:

> The fixed emission standard for cadmium for. . . factories doing electroplating. . . is two parts per million in waste discharged. But that discharge has to be diluted by something like a thousand times in order to reach the environmental standard which it is British policy to take as a basis.

He considered that the conclusion to be drawn was that either the Commission had got its arithmetic wrong or was deliberately weighting the choice heavily in favour of the preferred solution of fixed emission standards. The Lords' report also drew attention to the fact that the Commission's consultant had recommended a quality standard for salt water of 10 μg/litre in contrast to that proposed of 1 μg/litre. The Annex dealing with quality objectives as adopted is in very different form from that proposed. The main point is that figures set are somewhat higher than proposed.

Other developments
Adoption of this Directive enabled the Community to agree Council Decision 85/613 OJ L375 31.12.85 approving programmes and measures concerning cadmium under the Convention for the Protection of the Rhine against Chemical Pollution and the Convention for the Prevention of Marine Pollution from

Land-based Sources (Paris Convention). The Community is a signatory to both Conventions (see Chapter 11).

Formal compliance

The general requirements are described in Section 4.8 on dangerous substances in water. The DoE Circular 18/85 directs water authorities as a first priority to authorize discharges of cadmium which exceed or will exceed 3 kg a year; or will increase the concentration of cadmium in the receiving water either by 10 per cent of the relevant environmental quality standard (EQS) or to a concentration in excess of 50 per cent of the relevant EQS; or will increase the concentration of cadmium in the receiving water by more than 3 per cent of the relevant EQS and where, in the absence of the discharge, the concentration of cadmium was already greater than 50 per cent of that standard.

Two exemptions are listed: one, discharges from sewage works to which there is no significant industrial input; and, two, discharges of cadmium in water taken for cooling or use in an industrial process which is returned to the same body of water and to which no cadmium has been added.

Water authorities will need to ascertain the cadmium handling capacity of each plant. This information will also be needed to determine whether expansion of an existing plant requires it to be considered as a new plant. In determining capacity, account should be taken of cadmium actually used in the processes as well as that incidentally present in raw materials.

In setting consents for discharges to sewers it may be assumed that 50 per cent of cadmium will be removed by the sewage treatment works, but in due course an appropriate figure should be ascertained for each works.

Effect on UK practice

The UK notified the Commission in its return for 1985 of 506 discharges of cadmium in the UK. The UK elected to apply quality objectives in all cases and demonstrated with monitoring data compliance with the quality objectives specified in the Directive in all except five cases. Two of these were in Cornwall and were the result of pumping water from tin mines high in natural cadmium deposits directly into rivers. One was from a sewage treatment works which received two industrial discharges; one high result produced an annual mean slightly over the limit. The other two were in Scotland (both Firth of Forth) where monitoring showed that the internal coastal water quality standard had been exceeded; improvements are expected to show compliance in the next return. Of the 506 discharges, 244 were those of industrial firms discharging to 160 sewage treatment works. One hundred and two industrial firms made direct discharges of one kind or another. Total discharges to receiving waters therefore amounted to 262. The information which had to be collected shows that water authorities are now much more aware of the incidence of cadmium in their discharges. With improvements this year it seems likely that the next return will show almost 100 per cent compliance with the specified quality standards.

These figures can be contrasted with those published in a DoE commissioned report by Environmental Resources Ltd (ERL)[1] into the economic implications of changing to a limit value approach. Few firms out of the 188 firms studied would comply with the Directive's limit values effective until 1989. Only 17 out of 51 firms interviewed would comply with the stricter limits applicable from 1989. Two large smelters which account for 60 per cent of the total load of cadmium discharged have discharge concentrations of more than five times the 1989 limit value. The annual cost of complying with the 1989 limits for all water authorities in England and Wales is estimated at £6–£6.7 million.

References
1   Environmental Resources Ltd 1987 *Comparison of environmental quality objectives and limit value approaches to control of dangerous substances.*

4.13 Lindane

84/491/EEC (OJ L274 17.10.84) proposed 7.7.83 – COM(83)422	Directive on limit values and quality objectives for discharges of hexachlorocyclohexane.
Binding dates	
Notification date	11 October 1984
Formal compliance	1 April 1986
Standards to be met	1 April 1986 and 1 October 1986
Commission's comparative assessment	11 October 1988, every five years thereafter.

Purpose of the Directive

This is another of the daughter Directives which flow from Directive 76/464 dealing with pollution of water (see Section 4.8). The present Directive is concerned with preventing pollution from discharges of hexachlorocyclohexane (HCH). HCH can form several isomers of which only one, the gamma isomer, commonly called lindane is used in the European Community mostly in agriculture as a pesticide. The Directive is directed specifically at plants producing HCH but covers indirectly any industrial process where HCH is present.

Summary of the Directive

As with the other Directives of this family Member States may authorize discharges of HCH from plants producing HCH (including lindane) either by setting limit values or establishing emission standards enabling quality objectives to be complied with, in accordance with those set in the Directive. Limit values will also apply to discharges from plants where formulation of lindane takes place on the same site. The Council will determine later limit values for plants treating HCH not mentioned, in particular for plants for lindane formulation producing protective agents for plants, wood and cables: emission standards for such plants will be set by Member States in the meantime using best technical means available. In the case of new plants authorizations may only be granted if the standards corresponding to the best technical means available are applied. No specific guidance is given as to the standards achievable.

Limit values
The limit values are summarized in Table 5. The authorizations by Member States must be at least as stringent as these limit values and must be reviewed every four years at least.

Different values are laid down for different industrial sectors.

In each sector values are expressed (a) in terms of quantity of production, ie grams of HCH discharged per tonne of HCH produced or treated and (b) in

Table 5   Limit values for HCH discharge

	1 April 1986		1 October 1988	
Industrial Sector	g/tonne HCH produced/ treated	mg/l HCH discharged	g/tonne HCH produced/ treated	mg/l HCH discharged
Plant for production of HCH	3	3	2	2
Plant for extraction of lindane	15	8	4	2
Plant where production of HCH and extraction of lindane is carried out	16	6	5	2

Note: Limit values also include any discharges from lindane formulation on the same site. Pending Council determination of limit values for sectors not mentioned, Member States will fix emission standards taking into account best technical means available.

terms of concentration, ie milligrams of HCH per litre discharged. The limit values correspond to a monthly average weight or to a monthly flow weighted average concentration. Those expressed as concentrations in principle should not be exceeded: those given by quantity must be complied with.

The daily average limit values are twice the corresponding monthly average limit values.

A sampling procedure must be set up based on taking a representative sample over a period of 24 hours. The quantity of HCH discharged over a month must be calculated on the basis of the daily quantities of HCH discharged. A simplified procedure may be instituted where discharges are less than 3 kg of HCH per annum.

Quality objectives
The following quality objectives are laid down.

the total HCH concentration in inland surface waters affected by discharges must not exceed 100 nanograms per litre;
the total concentration of HCH in estuary waters and territorial sea waters must not exceed 20 nanograms per litre;
in the case of water used for the abstraction of drinking water, the HCH content must conform to the requirements of Directive 75/440 (Drinking water – Section 4.4).

It is for the competent authority to determine the area affected by the discharge in each case and to select from among the above quality objectives those that it deems appropriate having regard to the area affected and bearing in mind that the purpose of the Directive is to eliminate pollution. Emission standards are to be set by the Member States so that the appropriate quality objective(s) is or are complied with in the area affected.

In addition, HCH concentrations in inland waters must be determined by the national network set up for this purpose and the results compared with a total HCH concentration of 50 nanograms per litre.

Furthermore, the concentration of HCH in sediments or in shellfish or in fish must not increase significantly in time and where several quality objectives are applied to waters in an area, the quality of the waters must be sufficient to comply with each of these objectives.

New plants
The same conditions apply to new plants as for the other daughter Directives: authorizations may only be granted if standards comply with the best technical means and where these are not used a Member State must first justify the exception to the Commission which has to report its opinion within three months.

Monitoring and analysis
The requirements for monitoring and analysis follow the pattern set in the previous daughter Directives.

Comparative assessments
The requirements are identical to those for the cadmium Directive (4.12): a comparative report every five years based on information supplied by Member States to be submitted to the Council, except that the first report will be submitted four years after notification.

Development of the Directive
By the time this proposal had been put forward, the first daughter Directive (on mercury) had been adopted and agreement had been reached on the cadmium Directive. Standard forms of wording had therefore been worked out and the proposal followed in the main the pattern set and agreed in Council. Nevertheless the Commission took the opportunity to introduce a new concept in requiring competent authorities to make discharges of HCH to air subject to authorization laying down emission standards. This was a matter of concern to the UK government and the House of Commons also expressed its objection to the inclusion of control of discharges to air in a Directive dealing with discharges to water. Other points of concern to the UK were the very stringent quality objectives proposed compared with the limit values. Since the proposal concerned production plants and those treating HCH in order to extract lindane (of

which there are none in the UK), the proposal did not directly affect any country without such plants in so far as limit values were laid down only for such plants.

As a result of negotiations and developments on other proposals, a number of changes were made which met the UK objections. Agreement on the proposal for a framework Directive on discharges to air (see Section 6.8 Emissions from industrial plants) meant that it was possible to modify the proposal concerning authorizations for discharges for air to a general requirement not to increase pollution in other media, notably air and soil. The quality objectives as agreed were less stringent than proposed whilst at the same time the limit values were made more stringent and thus more in line with the quality objectives set. More generally the opportunity was taken to ensure the application of the Directive to all types of HCH with less emphasis on lindane as a separate isomer. There was thus a requirement to fix emission standards for discharges of HCH from plants not specifically mentioned.

Formal compliance in UK

The general requirements for compliance follow those already described in Section 4.8 on dangerous substances in water.

The DoE Circular 18/85 directs water authorities as a first priority to authorize discharge of HCH which exceed or will exceed 1 kg a year; or will increase the concentration of HCH in receiving waters either by 10 per cent of the relevant EQS or to a concentration in excess of 50 per cent of the relevant EQS; or will increase the concentration of HCH in the receiving water by more than 3 per cent of the relevant EQS and where, in the absence of the discharge, the concentration of HCH was already greater than 50 per cent of that standard.

It points out two exemptions: one, discharges from sewage works to which there is no significant industrial input; and two, discharges of HCH in water taken for cooling or use in an industrial process which is returned to the same water body and to which no HCH has been added.

Water authorities will need to ascertain the HCH-handling capacity of each plant. This information will also be needed to determine whether expansion of an existing plant requires it to be considered as a new plant. The HCH actually used in the processes as well as that incidentally present in the raw materials should be taken into account in determining capacity. In setting consents for discharges to sewers, it may be assumed that 50 per cent of HCH will be removed by the sewage treatment works; in due course an appropriate figure should be ascertained for each works.

Data for the first full year 1986 will be required by 31 March 1987.

Effect on UK practice

There are no plants for the production and extraction of lindane in Britain but only for its formulation. Since the Directive does not set limit values for discharges from other than production and extraction plants, it could be argued that the Directive can have little or no effect in any country choosing to follow the limit value path which does not have such plants. However, Annex 1 requires Member States to fix emission standards for formulation plants so that even Member States with only formulation plants would be required to take action.

On the other hand, the quality objective path is all-embracing since it requires a Member State to fix emission standards in an area affected by discharges of HCH without specifying from what sort of plant or source this might come from.

As a result of the Directive water authorities have had to monitor for lindane and some have found concentrations which were not expected. The Yorkshire Water Authority has found lindane in the catchments of the Rivers Aire and Calder and has traced this back to sewage works. It has been discovered that there is considerable variation in the concentrations discharged so that sometimes the water quality standards are substantially exceeded. The water authority attributes this to the textile industry washing imported wool, from sheep that may have been dipped in lindane. The problem is still unresolved.

4.14 DDT, carbon tetrachloride and pentachlorophenol

86/280/EEC (OJ L181 4.7.86) proposed 28.1.85 – COM(84)772	Directive on limit values and quality objectives for discharges of certain dangerous substances included in List I of the Annex to Directive 76/464/EEC.

Binding dates
Notification date	16 June 1986
Formal compliance	1 January 1988
Commission's comparative assessment	June 1990 and subsequently every five years.

Purpose of the Directive

This is another of the daughter Directives which flow from Directive 76/464 dealing with pollution of water (see Section 4.8). The Directive is intended to provide swifter implementation of 76/464 by enabling substances to be added to an Annex. Initially it is concerned with three substances: DDT, carbon tetrachloride and pentachlorophenol (PCP). They are all organochlorinated compounds coming under the heading of organohalogens in List I of the Annex to 76/464. They have varying uses: carbon tetrachloride is used to manufacture CFC (see Section 7.4 on chloroflurocarbons) and solvents, the others mainly as pesticides.

Summary of the Directive

The articles of the Directive generally follow the form of other Directives in this series. There are differences, some of which relate to the covering of several substances and the possibility of subsequent additions; others extend the monitoring requirements to cover sources other than industrial discharges and the requirement for Member States to draw up programmes to avoid or eliminate pollution from sources of these substances which are not covered by Community or national standards. This latter point covers multiple and diffuse sources, for example from agriculture. The Directive provides for discharges of these substances to be controlled either by setting limit values or emission standards enabling quality objectives as specified in the Directive to be met. New plants have to apply the standards corresponding to the best technical means available, though these are not specified. The difference between existing and new plant is to be determined by a date twelve months after notification of the Directive or of subsequent ones. A comparative assessment is to be made by the Commission on the basis of information from Member States and submitted to the Council every five years. An Annex sets out the general principles concerning limit values, quality objectives and reference methods of measurement which are applicable to all substances and explains that these are amplified by specific provisions applicable to individual substances.

Details applicable to the three substances named are summarized in Table 6.

Development of the Directive

The proposal of the Commission was a direct response to Resolutions of the Council on 7 February 1983 which called for more rapid implementation of Directive 76/464 with more simplified procedures. The Council also called on the Commission to make proposals for dealing with indirect or diffuse discharges. The proposal therefore was aimed at swifter implementation of 76/464 by avoiding repetition in subsequent proposals of agreed forms of words which could now be stated as general principles applicable to all substances; additional substances could be added simply to the annexes of this Directive.

In the UK the government reaction was to support in principle the new approach based as it was on provisions which had been settled in earlier Directives but to raise doubts about the inclusion of carbon tetrachloride and chloroform which were not regarded as List I substances and to oppose the stringency of the values proposed for the other substances. Clarification was also sought on the monitoring responsibilities (particularly where there were many diffuse sources of pollution) with the object of ensuring that those applying the limit value approach monitored as much as those using quality objectives.

The debate in the Houses of Parliament was widened to examine the procedures for arriving at the priority list of substances and from there to question the system of control of either limit values or quality objectives. Of particular relevance to this issue was the problem of diffuse sources especially when the number of point sources were limited. A submission by the Institute for European Environmental Policy based on the ideas put forward in Appendix 4 to the first edition of this book, which would make limit values additional to quality objectives rather than alternatives, was the stimulus for this wider discussion. The House of Lords supported the basic concept of an approach which would apply to all Member States without a choice.

The Economic and Social Committee echoed somewhat similar reservations about the need to achieve a balanced combination of the use of both limit values and quality objectives and also about the selection of substances. The Resolution from the European Parliament made the same point in describing the two systems as complementary.

The final version of the Directive differed in a number of points from the original proposal: monitoring was to be applied to waters affected by other sources of discharge besides those from industrial establishments; the programmes to avoid or eliminate pollution from sources other than sources covered by Community or national standards was extended to cover diffuse sources; the proposals concerning chloroform were omitted; specific provisions concerning no significant increase in concentrations in DDT and PCP in sediments and animal life (standstill) were made generally applicable and not just to the quality objective approach; and both limit values and quality objectives were in many cases made less stringent.

It is reported that the United Kingdom dropped its opposition to the inclusion of carbon tetrachloride only after it had persuaded the other Member

Table 6 Control of discharges of carbon tetrachloride, DDT and pentachlorophenol

1. Carbon tetrachloride
A. *Limit values*

Type of plant	Weight		Concentration	Compliance by
Carbon tetrachloride production by perchlorination	*Involving washing:*			
	monthly	40g/tonne	1.5 mg/l	01.01.88
	daily	80g/tonne	3.0 mg/l	01.01.88
	No washing:			
	monthly	2.5g/tonne	1.5 mg/l	01.01.88
	daily	5.0g/tonne	3.0 mg/l	01.01.88
Chloromethane production by methane chlorination	monthly	10g/tonne	1.5 mg/l	01.01.88
	daily	20g/tonne	3.0 mg/l	01.01.88

Note: Figures for a third process, production of chlorofluorocarbons, are to follow.

B. *Quality objectives*

		Concentration	Compliance by
All waters		12 μg/l CCl$_4$	01.01.88

2. DDT
Specific provision. Standstill: the concentration of DDT in the aquatic environment, sediments and molluscs, shellfish and fish must not increase significantly in time.

A. *Limit values*

Type of plant	Weight		Concentration	Compliance by
Production of DDT incl. formulation on same site:				
	monthly:	8g/tonne	0.7 mg/l	01.01.88
		4g/tonne	0.2 mg/l	01.01.91
	daily:	16g/tonne	1.3 mg/l	01.01.88
		8g/tonne	0.4 mg/l	01.01.91

B. *Quality objectives*

		Concentration	Compliance by
All waters	Isomer para-para-DDT	10 ng/l	01.01.88
	Total DDT	25 ng/l	01.01.88

3. Pentachlorophenol (PCP)
Specific provision. Standstill: concentration of PCP in sediments, molluscs, shellfish and fish must not significantly increase with time.

A. *Limit values*

Type of plant	Weight		Concentration	Compliance by
Production of sodium pentachlorophenate by hydrolysis of hexachlorobenzene	monthly	25g/tonne	1mg/l	01.01.88
	daily	50g/tonne	2mg/l	01.01.88

B. *Quality objectives*

		Concentration	Compliance by
All waters		2 μg/l	01.01.88

States to agree a Council Minute instructing the Commission when issuing further proposals in the series to 'give priority to substances which are *likely* to be present in Community waters at levels which cause particularly important environmental problems'. The text of the Council Minute is set out in the reply by the Minister (William Waldegrave) to a parliamentary question on 10 March 1986.

Formal Compliance
Formal compliance is not until 1 January 1988 but it can be assumed it will follow the pattern of the earlier Directives.

Effect on UK practice
The UK has one carbon tetrachloride production plant and two formulation plants, one of which is also the production plant. In addition, there are a number of point sources resulting from the use of carbon tetrachloride for solvents. There are no production plants for DDT and PCP. In general, levels of all substances measured in the UK have been below the values set. The end effect of this Directive as far as the substances listed are concerned is likely to be very small. On the other hand, there has been some development in the recognition by the Community that the problem of controlling diffuse sources cannot be met by setting limit values. The relationship between monitoring and quality objectives is recognized and the case for the latter approach therefore strengthened.

4.15 Titanium dioxide

1. 78/176/EEC (OJ L54 25.2.78) proposed 14.7.75 – COM(75)339	Directive on waste from the titanium dioxide industry.
2. 83/29/EEC (OJ L32 3.2.83) proposed 8.7.82 – COM(82)430	(Amendment).
3. 82/883/EEC (OJ L378 31.12.82) proposed 17.12.80 – COM(82)831	Directive on procedures for the surveillance and monitoring of environments concerned by waste from the titanium dioxide industry.

Binding dates (78/176)

Notification date	22 February 1978
Formal compliance	22 February 1979
Pollution reduction programmes submitted to Commission	1 July 1980
Programmes to be introduced	1 January 1982
Programme targets to be met	1 July 1987
First three yearly report to be submitted to Commission	22 February 1981.

Purpose of Directive 78/176

The main aim of the Directive is the prevention and progressive reduction of pollution caused by waste from the titanium dioxide (TiO_2) industry. Eventually all pollution is to be eliminated. Titanium dioxide is a white pigment used in paints and for other purposes. Its manufacture may result in a much larger quantity of waste than product and this has frequently been dumped at sea or discharged into estuaries. 'Red mud' in the Mediterranean resulting from discharges from an Italian titanium dioxide plant drew strong protests from Corsica in 1972 resulting in a Court case and restrictions on the plant. A subsidiary aim of the Directive is to reduce the resulting distortion to competition.

Summary of Directive 78/176

General duties are placed on Member States to ensure that TiO_2 waste is disposed of without endangering human health or harming the environment and to encourage recycling.

All discharge, dumping, storage and injection of waste must be subjected to prior authorization by the competent authority. Authorization may be granted for a limited period only and may be renewed. Authorization may only be given if the waste cannot be disposed of by more appropriate means, and an assessment shows that no deleterious effects will result. An Annex I lists the particulars of the waste, the site and the methods of disposal that must be supplied in order to obtain an authorization.

Disposal must be accompanied by monitoring of the waste and of the environment in accordance with particulars laid down in an Annex II. The

Commission was to propose more precise monitoring procedures (this has resulted in Directive 82/883 – see below).

Member States must take steps to remedy unsatisfactory situations that may arise (five such are listed) if necessary by suspending disposal. Member States must send to the Commission programmes for the progressive reduction and eventual elimination of pollution. The programmes must be introduced by 1 January 1982 and must include targets to be achieved by 1 July 1987.

Within six months of receiving all the national programmes, the Commission may submit proposals to the Council for harmonizing them, both as regards pollution reduction and the conditions of competition. The word 'may' was amended to 'shall' by Directive 83/29 and the period for submitting proposals extended to 15 March 1983. However, the Commission having placed an obligation on itself then failed to meet the amended deadline – see below.

Where a Member State considered that in the case of an individual establishment no additional measures were necessary to fulfil the requirements of the Directive, it had to provide the Commission with the evidence leading to that conclusion by 20 August 1979. The Commission could indicate its agreement, but if it did not agree, additional measures had to be included in the programme (Article 10).

Prior authorization is required before any new industrial establishment can be built and an environmental impact survey (sic) must be conducted. Authorization may only be granted to firms giving an undertaking to use only such materials, processes and techniques available on the market as are least damaging to the environment.

Member States must supply the Commission with information relating to authorizations, the results of monitoring and any remedial measures taken. Every three years, Member States must submit a report to the Commission on the progressive reduction of pollution. The Commission must communicate this report to the other Member States. The Commission must in turn report every three years to the Council and Parliament.

Development of Directive 78/176

One of the wastes from titanium dioxide production is ferrous sulphate and there seems little doubt that it was the conflict between France and Italy in the early 1970s over the dumping at sea of this waste from the Montedison factory at Scarlino resulting in 'red mud' that gave rise to the Directive. Speaking in the European Parliament's debate on the Directive on 13 January 1976, Mr della Briotta described how in Corsica there had been something like an insurrection over the issue. He went on:

> . . .in the Scarlino case we find all the aspects of the problem: the movement among the population protesting against the pollution, the involvement of the press, the action by the authorities which, following judgment by the courts, ordered the company to stop the pollution and seized some ships, the consequent reprisals on the part of the company which first threatened to close its factory and finally actually did so, putting the workers on the dole.

Mr della Briotta explained how the measures eventually taken in Italy – thought to involve a purer ore and dumping deeper in the sea – had increased costs and resulted in a distortion to competition, and he went on to congratulate the Commission for tackling the problem since an effective solution could not be achieved by national action alone. Mr Premoli, speaking in the same debate, expressed approval of the Commission for not making a distinction between inland seas like the Mediterranean and open seas like the Atlantic but appeared not to notice that he was thereby contradicting the motion that he, as the rapporteur of the Environment Committee, was presenting to the Parliament. This motion regretted the absence of quality objectives in the Directive, and such objectives would inevitably have led to different disposal practices in the Atlantic with its larger tidal excursions than those needed in the Mediterranean.

The original proposal was much more stringent than the Directive as eventually agreed. As well as requiring authorization and monitoring, it also specified a phased reduction of emissions so that by 1985 only 5 per cent of the total untreated emissions would be allowed to be dumped at sea or in estuaries. The Minister, Denis Howell, declared in the Council on 16 October 1975 that Britain could not accept the proposal in that form since it embodied uniform standards for controlling discharges of waste, regardless of environmental circumstances. In the House of Lords' debate (1 April 1976) the Minister, Baroness Stedman, explained why:

> Discharges are said to present a problem in the Mediterranean,
> but we have no significant problems from our industry which
> discharges into the North Sea.

The argument of the government has been all along that since the British factories discharge continuously to estuaries with large tidal excursions and high flow rates, the acid in the waste is rapidly neutralized on mixing with sea water and the resulting precipitates, as well as the iron, titanium and other trace metals, are quickly dispersed. The British sites were in fact chosen so that discharges were to estuaries already high in suspended solids. The lack of tide in the Mediterranean, on the other hand, makes dispersion difficult and intermittent dumping of concentrated acids from ships – the acid is concentrated to reduce shipping costs – produces stronger concentrations in the sea water instantaneously than a continous discharge of dilute acid from a pipeline.

The view widely held in Britain was that there was no reason why the well-sited British titanium dioxide industry, producing 40 per cent of European output, should be made to suffer economically in an attempt to solve a problem of bad planning in Italy, especially when the loss-making Montedison factory was responsible for only 6 per cent of European production.

The titanium dioxide proposal was used in Britain to emphasize the disadvantages of the limit value approach embodied in part of Directive 76/464 (see Section 4.8). The further point was made that waste from titanium dioxide production did not include substances in List I of that Directive (except in trace amounts) and that all Member States had agreed that emissions of other substances were to be controlled by reference to environmental quality objectives. Commissioner Scarascia Mugnozza, speaking in the European Parliament's debate only a few weeks after the compromise decision reached by the Council on Directive 76/464, conceded that the compromise decision was a relevant factor in discussing the titanium dioxide proposal.

The solution eventually agreed for TiO$_2$, which a memorandum from the DoE to Parliament (14 November 1977) said had emerged under the British Presidency of the Council, was that Member States would draw up and submit to the Commission their own programmes for progressive reduction of pollution. There can be little doubt that Britain was the principal opponent of uniform controls, but the danger of excessively stringent standards was also very much in the minds of others. The Economic and Social Committee, for instance, in their report of 25 February 1976 pointed to the danger of the titanium dioxide industry moving to countries outside the Community, with an associated loss of jobs, if the financial consequences of complying with the Directive were too high.

Britain was also responsible for the abortive Article 10 which allowed Member States to submit to the Commission, in respect of a particular factory, that no pollution reduction programme was necessary if no pollution was being caused. This provision, introduced under pressure from the British industry, resulted in the first environmental case being brought before the European Court (see below). The Minister, Denis Howell, possibly had this in mind when he publicly quoted the titanium dioxide Directive as an example of how closely the government sometimes works with industry in defending their interests:

> As an environmental Minister I go to Brussels to meet my
> ministerial colleagues in the Common Market. In the three
> years since I have had those responsibilities there has been an
> increasing number of occasions when I have had to take up
> cudgels particularly on behalf of British industries in an
> attempt to demonstrate that the issues being discussed by the
> Environmental Comittee (sic) in Brussels, in which I try to
> protect the interests of British industry, are in no way in
> conflict with the philosophy and develoment of an environ-
> mental policy. I found myself splendidly isolated and one
> against eight on the subject of the paper pulp industry; I was
> in a similar position over titanium dioxide. . .

The titanium dioxide Directive is an example of the 'sectoral approach' envisaged in the first action programme of 1973 which grouped the titanium dioxide industry together with the paper pulp industry and the iron and steel industry for early attention. The 'sectoral approach' is shorthand for dealing with a particular industry rather than with a particular pollutant or a particular environment. With the failure to agree a proposed Directive on paper pulp (COM(74)2256 OJ C99 2.5.75), the sectoral approach appeared to have been abandoned but the fourth action programme suggests that it may be revived (the daughter Directives of 76/464 (see Section 4.8) follow the sectoral approach, eg mercury from the chloralkali industry). Though in 1983 the titanium dioxide Directive could have been considered as an exception to be explained as the product of exceptional circumstances (an acute local problem resulting in a dispute between two Member States), it can no longer be so described. It has continued to be a matter of Community if not international concern.

The development of the Directive was influenced not only by arguments about competition but also by doubts about the technical report on which it was based.

Technical issues

The Commission proposal for the Directive was published not just with the usual explanatory memorandum but also with a seventy-seven page technical report, COM(75)339. This report described the preparation and uses of titanium dioxide, the market situation, the processes for titanium dioxide production, the raw materials, the kinds of waste that arise, the methods of treatment, and both long-term and short-term environmental effects. The section on environmental effects quoted extensively from the French government's report published in connection with the Montedison case. It did not say, though in fairness it could have done, that the growth of the titanium dioxide industry has enabled the use of toxic substances such as lead and zinc to be reduced in paints. Titanium dioxide is itself believed to be harmless and has largely replaced the toxic pigments, though mainly because it is a better pigment.

Titanium dioxide is extracted from ore by one of two processes: the sulphate and chloride, the more recent chloride process generating less waste by allowing the use of a purer ore. This ore is scarce and expensive and in 1975 only 12 per cent of the EEC industry used the chloride process. The sulphate process gives rise to ferrous sulphate, acids and traces of some heavy metals. The technical report said that in the immediate vicinity of discharge of these wastes there was reduced oxygenation and increased acidity resulting in a local reduction of zooplankton biomass and departure of fish but that evidence of actual damage to fish was inconclusive. The House of Lords' Scrutiny Committee in their report said that members of the Committee had examined biological studies carried out under the auspices of a manufacturer (BTP) in the estuary of the Humber and near French discharges at Calais which indicated that effluent from titanium dioxide works did not appear to have any detrimental effect on the ecology of these two areas. The Committee remained 'in no doubt that the best way to get rid of titanium dioxide waste is in the sea. If this is done under the right conditions, no significant environmental damage need result.' The government's view was the same. A memorandum to Parliament dated 14 November 1977 said:

> all the scientific evidence indicates that TiO_2 waste can be disposed of to the sea without harming the environment; as the only feasible alternative would be neutralization using lime and dumping of the resultant solid waste on land, the net effect of the Commission's proposals would have been to increase pollution and impose unnecessary costs on the UK industry.

The Commission proposal that only 5 per cent of the untreated wastes was to be discharged to sea was based on the assertion that several feasible treatment processes existed to reduce pollution. The Lords' Scrutiny Committee commented tartly that the methods of treatment listed did not appear to justify this statement, and went on to point out that none of these methods had yet been put into commercial use.

Notwithstanding the arguments that disposal from British plants was not creating environmental problems, representatives of the two British producers of titanium dioxide in giving evidence before the Lords' Scrutiny Committee implied that any new plants would use the chloride process rather than the sulphate process partly because of the environmental problems associated with the sulphate process. Since then the switch from the sulphate to the chloride process has accelerated in Britain, while in Germany, Bayer AG, which still uses the sulphate process, has stopped discharging or dumping at sea altogether. It is thought that the acid wastes are used in other processes in the same complex rather than recycling them in the titanium dioxide operation.

Formal compliance in the UK – Directive 78/176

In February 1979 when the Directive had formally to be complied with there were four dischargers of titanium dioxide waste in Britain, two into the Humber estuary and two into the estuary of the River Tees (Table 7).

The Laporte plant included both a sulphate and a chloride process. In March 1981 the Tioxide plant at Billingham was closed and in the same year output from the Laporte sulphate process was curtailed by 80 per cent.

    The government wrote to the Commission on 14 February 1979 saying that it was satisfied that the Control of Pollution Act 1974 provided adequate powers to meet the objectives of the Directive but omitted to say that the relevant part of the Act was not then in force and that one plant was sufficiently old not to be covered by a consent and was therefore not 'authorized'. This was rectified when Part II of the Control of Pollution Act was brought into force, but for a time there was a formal failure to comply with the Directive.

    The government's letter of 14 February 1979 also said that the Control of Pollution Act 1974 allowed the preparation of the programmes for reduction of pollution. This seems to be a mistake since there is nothing in that Act which provides for plans or programmes although provision for these is made in Section 24 of the Water Act 1973.

    There is no dumping of British titanium dioxide waste at sea from ships at present, but should any such plans be put forward they could be controlled by

Table 7 Discharge of titanium dioxide in UK

Teesside (Northumbrian Water Authority)			Approx capacity in 1976 (tons per annum) (1982 in brackets)
1) Tioxide (UK) Ltd	Billingham	sulphate	27 000 (closed)
2) Tioxide (UK) Ltd	Seal Sands, Hartlepool	chloride	60 000 (50 000)
Humberside (Anglian Water Authority)			
3) Tioxide (UK) Ltd	Grimsby	sulphate	90 000 (100 000)
4) SCM Chemicals Ltd (formerly owned by Laporte Industries Ltd)	Stallingborough (Immingham)	a) sulphate b) chloride	55 000 (curtailed) 60 000 (combined 94 000)

Note: These capacity figures were given by the manufacturers in evidence to the House of Lords except for that from the Hartlepool plant; 1982 figures are based on those in the Commission proposal 83/29 and those given in evidence to the House of Lords in 1983.

the Dumping at Sea Act 1974. Some neutralized solid wastes from titanium dioxide production at BTP's Hartlepool plant is dumped on land in Britain and this is covered by Part I of the Control of Pollution Act 1974. The Directive has therefore required no new primary legislation but requires Part II of the Control of Pollution Act to be brought into force by secondary legislation.

The discharges to the Humber fall within the area of the Anglian Water Authority and the discharges to the Tees within the area of the Northumbrian Water Authority. Letters from the DoE formally appointed these two authorities as 'competent authorities' for the purposes of the Directive and explained that programmes would have to be drawn up for the reduction of pollution.

The Court case

The first official action taken in Britain following the notification of the Directive was a request from the government to the Commission for exemptions, under Article 10, from the need to prepare pollution reduction programmes in respect of the two establishments discharging into the Humber. This request was presumably made at the instigation of the two companies concerned. A similar request was also made by the West German government in respect of dumping in the North Sea.

The Commission did not accept the British government's argument and, in a letter of 19 February 1979, refused to grant exemptions to the two establishments. Since the Directive provides no appeal against the Commission's decision, the government had to accept the Commission's opinion that programmes were necessary and informed the relevant water authority accordingly. The two companies were less easily satisfied and on 17 May 1979 they simultaneously brought an action in the European Court against the Commission seeking annulment of the Commission's opinion that programmes were necessary. The Bulletin of the European Communities (No 5, 1979, p 118) asserted that this was the first action brought to the Court relating directly to environmental matters. The British government for its part has made it clear that it is not associated in any way with the action.

All that is publicly known of this action is contained in the brief statement of case published in the *Official Journal* (OJ C153 20.6.79). The statement claims that the Court should not only annul the opinion contained in the Commission's letter of 19 February 1979 but should also declare the Directive illegal. The second point is thought to turn on the extent to which a draft Directive can be modified by the Council before being agreed without having to be resubmitted to the Parliament for an opinion. It is a point of the greatest importance and goes well beyond environmental policy.

The action has now been suspended and neither party (the companies and the Commission) is seeking to activate it. Possibly the companies are waiting to see what happens to the Commission's proposal for harmonizing the pollution reduction programmes (see below) before deciding whether to proceed or not.

Effect on UK practice

A pollution reduction programme was submitted by the government to the Commission in respect of the Tees on 3 July 1980 and in respect of the Humber on 6 January 1981. These two programmes also constituted the first three-yearly report. The Humber programme was six months late but in this Britain was not alone – Commissioner Narjes, replying to a question in the European Parliament (OJ C87/21 16.4.81) said that all Member States had been late.

The programme in respect of the Humber argued that near neither discharge had any accumulation of heavy metal been found nor was there any significant effect on the estuary as a whole so that the only cause for concern was the local reduction of pH around the outfalls. The objective of the programme was therefore to effect a better dispersion of the effluent so that the area of low pH was significantly reduced. The first step in the programme was therefore research, to be completed by the end of 1982, to see which of three options, or a combination of them, would be the most effective:

1. storage facilities on land so that no discharge (which is presently continuous) takes place during periods of slack water;
2. the fitting of diffusers to the effluent pipeline;
3. alterations to the position of the pipeline outlet.

When the results of the research were available, works were to be put in hand to be completed during 1986. Some ferrous sulphate was already removed from the effluent and the programme says that research would continue into possible further uses for this byproduct.

Although not specifically mentioned as part of point 3 of the programme, a £15 million sewage outfall was being constructed and had been designed in such a way that it could receive at least a part of the effluent from the Tioxide factory, and thus discharge it further out to sea. (In the event this possibility has not been adopted). It is unlikely that any of the three options in the programme would readily have been undertaken in the absence of the Directive. A choice between them was delayed until the harmonizing Directive was proposed (see below).

In 1980/81 Laporte's sulphate plant was curtailed by 80 per cent resulting in 1000 redundancies, the reason given being overcapacity in the industry and reduced profitability. This cannot be regarded as part of a pollution reduction programme. However, later in 1981 plans were announced and put in effect for an expansion of the chloride process. The existence of the Directive is likely to have been one factor in the decision to expand the chloride rather than the sulphate process.

The programme for Teeside has not been made available but the view of the Northumbrian Water Authority is that the one remaining factory does not create any significant problems. This was confirmed again in 1984. Since it uses the relatively clean chloride process, there is no red or brown discharge and the only cause for concern is said to be the discharge of titanium dioxide pigment creating a whitish plume. To reduce this the company, in 1980 and 1981, improved filtration within the factory to reduce pigment being discharged and improved the settlement/storage capacity. It is arguable that these improvements would have been carried out anyway without the Directive.

On monitoring Tioxide's claim that the £100 000 per annum that they spend is double what they used to spend before the Directive. Both water authorities agree that the Directive has involved them in increased monitoring. The Anglian

E

Water Authority also believes the Directive has acted as a stimulus to thought about the Humber estuary generally.

In July 1985 the Anglian Water Authority announced their requirements for improvements in accordance with the Directive. This followed a study of the three options described above. SCM were required to extend their pipeline by 300 metres and to fit diffusers, and Tioxide were required to extend their pipeline by 500 metres. The building of storage facilities so that discharges were not made during slack water was found not to be helpful. These improvements were expected to reduce the area affected by 80 per cent. Tioxide, however, decided to build an entirely new pipeline of 2500 metres rather than to extend the existing 900 metre pipeline by 500 metres to 1400 metres. The new pipeline, which should be in use a little time after the Directive deadline of 1 July 1987 is expected to reduce the area affected by 95 per cent.

What must be an unanticipated side effect of the Directive has been a drawing together of the DoE, water authorities and the industry; a closing of ranks, as it were, when confronted with an outside stimulus. In the normal way there would be no reason for the DoE to be involved with the discharge of one industry among many, but since it is the DoE that is responsible for submitting the pollution reduction programmes to the Commission, the DoE has had to be involved in the work of the water authorities. For their part, the water authorities have been provided with extra leverage when dealing with the industrialists since formally it is the water authorities who have had to prepare the pollution reduction programmes. The industrialists have an interest in ensuring that these programmes satisfy the Commission in order to head off what they might regard as draconian proposals from the Commission harmonizing the various national programmes (see below). More is now known about the problems by all three parties and more information on the monitoring programmes carried out by the industry has been made available to the authorities.

The Monitoring Directive 82/883
This Directive fulfils the obligation placed on the Commission by Directive 78/176 to propose procedures for surveillance and monitoring (the parent Directive required a proposal within one year but the Commission overran the date by nearly two years).

The Directive lays down in five Annexes the steps to be taken in monitoring air, salt water, fresh water, storage and dumping on land, and injection into soil. The Directive will not affect the industries but only the competent authorities. The Anglian Water Authority in written evidence to the House of Lords' Scrutiny Committee expressed concern about the potential cost (£50 000 per annum) if a Directive was agreed as proposed but the Directive was amended so the costs are now probably reduced. In particular it was amended so that Member States may, without consulting the Commission, allow less frequent sampling once the behaviour, fate and effects of the waste are known. In addition, the requirement to monitor sulphur dioxide has been significantly modified so that an existing sulphur dioxide monitoring station will suffice.

Compliance was effected by the issue by the Department of the Environment of Circular 4/86 on Implementation of Directive 82/883 early in 1986. The Circular announced that responsibility for monitoring had been delegated to the water authorities, waste disposal authorities and district councils in whose areas the three UK titanium dioxide plants are located. The authorities have been left free to decide on sampling points and frequencies and which of the 'optional' parameters are to be measured. Monitoring results are to be submitted annually to the DoE for transmission to the Commission.

Harmonizing national programmes

Member States were to submit national programmes for reducing and eliminating pollution to the Commission by 1 July 1980 and six months after receipt of all these national programmes the Commission was to make proposals for harmonizing them. In fact the Commission did not receive all the national programmes until 15 October 1981 and found that they were neither comparable nor provided adequate information. The Commission, therefore, had to ask for extra information and proposed a Directive extending the time period (see European parliamentary question OJ C93 7.4.83). This proposal was agreed as Directive 83/29 which set a new deadline of 15 March 1983. There was some suggestion that a Directive harmonizing the national programmes could have been agreed by majority voting in the Council if it was made under the authority of the parent Directive 78/176, but that possibility – even if legally sustainable – disappeared when the Commission failed to produce a proposal by the revised deadline of 15 March 1983.

A proposed 'harmonizing' Directive was eventually proposed on 14 April 1983, COM(83)189. It proposes uniform reductions in discharges largely irrespective of the environments into which the discharges are being made. As we have seen this was a course rejected when the parent Directive was being negotiated. The expectation that this would reopen the original conflict and lead to Britain finding itself alone again has been borne out by events.

The UK made known its opposition to the proposal on the grounds of its incompatibility with UK policy and the economic difficulties it would produce. The House of Lords in its report supported the government in its objection in principle to the application of uniform limits on all discharges to the environment but criticized the government for failing to set environmental quality objectives earlier than it did (ie before the Commission finally produced a proposal) and also for their inadequacy when they did (no objective was set for suspended solids and no time limits were given). The European Parliament later (April 1984) proposed stricter and earlier measures which were largely picked up by the Commission in a proposal for amendments in May 1984 (COM(84)303 OJ C167, 27.7.84). The proposal has not been before the Council and has effectively been deadlocked by UK opposition so far. However, the Commission in February 1987 informed Member States that this proposal was one of those which it intended to reissue under the new Article 100A of the Single European Act (see Chapter 2) and which then would be subject to majority voting.

Further developments

Tioxide, which operates plants in several countries outside the UK, is building pilot waste recycling facilities and sites in USA and Spain in anticipation of extra regulations. It will presumably therefore be able to adopt that technology in the UK if forced to do so.

It is of interest that the Italian factory at Scarlino was eventually required to stop dumping at sea. It operates now using uprated ilmemite with partial removal of iron, neutralizing the acid on land and discharging waste through a pipeline 100 yards out to sea. Tioxide purchased the plant from Montedison and has continued to operate the plant under the revised conditions for the last two or three years. Tioxide is therefore in a position to assess directly the effects of different environmental restrictions on competition.

Other events which have a bearing on the issue have been the action of Greenpeace in Germany, the UK and elsewhere which have led to the stopping of dumping by Germany of TiO_2 wastes; and the efforts of the Paris Commission to limit discharges into areas coming under the Convention.

References
1   Seminar on Industry and the Environment, Royal Society of Arts, London, 31 May 1977.

4.16 Oil pollution at sea

OJ C162 8.7.78	Resolution setting up an action programme on control and reduction of pollution caused by hydrocarbons discharged at sea.
80/686 (OJ L188 22.7.80)	Commission Decision setting up an Advisory Committee (on oil pollution).
85/208 (OJ L 89 29.3.85)	Amendment
87/144 (OJ L 57 27.2.87)	Amendment.
86/85 (OJ L 77 22.2.86)	Council Decision setting up Community system of information for the control and reduction of pollution from oil spills at sea.
Binding dates Submission of information to the Commission	Initially by 10 December 1982 and subsequently in January of each year.

Purpose of Resolution and Decisions

The object of the programme and subsequent Decisions is to involve the Community in taking appropriate action to prevent and reduce damage from oil spills at sea.

Summary of Resolution and Decisions

Resolution and programme
The programme provided for the Commission to undertake studies in six areas to see what needed to be done:

1. computer processing of data on dealing with marine pollution;
2. availability of data on tankers liable to pollute Community waters;
3. measures to enhance cooperation and effectiveness of emergency teams;
4. design and development of clean-up vessels;
5. amendments and improvements to rules on insurance;
6. research programme on means of combating oil pollution.

Decision 80/686 and Amendments
The Commission Decision set up an Advisory Committee consisting of three (subsequently two) experts nominated by Member States to advise the Commission on marine pollution programmes.

Decision 86/85
In December 1981 the Council decided (Decision 81/971 OJ L355 10.21.81) to set up a Community information system to be run by the Commission covering three areas:

1.   an inventory of the means of combatting marine oil pollution;
2.   a list of national and joint contingency plans;
3.   a compendium of hydrocarbon properties and their behaviour and of methods of treatment.

This Decision was replaced by 86/85; the main changes were to add an inventory of resources for intervention in the event of a spillage at sea of harmful substances other than oil and the collection by the Commission of information on such substances.

Development of the programme and Decisions
Community action was sparked off by the accident to the Amoco Cadiz off the Brittany coast in March 1978. But the Commission had in the previous year proposed much of this programme in response to the blow-out of oil from an oil platform in the Ekofisk field in Norwegian waters. The subsequent Decisions followed, as well as other proposals concerning port state control of shipping and harmonization of contingency plans. The modest scale of Community action adopted reflects the doubts of the UK and other States about the need for a Community role in this field. The view had been taken that national and joint contingency plans together with action in wider regional and international organizations provided the better way forward without duplication at Community level. In particular under the Bonn Agreement (see Chapter 11) the North Sea countries including those outside the Community had come together to coordinate plans for combatting marine pollution problems and under the International Maritime Organization an agreement had been drawn up signed by fourteen states concerning Port State Control (Memorandum of Understanding on Port State Control dated 26 January 1982). The basic IMO convention on oil pollution is the International Convention for the Prevention of Pollution from Ships 1973 and is known as MARPOL.

Formal compliance
Compliance has been concerned solely with submission of information.

Other developments
Under the budget sums have been provided for research projects on marine pollution. Following the accident at the Sandoz plant at Basle which polluted the Rhine the Commission in April 1987 proposed an amendment to Decision 86/85 so that it also covers inland waters, COM(87)120 OJ C108, 23.4.87.

4.17 Exchange of information – water

77/795/EEC (OJ L334 24.12.77) proposed 1.4.78 – COM(76)118 and amended by 84/422/EEC (OJ L237 5.9.84) (Commission Decision)	Decision establishing a common procedure for the exchange of information on the quality of surface fresh water in the Community.
86/574/EEC (OJ L335 28.11.86) proposed 8.11.85 – COM(85)605	Decision amending Decision 77/795.

Binding dates

Notification date	12 December 1977
First submission of information	12 June 1978 (and every 12 months thereafter) – subsequently changed to before 1 October of the following year.
Commission reports	annually – subsequently changed to every three years starting from 1987.

Purpose of the Decisions

The Decisions set up a system for the exchange of information on the quality of rivers and watercourses in the Community. A separate Decision established an information system concerned with resources to combat pollution at sea, and the Commission has proposed, following the accident at the Sandoz plant at Basle that polluted the Rhine, to extend this to inland waters (see Section 4.16).

Summary of the Decisions

The system and procedures set up by Decision 77/795 provide for data on a number of parameters on water quality to be submitted by Member States annually from specified measuring stations. These stations cover the main rivers in each Member State. The Commission is required to draw up an annual report. There is also provision for amendment of the list of measuring stations at the request of a Member State. The parameters may also be changed through a Committee for adaptation to technical progress.

Decision 86/574 made a number of changes. The information received annually is to be sent by the Commission to those Member States requesting it. The Commission is to publish a report every three years commencing in 1987. A more detailed procedure for taking measurements is laid down. One more parameter (biological quality) has been added and an additional Annex specifies the reference methods of measurement to be used. A number of changes to measuring stations has also been made by Commission Decision.

Development of the Decision

The proposal appeared after a number of meetings with national experts and, as far as the UK was concerned, met with general approval. The amendment proposed in November 1985 was the result of some six years experience and designed to put right some of the weaknesses of the original scheme. In particular the procedures for sampling and monitoring were tightened up. Experience had also shown that an annual report for publication was beyond the capabilities of the Commission, who were dependent on national submissions and subsequent national approval. Annual reports have been prepared by the Commission covering 1976 to 1980. A consolidated report covers 1976 to 1981 and shows trends over time for each determinant at each measuring station. There is little discussion. The amending Directive requires a report only every three years.

Effect on UK practice

The UK has supplied information as required for the seventeen points listed in England and Scotland. No particular difficulties have been reported as the information was already being collected as part of the Harmonized Monitoring Scheme for the measurement of river quality.

CHAPTER 5

Waste

5.0 Relevant British legislation

Origins of current legislation

Before 1972 there was no legislation concerned primarily with the broad problems of waste disposal but local authorities have long had powers to control waste as an aspect of public health. The Public Health Act 1936, which consolidated much earlier legislation, empowers them to remove house and trade refuse and to require removal of 'any accumulation of noxious matter'. It also places on them a duty to inspect their areas to detect 'statutory nuisances' including 'any accumulation or deposit which is prejudicial to health or a nuisance' and gives them the concomitant power to serve abatement notices and prosecute offenders. The *power* to inspect first appears in the Public Health Act 1848 and the *duty* to do so in the Sanitary Act 1866. These powers and duties could not prevent a nuisance arising but at least they should have ensured that there are no unknown major toxic waste deposits in Britain similar to the dramatic discoveries made elsewhere. Indeed, the very idea of voluntary bodies organizing themselves with official encouragement to 'hunt the dump' as happens elsewhere rings strangely in British ears since local authority environmental health officers (or 'inspectors of nuisances', 'sanitary inspectors', 'public health inspectors' – their names have changed over time) have been doing this as part of their normal duties for over a century.

The first preventive legislation was contained in the Town and Country Planning Act 1947 which required any new development, including waste disposal sites or plants, to have planning permission. However, growing concern in the 1960s about the environmental effects of waste led the government to set up two working groups, one on toxic waste in 1964 and the other on refuse disposal in 1967. The resulting reports,[1,2] though largely technical, paved the way for Part I of the Control of Pollution Act 1974 which now deals comprehensively with both household and toxic waste. But before the 1974 Act was even drafted a well-publicized scare about the dumping of toxic waste – the story is told by Lord Ashby[3] – forced the government to rush the Deposit of Poisonous Waste Act 1972 onto the statute book. It was always the intention that the 1972 Act would be repealed when the more comprehensive system embodied in the Control of Pollution Act 1974 was fully in operation and this happened in 1981.

Waste disposal plans

The Control of Pollution Act 1974 requires each waste disposal authority (county councils in England, district councils in Wales, and Scotland) to prepare a plan for the disposal of all household, commercial and industrial waste (including toxic waste) likely to be situated in its area and to review the plan and modify it where appropriate. In preparing the plan the authority must consult water authorities, other levels of local government, and other relevant bodies and must give adequate publicity to the draft plan and provide opportunities for the public to make representations. The plan must include information about:

the kinds and quantities of waste which will arise in the area, or be brought into it, during the period of the plan;
what waste the authority expects to dispose of itself;
what waste others are expected to dispose of;
the methods of disposal, eg reclamation, incineration, landfill;
the sites and equipment being provided;
the cost.

The Act requires disposal authorities to consider what arrangements can reasonably be made for reclaiming waste materials. The plan does not require the approval of central government but a copy must be sent to DoE. (See Table 8 in Section 5.1 showing how many plans have been produced).

Site licensing
The Act also introduced a comprehensive licensing system for the disposal of wastes over and above existing planning controls. It makes it an offence to deposit household, commercial or industrial waste on land or to use waste disposal plant unless the land in question is licensed by the waste disposal authority. The authority must maintain a public register with particulars of all disposal licences – sometimes also known as site licences. A site licence, with any conditions, can only be issued by the authority if any required planning permission for the site is in force. An application for a licence must be referred to the water authority and any unresolved dispute between the water authority and the waste disposal authority is referred to the Secretary of State.

Site licences can be made subject to such conditions as the waste disposal authority sees fit and may relate, among other things, to:

duration of the licence;
supervision by the licence holder of licensed activities;
the kinds and quantities of waste, the methods of dealing with them, and the recording of information;
precautions to be taken;
the hours when waste may be dealt with;
the works to be carried out before licensed activities begin or while they continue.

Toxic waste
The Deposit of Poisonous Waste Act 1972 made it an offence to deposit on land poisonous, noxious or polluting waste in circumstances in which it can give rise to an environmental hazard. The 1972 Act also required those removing or disposing of toxic or dangerous waste to notify the waste disposal authority and

the water authority at least three days before doing so, giving details of the composition, quantity, and destination of the waste. The 'notifiable' waste was defined negatively as all toxic or dangerous waste not specifically excluded by regulations. The Act thus produced for the first time a substantial amount of information about industrial waste, and indeed was criticized for the amount of paper work involved.

The 1972 Act was repealed in 1981 and the notification system was replaced by the provisions of the Control of Pollution (Special Waste) Regulations 1980 made under Section 17 of the Control of Pollution Act 1974. The introduction of the Regulations caused some controversy because it was argued that the method of defining 'special waste' (an inclusive list and criteria approach – see below) was more restrictive than the 'negative' definition of notifiable waste under the 1972 Act. The government argued that the new Regulations concentrated controls where they were most needed, and that the site licensing system should provide sufficient control over actual disposal of wastes.

The Section 17 Regulations provide for a control system (sometimes said to apply 'from the cradle to the grave') including:

a requirement that a waste producer notifies the receiving waste disposal authority of the intention to dispose of a consignment of special waste at least three days but not more than one month in advance;

a consignment note system under which a consignment note travels with the waste and also provides confirmation that any particular consignment of special waste has been disposed of at a site licensed to receive it;

a register containing a record of the despatch, conveyance and disposal of the special waste by each of the parties handling it;

a permanent record of the location of disposals of special waste within a landfill or at an underground disposal site;

a power for the Secretary of State to direct acceptance and disposal of special waste at a particular site or plant.

The Section 17 Regulations define 'special waste' as waste which is a medicinal product or waste containing any of the substances listed in a Schedule to the Regulations in such concentrations that it has:

1. the ability to be likely to cause death or serious damage to tissue if a single dose of not more than 5 cm³ were to be ingested by a child of 20 kg bodyweight; or
2. the ability to be likely to cause serious damage to human tissue by inhalation, skin contact or eye contact on exposure to the substance for fifteen minutes or less; or
3. a flash point of 21°C or less.

Apart from the third item, the definition of 'special waste' is therefore essentially by reference to its possible effect on human health rather than on the environment (as when a lorry load is dumped or accidentally spilled so as to pollute water) and this point will be seen to have significance when discussing Directive 78/319 (see Section 5.2). Effects on the environment, particularly water, are an essential part of the site licence conditions but these conditions do not normally extend to waste while being transported (although there is nothing to prevent a waste disposal authority from making conditions about the movement of waste to the site in question).

Other legislation

The Health and Safety at Work etc Act 1974 lays responsibilities on employers concerning the safety of workers and this extends to workers handling waste. The Health and Safety Executive, a central government agency established under the Act, has powers to supervise safety at work. Under the Alkali Works etc Act 1906 and the Health and Safety at Work etc Act 1974, major industrial emitters to air, including all chemical waste incinerators, are registered with and controlled by the Industrial Air Pollution Inspectorate (see Section 6.0, Relevant British legislation).

The movement of hazardous materials, including waste, is controlled by a whole host of specific Regulations. The Refuse Disposal (Amenity) Act 1978 places a duty on a local authority to provide sites where residents may deposit bulky household refuse free of charge, and also governs the disposal of abandoned motor cars. Waste oils and polychlorinated biphenyls (PCBs) which are the subject of individual Directives are not covered by separate British legislation but are controlled under the general legislation described above.

Administration

From this brief outline of the legislation relevant to EEC Directives it follows that waste disposal is very largely a local government function. Central government has reserve powers and has an appellate role exercised, for example, when an applicant for a disposal (or site) licence appeals against conditions imposed by the waste disposal authority, or to resolve a dispute between a water authority and a waste disposal authority. Central government activity is otherwise confined to developing overall policy, promoting research and issuing advice and, of course, negotiating EC Directives and answering to the Commission for their implementation. Examples of government advice include the series of 'Waste Management Papers' issued by DoE on such topics as waste disposal plans, site licensing, disposing of particularly difficult wastes, and on the definition of 'special wastes'.

In 1981 the House of Lords' Select Committee on Science and Technology made an inquiry into hazardous waste disposal policy[4] and made a number of recommendations for strengthening the system including the formation of a small central Hazardous Waste Inspectorate. This was established within the Department of the Environment in 1983 with only the power to advise. It has issued critical reports.

An example of central government involvement in instigating research is the large-scale research programme on the behaviour of hazardous wastes in landfill sites[5] which considered the effects of the practice, known as 'codisposal', of mixing hazardous waste together with household waste. This concluded that sensible landfill is realistic and that an ultracautious approach to landfill is unjustified, although some substances are not suitable for landfill and each case has to be treated on its merits. A complaint by a local authority about the practice of 'codisposal' at Pitsea – one of Britain's largest landfill sites receiving toxic waste – led to the Lords' Report mentioned above, but the Lords' Report found codisposal to be a valid method if well executed.

Scotland and Northern Ireland

The legislation covering Scotland and Northern Ireland is not always identical to that for England and Wales but broadly the same provisions apply.

Further developments

In December 1985 the Royal Commission on Environmental Pollution published a wide-ranging and critical report on waste[6]. The government replied immediately to some points and then in September 1986 issued a consultation paper proposing new legislation[7]. Not all the Royal Commission's proposals have been accepted. A 'duty of care' is to be imposed on waste producers who will be obliged to take all reasonable steps to ensure satisfactory disposal of their wastes. A registration scheme is to be introduced for waste transporters, and registered vehicles will have to carry a standard card. Waste disposal authorities are to gain extra powers over site licensing, enforcement of conditions, and aftercare of disposal sites. The Hazardous Waste Inspectorate is to be given statutory backing.

These proposed changes to legislation have not been as influenced by Community legislation as have the recent proposals to amend air pollution legislation (see Section 6.0 Relevant British legislation). There are some failures fully to implement some Directives and the occasion of a change to British legislation could yet be taken to put right such matters as (a) the definition of toxic waste being by reference only to human health and not to environmental effects (see Section 5.2); (b) no obligation to keep records of toxic waste produced; (c) no obligation to dispose of waste PCBs (see Section 5.4); and (d) no obligation for producers of waste oils to keep records or to store contaminated oil separately (see Section 5.5).

References

1   Key Dr A (Chairman) 1970 *Disposal of solid toxic wastes*. Department of the Environment/Scottish Development Department, HMSO.

2   Sumner J (Chairman) 1971 *Refuse disposal*. Department of the Environment, HMSO.

3   Ashby Eric, 1978 *Reconciling man with the environment*. OUP.

4   House of Lords' Select Committee on Science and Technology 1981 *Hazardous waste disposal* 1st Report Session 1980–81. HMSO.

5   *Cooperative programme of research on the behaviour of hazardous wastes in landfill sites*. HMSO (1978).

6   Royal Commission on Environmental Pollution 1985 *Managing waste: the duty of care* 11th Report. HMSO.

7   Department of the Environment, September 1986 *Waste disposal law: amendments*.

5.1 Waste – framework Directive

75/442/EEC (OJ L194 25.7.75) proposed 10.9.74 – COM(74)1297	Directive on waste.

Binding dates
Notification date	18 July 1975
Formal compliance	18 July 1977
Situation reports	every three years – first report due 18 July 1980.

This is to assume that the first year period started with the date for formal compliance – an assumption made by the Commission (see reply to European parliamentary question OJ C178 16/7/80). But the Directive is ambiguous and periods normally run from the date of notification. This ambiguity does not arise with the Directive on toxic waste (see Section 5.2) which states that the three year period starts from the notification date.

Purpose of the Directive

In all Member States waste disposal was regarded as a local or regional problem until the early 1970s. Several Member States then introduced or proposed legislation to provide some kind of national framework for dealing with it and the Directive accordingly seeks to set out a coherent set of measures applicable in all Member States. The Directive is sometimes referred to as a framework Directive, more detailed measures being provided by other Directives, such as those on toxic waste and on polychlorinated biphenyls (PCBs) (see Sections 5.2 and 5.4).

Summary of the Directive

A general duty is placed on Member States to take the necessary measures to ensure that waste is disposed of without endangering human health and without harming the environment. 'Disposal' and 'waste' are defined, and certain categories of waste are excluded from the scope of the Directive (eg radioactive waste, mining waste, some agricultural wastes, waste waters and gaseous effluents).
    The Directive contains four main mandatory elements:

competent authorities with responsibility for waste are to be appointed;
waste disposal plans are to be prepared by these competent authorities;
permits from the competent authorites are to be obtained by installations or undertakings handling waste;
the 'polluter pays' principle is to apply.

In addition the Directive requires Member States to encourage recycling. Situation reports are to be prepared every three years.

Competent authorities

The competent authorities are to be responsible in a given zone for the planning, organization, authorization and supervision of waste disposal operations.

Plans

The plans which are to be drawn up by the competent authorities 'as soon as possible' must cover:

    the type and quantity of waste to be disposed of;
    general technical requirements;
    suitable disposal sites;
    any special arrangements for particular wastes,

and may cover:

    the body empowered to carry out the disposal of waste;
    the estimated costs;
    appropriate measures to encourage rationalization of the collection, sorting and treatment of waste.

Permits

Permits must be obtained by an installation or undertaking treating, storing or tipping waste on behalf of third parties relating in particular to:

    the type and quantity of waste to be treated;
    general technical requirements;
    precautions to be taken;
    the information to be made available at the request of the competent authority concerning the origin, destination and treatment of waste and the type and quantity of such waste;

The competent authorites must make periodic inspections to ensure that the conditions of the permit are being fulfilled.

It will be noted that undertakings storing, tipping or treating their own waste do not require permits. However, they must still be subject to supervision by the competent authority. Similarly, undertakings transporting and collecting their own waste or waste on behalf of third parties do not need permits but must be subject to supervision by the competent authority.

'Polluter pays' principle

The cost of disposing of waste is to be borne by the holder who has waste handled, and/or by the previous holders or the producer of the product from which the waste came.

Recycling
Member States are to encourage the prevention, recycling and processing of waste, the extraction of raw materials and possibly energy and any other process for the reuse of waste. They are to inform the Commission of any draft rules to such effect. In addition they are to inform the Commission of the use of products which might be a source of technical difficulties as regards disposal or might lead to excessive disposal costs.

Situation reports
Every three years Member States are to draw up a situation report on waste disposal and forward it to the Commission. In its turn the Commission is to report to the Council and the Parliament on the application of the Directive.

Development of the Directive

At the time that the Commission began work on the Directive, a German law of 1972 required regional authorities and private individuals to use special installations for the treatment, storage and removal of waste, these installations having to conform to regional waste disposal plans. The drawing up of waste disposal plans was also an important feature of the British Control of Pollution Act which was then under discussion as a Bill. The French government also had a preliminary draft law on waste disposal and the recovery and recycling of materials. The Directive, therefore, had to take account of these three items of existing or proposed legislation.

In Britain the responsible Minister, Denis Howell, claimed, when giving evidence to the House of Commons Scrutiny Committee in 1975, that the:

> Control of Pollution Act . . . was in fact a model for this
> Directive. It has the same aims. I think that we can claim that
> here the EEC has been following our Control of Pollution
> Act rather than the other way about.

He went on to say: 'May I sum up this Directive by saying that in general we believe that this is a very enlightened and acceptable document.'
The European Parliament welcomed the Directive although it suggested a number of minor changes. One of these was that the title should be changed from 'waste disposal' to 'the waste sector' since the Directive dealt with recycling as well as disposal. In the event the briefer title of 'waste' was adopted. The Directive was agreed ten months after being proposed and with very little change suggesting that no major objections were raised by any country during deliberations in Council.

Formal compliance in the UK

When the Minister told the Commons' Scrutiny Committee that he welcomed the Directive and that it was based on the Control of Pollution Act, he added one caveat: 'There is the question of timing, which is probably the only part of it which might cause us any slight doubts'. He went on to say that because of 'economic stringencies' there had been delay in bringing the relevant part of the Act into force but that the 'Government do not intend that it be delayed for very long'. In the event, Section 2 of the Act, which requires waste disposal authorities to prepare waste disposal plans, was delayed longer than originally thought and was not brought into force until 1 July 1978 (The Control of Pollution Act 1974 [Commencement No 11] Order 1977 – SI 1977 No 2164) so that Britain was one year late in implementing a major element of the Directive. This point was conceded in the statement of compliance sent by DoE to the Commission on 5 October 1977. The statement did however point out that most disposal authorities in England had already begun preparatory work for the plans on an extrastatutory basis.

A fuller statement of how each Article of the Directive is implemented in Britain was sent to the Commission in March 1982 with the first situation report on waste disposal required by the Directive. This shows that all the main elements of the Directive are now implemented in England, Wales and Scotland largely by the Control of Pollution Act 1974 and in Northern Ireland by the Pollution Control and Local Government (NI) Order 1978, although various other Acts, such as the Town and Country Planning Act 1971, the Local Government Act 1972, and the Health and Safety at Work Act 1974 are also relied upon for certain Articles.

In summary the position on implementation is as follows: the Local Goverment Act 1972 appointed as waste disposal authorities the County Councils in England and District Councils in Wales. In Scotland it is the District and Island Councils that are waste disposal authorities by virtue of the Control of Pollution Act. Section 2 of the Control of Pollution Act requires waste disposal authorities to draw up plans, and Sections 3–11 provide for the licensing of sites to receive waste (ie the 'permits' of the Directive).

The Control of Pollution Act in several places goes further than the Directive in that the licensing provisions apply to undertakings disposing of their own waste as well as waste being disposed of for third parties. Furthermore, the Directive says nothing about publishing the waste disposal plans or the need for any consultations during their preparation, both of which are features of the Control of Pollution Act.

It is worth noting that the Directive requires the waste disposal plans to be drawn up 'as soon as possible'. The Control of Pollution Act in contrast contains no words suggesting any such urgency although, as originally enacted, the Secretary of State was empowered 'to give to any authority a direction as to the time by which the authority is to perform any duty specified. . .' (Section 2).[7] No such direction has ever been made but a Circular issued to local authorities in 1978 (DoE Circular 29/78) expressed the hope that substantial progress would have been made with plans within eighteen months to two years. The power to make directions about the time by which plans must be produced was subsequently repealed by the Local Government Planning and Land Act 1980 (Schedule 2), but the Secretary of State still has broad reserve powers under Section 97 of the Control of Pollution Act to declare an authority to be in default if it has failed to perform any function and to direct the authority to perform that function.

The DoE never formally notified waste disposal authorities of the existence of the Directive until April 1978 when DoE Circular 29/78 which dealt with Directive 78/319 (see Section 5.2). The reason given for this is that there is nothing in the Directive that is not already covered by existing legislation and practice.

Effect on UK practice

It is most probable that the Minister was correct in saying that the Directive was modelled on the Control of Pollution Act. Certainly the two are broadly similar with the detailed requirements for plans in the Directive being closer to the British Act of 1974 than to the German Act of 1972. It follows that what is required by the Directive would have been done without its existence and the Directive cannot be expected to have had much practical effect in Britain. One effect, however, has already been noted. Implementation of some sections of the Control of Pollution Act were delayed and the Directive must have provided pressure for not deferring implementation of Section 2 of the Act (concerned with waste disposal plans) much longer. There is no knowing how long Section 2 would have been delayed but for the Directive.

Another effect of the Directive may be attributed to the requirement to supply the Commission every three years with a situation report on waste disposal. The first report was due in July 1980 but was not in fact submitted till March 1982. A second report was submitted in May 1986. Britain was not alone in being late with the first report, and part of the explanation for the delay is that the Commission let it be known that it would issue guidelines for the preparation of the situation reports and these were not issued until September 1981. The British situation reports contain a quantity of information and statistics about waste all of which was already available to the DoE and did not have to be collected specifically for the situation report. Similar information will continue to have to be collected every three years. The Commission has not yet submitted a report to the Council and the European Parliament apparently because it has not received situation reports from several Member States.

The first situation report set out the position on the preparation of waste disposal plans. It showed that in March 1982 three plans had been completed, three had been referred to the Secretary of State and more than half the remaining 159 were expected to be ready in draft form by the end of the year. Five years later many are still incomplete. The position at the end of March 1987 was as follows:

Table 8   Progress of waste disposal plans

	Complete	Draft referred to Secretary of State	Incomplete	Total
England	23	3	13	39
Wales	36	1	0	37
Scotland	39	12	5	56
N Ireland	18	0	8	26
Metropolitan	1 (5)	0	39 (35)	40
TOTAL	117 (121)	16	65 (61)	198

Note: The abolition of the Metropolitan counties has caused some confusion. In theory there could be forty separate plans prepared by the districts and London Boroughs but it is likely that joint plans will be produced for many areas. So far one joint draft plan is being produced by Tyne and Wear Waste Disposal Joint Committee

5.2 Toxic waste

78/319/EEC (OJ L84 31.3.78) 22.7.76 – COM(76)385	Directive on toxic and dangerous waste.

Binding dates

Notification date	22 March 1978
Formal compliance	22 March 1980
Situation reports	Every three years – first report due 22 March 1981.

Purpose of the Directive

An earlier Directive 75/442 (see Section 5.1) laid down a broad framework of control for both household and toxic wastes involving the establishment of competent authorities responsible for producing plans and authorizing installations handling waste. The present Directive lays down more stringent controls for toxic and dangerous waste within that framework. A separate Directive deals with transfrontier shipment of toxic waste (see Section 5.3).

Summary of the Directive

The main provision of the Directive is that toxic and dangerous waste may be stored, treated and/or deposited only by authorized undertakings and that anyone producing or holding such waste without an appropriate permit must then have it stored, treated or deposited by an undertaking that is so authorized. The Directive also makes provision for plans to be made, records kept, transport controlled, inspections made, and reports produced.

'Toxic and dangerous waste' is defined as:

> any waste containing or contaminated by the substances or materials listed in the Annex to this Directive of such a nature, in such quantities or in such concentrations as to constitute a risk to health or the environment,

but certain materials are excluded from the scope of the Directive such as radioactive waste, certain agricultural wastes, explosives and hospital waste. The Annex lists twenty-seven toxic or dangerous substances. 'Disposal' of toxic waste is defined to include 'the transformation operations necessary for its recovery, re-use or recycling'.

The Directive places a general duty on Member States to ensure that toxic and dangerous waste is disposed of without harming human health or the environment, and in particular without risk to water, air, soil, plants or animals. A general duty is also placed on them to encourage the prevention and re-use of toxic waste.

The Directive makes the following more specific provisions.

Competent authorities and plans

The requirement of Directive 75/442 that competent authorities be appointed to authorize and supervise waste disposal and to produce plans is repeated. This time there is no requirement that these plans be drawn up 'as soon as possible' but an addition to the earlier Directive is that they must be kept up to date and be made public. Another addition is that the plans must also be forwarded to the Commission which together with the Member States must arrange for regular comparisons to ensure sufficient coordination.

The plans may include the estimated costs of disposal operations, but must include:

the type and quantity of waste;
the methods of disposal;
specialized treatment centres where necessary;
suitable disposal sites.

Permits

Establishments storing, treating and/or depositing toxic and dangerous waste must obtain a permit from the competent authority. (Unlike Directive 75/442 this also applies to establishments handling their own waste.) Undertakings engaged in the carriage of toxic and dangerous waste do not require a permit but 'must be controlled by the competent authorities'.

The permits may include conditions and obligations. They may be granted for a specified period. They must cover:

the type and quantity of waste;
the technical requirements;
the precautions to be taken;
the disposal site(s);
the methods of disposal.

Records

Any undertaking which produces, holds and/or disposes of toxic and dangerous waste (but not apparently ones treating such waste) must:

keep a record of the quantity, nature, physical and chemical characteristics and origin of such waste, and of the methods and sites used for disposing of it, including the dates of receipt and disposal; and/or
make this information available to the competent authority on request.

Transport

When toxic and dangerous waste is transported in the course of disposal (which includes transformation operations necessary for recovery, re-use or recycling) it must be accompanied by an identification form containing the following details:

nature;
composition;
volume or mass of the waste;
name and address of the producer or of the previous holder(s);
name and address of the next holder or of the final disposer;
location of the site of final disposal where known.

Inspection

All undertakings producing, holding or disposing of toxic and dangerous waste must be subject to inspection and supervision by the competent authorities to ensure fulfilment of the provisions adopted under the Directive and the terms of any authorization.

Separation and packaging

Member States must take the necessary steps to ensure that:

toxic and dangerous waste is, when necessary, kept separate from other matter and residues when being collected, transported, stored or deposited;
the packaging of toxic and dangerous waste is appropriately labelled, indicating in particular the nature, composition and quantity of the waste;
such toxic and dangerous waste is recorded and identified in respect of each site where it is or has been deposited.

'Polluter pays' principle

The cost of disposing of toxic and dangerous waste is to be borne by the holder who has waste handled by a waste collector, and/or by the previous holders or the producer of the product from which the waste came. If Member States charge levies on the monies used to cover these costs the yield may be used for financing control measures relating to toxic and dangerous waste or for financing research pertaining to the elimination of such waste.

Situation reports

Every three years, and for the first time by 22 March 1981, Member States are to draw up a situation report on the disposal of toxic and dangerous waste and forward it to the Commission. In its turn the Commission is to report to the Council and the Parliament on the application of the Directive.

Adaptation

Provisions are made for amending the Annex to the Directive in order to adapt it to scientific and technical progress. This adaptation is to be done by a committee, chaired by a representative of the Commission, and able to take decisions by qualified majority.

Development of the Directive

In its memorandum accompanying the proposed Directive the Commission attributed its origins to no particular Member State but explained that several had recently introduced laws or draft laws of varying scope to control toxic wastes.

Some ideas can nevertheless be attributed to particular countries. The Belgian law of 1974 foreshadowed the proposal – subsequently deleted from the Directive before it was agreed – that liability for damage to a third party caused by toxic waste disposed of by an unauthorized undertaking be jointly shared by the original holder of the waste and that undertaking. To the French law of 1975 can probably be attributed the obligation that the holder of toxic waste must surrender it to an authorized establishment. Similar words appear in the Directive although strictly they are redundant since they are implicit in an authorization procedure.

A British official, giving evidence to the Lords' Scrutiny Committee, claimed that Britain was a major contributor: 'The Directive was quite deliberately based on the Control of Pollution Act. The Commission did use it as their main model. . .' and perhaps for this reason expressed herself broadly satisfied: 'I think that this Directive, with which we have been involved from the outset. . . has been approached in a sensible, logical and scientific manner and I have no grave misgivings about the way the thing has been handled. . .'.

The Directive as proposed differed in several ways from what was finally agreed by including:

a definition of toxic waste which would have included any waste containing the substances listed in the Annex, with no qualification about quantity or concentration so that trace quantities would also be covered;
the provision about liability for damage, mentioned above;
a prohibition on undertakings discriminating on the grounds of the origin of the waste;
a provision that transporters of toxic waste be authorized.

The Minister responsible, Denis Howell, speaking in the House of Commons' debate said:

There is nothing in the Directive which presents us with major difficulties of policy, although we shall have to obtain a few important amendments if we are to avoid administrative difficulties.

He went on to specify four main reservations about the Directive as proposed:

that recycling should be kept outside its scope on the grounds that toxic waste is no longer waste when it has been identified as suitable for recycling;
that the control of transport of toxic waste should be outside its scope on the grounds that the transport of dangerous material needs to be controlled whether the material being transported is waste or not;
that the definition of toxic waste should contain a qualification to ensure that it only applied when the toxic substance was present in such a concentration that there was a degree of hazard;
that the technical progress committee should not have excessive powers to amend the Annex.

The government was unsuccessful on the recycling point but seems to have secured some amendments on the other three points, the most important being the qualifications made to the definition of toxic waste. Britain was not alone: the Dutch government for instance took the same view on the authorization of transporters (according to evidence given to the House of Lords' Scrutiny Committee). Since then the government has proposed that transporters be licensed (see Section 5.0).

An explanation of how the list in the Annex was arrived at was given to the House of Lords' Scrutiny Committee:

> The list, which represents the distillation of the work that has been done by the scientific expert group the Commission set up, is really a condensation of a much longer list that was drawn up originally and now contains the materials of concern to one or other of the Member States. Problems have been identified in one or other of the Member States with the materials listed, . . . and although obviously, like all these things, we are perhaps not quite so concerned about some of the things on the list as others, on a scientific and technical basis we are reasonably happy that there are not any materials included here unnecessarily.

Among the points made by the European Parliament was the need for a supplementary proposal as soon as possible

> specifying in a uniform manner the levels of concentration of toxic and dangerous substances above which wastes fall within the field of application of the Directive.

The laying down of concentrations had been an issue between the Dutch and British governments during negotiations with the Dutch in favour and the British opposed. This conflict was deferred and the Commissioner, Mr Tugendhat, in replying to the debate in the European Parliament, undertook to bring forward a supplementary proposal on concentrations. This proposal has yet to emerge although it has been the subject of discussions.

The European Parliament were successful with their suggestion that asbestos be added to the Annex.

Formal compliance in the UK

According to the DoE, all Articles in the Directive were formally implemented by the due date of 22 March 1980 except for the Article concerned with the identification form to accompany waste being transported and the keeping of records. Implementation of that Article had to await the Regulations made under Section 17 of the Control of Pollution Act – the Control of Pollution (Special Waste) Regulations 1980 – which came into force on 16 March 1981, although, as explained below, there is uncertainty as to whether the Article is yet fully complied with. The Directive was drawn to the attention of waste disposal authorities, within a few days of being agreed, by DoE Circular 29/78 dated 5 April 1978 and the Section 17 Regulations was drawn to their attention by DoE Circular 4/81 dated 20 February 1981.

A full statement of how each Article in the Directive is implemented was sent to the Commission in March 1982 with the first situation report on toxic waste disposal required by the Directive. Compliance has largely been achieved in England, Wales and Scotland under the Control of Pollution Act 1974 and in Northern Ireland by the Pollution Control and Local Government (NI) Order 1978 although various other Acts and Regulations have also been relied upon (a total of twenty-eight in all).

In summary, the requirement to appoint competent authorities, to draw up waste disposal plans, and to issue permits is covered by the same legislation that covers the similar requirements of Directive 75/442 (see Section 5.1). The keeping of records for toxic wastes leaving a producer's premises or being disposed of to land is covered by the Section 17 Regulations, as is the requirement of an identification form when toxic waste is being transported. The Article concerned with separation and packaging of toxic waste is covered by a large number of separate Regulations (eg, concerned with asbestos, corrosive substances, inflammable substances).

One gap in the implementation of the Directive is that there is no British legislation explicitly requiring records to be kept of toxic waste *produced* or *stored*, since the Control of Pollution (Special Waste) Regulations 1980 only require records for waste deposited on land (Regulation 14) or before the waste *leaves* the producer's premises (Regulation 4). Article 14(1) of the Directive is, however, clear that records are to be kept by 'any installation, establishment or undertaking which *produces*, *holds* and/or disposes of toxic and dangerous waste'. Under existing British Regulations, if the producer stores (holds) toxic waste for a long time without disposing of it he need keep no records and indeed the producer may argue that he is only holding the toxic waste because he does not regard it as waste. If, however, the producer disposes of toxic waste on land within the curtilage of his factory he may be required to have a licence under Section 3 of the Control of Pollution Act and will then have to keep records. The House of Lords' Select Committee on Science and Technology recommended in 1981[1] that all producers of hazardous waste should be registered and should make a quarterly report of waste produced. However, the government is not apparently proposing to implement this recommendation. The argument is that the records that now have to be kept for disposal and movement effectively mean that there is information about production.

The British Regulations are more stringent than the Directive in some respects. For instance, the Directive places no requirement on the producer of waste to notify the disposal authority in advance that a consignment is coming.

When the Control of Pollution (Special Waste) Regulations 1980 were laid before Parliament a campaign was launched by the County Councils to have them withdrawn and amended leading to debates in both the House of Lords and Commons. In the Commons a motion to revoke the Regulations was moved unsuccessfully by the Opposition spokesman on the environment, Denis Howell, who, as we have seen, happened to have been the responsible Minister at the time the Directive was being negotiated and agreed. In the debate he alleged that the Regulations were contrary to the Directive, and given the source of the allegation it must be considered seriously.

Mr Howell has not publicly elaborated on his reasons for believing that the Directive is not complied with but in a personal letter to the author he said it was because the substances controlled during transport by the Regulations are defined as having to be dangerous to human life or health, whereas the Directive also covers risk to the environment.

The point that the Regulations do not cover environmental considerations has been conceded by the DoE in Waste Management Paper No 23 (para 3):

> The Section 17 controls are not mainly concerned with wider environmental issues such as water pollution, site sterilization and damage to vegetation, which are matters already dealt with by site licensing, and are covered in other technical memoranda in the Waste Management Paper series.

Thus a load of waste which could pose a risk to water can be moved by lorry without being accompanied by the consignment note (British terminology) or identification form (terminology of the Directive) so long as it is not a 'special waste' defined by reference to danger to human life if ingested (see Section 5.0). As the National Water Council put it in evidence to the House of Lords Select Committee on Science and Technology[1]:

> . . .special waste is primarily defined by reference to the toxicity to a child of an ingested five cubic centimetres of the material. This is most unsatisfactory from the Council's point of view; for example, waste containing up to 40 000 mg/kg mercury might not require notice under these regulations (the Section 17 Regulations) yet a lorry load might contain, say, 300–400 kilogrammes of mercury compounds. Such a quantity would be sufficient to contaminate well over 100 million cubic metres of water beyond the limit of the EEC Directive on Surface Water for Abstraction for Drinking. It is therefore clearly the total toxic content of a load that is critical. . .

The Directive (Article 5) says that Member States are to:

> take the necessary measures to ensure that toxic and dangerous waste is disposed of without endangering human health and without harming the environment, and in particular without risk to water, air, soil, plants or animals,

and (Article 14[2]) that: 'when toxic and dangerous waste is transported in the course of disposal it shall be accompanied by an identification form. . .'

Is 'transport' part of 'disposal'? On this the Directive is quite clear. Article 1 defines 'disposal' to include collection and carriage as well as tipping from which it must follow that identification forms are required for waste being transported if there is a risk to the environment as well as to human health. Furthermore, the Directive defines toxic waste as meaning any waste containing the substances in the Annex in *such quantities* or in such concentrations as to constitute a risk to health or the environment. The example given by the National Water Council shows that it is possible for a large quantity of waste to be transported creating a risk to the environment without the waste falling within the British definition of 'special waste'. It seems that Mr Howell is right in that Article 14[2] concerning notification forms has not been fully complied with. The Regulations are being revised, and the revised version may be such that effects on the environment are specifically covered. If the amendments are not satisfactory, the matter could eventually be tested in the Courts. Thus a waste disposal authority could interpret 'special waste' in accordance with the Directive and more stringently than the Section 17 Regulations. If a resulting dispute reached a British court, the British court could then apply, under Article 177 of the Treaty of Rome, to the European Court for a ruling on the interpretation of the Directive.

It has to be added that the wording of the Directive has been drafted very widely indeed since any toxic substance, however dilute and however small in quantity, can pose some risks to the environment. Nevertheless, it should be possible to include within the definition of 'special waste' not only a reference to concentration but also a reference to the total quantity. This would meet the point made by the National Water Council in a practical way and would go some way to meeting the requirements of legal implementation. DoE officials for their part maintain that wherever the line is drawn some waste will fall outside the scope of the Directive which could have some harmful effects on the environment, and that although the line they have drawn is primarily by reference to human health, it also ensures that waste most harmful to the environment is covered.

Another gap in implementation is that the Special Waste Regulations do not apply to wastes that are to be recycled whereas these are covered by the Directive. Having failed to get the Directive narrowed during negotiations the government has effectively decided to ignore what it must regard as an unnecessary provision. However, recyclable wastes carried in road tankers have to be accompanied by details of the substances carried – under the Dangerous Substances (Conveyance by Road in Road Tankers and Tank Containers) Regulations 1981 – and it is the government's intention to extend the requirements to other types of vehicle.

There are two further gaps in the implementation of the Directive. British legislation does not cover waste produced by the Crown (for example, the armed services) while the Directive makes no exemption for them. This problem has arisen with Directive 76/464 (see Section 4.8) on discharge of dangerous substances to water, and presumably the Commission turns a blind eye. However, it is possible that problems could arise if a third party adversely affected by Crown waste sought to have the Directive enforced in the courts. DoE Circular 4/81 says that 'the Secretary of State believes that the Armed Services and Government Departments will wish to take account of the Provisions of the (Control of Pollution) Act and the new Regulations under Section 17'. The other gap in implementation is that the Directive does not exclude all agricultural waste while the Section 17 Regulations do.

Effect on UK practice

The site licensing provisions of the Control of Pollution Act were brought into force in June 1976 before the Directive was proposed and will not have been influenced by it. The effect of the Directive will therefore largely have been on the form of the Section 17 Regulations made after the Directive was agreed, and the possibility of influence was explicitly stated by an official giving evidence to the House of Lords' Scrutiny Committee in 1977:

> We are hoping to make regulations. . . under Section 17. . ..
> We have deliberately not put firm recommendations to Min-
> isters at this stage because it seemed sensible at the least to
> listen to what people had to say in the course of the Brussels'

discussions. They are knowledgeable and sensible and if they make good points we want to take them into account. We clearly want the two things [the Directive and the British Regulations] to be in line. We have our own ideas and we know what we do not want and what we would want to resist in the Brussels' discussions, but the two things are really marching in parallel and we have deliberately kept to ourselves a degree of flexibility at this stage.

We have already seen how the Annex to the Directive listing the substances to which the Directive applies was arrived at collectively by the Member States and the substances listed in the Section 17 Regulations include all of these and some others. There must therefore have been some influence here. As is to be expected, DoE officials play down the overall effect of the Directive on the Section 17 Regulations maintaining that its basic tenets were unchanged while Commission officials emphasize that the Directive helped to clarify British thinking and point out that the British legislation did not exist even in draft before the Directive.

The Directive requires Member States to forward the waste disposal plans to the Commission which will then, together with the Member States, arrange for regular comparisons. This has not been done nor has the Commission asked for them possibly because so few plans are complete both in Britain (see Table 8) and in other countries.[2] When comparison comes to be made it could have a long-term effect on British practice as authorities in countries learn from each other.

Other effects of the Directive include the pressure generated to introduce the Section 17 Regulations without excessive delay and the pressure it has created to require producers of waste to keep records.

Situation reports were submitted to the Commission in March 1982 and March 1986.

References

1   House of Lords' Select Committee on Science and Technology 1981 *Hazardous waste disposal* 1st Report Session 1980–81. HMSO.

2   Haigh N, Bennett G, Kromarek P, and Lavoux T 1986 *EC environmental policy in practice. Vol I comparative report: water and waste in four countries.* Graham and Trotman.

5.3 Transfrontier shipment of toxic waste

84/631/EEC (OJ L326 13.12.84) proposed 10.1.83 – COM(82)892	Directive on the supervision and control within the European Community of the transfrontier shipment of hazardous waste.
85/469/EEC (OJ L272 12.10.85)	Adaptation (Commission Directive).
86/279/EEC (OJ L181 4.7.86) proposed 3.10.85 – COM(85)511	Amendment (Council Directive).
87/112/EEC (OJ L48 17.2.87)	Adaptation (Commission Directive).

Binding dates
Notification date	6 December 1984 and 17 June 1986
Formal compliance	1 October 1985 and 1 January 1987
Information on permits	31 December 1985
Situation report	1 October 1987, biennially thereafter.

Purpose of the Directive

The existing Directive on toxic waste (see Section 5.2) makes no provisions concerning control of transfrontier shipment. This Directive sets up a system for controls and safety regulations for movement of hazardous wastes across frontiers from collection to disposal. It covers movement within the Community and in and out of the Community.

Summary of the Directive

The Directive (as amended) adopts the definition of toxic and dangerous waste found in the toxic waste Directive except for chlorinated solvents and organic solvents and includes PCB as defined in the PCB disposal Directive. The basic provision is that the holder of any such waste who intends to move it across a frontier is required to notify the competent authority of the Member State or States concerned and where applicable any third State by means of a consignment note as set out in an Annex. The consignment note gives details of the source and composition of the waste, routes, insurance against damage to third parties, measures for safe transport and compliance with conditions required by Member States, and on the existence of a contractual agreement with the consignee of the waste. Where waste is being shipped to a third State, the holder of the waste must obtain the agreement of that State before starting the notification procedure and the notification must include satisfactory information on the agreement. No movement may take place before the competent authorities of the Member State(s) concerned have acknowledged receipt of the notification. Such acknowledgement or objection must be sent within one month of receipt of notification to the holder of the waste, with copies also to the consignee and all other States concerned. Any objection must be based on legislation in accordance with

Community Directives or international conventions on this subject. The competent authorities of the despatching Member State and of any transit state have fifteen days after receipt of notification in which to set particular conditions concerning transport of the waste; they must not be more stringent than those normally laid down by the State concerned. There is provision for using a general procedure when there are regular shipments of the same kind of waste.

The holder of the waste on receipt of acknowledgement of the notification is required to complete the consignment note and send copies to all competent authorities concerned. The consignee of the waste is required to send, within fifteen days of receipt of the waste, copies of the completed consignment note to the holder and all other concerned authorities.

Conditions are laid down covering packaging, labelling and instructions in the event of danger or accident. The cost of implementing the procedures, in accordance with the 'polluter pays principle', is chargeable to the holder and/or the producer of the waste. The producer of the waste is also responsible for ensuring that disposal is carried out in accordance with Directives on waste so as to protect the environment. (The Commission is to determine by 30 September 1988 the conditions for implementing the civil liability of the producer in the event of damage and for setting up a system of insurance).

Details of competent authorities and permitted installations are to be notified to the Commission by 31 December 1985 and passed on to other Member States. (They are now listed in the *Official Journal* (OJ C64 11.3.87) together with the code numbers to be used on the notification and shipment documents). Member States are also to submit biennial reports to the Commission (the first on 1 October 1987) on operation of the scheme. The Commission using these reports is to submit a summary report every two years to the Council, Parliament and the Economic and Social Committee.

Provision is made for exemption from the Directive of waste from nonferrous metals which are destined for recycling. A form of declaration is set out in an Annex and has to be completed to enable exemption to be claimed. Another Annex gives details of international transport conventions.

The technical adaptation committee under the toxic waste Directive is empowered to draw up the consignment note and the declaration document concerning waste for recycling and to amend them.

The original Directive required Member States to comply with it by 1 October 1985 but the amendments in Directive 86/279 affecting five articles of the original Directive required compliance by 1 January 1987, which must therefore be considered as the effective date.

Development of the Directive

Though concern was expressed during negotiations on the toxic waste Directive about problems of waste being transported over frontiers, it was then argued that existing legislation and conventions concerning international transport provided sufficient safeguards. However, it became clear after its adoption that further Community action was needed. In the United Kingdom one incident which raised much publicity concerned a £100 company which imported wastes from the Netherlands and stored them temporarily in this country. The company subsequently went into liquidation with debts of nearly £3 million leaving behind it considerable amounts of hazardous waste to be disposed of at other people's expense. The incident coincided with the investigation by the House of Lords' Science and Technology Committee into hazardous waste disposal and is covered in its report.[1] This recommended that controls on imported waste be the same as for home produced waste. The government announced in June 1981 that a review was under way and in July 1982 proposed legislation tightening up controls on storage in this country, but decided to leave additional controls on notification of imports of wastes to the Directive then being prepared by the Commission.

Shortly after the proposal was published, forty-one drums of waste, originating from Seveso and thought to be contaminated with dioxin, were temporarily lost in transit from Italy to France; they later were found in France. There was considerable publicity and concern was widespread. The European Parliament reacted quickly and put forward suggested amendments to the proposal aimed at strengthening its provisions. They included changing the form to a Regulation which would be directly applicable instead of a Directive. As a consequence the Commission published amendments providing for a Regulation and making more stringent conditions for shipment covering the use of specially reserved routes, insurance, licensing of shippers and no fault liability on the producer until disposal. The Economic and Social Committee also advocated a Regulation and pressed for early adoption and implementation.

The Minister responsible, Mr William Waldegrave, speaking in the House of Commons' debate said that the proposal complemented and enhanced the existing UK controls and he welcomed the basis of the proposal. The main objections by the government appeared to concern the inclusion of waste for recycling within the proposal and the requirement for strict liability on the part of the producer. On both of these issues the government seems to have been successful in achieving changes. On the amended proposal for a Regulation, the government took a relaxed view on what would have been something of a precedent in the environmental field: they preferred the Directive form. The House of Lords in its report had reviewed at length the relative merits of a Regulation and a Directive and favoured a Directive.

The various well-publicized incidents of problems of transfrontier movement of hazardous wastes made for general acceptance of the need for the Directive but there proved to be considerable differences of views over the freedom to object to or control transfrontier shipments, the inclusion of material for recycling and the question of liability. Discussions took place at three Councils before agreement was reached in June 1984.

The final Directive differed in certain respects from the Commission's proposals. The most significant changes were:

> omission of the requirement for shippers of hazardous waste to be licensed;
> omission of requirement for insurance cover and liability (left for subsequent proposals);
> form of notification and consignment note not specified (this was settled later – see below);
> reports to be two yearly, not three yearly;
> exclusion of material for recycling from the Directive.

The idea of a Regulation was rejected.

Following agreement on the Directive, United Nations Environment Programme (UNEP) experts examining the problems of Third World countries importing hazardous wastes from industrialized countries recommended that export should only take place when importing countries have the necessary disposal facilities. An Organization for Economic Cooperation and Development (OECD) conference in March 1985 recommended that OECD member countries should not apply any less strict controls than they do for movement of hazardous wastes involving member countries. The conference also recommended that such movements should not be allowed without the consent of the importing country and without ensuring that adequate disposal facilities existed.

As a result, the Commission put forward a proposal amending Directive 84/631 which would require a Member State to object to shipment of waste unless the holder could show proof that the importing country had signified its agreement to importation and that the importing country was able to dispose of the waste adequately. Agreement in principle was reached at the Environment Council in March 1986 though there was some difficulty over the implications for a similar procedure covering exports of hazardous goods. The UK insisted on a Council minute which recorded that the retention of 'prior informed consent' in the Directive was without prejudice to future consideration of controls of exports of hazardous goods. The amending Directive 86/279 was adopted on 4 July 1986.

The Commission, after setting in train the procedures for the Technical Adaptation Committee, published Directive 85/469 amending the original Council Directive 84/631. The Annexes covering notification information and the declaration on waste for recycling were replaced by respectively a four-page uniform Community consignment note and a Community form for declaration concerning waste for recycling. Though the Commission Directive was not published in the *Official Journal* until 12 October 1985, compliance was required by 1 October 1985. A second Commission Directive 87/112 makes changes to forms and instructions for their completion which were made necessary by the amending Council Directive 86/279.

Formal compliance in the UK

No Member State found it possible to introduce legislation to ensure that controls would be in operation by the due date of 1 October 1985. One reason was the technical committee charged with drawing up the consignment note and declaration concerning waste for recycling continued its deliberations until July of that year and the Commission Directive giving effect was not published until 12 October. On 10 October 1985 the DoE sought comments on its proposals for Statutory Instruments to implement the Directives. The intention then was to have the Regulations in operation by the end of the year. The proposal which appeared in October 1985 and resulted in the amending Directive 86/279 and the consequent Commission Directive 87/112 have further delayed completion. The intention is to implement all four Directives by Regulations under the European Communities (Designation) (No 3) Order (1985 1195) to come into force in the spring of 1987.

Effect on UK practice

It is not easy to predict any particular effect that this Directive will have on UK practice. The climate to institute controls of the type provided for in the

Directive already existed. The 'cradle to grave' system of control by means of documentation had already been instituted for special wastes as a result of the toxic waste Directive 78/319 (see Section 5.2) and though there has been room for doubts over its full compliance with the Directive the principle has not been a point of issue. Since rather little waste is exported from Britain, the biggest effect of the Directive is likely to be in providing information in advance about imports.

References
1   House of Lords' Select Committee on Science and Technology 1981 *Hazardous waste disposal* 1st Report Session 1980–81. HMSO.

5.4 Disposal of PCBs

76/403/EEC (OJ L108 26.4.76) proposed 10.2.75 – COM(75)38	Directive on the disposal of polychlorinated biphenyls and polychlorinated terphenyls.

Binding dates
Notification date	9 April 1976
Formal compliance	9 April 1978
Situation reports	every three years – first report due 18 July 1980.

This is to assume that the report is due on the same date as the report under Directive 75/442. The Directive is not clear on the point but Article 10 says the report is to be drawn up within the framework of the 75/442 report (see Section 5.1).

Purpose of the Directive
Polychlorinated biphenyls (PCBs) are organohalogen compounds which are now used mainly as dielectric fluids but which were also more widely used before 1973 as hydraulic fluids, heat transfer fluids, lubricants and as plasticizers in such products as paints and carbonless copying paper. PCBs are not believed to occur naturally, but being very resistent to degradation they have been widely detected in the environment, particularly in predatory birds feeding on aquatic organisms. PCBs may have accounted for the spectacular catastrophe among wild birds in the Irish Sea in 1969. It is known that some aquatic organisms such as shrimps may be killed at very low concentrations of PCBs in water. PCBs can be destroyed in high-temperature incinerators.

Separate Directives 76/769 and 85/467 (see Section 7.2 Restrictions on marketing and use) restrict the sale and use of PCBs and the present Directive sets out a system of control over the disposal of PCBs within the framework of Directive 75/442 (see Section 5.1).

Summary of the Directive
PCB is defined to include polychlorinated terphenyls and mixtures containing one or both substances. The definition of 'disposal' does not include the words dumping or tipping but refers to the collection and/or destruction of PCB, or transformation operations necessary for regenerating PCB. There is an ambiguity in the use of the words 'and/or'. If the definition is interpreted to include collection without destruction the purpose of the Directive would be nullified. It must be intended to mean destruction with or without prior collection.

Four duties are placed on Member States:

to prohibit the uncontrolled discharge, dumping and tipping of PCB and of objects and equipment containing PCB;
to make compulsory the disposal (ie collection and/or destruction, regeneration) of waste PCB and PCB contained in equipment no longer capable of being used;

F

to ensure that PCB is disposed of (ie collected and/or destroyed, regenerated) without endangering human health and without harming the environment; to ensure, as far as possible, the promotion of the regeneration of waste PCB.

In order to carry out these duties the competent authorities are to set up or designate the undertakings authorized to 'dispose of' PCB on their own account or on behalf of third parties. Anyone holding PCB who is not so authorized is to hold it available for 'disposal' by an authorized undertaking. Member States are themselves to lay down the specific provisions with which the holders of PCB and the authorized undertakings must comply. The 'polluter pays principle' is to apply.

Situation reports on the 'disposal' of PCB are to be drawn up every three years within the framework of the report required by Directive 75/442 (see Section 5.1). This may be intended to mean that the two reports are due at the same time. The Commission is to circulate the reports to the other Member States. In its turn, the Commission is to report to the Council and to the Parliament on the application of the Directive.

Development of the Directive

Following a number of incidents including one in Japan where rice oil contaminated by PCB caused injury to humans and death to poultry, the Council of the OECD issued a Decision in February 1973 requiring Member States of the OECD to regulate both the use and disposal of PCBs. An OECD Decision places an obligation on Member States to put it into effect but there is no court to ensure that effective action is taken as with an EEC Directive. It is significant that notwithstanding the OECD Decision the Community nevertheless felt the need for a Directive.

Following that OECD Decision, the French government forwarded to the Commission a preliminary draft, 'Conditions of the Use of PCBs', which also dealt with PCB disposal. The Commission decided to propose two separate Directives, one dealing with the use of PCB and the other with its disposal.

In July 1974 a Directive was proposed (Directive 76/769 see Section 7.2 Restrictions on marketing and use) restricting the sale and use of PCBs to closed circuit electrical equipment (transformers, resistors and inductors), condensers (capacitors) and a few other limited applications. Seven months later the Commission proposed the present Directive.

Neither the House of Commons nor the House of Lords commented on the proposed Directive so there is no publicly available record of the attitude of the British government to the proposal.

The European Parliament welcomed the proposal but suggested that the Commission should report on the application of the Directive to the Parliament and to the Council. This is one of only two amendments (other than drafting amendments) made before the Directive was agreed, the other being the insertion of the duty to promote regeneration of PCBs.

Formal compliance in the UK

In December 1978, that is to say some eight months after the due date, the government submitted a statement to the Commission of how it had complied with the Directive. This referred to the site licensing provisions of the Control of Pollution Act 1974 as providing the powers to control the disposal of waste generally (the word 'dispose' being used in the usual sense to include tipping and not being restricted to the special sense of the Directive). These site licensing provisions were brought into force in England and Wales in June 1976 and in Scotland in January 1978, well before the due date. The statement of compliance also referred to the forthcoming Regulations to be made under Section 17 of the Act and to the Deposit of Poisonous Waste Act 1972. Under the 1972 Act any transport of PCB for the purpose of being deposited on land (which included delivery to an incinerator) had to be notified in advance. The 1972 Act was replaced in 1981 by the Section 17 Regulations which provide a more precise definition of toxic waste and more precise control arrangements. Any transport of waste containing at least 1 per cent by weight of PCB, including transport to a high-temperature incinerator, now has to be notified in advance and must be accompanied by a consignment note.

In July 1979 the Commission wrote formally to the government asking it to submit observations for its failure fully to implement the Directive, and in October 1979 the government replied that it intended to lay Regulations under Section 17 of the 1974 Act before Parliament by mid-1980. Despite this letter the Commission issued a Reasoned Opinion in May 1980 to the effect that since it had not been informed of all the provisions adopted to comply with the Directive, it was compelled to assume that the United Kingdom had failed to fulfil its obligations.

In July 1980 the government replied by letter that it was now the hope that the Section 17 Regulations would be laid before Parliament by the end of the month. The letter referred again to the Deposit of Poisonous Waste Act 1972 and stated that it was the government's view (an erroneous view, see below) that it already had the necessary legislation to enable it to fulfil its strict obligations under the Directive. After some further delay, the Section 17 Regulations were laid before Parliament in November 1980 and came into operation on 16 March 1981. This is not the only Directive which will have created a pressure for the introduction of the Regulations (see also Section 5.2).

The government sent the Regulations to the Commission in April 1981 in a letter which carefully specified those Articles of the Directive that were implemented by the 1974 Act and the new Regulations made under it. The Article concerned with compulsory 'disposal' was not mentioned.

In March 1982 the DoE submitted a situation report to the Commission, as required by the Directive, containing a further statement of the legislation under which the Directive is implemented. This referred incidentally to the Alkali Act 1906 and to the duty on the Alkali Inspectorate to control high-temperature incinerators. A second situation report was submitted in March 1986.

Neither the letter of April 1981 nor the original statement of compliance sent in December 1978, nor the situation report of March 1982, made any reference to measures implementing the duty to make *compulsory* the 'disposal' (collection and/or destruction, regeneration) of waste PCB. There is at present no British legislation preventing someone holding a quantity of waste PCBs on his premises (for example in an old transformer which may begin to leak) until an occupational hazard is posed. There is also nothing to compel someone holding an old transformer to have it collected for destruction or regeneration although it may not be sold (SI 1986 No 902 – see Section 7.2 Restrictions on marketing and use). If, however, the holder has the waste transported he must, under the Section 17 Regulations, prenotify the recipient and disposal may only take place at a licensed plant or site. The duty in the Directive to make 'disposal' compulsory has therefore only partly been implemented by legislation and if there has been full implementation of this duty it must be by some nonlegislative means, although it is hard to see how the word 'compulsory' in the Directive can allow for nonmandatory action. In 1976 the DoE issued a Code of Practice contained in a Waste Management Paper[1] but since this provides nothing which could fulfil the duty, it must be concluded that full compliance has not been achieved.

Another difficulty over compliance arises from ambiguity in the text. It is the practice in Britain, and presumably in other Member States, for small capacitors (for example from domestic fluorescent lights) to be deposited with household waste into landfill sites. This is 'controlled tipping' in the language of the Directive and hence permitted since the relevant Article only prohibits 'uncontrolled tipping'. However, another Article also lays a duty on Member States to make compulsory the 'disposal' (collection and/or destruction, regeneration) of waste PCB contained in equipment no longer capable of being used. This duty, on its own and unqualified by the other prohibition, should result in a prohibition of the practice of tipping even small capacitors on landfill sites. This inconsistency must have been overlooked or ignored when the Directive was being agreed since it leads logically to a meaningless interpretation of the Directive. Thus if the deposit of small capacitors in landfill sites is 'controlled tipping' and hence is permitted by the Directive then, by the same token, there is nothing to prevent a Member State allowing the 'controlled tipping' of large capacitors or even large transformers on landfill sites. This cannot be the intention of the Directive. The conflict between the two prohibitions could be resolved by an amending Directive qualifying the duty to destroy or regenerate PCB-filled equipment to cases where this can reasonably be done, and additionally or alternatively indicating a maximum volume or weight permitted for landfill. (British government officials, however, argue that tipping of small capacitors constitutes 'destruction' since eventually PCBs degenerate. This is an interesting argument but does not overcome the difficulty: if PCB in small capacitors eventually degenerates so will PCB in larger equipment. Yet a purpose of the Directive is to prevent tipping of such equipment).

The existence of the Directive has never been formally drawn to the attention of waste disposal authorities. The Waste Management Paper[1] which was sent to all waste disposal authorities merely said that the EEC would shortly be publishing two Directives relating to PCBs.

Effect on UK practice

The DoE Waste Management Paper of 1976 described the uses of PCBs, the amount of wastes arising, their toxicity, methods of disposal, and set out a code of practice. The DoE plans to revise the Paper.

The major uses of PCBs are now in transformers and large capacitors. Small capacitors for domestic use are virtually no longer filled with PCB. From 1971 the sole British manufacturer restricted sales to dielectric applications and for research purposes and Directive 76/769 (see Section 7.2 Restrictions on marketing and use) made that mandatory. Production of PCB in Britain ceased in 1977. All new uses are now banned.

Small capacitors were used on fluorescent lights and so are bound to find their way into household and commercial waste. The code of practice says that no special precautions need be taken in the disposal of these small capacitors unless there is undue concentration (more than one capacitor per tonne of refuse) at one particular landfill site. The tipping of small capacitors in landfill sites is therefore controlled for the purposes of the Directive by the site licence (or its equivalent for a local authority owned site) and by the normal supervision that takes place at any landfill site and no change has resulted from the Directive.

The code of practice recommends that waste PCBs from transformers and large capacitors be removed for reclamation or incineration. Incineration is to be carried out at over 1100°C for at least two seconds with a minimum excess oxygen content of 3 per cent. The first situation report stated that one firm is licensed for the storage of PCB waste from the refilling of existing electrical equipment, and five high temperature incinerators were licensed for the disposal of PCB waste. These incinerators were all registered under the Alkali Act and controlled by the Inspectorate. The total quantity of PCB incinerated at these five incinerators in the twenty months from 1980 to August 1981 was 227 tonnes at a cost to the disposer of around £600 per tonne of concentrated PCB waste. Some of this waste PCB was imported since most Member States have inadequate incinerator capacity. The practice of incineration will not have been effected by the provisions of the Directive. In 1987 there were three incinerators licensed for disposal of PCB waste.

The Waste Management Paper[1] explained that since 1971 new transformers in Britain containing PCBs had been labelled by the manufacturers. This has been done on a voluntary basis. Some manufacturers have contacted all their customers, even those who bought articles in the 1940s, advising them of the need for adequate disposal. Some retrospective labelling has been carried out on the older equipment still in use but difficulties arise when there are no adequate records. The Waste Management Paper says that identification can be assisted by an examination of the original capital cost and siting of the unit and by the fact that the operating and maintenance procedures for PCB-filled units are different from those filled with hydrocarbon oils.

Despite this advice, instances have been known of PCB-filled transformers being sold for scrap without the scrap merchant being notified of the contents. Since 1981 the movement of such transformers to the scrap merchant will have been an offence under the Section 17 Regulations but the holding of an unused transformer is not an offence. Since 1986 sales of secondhand transformers have been banned. If a transformer begins to leak, and thus creates a hazard, an employer will have obligations to his employees under the Health and Safety at Work etc Act 1974.

In a House of Commons' debate on 16 March 1982 the Minister (Giles Shaw) said that there was no complete record of the number of transformers still in use containing PCBs and that the government was trying to find out. He also explained that factory inspectors have written instructions on the hazards of PCBs and the precautions to be observed, and that if plant containing PCBs is found in the course of inspection appropriate advice is given. The government believes that there are about 3000 transformers with PCB still in use.

Whatever the difficulties in legislating to prevent people unknowingly holding old transformers, the fact remains that the Directive places a duty on

Member States to make *compulsory* the collection and/or destruction, or regeneration, of PCB contained in equipment no longer capable of being used, and this duty has not been fully complied with. This problem must have arisen in other Member States and it would be extremely helpful if the Commission were to compare legislation on the subject. New British legislation could for instance take the form of a requirement on all owners of transformers which are not marked with their contents to have them examined and to 'dispose' of any containing PCB which are no longer in use: if such legislation were to be introduced it would of course be one effect of the Directive.

The Waste Management Paper[1] of 1976 reported that one centre in Britain offered a PCB reclamation service (regeneration in the language of the Directive) but this has since closed and the situation report of 1982 says that there is no regeneration facility in Britain at present. The duty on Member States to promote regeneration is qualified by the words 'as far as possible' and in the absence of facilities regeneration must now be regarded as not possible in Britain.

As with the other waste Directives, the DoE is now obliged to continue to collect information about PCB disposal for the purposes of the three yearly situation reports. The Commission has yet to draw up its own report consolidating the information gathered from the national situation reports.

Further developments

In reply to a European parliamentary question in January 1987, Commissioner Clinton-Davis announced that as a result of a complaint about excessive PCB-related pollution in the Toerfan area of Wales, the Commission had decided to open an infraction procedure against the UK under the Directive. This relates to an incinerator operated by Re-chem International Ltd. The proceedings have not yet been started although there have been discussions between Commission and government officials. The Commissioner also announced that the Commission intended to propose amendments to the Directive relating to a tighter definition of PCB and the need for an inventory of PCBs currently in use.

References
1   Department of the Environment 1976 *Polychlorinated biphenyl (PCB) waste*. HMSO, No 6. (Waste Management Paper).

5.5 Waste oils

75/439/EEC (OJ L194 25.7.75) proposed 20/3/74 – COM(74)334	Directive on the disposal of waste oils.
87/101/EEC (OJ L42 12.2.87) proposed 24.1.85 – COM(85)757	Amendment.
Binding dates	
Notification date	18 June 1975 and 13 January 1987 (87/101)
Formal compliance	18 June 1977 and as amended 1 January 1990
Final date for permits	18 June 1979
Situation reports	every three years – first report due 18 June 1980 assuming the period runs from the date for compliance (see Section 5.1).

Purpose of the Directives

A survey before the first Directive was proposed showed that in some Member States as much as 20 to 60 per cent of all waste oils were disposed of without any control, resulting in a significant proportion of all industrial pollution. The Directives not only deal with this environmental problem but also seek to prevent waste of resources by encouraging regeneration rather than burning of waste oils, to ensure that different financial arrangements adopted to promote safe disposal and recycling do not create barriers to the common market and to prevent the uncontrolled burning of waste oil as fuel.

Summary of the Directives

A general duty is placed on Member States to ensure that the collection and disposal of waste oils causes no avoidable damage to man and the environment. The definition of 'waste oils' is not restricted to lubricating oils but by including the words 'used oils' it excludes wastes from oil refineries for example.

They are also required to give priority to regeneration (producing base oils) 'where technical, economic and organizational constraints so allow'. Burning of waste oils which cannot be regenerated is to be carried out under environmentally acceptable conditions as set out in the Directive with the proviso that it is technically, economically and organizationally feasible. Waste oils that are neither regenerated nor burnt must be safely destroyed or their dumping controlled.

The following are to be prohibited:

discharge of waste oils to any water and drainage systems;
any deposit and/or discharge harmful to the soil;
any uncontrolled discharge of residues from processing;
any processing of waste oils causing air pollution which exceeds the level prescribed by existing provisions.

Where the above aims cannot otherwise be achieved, Member States are to ensure that one or more undertakings carry out the collection and/or disposal of waste oils in assigned zones. Holders of waste oils who cannot comply with the above prohibitions must place the oils at the disposal of these undertakings.

Indemnities may be granted to these collection and disposal undertakings as a reciprocal concession for the obligations imposed on them. These indemnities must not exceed annual uncovered costs and must not cause any significant distortion to competition or give rise to artificial patterns of trade in the products. The indemnities may be financed by a charge on waste oils or on products which after use are transformed into waste oils. The 'polluter pays principle' is to apply.

Member States are required, where necessary to achieve the objectives of the Directive, to carry out public information and promotional campaigns to ensure that waste oils are stored appropriately and collected as far as possible.

Any undertaking *disposing* of waste oil must obtain a permit from the competent authority. The permit may be subject to conditions. The undertakings must supply certain information to the competent authority on request and must be periodically inspected. Any undertaking *collecting* waste oils must be registered and be adequately supervised; a system of permits may be required. Undertakings *regenerating or burning* waste oils may be granted a permit only when the competent authority is satisfied that all appropriate preventive measures have been taken. In the case of regeneration plants, Member States are required to ensure that their operation will cause no avoidable damage to the environment by requiring that the risks from residues are reduced to the minimum and that such residues are disposed of as required by the toxic wastes Directive.

Member States must also take the following measures where waste oils are burnt: plants with a capacity of more than 3 MW must observe emission limits set in the amending Directive (these include heavy metals, chlorine and fluorine but sulphur dioxide and smoke limits are to be set by each Member State); plants under 3 MW must be subject to adequate control. The Commission must be informed of the measures taken for both regeneration and combustion plants. There are further provisions to ensure that PCB/PCTs do not cause hazards. A limit of 50 ppm is laid down for the content of PCB/PCTs in regenerated waste oil.

Every three years Member States must submit a situation report on the disposal of waste oils to the Commission. (Unlike the other waste Directives, there is no obligation on the Commission to submit a consolidated report to the Council or Parliament). In addition, Member States must periodically convey to the Commission their technical expertise, experience gained and results obtained through the application of the measures taken under the Directive. The Commission is to send an overall summary of such information to the Member States. The Commission is also to report to the Council by January 1992 on the measures taken by Member States concerning the operation of regeneration and combustion plants.

Development of the Directives

Under a German law of 1968 controlling the disposal of waste oil, a levy on the sale of lubricants is used to cover losses during waste oil disposal operations. This law provided one inspiration for the Directive but the Commission's work was initiated by a legislative proposal from the Dutch government rather similar to the scheme in Germany and by French draft legislation. This explains why the Directive preceded the framework Directive (Section 5.1). In fact the Directive – agreed at the Council meeting of 7 November 1974 – was the very first to be agreed under the action programme on the environment.

Since the proposed Directive was not considered by either the House of Commons or the House of Lords, there is no parliamentary record of the attitude of the British government at that time other than the inference that can be drawn from the comment of a British member (James Hill) made during the European Parliament's debate. He said that it was not the British government's intention to take powers to pay subsidies to firms which collect or dispose of waste oils, and pointed out that the proposed Directive made it clear that such subsidies were payable at the discretion of the Member States. The lack of parliamentary scrutiny may also explain how Britain came to accept obligations which it has subsequently not completely fulfilled.

The European Parliament welcomed without reservation the provisions aimed at 'banning the destruction of waste oils' and 'making regeneration of waste oils obligatory', thus giving a much more stringent interpretation to the language of the Directive than it bears. The general tone of the European Parliament's resolution was to make the Directive yet more stringent. The Economic and Social Committee concentrated largely on the financial arrangements and proposed an alternative scheme which, in their view, applied the 'polluter pays' principle more rigidly.

Before the Directive was agreed it underwent some changes including an increase from 200 to 500 litres per annum of the threshold above which records have to be kept by establishments producing, collecting or disposing of waste oils.

The major amendments proposed by the Commission in January 1985 were based on the inadequate collection of waste oils and the problems of uncontrolled burning. The proposals were rather more stringent than those adopted: they would have required an unqualified advertising campaign to ensure the maximum collection of waste oils. The UK government took the line that there was no need to change current policy and practice and that there was no evidence that potentially harmful substances in waste oils were likely to cause major problems in combustion. The House of Lords also concluded that the proposals in most respects were not justified; they considered that there was no evidence to support the stringent controls on burning waste oils put forward by the Commission. They thought that regeneration of waste oil was desirable but that the industry itself should promote such action. The regeneration industry wanted the proposed controls on burning because the lack of such controls was forcing them out of business.

Formal compliance in the UK

In October 1977, that is to say nearly four months after the due date, the government submitted a statement to the Commission of how it complied with the first Directive. This referred to the site licensing provisions of the Control of Pollution Act which had been brought into force in June 1976 and to the Deposit of Poisonous Waste Act 1972. It referred to the DoE's advisory Waste Management Paper No 7 on 'mineral oil wastes'[1] dated 1976, and it also referred to the forthcoming Regulations to be made under Section 17 of the Control of Pollution Act. Additionally, the statement referred to various other pieces of legislation controlling the discharge of waste oils to water or soil and controlling air pollution. The reference to the Section 17 Regulations said that these would 'control the handling, storage and disposal of waste oils containing certain impurities in significant quantities', a promise which has since been only partially fulfilled. The statement also referred to the Section 17 Regulations in connection both with the duty on establishments handling more than 500 litres per annum to keep records, and with the duty on holders of waste oil containing impurities to handle them separately. These statements indicate that it was then the intention of the government to implement these provisions of the Directive.

The waste disposal authorities were only informed of the existence of the Directive by being sent a copy of the Waste Management Paper.[1] It contains a reference to the Directive.

In May 1980 the Commission issued a Reasoned Opinion to the effect that since it had not been informed of all the provisions adopted to comply with the Directive, it was compelled to assume that Britain had failed to fulfil its obligations. In July 1980 the government replied by letter that it was now the hope that the Section 17 Regulations would be laid before Parliament by the end of the month, but also went on to argue that the requirements for records and separate handling were already covered by the site licensing provisions of the Control of Pollution Act. The letter concluded (erroneously as is now admitted, see below) that they had the necessary legislation to enable them to fulfil their strict obligations under the Directive. After some further delay, the Section 17 Regulations were laid before Parliament in November 1980, and came into operation on 16 March 1981. They were sent to the Commission in April 1981.

In March 1982 the DoE submitted a situation report to the Commission, as required by the Directive, containing a further statement of how the Directive was implemented. This explained that the discretionary provisions for indemnities to be paid to waste oil collection and disposal undertakings specially authorized on a zonal basis have not been used in Britain:

> The disposal of waste oil to various outlets is not regulated other than in conformity with legislative measures for the protection of the environment. The functions of collection, reclamation and ultimate disposal of waste oils are exercised by producers and private (and public) undertakings within the market economy system.

All other provisions of the first Directive (apart from those requiring separate handling of oil containing impurities, and the keeping of records) including the requirements for permits, were said to be covered by general environmental legislation including the Town and Country Planning Acts, the Alkali Act, the Health and Safety at Work Act, and the Control of Pollution Act. In fact there are no powers to license any category of waste handler, including those who dispose of waste oil. The government is therefore in breach of the Directive. The draft Regulations on waste collection and disposal due to take effect from 1 July 1987 will require licensing of those treating waste oils with a view to their re-use.

The situation report admitted that the requirement that establishments *producing* and *collecting* waste oils should keep records (originally Article 10 – now Article 11) has not been complied with:

Producers are not currently required to maintain records of
the quantity, quality, origin and location of the waste oils they
generate.

Undertakings collecting waste oil are not currently required
to maintain records of the quantity quality, origin of the waste
oil other than to meet the requirements of HM Customs and
Excise in respect of oil purchased for onward sale and subject
to liability for Value Added Tax.

For establishments *disposing* of waste oils the position is different since
waste disposal authorities are empowered to specify in the site licence that
records be kept of the characteristics and qualities of waste oil and oil-bearing
residues handled on site. Additionally, requirements for records apply if the
waste oils contain toxic impurities and so become 'special waste' under the
Section 17 Regulations.

The situation report also admits failure to comply with another provision of
the Directive (Article 8 – which has since been deleted and replaced by more
specific provisons concerning PCB/PCTs and toxic wastes):

There is no specific legal requirement for holders of waste oils
to handle and store these separately according to the content
of impurities.

The draft Regulations on waste collection and disposal due to take effect on 1
July 1987 do not appear to implement the provisions of original Articles 8 and 10
(now Article 11).

There is a further difficulty over implementation since the Directive places a
prohibition on discharges of waste oils to water and drainage systems. Such an
absolute ban – there is no provision for exceptions – must be regarded as
impractical since some waste oils are bound to find their way into industrial
discharges. This is admitted in the Waste Management Paper:[1]

At most premises where oil is used, interceptors are provided
in the drainage system in order to minimize the discharge of
oil to sewers and rivers. . . (para 1.9).

In the past there has tended to be a small chronic contamination of the environment via drainage systems and rivers
but the greater care now exercized in the handling of oil
products has generally resulted in an improvement of the
situation (para 1.10).

Where a discharge to a watercourse is inevitable, the requirement 'no visible oil' is often specified: this in effect may mean
up to 20 ppm depending on the droplet size (para 2.3.1).

The situation report further confirms this by giving figures of over 100 000
tonnes per annum of waste oils disposed to the environment and commenting
that these 'include oily wastes deposited at licensed landfills and oil also contained
in consented effluents discharged to water systems'.

It is clear from these official statements that not only is the prohibition not complied with formally in the sense that there is no legislation banning such discharges but also that such a ban could anyway not be complied with. The fault here lies in the drafting of the Directive and again raises the problem of outright bans which we have encountered in the case of the groundwater Directive (see Section 4.9). On that occasion the House of Commons adopted a resolution that 'This House. . . cannot accept proposals that require a ban on all types of direct discharge, particularly those found acceptable in the United Kingdom'. It is interesting to speculate whether, if the first waste oils Directive had been scrutinized by either of the two Houses of Parliament, it would have passed unscathed.

There is a more general difficulty that goes to the very root of the original Directive and concerns the duty to ensure that 'as far as possible' 'disposal' is to be carried out by recycling. The Directive, inspired as it was by German legislation, envisaged the possibility of a special regime to deal with the recycling of waste oils. If in Britain a significant amount of oil has not been recycled which could and would have been recycled with a system similar to that in Germany, can the government argue that it has indeed ensured that 'as far as possible' waste oils are being recycled?

The German system has been described in an OECD report of 1981.[2] A charge on both virgin and reprocessed oil provides a fund from which aid is distributed to firms which must agree to collect, within specified zones, all waste oils in quantities exceeding 200 litres, and arrange storage when smaller quantities are involved. The oil recovery industry in Britain, as represented by the Chemical Recovery Association, on the other hand believes that the intense competition among a large number of small specialist recovery firms ensures that all recoverable oil in Britain is indeed recovered. The Association would strongly resist the introduction of a system similar to the German system in Britain. A system with some similarities exists in France.

If the claim that all recoverable oil is indeed recovered in Britain is correct then the main obligation of the Directive is complied with, since the indemnity provision of the Directive is an optional one. There is obviously a need for an objective assessment of the merits of the British and German system not merely for the intrinsic interest of such a comparison but also to be able to judge whether a legal obligation has been fulfilled.

The failure of Britain to implement the original Articles 8 and 10 (records for producers of waste oils and separate storage according to the impurity content) has yet to be fully explained. One explanation is that the Directive was rushed through immediately after an oil crisis when all governments were possibly more ready to undertake new obligations. Another is that being the first environmental Directive the British officials concerned were unfamiliar with the procedures and did not fully realize the consequence of a failure to comply with every detailed Article. Parliamentary scrutiny could have led to a discussion of the value of the two provisions. Whatever the reasons, this Directive is the only environmental Directive where failure to implement is not only clear and admitted, but also where there is no stated intention of remedying the deficiency. Despite this admitted deficiency the Commission is turning a blind eye. In reply to a European parliamentary question the Commissioner, Mr Narjes, said that Belgium is the only Member State which has not yet fully implemented the Directive (OJ C177 4.7.83). The adoption of the amending Directive – whose formal compliance date is not till 1990 – provides the occasion for a review in Britain of implementation.

Effect on UK practice

There have been no changes to British practice caused by changes in legislation attributable to the Directive since there have been no such legislative changes. Although the Section 17 Regulations were introduced after the Directive they were not introduced primarily for the purpose of implementing this Directive (see Section 5.2).

In 1977, after the Directive was agreed, the DoE published a Waste Management Paper on mineral oil wastes[1] which included a statement in the foreword that the advice given accorded with the approach established in the Directive. The Paper ended with a code of practice dealing with minimizing environmental problems and encouraging recovery. There is no advice to establishments handling oils to keep records, nor to stock separately oils containing impurities, although caution is urged when burning contaminated oils. Advice on recycling includes the following:

> The total of potentially recoverable oil, generated as small arisings, is considerable and the collection of this oil warrants closer examination: in particular the economics of collection could be improved by the provision of reception points at Civic Amenity Sites and of joint storage facilities for example on industrial trading estates. The dissemination of information on the available reception (collection) facilities for spent oils in local areas is strongly recommended.

The production of the Waste Management Paper may be regarded as one consequence of the Directive.

The situation report submitted to the Commission in March 1982 contains the following figures for Britain to which have been added those reported for 1984 (Table 9).

One effect of the Directive is that the DoE will have to produce comparable figures every three years for further situation reports. The Commission is under no obligation to publish a report comparing figures in the Member States and unless it chooses to do so it will not be easy to tell whether a higher or lower proportion of waste oils is recycled in Britain compared with other countries. Figures from other countries published in the Explanatory Memorandum to the Commission amending the proposal in 1985 – COM(85)757 – are incomplete and not very comparable; in Germany 'most' is recycled; some countries report about 70 per cent re-used, others much less.

If new legislation is introduced, as it should be, to implement the amending Directive – particularly the provisions for adequate supervision for waste oil collectors possibly including a system of permits – then there will have to be changes in practice in Britain.

References

1   Department of the Environment 1979 *Mineral oil wastes*. Waste Management Paper.

2   Organization for Economic Cooperation and Development 1981 *Economic instruments in solid waste management*.

Table 9

| | (in thousand tonnes) | | |
	1979	1980	1984
Lubricating oil sales	1031	896	818
Waste oil generation	533	443	430
Waste oil collection collected for disposal by commercial undertakings	280	270	200
Recycling (by type of undertaking) Recycled in house by generators as fuel/lubricant	160	120	120
Recycled by commercial under- takings as lubricants or fuel	210	200	200
	370	320	320
Recycling: (by type of use) Waste oil to fuel use	280	240	260
Waste oil reprocessed as lubricants and other oil fractions	90	80	60
	370	320	320
Final disposal Incineration	20	10	10
Disposal to the environment	133	113	100
	153	123	110

5.6 Containers for liquids

85/339/EEC (OJ L176 6.7.85) proposed 23.4.81 – COM(81)187 and 28.10.83 – COM(83)638	Directive on containers of liquids for human consumption.

Binding dates

Notification date	3 July 1985
Formal compliance	3 July 1987
Programmes to be communicated to Commission	1 January 1987
Reports to Commission	every four years

Purpose of the Directive

The purpose of the Directive is to reduce the burden on the environment and to save energy and raw materials by reducing the number of containers in waste for disposal.

Summary of the Directive

Member States are to draw up programmes for reducing the tonnage and/or volume of containers in waste for disposal. The Directive applies to sealed containers of all types (excluding barrels and casks) containing liquids for human consumption set out in an Annex (yoghurt is excluded but ethyl alcohol and vinegar are specifically included). The first programme is to start from 1 January 1987 and will be revised and updated at least every four years. Measures include: developing consumer education, facilitating refilling and recycling of containers; promoting selective collection of nonrefillable containers and recovery of materials used; encouraging technical development and marketing of new containers and maintaining and if possible increasing the proportion of refilled and recycled containers. Member States may take these measures either by legislative or administrative means or by voluntary agreements. New refillable containers must be clearly marked to indicate that they are refillable. Existing glass bottle systems are exempted for ten years from this requirement: well-established systems (such as in the UK) for recovery of glass milk bottles are also exempted. Draft programmes have to be submitted to the Commission in advance for vetting, and reports have to be sent every four years to the Commission on the results achieved in accordance with guidelines set out in an Annex.

Development of the Directive

Though the proposal had its origin in the Commission's general programme on waste, the Danish government's subsequent proposal to introduce legislation making compulsory standardized returnable containers for beer and soft drinks undoubtedly had some influence on subsequent discussions. The Danish legislation was declared to be a barrier to trade, but the proposal might have legitimized it. One influence was a 'Bottle Bill' which came into force in the State of Oregon, USA in 1972.

The process of getting this Directive adopted proved to be among the longer drawn out ones. There was much discussion with representatives of industry and consumer protection as well as between governments before the Commission made its original proposal and their original ideas were much modified. (Nine drafts were produced.) In June 1980 it was reported that the proposal would provide for a ban on ring-pull cans and mandatory recycling measures. The proposal when it appeared in April 1981 did not contain these provisions. It did propose setting specific obligations on Member States to fix estimates for each type of material each year for the increase in recycled and refillable containers and for the reduction in containers in household waste. The measures by which Member States achieved these targets were left to them, but if for example they were to decide to introduce a deposit system, containers should bear the symbol 'R' and consumers informed of the amount of the deposit. There was also a provision for encouraging the standardization of containers and for subsequent proposals by the Commission to this end. The proposal aroused much controversy and little support. Generally trade and industry representatives were opposed to it, environmental interests thought it did not go far enough and consumer protection groups were concerned about consumer choice. There were also concerns expressed about barriers to trade being erected. On the other hand, support was usually given to the aims of the proposal.

The progress through the European Parliament well illustrates the differences in views. After nearly a year in preparation a draft report was looked at three times in the course of 1982 by the Committee on the Environment, Public Health and Consumer Protection. The Committee rejected the Commission's proposal and asked the rapporteur for a new motion for a resolution. In January 1983 the Committee rejected the new motion for a resolution. Instead they narrowly voted for a motion calling on the Commission to replace the proposal for a Directive but tried to find a compromise with the Commission. Subsequently after discussion with the Commission, the Environment Committee agreed a simplified form of a Directive. This was put to the Parliament which in July 1983 finally agreed to the simplified form but only as a Recommendation; it would require Member States to draw up four-yearly programmes to reduce container waste and encourage refillable and recyclable containers.

Rather earlier the House of Lords had produced their own report which made clear the very differing views summarized above. The Lords believed the proposed Directive would be unenforceable and rejected it outright. They saw some virtue in a Directive which would oblige each Member State to formulate and publish a policy to carry out the objectives of reducing waste and encouraging refilling and recycling. One point that led to further discussion was the belief that the proposal would mean that the objectives set would be legally binding, a measure opposed by the UK Government. The Commission apparently had in mind the legally enforceable 'contrats de branche' in France, but were prepared to consider an amendment which would refer to the objectives being ones which Member States would endeavour to attain.

In October 1983 the Commission put forward an amended proposal which followed the European Parliament's proposal except for maintaining it as a Directive and retaining milk, vinegar and edible oils in the Annex. The House of Commons continued to support the government view that no Directive was needed but the House of Lords reported in favour of the amended proposal. In the event it was negotiation in the Council machinery that decided the final form. One particular UK point was met by the requirement that Member States give advance notice of the measures which they intended to take to the Commission for vetting. The UK had feared that barriers to trade in containers could be erected and obtained an assurance from the Commission that when examining these draft programmes, they would seek to ensure that there would be no discrimination between different types of container systems or between different types of packaging.

Formal compliance by the UK

Compliance is required by 3 July 1987. The Department of Trade and Industry, after consultation with some sixty-five organizations with an interest in the subject, submitted to the Commission in March 1987 an outline programme to show how the UK proposed to implement the Directive. This outline covers the six programme items under four separate types of material (glass, metals, plastic and paper/composites) outlining the measures to be taken and by whom. Guidelines stress that the programme is based on what is feasible in present economic, industrial and market conditions and will be implemented by voluntary agreements without recourse to legislation. Additional costs for all concerned are to be kept to a minimum. It is intended to submit further details of the measures to be taken, including availability of the information required for the four-yearly report before 3 July 1987, the deadline for compliance.

Effect on UK practice

It is too early to consider any direct effect, but comparisons of figures for recycling and re-use of containers with other Member States, show that there appears to be much that can be done in this country. One view, that of the Local Authority Recycling Advisory Committee (LARAC) is that a 50 per cent recycling target for each packaging material should be set to be achieved by the end of the century by means of voluntary agreements between the government and container manufacturers.[1] The government believes, as does UK industry, that market forces are already promoting savings in energy and raw materials and reduction in waste arising. To keep costs down industry has been maintaining a development programme aimed at producing lighter, thinner containers and progressive improvements can be expected.

References

1   LARAC Working Paper No 1 1986 *Recommendations on the EC Directive on containers of liquids for human consumption.*

5.7 Sewage sludge

86/278/EEC (OJ L181 4.7.86)
proposed 13.9.82 – COM(82)527
and 25.5.84 – COM(84)240

Directive on the protection of the
environment and in particular of the
soil, when sewage sludge is used in
agriculture.

Binding dates
   Notification date   17 June 1986
   Formal compliance   17 June 1989
   Situation reports   17 June 1991 and subsequently every
                                      four years.

Purpose of the Directive

The Directive has a double purpose: to ensure that human beings, animals, plants and the environment are fully safeguarded against the possibility of harmful effects from the uncontrolled spreading of sewage sludge on agricultural land; and to promote the correct use of sewage sludge on such land. The Directive could prove to be a first step in a Community policy on soil protection.

Summary of the Directive

Sewage sludge application must be banned whenever the concentration of one or more metals in the soil already exceeds the limits laid down at national level in compliance with the Directive. The use of sludge must also be regulated to ensure that heavy metal accumulation in the soil shall not exceed these limits. Regulation by Member States may be by either of two methods. Upper limits can be set on the maximum quantity of sewage sludge which may be applied per unit area per year while observing the limits for metal concentrations in sludge selected from the ranges laid down in the Directive. Alternatively, the limits on metal addition per unit area per year, as laid down in the Directive, can be applied. Limit values for concentrations of heavy metals to be observed are set out in three Annexes covering soil, sludge for use in agriculture, and amounts which may be added annually to agricultural land, based on a ten-year average.

Sludge must be treated before use but Member States may authorize under their own conditions the use of untreated sludge if it is injected or worked into the soil. Member States are to set a minimum period of not less than three weeks after sludge has been spread before grazing or harvesting can take place. Its use is also banned on soil in which fruit and vegetable crops (except fruit trees) are grown, as well as for ten months preceding harvesting of fruit and vegetables which are normally in direct contact with the soil and eaten raw.

Where the pH of soil is below 6, Member States are required to take account of the increased mobility and availability of metals and if necessary set tighter limits than they have laid down elsewhere.

The requirements for analysis and sampling of soil are specified in two Annexes. Comprehensive records are to be kept of quantities of sludge produced and used in agriculture, its composition, how treated and where used. Records of analyses must regularly be provided to users of sludge. Information on methods of treatment and results of analyses must be released to competent authorities upon request.

The usual Committee for adaptation to technical progress is set up to allow changes to the Annexes but is limited to those concerning sampling and analysis methods only.

Member States are to submit a first consolidated report on the operation of the Directive five years after notification; subsequent ones are to be every four years.

Development of the Directive

The subject of sewage sludge has been of concern to the Community before even the Community Environment Programme came into existence. In 1971 a research project on certain aspects of sewage sludge was initiated as part of the work of European Cooperation in the field of Scientific and Technical Research (COST) and became known as COST project 68. This was extended in 1977 (Decision 77/651/EEC OJ L267 19.10.1977) by a three-year research project which became part of the environment research programme and a third phase was begun in 1983. It is claimed that this proposal for a Directive followed from the conclusion of the COST 68 project but references in the second Community environment programme and the report on 'Progress made in connection with the Environment Programme' (COM(80)222) had foreshadowed it.

Drafts of the Commission proposal were widely discussed before the final proposal was submitted. The main elements of the proposal were the application of uniform limits on the metal content of sewage sludge used for agriculture, on the rate at which metals could be disposed on such land by means of sludge, and on the metal content of soils to which sludge was applied. In other words, not only were the quality standards to be applied to the receiving medium specified but also limit values on the content of the material discharged at any one time and over a period. Also proposed were curbs on sludge use in parks and woodlands and a no-grazing period of six weeks after sludge application.

The UK with by far the largest proportion of the population and industry connected to sewage works in the Community and with a consequent large amount of sewage sludge produced and used for agricultural land, had a particular interest. It also felt that it had considerable experience of controlling the use of sewage sludge. Since 1977 there had been guidelines for disposal of sewage sludge to land which were revised and extended in 1981.[1] The Royal Commission on Environmental Pollution in its *Seventh report on agriculture and pollution*[2] in 1979 showed its concern and made several recommendations which were considered and reported on in the *Report of the sub-committee on the disposal of sewage sludge to land*.

The main element of the UK guidelines consisted of recommendations for maximum permissible additions of potentially toxic elements to types of soil over a period of thirty years. Compared with the Commission's proposals they were very flexible and enabled users to take account of very varying conditions. The UK was from the start opposed to the proposal's rigidity in applying uniform limits throughout the Community. The government was also opposed to the following six-week no-grazing limit, arguing for a three-week period as in its own guidelines; relaxation of some of the proposed limits on metals in soils; an exemption for 'sludge farms', areas of land adjacent to sewage works; and removal of the proposal to ban sludge from land with a pH below 6. It was claimed that additional costs otherwise would be £20 million a year. In the main the government's objections were supported by the House of Lords in its report and debate on the proposal.

Four years of negotiations led to a Directive which met a great many of the UK objections. Member States may now select from a range of limit values for metal concentrations in setting national standards. The emphasis has shifted from a rigid control of sludge quality by mandatory limits towards preventing a build-up of metals in soils. Other changes include a provision allowing certain upper limits to be exceeded on strictly monitored sludge farms; an exemption from normal limits for some metals on soils with a pH above 7; three-week no-grazing period limit and dropping of any reference to curbs on the uses of sewage sludge in parks and woodlands. In addition the banning of sludge application of soils with a pH below 6 was replaced by a requirement for Member States to impose tighter restrictions on such soils where found necessary. On the other hand, the Directive applies to all sewage works (except in certain reporting requirements) whereas the proposal provided for exemption for such works serving populations of 5000 or less.

Formal compliance in the UK

Government has not yet indicated how the Directive is to be implemented. Clearly the first step will be to review and update as necessary the existing guidelines for water authorities and other sludge disposal authorities (see above – Development of the Directive). The guidelines are however contained in a sub Committee's report; there would be advantage in spelling out the new requirements for guidelines as such in a separate document, for instance as part of a Circular, which can be related to the Directive.

Effect on UK practice

In general, the Directive is unlikely to have much impact on current practices. Metal levels in most sewage sludges are well within the limit values in the Directive and the Directive otherwise gives the discretion to operate the current guidelines with certain revisions, and most sludge producers are already introducing recording systems which can cope with the requirements of the Directive.

References

1   Standing Technical Committee 1981 *Report No 20 – Report of the sub-committee on the disposal of sewage sludge to land*. Department of the Environment/National Water Council, June 1981.

2   Royal Commission on Environmental Pollution 1979 *Seventh Report. Agriculture and pollution*. HMSO.

CHAPTER 6

Air

6.0 Relevant British Legislation

British air pollution policy is marked by a great divide, but to assume that the division lies between industrial emissions on the one hand and domestic emissions on the other, or between 'noxious gas' – as the legislation calls it – and smoke is to come sufficiently close to the mark as to cause confusion. These divisions are important but not so important for the shaping of British policy as the division of responsibility for controlling emissions between the national inspectorates and local authorities. Thus unlike both water pollution and waste disposal, responsibility for air pollution is only partly a local or regional matter. But even at the national level the task of controlling air pollution has been devolved to administrative agencies: the Industrial Air Pollution Inspectorate in England and Wales (formerly the Alkali Inspectorate) and the Industrial Pollution Inspectorate in Scotland. Indeed, the Secretary of State has rather limited powers over air pollution and although he has some powers to set emission standards (for grit and dust under the Clean Air Act 1968) and product standards for fuels, he has no general powers to set emission standards or air quality standards, to direct industries to use one fuel rather than another even in an emergency, or to set ceilings on total emissions in particular areas or nationally. This may change if proposals made in December 1986 are implemented (see below – Further developments).

A history of the separate development of controls over 'noxious gases' and smoke and of the powers of the Alkali Inspectorate and local authorities has been written by Eric Ashby and Mary Anderson[1] and it is by reference to its origins that British air pollution policy is best understood.

'Scheduled' processes
The Inspectorate is responsible for 'scheduled' processes giving rise to particularly noxious or offensive emissions. Once a process is scheduled the Inspectorate is responsible for all emissions from it including smoke. The number of scheduled processes has increased steadily since 1863 when the first Alkali Act was passed, so as to cover today over sixty processes involving over two thousand plants. The Inspectorate now operates partly under the Alkali etc Works Regulation Act 1906, which consolidated various Acts passed after 1863, and partly under the Health and Safety at Work etc Act 1974 which will eventually replace the 1906 Act completely. The Inspectorate became part of the Health and Safety Executive when it was established under the 1974 Act but in 1986 was transferred to the Department of the Environment. The 1906 and 1974 Acts allow the Secretary of State by regulation to extend the Schedule in the 1906 Act listing the processes under the Inspectorate's control.

Scheduled processes must be registered annually with the Inspectorate and any changes in the process and ownership must be notified. Registration is not, however, the equivalent of the granting of a licence to emit a certain quantity or quality of gases (similar to the 'consent' given subject to conditions for a discharge to a river), but instead there is a statutory duty on the operator of the process, and on the Inspectorate, to ensure that the process is operated using the 'best practicable means for preventing the escape of noxious or offensive gases. . . and for rendering such gases where discharged harmless and inoffensive'. One of the conditions of first registration is that the plant must have such appliances as the Inspectorate considers necessary to comply with the requirements of the Act.

The way the term 'best practicable means' (bpm) is interpreted is therefore of considerable importance. It has never been more concisely defended than by an assistant alkali inspector in 1876:

> Some persons have expressed a fear that this bpm is not sufficiently definite and binding on the manufacturer. For my part I feel it to be more binding than a definite figure, even if that could be given, for it is an elastic band, and may be kept always tight as the knowledge of the methods of suppressing the evils complained of increases[1]

The way the elastic band is kept tight is by the Inspectorate from time to time redefining what they mean by bpm. In practice the Inspectorate discusses the ways of reducing emissions with representatives of the industry concerned and brings to bear its own technical knowledge and knowledge of what has been done abroad. The Inspectorate then publishes the conclusions in *Notes on best practicable means*. These *Notes* will describe treatment plant to be used and its maintenance; methods of operation; and also may include a 'presumptive limit' for emissions, that is, a numerical limit on the amount of a pollutant per cubic metre of gases emitted from a chimney stack. If the limit is being met then there is normally a presumption that the 'best practicable means' are being used. These 'presumptive limits' are therefore emission standards, but since they are not enshrined in legislation but are set administratively they can be tightened by the Inspectorate as required in keeping with advances in abatement technology. The *Notes on best practicable means* including the 'presumptive limits' apply nationally although inspectors can exercise discretion in modifying them to take into account the circumstances of particular plants and local conditions. Cost is a major factor taken into account. The Chief Alkali Inspector in his 1966 Annual Report explained that:

> the expression 'best practicable means' takes into account economics in all its financial implications, and we interpret this not just in the narrow sense of a works dipping into its own pockets, but including the wider effect on the community[2]

The term 'best practicable means' has been authoritatively discussed most recently in the Chief Inspector's report for 1981.[3] However, it is not abundantly clear from that description or from other literature to what extent the Inspectorate takes into account local environmental conditions in deciding on the 'best practicable means' for a particular plant although it is the view of the Inspectorate that it should be taken into account and that there should be some variation. The Royal Commission on Environmental Pollution in its fifth report[4] explained (para 91) that the District Inspector 'has discretion to impose tighter (but not laxer) requirements than the general best practicable means would call for if this is justified by particular local conditions'. Since the duty under the Act is first to prevent 'the escape of noxious or offensive gases' whether harm is being caused or not, it can indeed be inferred that the 'presumptive limit' should not be relaxed merely because a particular plant is remote from a centre of population. The position seems to be that laxer standards than the 'presumptive limits' are permitted for existing plant and that for new plant more stringent conditions are sometimes applied but that less than the 'presumptive limit' is not permitted. The provisions of 'best practicable means', other than the 'presumptive limits', appear to be more open to variation including the height of chimneys. The desirability of having some uniformity across the country was nevertheless explained by one Chief Inspector in the following words:

> It is to the trade's advantage to have uniformity of application
> of control measures and it would be unjust to give one works a
> commercial advantage over another.[5]

The term 'best technical means' or equivalent words are not be found in British legislation although they are used in other countries. The term 'best technical means' could be expected to differ from 'best practicable means' by taking no account of local circumstances and less account of cost. It cannot presumably take no account of cost since almost any amount of abatement is theoretically possible but at a price which no one would be prepared to pay. All such phrases as 'best practicable means' or 'best technical means' can only be understood by a close examination of how they are interpreted and applied which are bound to be matters of tradition that evolve within an inspectorate or agency. They are therefore likely to cause considerable problems in Community legislation.

Processes not 'scheduled'

All processes that are not scheduled are the responsibility of local authorities whose powers are exercised by environmental health officers. The Clean Air Act 1956 (amended in 1968) strengthened the powers of local authorities previously contained in the Public Health Act 1936 to control nonscheduled processes. However, the Clean Air Acts only cover combustion processes and the emissions of smoke, grit and dust.

The 1956 Act prohibits dark smoke from being emitted from any trade or industrial premises. Any new furnace (other than domestic boilers) must be capable so far as practicable of being operated continuously without emitting smoke, and local authorities must be notified of any proposal to install a new furnace. Plants over a certain size must be equipped to the satisfaction of the local authority with plant to arrest the emission of grit and dust, and the height of a new chimney must be approved by the local authority who must be satisfied that it will be high enough to prevent the emissions becoming prejudicial to health or a nuisance.[6] The Secretary of State has made Regulations setting limits on the emission of grit and dust from furnaces.

Emissions other than smoke, grit and dust from processes that are not scheduled can only be controlled by the statutory nuisance provisions of the Public Health Act 1936 or the Public Health (Scotland) Act 1897. If a local authority is satisfied that a nuisance exists it must serve on the person responsible a notice requiring him to take whatever steps are necessary to abate the nuisance. This procedure cannot be used to anticipate a nuisance so that control over gases from nonscheduled processes are limited (eg the emissions of metals from foundries).

The Control of Pollution Act 1974 includes a Part IV dealing with air. This part does not have the same comprehensive character as the parts on water and waste but it does extend the powers of local authorities to obtain information about emissions – though these are difficult to use.

Domestic smoke

Smoke from domestic chimneys is also the responsibility of local authorities. Under the Clean Air Acts local authorities may make smoke control orders prohibiting the emission of smoke from any building in a specified area although specific buildings may be exempted. In these areas householders who have to change their means of cooking or heating may receive grants. The 'smoke control order' has been the principal instrument of policy to reduce pollution of air by smoke that was such a feature of British towns within even the last twenty-five years, but it remains a matter for conjecture to what extent the marked improvement has been advanced by smoke control orders and to what extent it is the consequence of a spontaneous change from open fires to other forms of heating. As we will see in Section 6.2 the smoke control order is the principal instrument being used to implement Directive 80/779 setting air quality standards for smoke and sulphur dioxide.

Composition of fuels

The Control of Pollution Act 1974 also gives the Secretary of State power to make Regulations controlling the sulphur content of oil fuels and the composition of motor fuels including lead in petrol and sulphur in diesel fuel. These have been used to implement Directives (see below).

Vehicle emissions

Vehicle emissions can be controlled by specifying the construction of the vehicle itself as well as by specifying the composition of the fuel. The Secretary of State for Transport has powers under the Road Traffic Act 1972 to make Regulations on vehicle emissions and, as will be seen, a whole series of such Regulations has been made to implement various Directives.

Further developments

In December 1982 the government announced a comprehensive review of air pollution legislation but a consultation[7] paper setting out proposed changes did not appear until four years later. There were two reasons for this delay: first the officials responsible had to devote much of their time to negotiating EC legislation; and second, there was a battle, in which the Royal Commission on Environmental Pollution played a major part, to move the Industrial Air Pollution Inspectorate from the Health and Safety Executive to the Department of the Environment. This move was made in 1986. At the same time the government announced that it was creating a unified pollution inspectorate (to be known as Her Majesty's Inspectorate of Pollution) from the existing Industrial Air Pollution Inspectorate, the Hazardous Waste Inspectorate, the radiochemical Inspectorate and a new Water Inspectorate (being formed to supplement the work of the water authorities). The new unified inspectorate began to operate on 1 April 1987, one of its aims being to apply the knowledge of process technology to reduce waste generation by industry so as to minimize its overall impact on air, water and land. The new inspectorate will rely initially on existing legislation, but it is foreseen that new legislation may be required since the existing powers of the different inspectorates are so different and there is no requirement on them to consider effects on the other environmental media. Any new legislation to be introduced as a result of the creation of the unified inspectorate will be additional to that proposed in the December 1986 consultation paper on new air pollution legislation.

The proposals in the consultation paper[7] issued in December 1986 have been much influenced by Community legislation. The Secretary of State would be empowered to set air quality standards (whether nationally or by area) by Regulations, and would also be empowered to set emission limits (whether nationally or by area) by Regulations for specified emissions or from specified processes. This significant change can be achieved, the government believes, without abandoning the principle of 'best practicable means'. Another significant change is that the schedule of processes giving rise to particularly noxious or offensive emissions will be divided into two parts A and B, and the local authorities would be given powers to control and to grant prior approval to plants in part B. A system of written consents would also be introduced which would be accessible to the public.

References

1   Ashby Eric and Anderson Mary 1981 *The politics of clean air*. Clarendon Press, Oxford.

2   McLaughlin J and Foster M J 1982 *The law and practice relating to pollution control in the United Kingdom*. Graham and Trotman.

3   Health and Safety Executive 1982 *Industrial air pollution 1981*. HMSO.

4   Royal Commission on Environmental Pollution 1976 *Air pollution control: an integrated approach. Fifth Report*. HMSO.

5   Ireland F E 1971 *Control of special industrial emissions in Britain*. Proceedings of the Second International Clean Air Congress. Academic Press, London and New York.

6   Department of the Environment 1976 *Pollution control in Britain: how it works*. HMSO, No 9 (Pollution paper).

7   Department of the Environment, December 1986 *Air pollution control in Great Britain – review and proposals – a consultation paper*.

6.1 Sulphur content of gas oil

75/716/EEC (OJ L307 27.11.75) proposed 11.2.74 – COM(74)158	Directive on the approximation of the laws of the Member States relating to the sulphur content of certain liquid fuels.
87/219/EEC (OJ L91 3.4.87) proposed 16.7.85 – COM(85)377	Amendment.

Binding dates
75/716
Notification date	25 November 1975
Formal compliance	25 August 1976
Limits to be met	1 October 1976
	1 October 1980

87/219
Notification date	2 April 1987
Formal compliance	31 December 1988
Limits to be met	1 January 1989

Purpose of the Directives

A limit is set on the sulphur content of gas oil both to eliminate barriers to trade resulting from different limits in different countries and also to reduce air pollution by sulphur dioxide.

'Gas oil' is a term of art used to describe certain medium distillates used mostly for domestic heating and cooking and also 'Derv' for diesel-engined motor vehicles. Gas oil differs from 'fuel oil' which is a term of art for heavier oil used for industrial heating and in power stations. Gas oil is also sometimes referred to as 'light fuel oil'. A Directive on the sulphur content of fuel oil was proposed but never agreed (see Section 6.2).

Summary of the Directives

75/716
The earlier Directive 75/716 allows only two grades of gas oil to be sold in the Community. Type A, having the lower sulphur content, may be used without restriction, while Type B is only to be used in zones designated by Member States. These zones are to be either where ground level concentrations of atmospheric sulphur dioxide are sufficiently low, or where gas oil accounts for an insignificant proportion of sulphur dioxide pollution. Member States must inform the Commission and the other Member States of the Type B zones they have designated with their reasons.

The sulphur compound content of both types is to be reduced in two stages: from 1 October 1976 0.5 per cent (by weight) for type A, 0.8 per cent for type B; from October 1980 (1985 for Ireland) 0.3 per cent for type A and 0.5 per cent for type B. Member States are to ensure sampling of the sulphur content. A reference method for determining the sulphur content is specified.

If, as a result of sudden changes in crude oil supplies, there is a shortage of desulphurization capacity, a Member State may allow the use of gas oil with more than the specified sulphur content but must inform the Commission. The Commission, after consulting the other Member States, must decide within three months on the duration and details of the derogation.

Gas oil used in power stations and shipping and contained in the tanks of inland waterway vessels or motor vehicles crossing zones or crossing a frontier into the Community is excluded from the Directive.

87/219
The text of Directive 75/716 is entirely replaced by a new text. From 1 January 1989 the distinction between types A and B is dropped and the sulphur content is not to exceed 0.3 per cent. Member States may set a limit of 0.2 per cent in certain circumstances, but may not prohibit marketing of gas oil with a sulphur content of less than 0.2 per cent. The circumstances in which a sulphur content of 0.2 per cent is required includes the need to meet air quality standards in the zones provided by Article 4 of Directive 80/779 (see Section 6.2) and where damage to the environment or the national heritage caused by total sulphur dioxide emissions requires a lower sulphur content than 0.3 per cent.

By April 1990 the Commission is to submit a proposal with a view to the establishment of a single value.

Development of the Directives
In 1969 the Commission had instituted a general programme of measures to eliminate technical or nontariff barriers to trade. As a result of a study of the difficulties encountered by the oil industry in adjusting to the different requirements of different Member States the Commission incorporated 'petroleum oils used for heating or for the propulsion of motor vehicles' into the general programme in May 1973. This step preceded the first action programme on the environment of November 1973 which, however, mentioned the general programme as a possible instrument of environmental policy and, by way of example, referred to a limit on the sulphur content of gas oil. By the time it was formally proposed, the Directive was therefore seen both as an environmental protection measure and as a measure to facilitate trade. From a trade point of view, what matters is that the limits are the same in the different Member States, and the contribution of the Community's environmental policy has been to ensure that the limits are as low as reasonably possible.

A spur to action was provided by information supplied in 1973 by the Dutch, French, Italian and German governments of proposals for further legislation concerned with fuels and it may be assumed that the idea of Type A and B gas oils with Type B being restricted to certain zones stems from one or more of these proposals for domestic legislation. The principle is in some respects the same as the smoke control areas of the Clean Air Act 1956.

The Economic and Social Committee and the European Parliament both welcomed the proposal while criticizing points of detail. Both agreed with the opinion of the Commission that implementation of the Directive would not entail any appreciable increase in costs for the refining industry nor any significant increase in fuel consumption. The Commissioner, Mr Gundelach, in the Parliament's debate contrasted this with heavy fuel oils for which desulphurization would create greater problems. He promised to propose a Directive on fuel oil and although he did not specifically mention a proposed Directive on air quality standards for sulphur dioxide (see Section 6.2), an obligation to consider this possibility was placed on the Commission by Article 6 of Directive 75/716.

The Economic and Social Committee made the point that Type A gas oil should be prescribed throughout the Community for use in road and rail transport without the establishment of special zones because of the difficulties of changing fuel and marketing two grades of fuel. This suggestion was not adopted in the Directive but has been adopted in Britain.

There can have been little argument about the proposed Directive in the Council of Ministers because the Directive was agreed within two years of being proposed and differs only in detail from the proposal.

In proposing an amending Directive in 1985 the main points made by the Commission were that gas oil amounted to only 6 per cent of total sulphur emissions in the Community, that the average sulphur content was already 0.34 per cent so that the lower limit would cause few problems to industry and the consumer, and that as costs at the refinery increased steeply only when the sulphur content was reduced below 0.2 per cent, there was no justification for going below that figure. Adoption at the June 1986 Environment Council was blocked by Denmark whose Parliament insisted on being able to impose a lower limit than 0.2 per cent, a view supported by the European Parliament. In November 1986 it was Spain that blocked adoption by objecting to States being permitted to fix a 0.2 per cent limit. Both these objections were withdrawn.

Formal compliance in the UK

No new primary legislation was introduced after the Directive was agreed in order to implement it because Sections 75 to 77 of the Control of Pollution Act 1974 already gives the Secretary of State powers to make regulations controlling the content of liquid fuels. These powers, however, had been introduced in anticipation of a Directive as was explained by the Minister, Baroness Young, during the Committee stage (4 February 1974) in the House of Lords on the Protection of the Environment Bill:

> It is perfectly true that one reason why it (the clause) is included is because the Commission of the European Economic Communities are preparing a draft Directive on the sulphur content of gas oil, which is a kind of fuel oil; and, on the assumption that a Directive on those or similar lines will eventually emerge, this clause provides the necessary powers for its implementation in the United Kingdom.

Although the Protection of the Environment Bill never reached the Statute Books because of the resignation of the government in February 1974, the Control of Pollution Act introduced by the new government was very similar to the earlier Bill.

On 8 December 1976, that is three and a half months after the due date for compliance, two Regulations made under the Control of Pollution Act 1974 were laid before Parliament:

SI 1976 No 1988 The Oil Fuel (Sulphur Content of Gas Oil) Regulations 1976; SI 1976 No 1989 The Motor Fuel (Sulphur Content of Gas Oil) Regulations 1976.

On 10 December a circular letter to local authorities (DoE Circular 105/76) was jointly published by the Departments of the Environment, Transport and the Welsh Office summarizing the Directive and explaining that the Regulations had been made to implement it. The circular stated that it had been decided that only the lower sulphur content (Type A) gas oil was to be used on roads and that the rest of the UK was to be regarded as a zone in which the higher sulphur content (Type B) gas oil was to be permitted. The circular stated that weights and measures' authorities were to be responsible for enforcing the Motor Fuel Regulations and that the Oil Fuel Regulations were to be enforced in England and Wales by the Alkali Inspectorate and by district councils.

The Commission had earlier asked why the government had not complied with the Directive by the due date. In the letter of reply of 22 December 1976 the government enclosed the two Regulations and regretted the delay. It seems that this was caused by the lawyers in the DoE being involved with the consequences of that year's drought, but the letter to the Commission explained that no adverse consequences had resulted because the sulphur content of the relevant fuels was already below the permitted levels.

In March 1977 the Commission asked for an explanation of the designation of the zones which the Directive required Member States to provide it with. The government explained in reply that in the UK ground level concentrations of atmospheric sulphur dioxide were sufficiently low to permit the general use of Type B gas oil apart from the road system where concentrations were higher. For this reason, the road system had been made a zone for Type A only (an exception being made for the Orkney and Shetland Islands because of the low volume of traffic there). This letter of explanation was then sent to all other Member States as required by the Directive.

It is not clear whether such an extraordinarily shaped zone – the whole of the UK minus the road system – was ever anticipated by the Commission in drafting the Directive. The desirability of allowing only low-sulphur content fuel for motor vehicles had been set out in the report of the Economic and Social Committee and the simpler way to have introduced this possibility into the Directive would have been to provide for restrictions on Type B gas oil by use as well as by geographical zone.

The Motor Fuel Regulations extend to Northern Ireland but the Oil Fuel Regulations do not. Separate Regulations were therefore made for Northern Ireland for Oil Fuel under the Pollution Control and Local Government (Northern Ireland) Order 1978 but these did not come into operation until 5 March 1979, two and a half years after the due date.

New Regulations will be required to implement the amending Directive 87/219.

Effect on UK practice

According to an explanatory memorandum submitted by the DoE to the House of Commons in December 1974 gas oil, including 'Derv', then represented about 20 per cent of the total inland market for oil fuels. The memorandum explained that the sulphur content of Derv, which represented 5 per cent of the total, was already 0.3 per cent while that of the rest of the gas oil was then about 0.8 per cent. This suggests that there was no difficulty in meeting the standards set by the Directive from 1 October 1976. (A British Standard 2869 had previously specified non-mandatory requirements for petroleum fuels for diesel engines with a sulphur content limit of 0.5 per cent, but notwithstanding this standard the majority of oil companies were supplying diesel with less.)

The explanatory memorandum further explained that as North Sea oil has a sulphur content of about 0.2 per cent, its use in Britain would lessen the demand for desulphurization of gas oil obtained from Middle East crude. The Directive was therefore 'likely to have relatively small effects in the United Kingdom in terms of desulphurization costs to the industry'. The explanatory memorandum went on to say that the use of low-sulphur content fuels should secure some small environmental improvement, although this was difficult to quantify. Since Middle East crude continues to be refined in Britain the Directive's second stage reduction to 0.5 per cent will have had some effects on the amount of desulphurization required in Britain.

In Britain a large proportion of domestic heating is by North Sea gas, and cooking is by gas or electricity. Gas oil is used in Britain to some extent for central heating and is also used as a starter fuel for generating plant which normally runs on fuel oil. In some other Member States gas oil is much more widely used for domestic heating and cooking and has been the source of much sulphur dioxide pollution in towns. The Directive can be expected to have had a more substantial effect in those countries particularly if they use Middle East crude.

The government did not justify its decision to designate the whole of the UK – except the road system – for Type B gas oil by arguing that gas oil accounts for only an insignificant proportion of atmospheric pollution. Instead it argued that ground level concentrations of sulphur dioxide are sufficiently low (except on roads).

6.2 Air quality – smoke and sulphur dioxide

80/779/EEC (OJ L229 30.8.80) proposed 25.2.76 – COM(76)48	Directive on air quality limit values and guide values for sulphur dioxide and suspended particulates.

Binding dates

Notification date	17 July 1980
Formal compliance	17 July 1982
Limit values to be met, if possible	1 April 1983
Improvement plans to be submitted to	1 October 1982
Commission where limit values not met	
Limit values must be met	1 April 1993

Purpose of the Directive

Although air quality guidelines had previously been set in some Member States, and had been set mandatorily in the Federal Republic of Germany, the Directive is the first piece of Communitywide legislation to lay down mandatory air quality standards. The standards relate to sulphur dioxide and smoke and are intended to protect human health and the environment, but the Directive foresees Member States setting more stringent standards in zones needing special environmental protection. This Directive is only very indirectly connected with the problem of acid rain and forest damage. The Community's principle responses to these problems are attempts to reduce emissions from vehicles and stationary plants (see Sections 6.7 and 6.8). A separate Decision (see Section 6.10) establishes an exchange of information on air quality.

Summary of the Directive

An Annex I sets limit values for the ground level concentration of sulphur dioxide and suspended particulates (smoke) which must be met throughout Member States during specified periods as shown in Table 10.

Table 10 contains all the information in Annex I but in a more comprehensible form. It is taken from DoE Circular 11/81. Figure 2 below and the associated discussion help to explain the table.

The limit values are given in microgrammes per cubic metre using a prescribed measuring method for sulphur dioxide and an OECD method of measurement for smoke – the 'black smoke' method – which differs from the method usually used in Britain. The Directive allows another method – the gravimetric method – to be used also, in which case different limit values apply. The limit values should be met by 1 April 1983, but if that seems unlikely in certain zones the Commission is to be informed and plans for the progressive improvement of those zones are to be submitted to the Commission by 1 October 1982. The limit values must, at the latest, be met by 1 April 1993.

Table 10

Reference Period	Limit values – air	
	Smoke	Sulphur dioxide
Year (Median of daily values)	80	If smoke less than 40:120 If smoke more than 40:80
Winter (Median of daily values 1 October–31 March)	130	If smoke less than 60:180 If smoke more than 60:130
Year (peak) (98 percentile of daily values)	250	If smoke less than 150:350 If smoke more than 150:250

A general duty is also laid on Member States to endeavour to move towards more stringent guide values set out in an Annex II. These guide values can also be used as reference points for the establishment of specific schemes in two types of zone which Member States may designate:

zones where the Member State considers it necessary to prevent a foreseeable increase in pollution in the wake of urban or industrial development (Article 4(1));
special environmental protection zones (Article 4(2)).

What is known as the 'standstill principle' is also enunciated: air quality is not to be allowed to deteriorate significantly even in areas where pollution is well below the limit values. However, a minute of a Council meeting records a declaration of both Council and Commission that this is not to be interpreted as prohibiting the siting in such areas of new plants that may be sources of smoke or sulphur dioxide. (Council minutes are not usually published but the essence of this declaration is given in published DoE Circular 11/81.)

Member States must establish monitoring stations designed to supply data necessary for the application of the Directive, in particular in zones where the limit values are likely to be approached or exceeded. Member States fixing values in border regions must consult one another and the Commission may attend these consultations. Once a year Member States must inform the Commission of instances when limit values have been exceeded, together with the reasons and the measures which have been taken to avoid recurrences. Each year the Commission must publish a summary report of the application of the Directive.

Development of the Directive

Following agreement on the sulphur content of gas oil Directive (Section 6.1) the Commission proposed two more Directives on sulphur dioxide which came to be considered together. Initially the British government was opposed to both proposals but then changed its attitude to one of general support for the air quality proposal while maintaining its opposition to the proposed Directive on the sulphur content of fuel oil (COM(75)681). A DoE witness before the Lords' Scrutiny Committee put it like this, introducing incidentally a note of scientific nationalism:

> These two Directives. . . are very closely related. Our view. . . is that they are of very unequal weight and indeed of unequal merit. The (air quality) Directive is medically based and does seem to us to be sensible. We might clearly want to argue about the phraseology in the Directive, but since it is based upon the World Health Organization Report 506, which was very largely written by Professor Lawther on the basis of UK material we do not wish to oppose that Directive fundamentally. The fuel oil Directive is quite another matter.

The fuel oil proposal would have required Member States to designate 'special protection zones' wherever specified pollution levels were exceeded. Oil burning installations inside these zones would then be required to use low-sulphur fuel oil, although plants with tall stacks could be exempted. In addition, large oil burning installations wherever sited would be required to maintain a stock of low-sulphur oil to which they would have to switch when high levels of pollution had been recorded for twenty-four hours.

The fuel oil proposal was an attempt by the Commission to prevent distortion to competition following similar national legislation proposed in the Netherlands, but the proposal effectively died in early 1978 when only four Member States were found to support it even in principle. The British government was opposed on the grounds that the cost to industry would have produced little environmental benefit, since a switch to low-sulphur fuel oil would have to be made even if coal was the major cause of the pollution. The government took the view that the air quality proposal effectively achieved the same desired end but left Member States free to use the most appropriate means. A fear not far below the surface was that agreement on a fuel oil Directive would be followed by a proposal for a coal Directive which would involve considerably greater costs for Britain. There is no reason to suppose that the fuel oil proposal was intended as a stalking horse for the air quality proposal but it came close to being just that, at least in Britain.

Opposition in principle to the air quality proposal came from the French government which felt that the proposed standards were at once too strict (some French industrial zones did not meet the limit values) and not strict enough (most rural areas had better air quality and the limit values would then be seen as a licence to pollute). These points were met by amending the proposal to include:

the derogation provision allowing time (till 1993) for meeting the values;
provisions for Member States at their own discretion to set more stringent values.

The European Parliament welcomed the proposal but in one of its detailed points of criticism revealed a lack of understanding of what is meant by an environmental quality standard. The Parliament's Resolution called for an amendment requiring Member States to ensure that their national legislation made provision 'for the imposition of fines on undertakings which do not comply with the norms'. This Resolution failed to take into account the difficulty of separating quantitatively the effects of the different sources of pollution, a problem inherent in any mandatory quality standard. In London, for example, failure to meet a quality standard is as likely as not to be the result of innumerable domestic fires or road traffic. An individual householder can be fined for producing dark smoke by burning raw coal in a smoke control area designated under the Clean Air Act, as can an industrialist, but except in the case of a very large emitter it is hard to see how proof can be established that a particular installation has been responsible for breaking an air quality standard covering a large area. Therefore although there is a distinction between a mandatory air quality standard and a mere guideline it is not so sharp a distinction as between a mandatory emission standard and a guideline: whereas a mandatory emission standard can be legally enforced, this is not so easy with a mandatory air quality standard.

The House of Lords' Scrutiny Committee considered the fuel oil and air quality proposals together and perhaps for that reason gave less attention to the air quality proposal than it deserved. Although they heard evidence from Professor Lawther (from whose epidemiological work the limit values are said to have been largely derived), from the DoE, from British Petroleum, from the Central Electricity Generating Board and from the National Society for Clean Air, their report did not express any definite view on the proposal as a whole. The report made detailed suggestions for improvement – with the implication that the Committee were not totally opposed to it; on the other hand, the report included in an Annex, without comment, an excerpt from the Fifth Report of the Royal Commission on Environmental Pollution[1] which had dealt with the same subject six months earlier (the Scrutiny Committee and Royal Commission had overlapping memberships) saying 'we are also opposed to the imposition of air quality standards'. The final paragraph of the Committee's report asked the government to present an account of any significant changes which might be agreed, implying that the Committee might return to the subject. However, despite a letter from the DoE some seventeen months later, the Committee did not do so, nor did the House debate the report.

The consequence was that a significant turning point in British air pollution policy was allowed to pass largely unremarked in Parliament. It is true that in the Commons' debate (18 May 1977) the Minister, Denis Howell, drew attention to what he called matters of principle, but no one in the Commons' debate, apart from the Minister, showed any realization that to introduce mandatory air quality standards was a departure from current British practice and worthy of comment. Since some members of the Royal Commission sat in the House of Lords, it is hard to believe that if a debate had been held in the Lords some explanation would not have been forthcoming of the apparent conflict between the Directive and the opposition of the Royal Commission to 'the imposition of air quality standards'. The Royal Commission had instead recommended guidelines but there can be no doubt that the Directive does indeed impose standards which have to be met by a certain date – with the Commission and the Court of Justice ready to ensure compliance. The words that the Minister, Denis Howell, used in the Commons' debate did not conceal the point, nor it must be said, did they draw particular attention to the change of policy. He said:

> There are matters of principle which I must draw to the attention of the House. The use of air quality standards to be achieved by a stated time represents a new departure for us. But there are no legal penalties involved for individuals. It is

left to us to determine how we must meet the required standard.

In addition to the changes made to satisfy the French objections some changes to the limit values were also made in response to British pressure. The German government insisted on being able to continue using the gravimetric method of measurement rather than that proposed by the Commission and as a result the Directive allows either to be used despite the fact that the two methods are hard to compare.

Technical issues

Some important technical criticisms of the proposal for the Directive were never answered publicly, at least in Britain, before it was agreed and have not been answered since by the Commission or by the British government.

The limit values set by the Directive are for the two pollutants (smoke and sulphur dioxide) considered together. If one is low, more is allowed of the other. The fifth report of the Royal Commission[1] gave some tentative support to this kind of trade-off between the two pollutants:

> Moreover, some pollutants have a combined effect which is much more serious than that of each by itself and cannot sensibly be considered apart. The classic example is smoke and sulphur dioxide. Together they can affect health at concentrations which used to be common in British cities. However, now that in many urban areas smoke has reached low levels the acceptable levels of SO_2, less damaging by itself, are probably much higher. (para 171)

Professor Lawther roundly contradicted this when giving evidence to the Lord's Scrutiny Committee. Referring to the Commission's proposal and its authors, he said:

> There is another failure in the documents, a fundamental error, which I think is the only serious fundamental error; that is, they still have not got the message which we have given them repeatedly and that is that there is no evidence of synergism between sulphur dioxide and smoke. They have always confused the idea that sulphur dioxide acting with smoke gives an effect greater than either acting singly. They seem incapable of getting hold of the idea that the only reason why we bracket smoke and sulphur dioxide is that in the epidemiological work they exist together. This has led to an absurdity in the latter part of the document in which they say that they suggest criteria for smoke and sulphur dioxide, but then say if, in certain situations, the sulphur dioxide is low, then that allows us to have more smoke, and the reverse: that if smoke is low, we can tolerate more sulphur dioxide. This ridiculous suggestion implies that we know which is the villain and that I suppose implies further that they are equal in

effect. We have repeatedly told them that all we can say is that in the most sensitive methods available, the epidemiological surveillance of very susceptible people, then the things occur together and we are not able yet to separate them.

This damaging criticism was left unanswered.

To understand the way in which the two pollutants are traded off against each other in the Directive it helps to consider the limits in the graphical form shown in Figure 2, where the sulphur dioxide concentration and smoke concentration at various notional sites are plotted against each other. The dashed line represents the winter mean limit values set by the Directive by way of example. Notional sites A, B and C would be in breach of the values, while sites D, E and F would not. Site G might be said to be at risk of exceeding the limits given the variability of pollution from year to year.

It is immediately apparent that the step form of the dashed line must be arbitrary. Rather than having a step form – which is an inevitable consequence of having smoke value 'trigger points' (40, 60 and 150) with different sulphur dioxide limit values associated with them – one could as easily have postulated an equally arbitrary curved line which could not then so easily be represented in the tabular form adopted in the Directive.

Lord Ashby, when the DoE gave evidence to the Lords' Scrutiny Committee, pointed to the arbitrary nature of these 'trigger points':

> I would be very surprised, I was not present when Professor Lawther spoke, if he was happy about the splitting down into more than 40 micrograms or less than 40. Anyone who has done science knows you cannot do this. This is just nonsense.

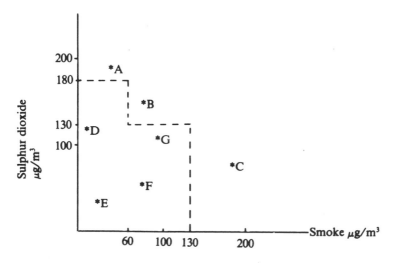

Figure 2: Graphical presentation of winter mean limit values

Source: Paper by P. Evans of the DoE (with author's permission).[2]

> I would hope you would not accept this list and put up the
> best defence you can against it and get something much
> simpler like the original WHO one.

Dr Reed of the DoE (subsequently the head of the Industrial Air Pollution
Inspectorate) replied:

> . . .I do not think there is any evidence to say that the smoke
> and SO_2 act together synergistically. All one knows is that
> when these are together in combination and probably with a
> number of other pollutants as well, because you cannot isolate
> them, certain effects can be demonstrated. One has then
> picked out smoke and sulphur together as two pollutants we
> know most about and can do something about.

And there the matter was allowed to rest, the discussion moving on to other
subjects. It is hard to imagine a comparable scientific assault on a proposed piece
of purely domestic legislation that was establishing a wholly new principle in air
pollution policy not drawing a stronger justification in public before it was
allowed to become law.

The justification could have come from the Commission which proposed
the limits, or from the governments which agreed to them. The parliamentary
record in countries other than Britain has not been studied. It is possible that a
justification was attempted by some other government. Such a justification could
have been in these terms: 'These are pollutants that need to be controlled and that
we can do something about. Rough and ready as the selected boundaries are, they
provide a spur to action and are the best that we can propose by way of
legislation.' Such a reply would at least be frank and is much to be preferred to the
bald assertion of the responsible Commissioner, Mr Burke, in the European
Parliament's debate (11 March 1977) that the Commission had produced proposals 'with an incontrovertible scientific basis'.

Formal compliance in the UK

Although the Directive represents a turning point in British air pollution policy,
it was not, until 1986, the intention of the Government to introduce any new
legislation to implement it, despite the absence of legislation either setting air
quality standards or empowering a minister to set such standards. This was the
view set out in an explanatory memorandum that the DoE submitted to Parliament in 1976, and ten years later this remains the position: 'It is thought that if the
Council adopted this Directive it could be implemented in the UK without
further legislation.'

In July 1982 the government wrote formally to the Commission enclosing a
memorandum listing the legislation and other measures that, in the government's
view, fulfilled the formal requirements of the Directive. This included:

Clean Air Acts 1956 and 1968
Alkali etc Works Regulation Act 1906
Control of Pollution Act 1974
Pollution Control and Local Government (Northern Ireland) Order 1978

together with various Regulations made under these laws and various government circulars. The Clean Air Acts give local authorities power to control domestic and industrial smoke and empower the Secretary of State to direct local authorities to submit smoke control programmes and carry them out. The Alkali Act empowers the Inspectorate to control emissions from registered chemical and industrial processes. The Control of Pollution Act empowers the Secretary of State to control the composition of motor fuel and the sulphur content of oil fuel, and also empowers local authorities to obtain information about air pollution.

One Act which could have been, but was not, mentioned is the Road Traffic Act 1972 which empowers the Secretary of State for Transport to regulate the construction of vehicles to avoid smoke and other emissions and gives powers for authorized examiners to check vehicles. Since smoke from an increasing fleet of vehicles, particularly from diesel engines, is now responsible for a significant proportion of smoke emissions in some larger cities, including London, it could be that strict enforcement of the vehicle smoke emissions will prove to be an important means of achieving the limits of the Directive. The ability of Member States individually to set more stringent emission limits to smoke from vehicles is however constrained by the Directives on vehicle emissions (see Section 6.7).

It follows from this array of different powers in different hands that achieving the objective of the Directive is largely a task of coordination so that the appropriate powers are used by the appropriate authority, when and where required. Monitoring thus plays an important part. In its memorandum to the Commission the government explained that:

> . . .the UK has had an extensive network of monitoring stations for smoke and sulphur dioxide for many years and measurements will continue in all areas where there is a possibility of approaching or exceeding the limit values. Measurements are carried out by the local authorities but the measurements are supervized and the results received and analysed centrally by the Warren Spring Laboratory (Department of Industry). Powers exist to require measurements to be taken wherever necessary.

Although the Secretary of State can issue guidelines and can ask the appropriate authorities to try to ensure that the mandatory air quality standards are met (and in the case of smoke control has the power of direction), the question nevertheless must be asked whether the existing powers are sufficient to comply with standards that are mandatory.

The difference between a guideline and a mandatory standard is the existence of some kind of sanction, and the sanction in this case is that the government is answerable for achieving the limit values to the Commission, and the Commission can in the extreme have recourse to the European Court for a declaration that the Directive must be implemented.

In a letter to the Commission dated 15 February 1983 (see below) the DoE listed certain areas that would not comply with the standards by April 1983, but went on to say that the extension of smoke control areas would ensure that the requirements of the Directive would be met by 1993 at the latest. In the absence of evidence to the contrary it is hard to see how the Commission can question this opinion, and if the standards can be achieved then it must follow that no new legislation is required.

The Directive also requires Member States to endeavour to move towards more stringent guide values set out in Annex II and to fix values for smoke and sulphur dioxide lower than the limit values in two kinds of zone (Article 4(1) and 4(2)) if the Member State considers they are in need of such protection. Until there are powers to set such mandatory limits use cannot be made of Article 4. The DoE has stated in Circular 11/81 drawing the attention of local authorities to the Directive that 'the government does not see any areas in which it would be either desirable or economically feasible for it to set up either type of zone' and so would presumably argue that the absence of the necessary powers does not prevent it from complying with the Directive in law, since even if it had the powers it would not use them. Article 4 serves to underline the desirability of new legislation, but does not make it essential.

The obligation to endeavour to move towards more stringent guide values can clearly be achieved without the power to set mandatory standards. DoE Circular 11/81 has merely asked local authorities to note this objective and, where pollution is below the mandatory standards, to consider whether any further progress towards the guide values is desirable and economically feasible.

As explained in Section 6.0 the DoE, in 1986, issued a consultation document, proposing a major reform of air pollution legislation which would include powers for the Secretary of State to lay down mandatory air quality standards either nationally or by area. The consultation document concedes that a major pressure for this change has been this and other Directives setting air quality standards. If these powers are created it means that the major change of policy brought about by the Directive will have been formalized in legislation.

Effect on UK practice

The DoE issued Circular 11/81 on 27 March 1981 drawing the attention of local authorities to the Directive and setting out action 'thought likely to be necessary to implement the Directive'. The Circular listed seventy-one district councils in England and Wales containing sites where it was thought that the limit values of the Directive might be exceeded – mostly because of insufficient coverage by smoke control orders under the Clean Air Acts. In addition, districts in Scotland and Northern Ireland were also identified. These local authorities were asked to:

> . . .order their priorities within the general restraint on public expenditure so as to complete any necessary extension of smoke control by 1983. Where this is not possible, authorities should aim to complete any necessary programme as soon as possible after that date and at the latest by 1993.

In addition, the Circular said that the government would allocate its financial contribution to local authorities for smoke control by reference to areas exceeding the limit values. The Circular asked local authorities who considered that sulphur dioxide alone might be a problem to contact the DoE but only one did so and then decided that the standards were indeed met.

In February 1983 the DoE wrote to the Commission listing twenty-one district councils in England, four in Scotland and three in Northern Ireland (but none in Wales) which, on the basis of monitoring results over the years, contained areas which would not comply with the limit values by April 1983. An extra district was added in England in August 1983. In all cases the cause was smoke alone and the smoke was said to arise primarily from dometic coal burning. The discrepancy in number between the seventy-one districts in England and Wales said to be at risk in 1981 and the twenty-nine for the whole of Great Britain communicated to the Commission is partly explained by the original list being over cautious, partly by the introduction of smoke control in some districts, and partly by the improvement in air quality that is taking place as householders spontaneously switch from coal to other fuels such as North Sea gas.

The DoE letter to the Commission said it was the government's intention to ensure that additional smoke control programmes would be introduced so as to ensure that the limits would be met by 1993 at the latest. This letter constituted, in the government's view, the 'plans for the progressive improvement of the quality of air in those zones' required by the Directive. The DoE subsequently notified the Commission that in the reference period ending 31 March 1984 seven districts were identified as zones where air quality did not meet the limit values – Doncaster, Barnsley, Mansfield, Wansbeck, Copeland, Sunderland and Wakefield. In all cases the government gave details of the smoke control programmes which were under way or planned. In Sunderland and Wakefield it was reported in 1985 that there was some way to go in completing these programmes and that the local authorities appeared to feel that they had other expenditure priorities. The Commission had reported in its first annual report to the Council of 1985 on the implementation of the Directive[3] that the UK had not submitted the plans for the progressive improvement of the twenty-nine zones mentioned above. The Commission is still pursuing this matter and has issued a letter under Article 169 of the Treaty; talks are continuing (March 1987).

From what has happened so far it follows that the major effect of the Directive has been to provide an impetus and a strategic framework for the completion of smoke control that began with the 1956 Act. Areas likely to exceed the limits have had to be identified and pressure has been generated for the introduction of smoke control. There may well not be any effect on sulphur dioxide control except as a result of controlling the burning of coal primarily to reduce smoke.

Some tricky issues may be arising in implementing the Directive. If, for instance, a local authority, perhaps a mining area where domestic coal burning is encouraged by free allowances of coal for miners, does not of its own volition introduce smoke control in time because it has higher priorities for spending its money, central government will then have to direct the local authority to do so under the Clean Air Act of 1968. Those powers have never previously been used – which does not mean they have not been having a persuasive effect. In the discussions that will ensue, the local authority may well argue that on the one hand it is being told to cut back on expenditure while, on the other hand, it is being directed to adopt a policy that entails increased expenditure. Sunderland and Wakefield have indeed so argued and in South Yorkshire in 1983 it was recommended that the government and the Community should give greater financial support to coal mining areas such as Barnsley, Rotherham and Doncaster.

It is because responsibility lies primarily with the local authority that the government may well be having difficulty in submitting the precise plans for improvement that the Commission would prefer to have, and the Commission will need to recognize the importance of not upsetting the delicate balance between central and local government.

Another effect of the Directive has been on monitoring. The National Survey of Smoke and Sulphur Dioxide has been in operation since 1961. Initially there were some 500 monitoring sites, increasing to about 1200 by 1966 and at that time providing the most comprehensive survey in the world. The monitoring is carried out largely by local authorities but is coordinated by the Warren Spring Laboratory which falls under the Department of Industry. It so happened that this survey was in the process of being reviewed when the Directive was agreed. The long term plan is to reduce the network to about 150 stations[4] but Circular 11/81 said that the adequacy of existing monitoring stations was being considered in relation to the requirements of the Directive. As a result around 400 sites are being maintained for the time being where areas are at risk of breaching the standards in the Directive. The number of sites will be progressively reduced as the areas at risk diminish, but without the Directive these 400 sites would not all have been maintained.

One possible effect of the Directive is the influence it could have on town and country planning. An attempt by Cheshire County Council to include air quality standards in a structure plan was struck out by the Secretary of State in 1978 at a time when there were no national air quality standards and no policy on the subject. Now that the Directive exists it is possible that the arguments would come out differently. Circular 11/81 went so far as to advise local authorities with areas exceeding the limit values to take into account the need to attain the limit values when preparing or reviewing structure plans or local plans. At least one local authority (Middlesborough) has already adopted an air quality management system which is based on an absolute maximum ceiling level of 40 μg per cubic metre for both smoke and sulphur dioxide.

The Commission's first annual report on implementation of the Directive throughout the Community[3] reveals that progress made so far is anything but satisfactory. In two cases infraction proceedings had been taken (Netherlands and Ireland) and in the case of all other countries discussions were taking place on interpretation of the Directive. Monitoring methods and instruments vary widely and little can be said about comparability between countries.

Transboundary air pollution

The effect of the Directive on long range transboundary air pollution – the only form of relevance to Britain – is problematic. This is because the Directive is concerned with ground level concentrations and not with the total quantity of smoke or sulphur dioxide emitted. Nevertheless, a connection is sometimes assumed because following agreement on the Directive, a Council Resolution was adopted on 15 July 1980 (OJ C222 30.8.80) in the following terms:

> Taking due account of the facts and problems involved, the Member States will endeavour, in accordance with the objective of Council Directive 80/779/EEC of 15 July 1980 on air quality limit values and guide values for sulphur dioxide and suspended particulates to limit and as far as possible gradually

reduce and prevent transboundary air pollution by sulphur dioxide and suspended particulates.

Action under the Directive should to a small extent reduce total emissions which should in turn reduce long-range movements. On the other hand, if to achieve the ground level limits, more sulphur dioxide were to be emitted at a high level this could increase long-range pollution, although the point has been partly disputed by the government-appointed Commission on Energy and the Environment. Its report on *Coal and the Environment*[5] said (para 17.52):

> There appears to be some misunderstanding about the contribution made by tall stacks to long range air pollution, namely that large emitters using tall stacks greatly enhance the transport of sulphur dioxide for long distances. This is not so: the long distance transport of sulphur dioxide is almost independent of chimney height. The main effect of tall stacks is to delay the time and distance before the plume returns to the ground and thus reduce the ground path for sulphur dioxide absorption by some 10 kilometres. In exceptional weather, however, it appears possible that plumes can be isolated above an inversion layer and carried relatively rapidly for some hundreds of kilometres.

In June 1981 by a Council Decision (OJ L171/11 27.6.81) the European Community concluded the Convention on long-range transboundary air pollution to which the UK had already adhered see Chapter 11.

There has been much further action both within the Community and in other international organizations to try and deal with the transfrontier air pollution problem and to reduce emissions of sulphur dioxide and other air pollutants. The German government in 1983 became increasingly concerned with the effects of air pollution on its forests and, as a result, a number of Directives have been proposed and some agreed (see Emissions from industrial plants).

References

1   Royal Commission on Environmental Pollution 1976 *Air pollution control: an integrated approach. Fifth Report.* HMSO.

2   Evans P 1980 *The EC Directive on smoke and sulphur dioxide: The future for smoke control.* 47th Annual Conference of the National Society for Clean Air.

3   Commission of the European Communities March 1985 *First annual report of the Commission to the Council on implementation of Directive 80/779 – COM(85)368.*

4   Keddie A W C, Williams F P and Gooriah B D (Warren Spring Laboratory)
    1981 *Monitoring – where next?* National Society for Clean Air Workshop.

5   Commission on Energy and the Environment 1981 *Coal and the Environment*. HMSO.

6.3 Air quality – nitrogen dioxide

85/203/EEC (OJ L87 27.3.85) proposed 7.9.83 – COM(83)498	Directive on air quality standards for nitrogen dioxide.

Binding dates
Notification date	3 March 1985
Formal compliance	1 January 1987
Limits to be met	1 July 1987
Report to Commission	annually from December 1988

Purpose of the Directive

An air quality standard is set for nitrogen dioxide (NO_2) in air in order to protect human health and to contribute towards protection of the environment. It only relates to the ambient atmosphere and does not cover indoor or workplace conditions.

Nitrogen dioxide is mainly a secondary pollutant. Most is formed in the atmosphere as a result of the chemical interaction of nitric oxide emitted from combustion processes with ozone and other oxidants. Hydrocarbons emitted from combustion processes add to the quantity of oxidants available in the atmosphere. Countries may be effected by oxidants from well beyond their own borders. Some nitrogen dioxide is emitted as a primary pollutant from vehicle exhausts.

Summary of the Directive

The Directive sets a limit value of 200 μg/m³ for nitrogen dioxide in the atmosphere (calculated as the 98th percentile of mean values per hour recorded throughout the year) to be observed from 1 July 1987. It also sets guide values of 50 μg/m³ (50th percentile of mean values) and 135 μg/m³ (98th percentile of mean values) which are intended to serve as reference points for the establishment of particular schemes within zones in Member States with the object of improving protection of the environment in the long term.

Provision is made for Member States, if unable to meet the limit value by the due date in certain zones, to report the circumstances to the Commission with plans for gradual improvement of the air as soon as possible and in any case by 1 January 1994 at the latest. In such cases a lower limit may be fixed by the Member State. Member States may also fix more stringent limits than the guide values in zones which are considered to need special environmental protection. Member States may at any time fix more stringent values. Annexes establish how the limit values shall be measured and monitored.

Measuring stations are required to be set up, particularly in the zones where the limit values are relaxed or made more stringent. Member States are to notify the Commission in annual reports (the first to be submitted presumably by 31 December 1988) of instances where the limit value has been exceeded. The Commission is also to be notified of the reasons and the measures taken to deal with such incidents. These details have to be submitted within one year of the end of the reference period. The Commission may also request additional information on the zones where lower or more stringent limits are set. The Commission will report periodically.

In regions near the border with other Member States where it is intended to fix lower or higher limit values prior consultations are to take place; the Commission is to be informed and may take part. Where significant pollution originating from another Member State leads to limit values being exceeded, consultation shall also take place with a view to remedying the situation.

The usual Committee for adaptation to scientific and technical progress is established to allow amendments to the reference methods of analysis laid down. It has no power over the limit values.

Development of the Directive

The first environmental action programme of 1973 provided for investigation of nitrogen oxides as one of the air pollutants in the first category in order to determine 'criteria' and harmonize measuring methods. The second programme endorsed this priority and the need to formulate quality objectives. A Council Resolution of 7 February 1983 (OJ C146 17.2.83) reinforced the move towards establishing quality standards for nitrogen oxides. The effects of air pollution on forests in Germany (and the 'acid rain' problem in general) in which nitrogen oxides play an important part gave added impetus to producing the proposal.

In the UK the view taken by the government was an unfavourable one. The 200 $\mu g/m^3$ level was considered to be too stringent and to be questionably founded both on medical grounds and those of practical implementation. The monitoring costs were considered to be too high. The House of Lords expressed similar concerns.

The original proposal was not greatly changed in the course of negotiation. In particular the limit values proposed remained. The main change was to defer compliance dates by fifteen months which presumably reflected the delay in achieving agreement. Another significant change was limiting monitoring to areas representative of human health risk and requiring compliance at monitoring sites rather than countrywide. Thus kerbside monitoring was not required and compliance will be considerably less costly than under the original proposal.

This is another example of where the Council reached agreement on the proposal but had to wait for the European Parliament's opinion before formally adopting it. The Parliament's opinion was only published six months after the Council had reached agreement. Although the Commission then proposed certain amendments put forward by the Parliament these were not adopted.

One consequence of the Council's consideration was an examination into the need for a long-term limit value for nitrogen dioxide which certain Member States wanted. The Commission reported (COM(85)371 11.7.85) that it was of the opinion that neither could a long-term value be set nor did the guide value in the Directive need adaptation at present.

Formal compliance in UK

The compliance letter to the Commission dated 22 December 1986 explains that steps are in hand to establish measuring stations in accordance with the Directive to measure concentrations where there is greatest risk of individuals being exposed to levels in excess of the limit value. These points will be selected both from areas predominantly affected by emissions from motor vehicles and those from fixed sources. It states that a monitoring network will be located in London, Birmingham, Manchester, Glasgow and Teesside. It adds that measurements over the past three years indicate that the limit values in the Directive will not be breached. No mention is made of how limit values or quality standards would be set or enforced if breached beyond explaining the responsibilities of the pollution inspectorates and local authorities in controlling emissions under present legislation.

Under the proposals for new legislation in the Consultation Paper for Air Pollution Control issued in December 1986 (see Relevant British Legislation) powers would be provided to set air quality standards by Regulations. Such legislation would enable the Directive to be fully complied with but this could not be before the implementation date. It is assumed that if the new legislation is not introduced shortly because of lack of parliamentary time, recourse would have to be made to a Circular as was done with the Directive on smoke and sulphur (see Section 6.2).

Effect on UK practice

Since such monitoring as has been carried out in the UK showed that only in one heavily trafficked locality was the limit of 200 $\mu g/m^3$ exceeded and that in general levels were considerably lower, the effect on the UK is likely to be limited. Indeed it is not clear why there was a general objection to the level proposed and eventually agreed. Other Directives (for example on vehicle emissions) may well have more important effects both in general and in particular places with high concentrations. Controls on nitrogen oxide emission from major industrial plants have been controlled by the Industrial Air Pollution Inspectorate and its predecessor for many years.

6.4 Air quality – lead

82/884/EEC (OJ L378 31.12.82) proposed 16.4.75 – COM(75)166	Directive on a limit value for lead in the air.

Binding dates
Notification date	9 December 1982
Formal compliance	9 December 1984
Report to Commission if limits exceeded	annually from 1 July 1985*
Commission to publish report	annually from 9 December 1986*
Commission to be informed of places likely to exceed limits and of improvement plans	9 December 1986*
Limit values should be met	9 December 1987
Plans must ensure limits achieved by	9 December 1989

* There is ambiguity about these dates because although the Directive sometimes refers to the date of notification, which is clear enough, it sometimes refers to the date of 'implementation' which could mean the date of formal compliance (December 1984) or the date by which the limit is to be met (December 1987). Here it is assumed that that date of formal compliance is intended. In Article 3(2) a date of four years after 'notification' is given and in Article 3(3) a date of two years after 'implementation': they turn out to be the same date (December 1986).

Purpose of the Directive
Breathing air containing lead contributes to the body burden of lead, and in order to protect human health an air quality standard is laid down.

Summary of the Directive
The concentration of lead in the air is not to exceed two micrograms per cubic metre, expressed as an annual average mean concentration, as from December 1987. This limit value does not apply to occupational exposure (such as inside factories). Member States may set more stringent values.

Where a Member State considers that the limit value may be exceeded in December 1986 it must inform the Commission, and must by December 1986 send the Commission plans for the progressive improvement of the quality of the air in those places. These plans, drawn up on the basis of information as to the nature, origin and development of the pollution, must describe the measures already taken or envisaged and the procedures implemented or planned. (The difference between a 'measure' and a 'procedure' is not explained.) The objective must be to bring air in those places within the limit as soon as possible and at the latest by December 1989.

Sampling stations are to be installed and operated at places where individuals may be exposed continually for a long period and where there is a possibility that the limit value will not be observed. Member States are to supply the Commission, at its request, with information on the sampling sites and sampling and analysis procedure. An Annex sets out how to choose the sampling method, and also a reference method of analysis. If Member States use some other method of analysis they must prove to the Commission beforehand that it will produce equivalent results.

Annually from 1 July 1985 Member States must inform the Commission of the places where the limit has been exceeded in the previous year and of the concentrations recorded. Within a further year they must notify the Commission of the measures taken to avoid recurrence. Annually the Commission is to publish a summary report on the application of the Directive.

Measures taken as a result of the Directive are not to bring about a significant reduction in the quality of the air where the level of lead is low compared to the limit.

The usual Committee is established for the adaptation to scientific and technical progress of the sampling method and the reference method of analysis.

Development of the Directive

More than six years elapsed between the Directive being proposed and being agreed, largely because it was blocked by Britain, although other Member States were not enthusiastic for it either. The proposal was made at the same time as a proposed Directive on biological screening of the population for lead (see Section 6.6) and, as a result, the air quality proposal was rather neglected in parliamentary discussion. Thus, although the House of Commons held a debate (5 April 1976) to take note of the two proposed Directives as well as the proposed lead in petrol Directive (see Section 6.5) no one mentioned the proposed air quality standard. In a House of Lords' debate (1 April 1976), however, the Minister (Baroness Stedman) made clear the government's opposition to both proposals:

> The Commission's proposals on biological standards for lead in blood and air quality standards for lead go, in our view, too far. . . The scientific evidence, despite the effort put in over a number of years, is still not such that we can advance to the point where we should lay down, in legislation, precise standards. Such a step would imply in law that every individual exceeding the blood lead limit and everybody in an area in which the air quality standard was exceeded would be in danger. We would not dissent from the view that the sort of figures for the standards proposed are reasonably reliable indicators of where investigation of the sources of lead should be initiated and action taken. We are, however, opposed to the rigidity and overemphasis on particular figures which would be consequent on enshrining them in legislation and which would carry with them the absolute obligation that they should not be exceeded. Until we know more, therefore, we should prefer something less rigid in the form of guidelines, or possibly quality objectives. These would set targets to be achieved which, in the light of further evidence, may be further modified or possibly adopted as standards. . .

The proposed biological standard was turned into a screening campaign and the air quality standard was deferred. In 1978 the government established a working party to consider the health effects of environmental lead pollution under the Chairmanship of Professor Lawther. The report[1] was published in 1980 and effectively provided the further evidence that the Minister had said was necessary. It recommended an air quality standard for lead of two micrograms per cubic metre. On 11 May 1981 the Minister, Tom King, announced in the Commons that the government agreed with this standard which was the same as that in the proposed Directive, and on 30 June 1981 at a press conference at the start of the British Presidency of the Council, he announced that he hoped to reactivate the proposed Directive.

As originally proposed the Directive would have had two standards:

an annual mean of 2 $\mu g/m^3$ in urban residential areas and areas exposed to atmospheric lead other than motor vehicle traffic;
a monthly median of 8 $\mu g/m^3$ in areas particularly exposed to motor vehicle traffic.

A specific proposal about roadside sampling stations being between 1 and 2 metres from the kerb and between 1.5 and 2 metres above the ground was heavily criticized in the House of Lords' Scrutiny Committee's report as producing results unrepresentative of air actually breathed in. This argument must have prevailed since the Directive as agreed instead requires that 'sampling stations are installed and operated at places where individuals may be exposed continually for a long period. . .'. In the case of roadside locations this presumably means where people live rather than pavements where they may walk for only brief periods each day. The monthly limit of 8 $\mu g/m^3$ was dropped.

Formal compliance in UK
The Commission was informed by a letter nearly two months after the due date about how the UK was complying with the Directive. The following powers were listed:

Control of Pollution Act 1974, Section 79 – power of local authorities to monitor levels of lead in air;
Control of Pollution Act 1974 Section 75 – power to regulate lead content of petrol;
Health and Safety at Work etc Act 1974 – Inspectorate's power to control industrial emissions from scheduled processes;
Public Health Act 1936 and Public Health (Recurring Nuisances) Act 1969 Sections 92–100 – power of local authorities to require action to abate public nuisances.

The government stated that arrangements were being made for monitoring by local authorities where there were risks of the limit of 2 μg of lead per cubic metre being breached. The belief was expressed that these measures (including the reduction of lead in petrol to 0.15 g/l) would be sufficient. It was also intended to issue, before the end of 1986, a Departmental Circular to give a clear explanation of how the legislation operates to fulfil the obligations of the Directive. A Circular has not yet been issued, though the Department has been in touch with local authorities where levels are close to the limit.

The legislation proposed in the Consultation Paper on Air Pollution Control (see Section 6.0) would enable mandatory air quality standards to be set in Regulations. Until such Regulations exist or until a Circular is published making it clear to all the responsible authorities that the standards must be achieved the Directive will not have been formally complied with.

Effect on UK practice

Local authorities will be carrying out monitoring to check possible areas at risk. Arrangements will also have to be made to ensure that appropriate action is taken if levels are found to be above 2 μg/m^3. DoE Circular 22/82 issued to local authorities on 7 September 1982 said that the decision to reduce the lead content of petrol to 0.15 g/l should bring about a proportionate reduction in lead in air near main roads and enable the 2 μg/m^3 standard recommended in the Lawther Report[1] to be achieved virtually everywhere. It added that breaches of this standard in places where people are exposed for long periods, even close to main roads, are rare even at present.

In anticipation of the obligation arising from the Directive and to discover what evidence about possible breaches of the standard existed the Institution of environmental health officers sent a questionnaire to local authority environmental health officers asking whether, by December 1982, any surveys showed that the 2 μg/m^3 standard had been exceeded at any time. Of the responding authorities 19 said Yes and 182 said No. It is difficult to draw conclusions from this rather preliminary survey since information is not given about the way, and where, the samples were taken.

A survey in 1984 by Warren Spring Laboratory (WSL) on background levels of lead in air from eight metal refining and processing works showed that emissions from only one (in Walsall) exceeded the Directive's limit with levels of 2.6 μg/m^3 (three month mean concentration). A further survey of four sites in 1985 showed similar results. Another survey from WSL based on twenty-one kerbside urban and rural monitoring sites in the first three months of 1986 showed a 50 per cent reduction in air lead levels. The reduction is closely linked to the reduction of lead in petrol from 1 January 1986 to 0.15 g/l. Average concentrations were 0.29 μg/m^3.

References
1   Lawther Professor P J (chairman) 1980 *Lead and health: the report of a DHSS working party on lead in the environment.* HMSO.

6.5 Lead in petrol

85/210/EEC (OJ L96 3.4.85)
proposed 6.6.84 – COM(84)226

Directive on the approximation of the
laws of the Member States concerning
the lead content of petrol.

Binding dates
Notification date
Formal compliance
Limits to be met

26 March 1985
1 January 1986
unleaded petrol by 1 October 1989

This Directive replaced Directive 78/611/EEC – OJ L197 22.7.78 – which ceased to be
applicable on 31 December 1985.

Purpose of the Directive
An earlier Directive 78/611 set limits on the lead content of petrol both to
prevent barriers to trade in petrol and motor cars resulting from different limits in
different countries and also to reduce air pollution by lead. This Directive takes
these aims a stage further by requiring the availability of unleaded petrol and
promoting its widest possible use. A proposed Directive amending the limits on
vehicle emissions (see Section 6.7) needs to be agreed before all new cars must be
capable of running on unleaded petrol. Another Directive 85/536 (OJ L334
12.12.85) deals with crude oil savings through the use of substitute fuel components in petrol.

Summary of the Directive
The original Directive 78/611 adopted in July 1978 set a maximum permitted lead
content of petrol sold within the Community at 0.40 grams per litre. Member
States could set an upper limit between 0.40 g/l and 0.15 g/l but could not insist
on less than 0.15 g/l. The current Directive provides for the continuation of
availability and balanced distribution of leaded petrol (which is defined as containing between 0.4 g/l and 0.15 g/l) within the territories of Member States but
requires them as soon as they consider it appropriate to reduce the maximum
limit to 0.15 g/l. Member States are also to ensure the availability and balanced
distribution of premium grade unleaded petrol within their territories from
1 October 1989 but may take measures to introduce unleaded petrol before that
date. From 1 October 1989 the benzene content of leaded and unleaded petrol
shall not exceed 5.0 per cent by volume. There are provisions for waivers from
limits both for leaded and unleaded petrol for a period of four months by
Member States in the event of a sudden change in supply of oil or petroleum
products; the period may be extended by the Council. Premium grade unleaded
petrol is required to meet a minimum motor octane number (MON) of 85 and
research octane number (RON) of 95. Technical Annexes provide for determining the lead and benzene contents of petrol and octane numbers. Amendments

arising from scientific and technical progress may be made through the usual Technical and Scientific Committee set up by the Directive.

Member States are invited to promote the widest possible use of unleaded petrol in all existing vehicles. They are also to provide the Commission at its request with information on supplies of petrol on the market and on the results and effects of the Directive on air pollution and energy policy in particular.

Development of the Directives

The earlier Directive 78/611
The development of the earlier Directive shows that in favourable circumstances a determined Member State can pull the rest of the Community along behind it so that higher environmental standards are achieved throughout the Community more quickly than if the Member States had proceeded at their own pace. From 1 January 1972 the lead content of petrol sold in the Federal Republic of Germany was restricted to 0.40 g/l and it was the knowledge that Germany was proposing to make this reduction that stimulated the Commission into proposing a Directive requiring a limit of 0.40 g/l by 1 January 1976.

In 1971 the Commission, learning of the German government's plans, established two committees to study the health and technical aspects of lead pollution from motor vehicles, and the work of these committees is summarized in the explanatory memorandum (COM(73)2050) accompanying the proposal for a Directive issued in December 1973. The memorandum includes a table showing that permitted lead levels at that time differed considerably in the different Member States, some having limits up to 0.84 g/l and some having no limits at all. The memorandum concluded that although there was no immediate danger for public health, it was desirable to prevent an increase of air pollution by lead and hence to limit lead because of the increase in car use. The other reasons were to prevent technical barriers to trade.

The German government, in addition to reducing lead to 0.40 g/l in 1972, also announced its intention of making a second stage reduction from 1 January 1976 to 0.15 g/l. A level of 0.15 g/l seems to have been chosen because it is near the lowest level useable in many existing petrol engines without special adaptations. The Commission proposed a rather less severe second stage reduction with a limit of 0.15 g/l from 1 January 1978 for regular grade petrol but leaving the limit for premium grade at 0.40 g/l.

Shortly after the Directive was proposed and during discussions in the House of Lords (4 February 1974) on the Protection of the Environment Bill the Minister, Baroness Young, referred to the proposed Directive and said:

> I should perhaps make it quite clear that this Directive is supported by us. I hope I can assure the noble Baroness, Lady White, who asked whether we took a lead in these matters, that in fact we have taken a leading part in the drafting of the European Community Directive on lead in petrol. The standards set in this draft are largely the outcome of British initiative. The noble Baroness is of course quite right in saying that the Federal Republic of Germany has asked for more stringent measures. . .

In the debate in the European Parliament (10 November 1975) the rapporteur of the Environment Committee said that the proposed second stage reduction (to 0.15 g/l for regular grade petrol) had 'met with insurmountable opposition in the Committee' because it would have involved the industry in substantial investment as well as increasing petrol consumption. 'Since', he went on, 'these objections could not be refuted, the committee preferred to require the Commission to postpone the introduction of the second stage.' The limit of 0.40 g/l was, however, approved by the Committee. Spokesmen for four political groups in the Parliament supported the Committee's resolution but James Spicer, speaking for the European Conservative Group (the British Conservatives) explained that his group would be voting against the proposal largely because of the costs entailed and the absence of proof that there was any harm to health from lead in petrol.

The Commissioner, Mr Gundelach, in defending the Commission's proposal referred to the studies that had been done and said:

> . . .our proposals are built to the best of our or anyone else's ability on the probabilities presented by these studies – I say probabilities because nothing beyond that exists, neither here nor a few hundred kilometres away in the Federal Republic of Germany.

He explained that the Commission was not convinced that it was necessary to go as far as the German government was proposing, but pointed out that the delay in obtaining an opinion from the Parliament meant that it would not now be possible to obtain a Council decision on the proposal before the second stage reduction took effect in Germany on 1 January 1976. All the subsequent discussion in the Council was therefore coloured by an existing German limit of 0.15 g/l. The Directive finally agreed in 1978 therefore had to allow Member State to introduce a national limit of 0.15 g/l but its main provision was an upper limit of 0.40 g/l. The provision in the Directive to prevent a limit less than 0.15 g/l which is not to be found in the original proposal was put in at the suggestion of the British government among others, presumably to ensure that no barriers to trade in motor cars would be created by any one Member State insisting on lead free petrol. As a result, the earlier Directive lost some of its claim to be an environmental protection measure.

The House of Commons debated the proposal on 4 March and 5 April 1976 and resolved:

> that this House...accepts the principle of reducing the maximum lead content of petrol to 0.40 grams per litre...and, whilst recognizing that this will have an adverse effect on the United Kingdom balance of payments, nevertheless calls on Her Majesty's Government to achieve this aim by staged reductions.

Given that the limit in Britain at the time of the debate was 0.55 g/l and that the government had already announced three years before that it intended to reduce the limit to 0.45 g/l (see below) the debates were surprisingly heated. Several speakers argued that expenditure should not be incurred in the absence of proof of medical ill-effects, and many who supported the motion acknowledged that the medical evidence was not conclusive.

The Minister, Denis Howell, explained that the government had already decided in 1972 that air lead levels should not increase above the 1971 levels (see below) and that given current trends in petrol consumption a reduction to 0.40 g/l would have to be made in 1981. This therefore was the government's policy so far as the timing of the earlier Directive was concerned, and it seems unlikely to be a coincidence that it is this same date that appears in the Directive – a date five years later than that originally proposed. Notwithstanding the comments made two years earlier by Baroness Young that the government supported the proposed Directive the British government succeeded in slowing down its introduction, though it is probable that other countries were also anxious not to be compelled to move too fast.

The present Directive 85/210

A number of threads come together to explain why the Commission's proposal for lead-free petrol was to take so little time (in contrast to so many proposals discussed in this book) before it was agreed in Council – effectively less than six months. One starting point is the decision by the UK government in May 1981 in the light of the recommendations of the Lawther Report[1] that emissions of lead to the atmosphere should be reduced by lowering the lead content of petrol to the limit then allowed of 0.15 g/l; and to support the figure of 2 $\mu g/m^3$ of lead in air proposed in the Commission draft Directive on air quality for lead (see Air quality – lead). From then on the UK took a very much more positive line on limiting emissions from lead. This was given further impetus in April 1983 by a recommendation of the Royal Commission on Environmental Pollution[2] that the government should initiate negotiations with the Commission and other Member States to secure removal of the lower limit of lead in petrol from Directive 78/611. The objective of these negotiations would be that from the earliest practicable date all new petrol-engined vehicles sold in the UK should be required to run on unleaded petrol. The Royal Commission's investigation had coincided with a vigorous public campaign called CLEAR (Campaign for Lead Free Air) and it was as a result of this campaign that the government took the unusual step of accepting the Royal Commission's recommendation the same day that it was made public.

The government then immediately asked the Community to amend Directive 78/611, a move that was supported by the German government that realized that it needed lead free petrol if it was to realize its ambitions in reducing other emissions from vehicles by the use of catalytic converters that are 'poisoned' by lead in petrol.

By September 1981 the European Parliament had under consideration a motion to take action to achieve lead-free petrol by the progressive reduction of the maximum levels permitted under the earlier Directive. Another motion in February 1982 called on the Commission to propose that all new cars put on to the Community market after 1 January 1985 be manufactured to run on lead-free petrol and that from the same date lead-free petrol should be generally available. But it was not until June 1983 that the European Parliament passed a Resolution calling on the Commission to present proposals to abolish the prohibition on setting a level below 0.15 g/l, to reduce the maximum permitted level to 0.15 g/l by 1985 and to make lead-free petrol available as soon as possible.

The Commission had also been active. Under pressure from a number of sources concerned at the ad hoc approach to vehicle emissions that paid too little attention to the possible economic consequences for the important motor industry in the Community, it had brought together in January 1982 a group of experts – to become known as ERGA I (Evolution of Regulations, Global Approach). ERGA I was to assess the various ways of reducing gaseous pollutants emitted by passenger cars taking into account technological, environmental, health, energy and economic considerations.

At the European Council at Stuttgart in June 1983, and the Environment Council in the same month, the decision in principle was taken to reduce or eliminate the use of lead in petrol. This decision is unlikely to have been taken had two large countries (the UK and the Federal Republic of Germany) not both wanted lead-free petrol at the same time but for different reasons. ERGA II was then set up to consider the possible consequences of this decision from the technical, energy and economic points of view. ERGA I reported in August 1983 and ERGA II in May 1984.

Thus the Commission published on 30 May 1984, in the same document, two proposals for amending Directives on the lead content of petrol and on motor vehicle emissions. The proposal on petrol provided for:

further reduction of lead use by making it obligatory to market premium grade unleaded petrol alongside leaded petrol from 1 July 1989;
for a reduction in the maximum lead content of petrol used in existing vehicles to 0.15 g/l;
for the benzene content of petrol to be limited to 5 per cent by volume.

Though the proposal had only been issued less than a month before, the Environment Council on 28 June were able to take a decision in principle that unleaded petrol should be available throughout the Community by 1989 as proposed. Points of difficulty were revealed on the case for an earlier date both for unleaded petrol, and the deadline for new vehicles to run on lead free petrol. A linked issue on the vehicle emissions proposal showed difference of views on the use of catalytic converters and thus the use of lead-free petrol. In September the Commission completed its proposal by publishing an amendment covering the definition of octane levels.

On 10 December the European Parliament recommended an earlier date – 1 July 1986 – for the introduction of lead-free petrol. The Commission took note of this by putting forward amendments in March. However, the Environment Council had already agreed the text of the Directive on 6 December 1984, subject to the opinion of Parliament. Subsequently, the Environment Council on 20 March 1985 adopted the text in the form agreed in December.

There were some important differences with the original proposal: leaded petrol continued to be defined as petrol with a lead content of between 0.4 and 0.15 g/l with the reduction to a maximum of 0.15 g/l to be left to Member States to put into effect as soon as they considered it appropriate; the date by which unleaded petrol was to be made generally available was deferred by three months to 1 October 1989 (to conform to the usual date for changes to vehicle requirements); and derogations for a limited period of four months were provided for in the event of unforeseen changes in the supply of oil products.

Agreement on the linked proposal on vehicle emissions which set a date by which new cars must be capable of running on unleaded petrol (see Section 6.7) was not, however, achieved due on the one hand to Denmark which wanted more severe controls and Greece which looked for aid to combat the serious atmospheric pollution in Athens.

Formal compliance in the UK

No new primary legislation had to be introduced following agreement on the earlier Directive 78/611 because Section 75 of the Control of Pollution Act 1974 already gives the Secretary of State powers to control the composition of motor fuel for the purpose of limiting or reducing air pollution. We have already seen (see Section 6.1) how the power to control the sulphur content of fuel oil was introduced in order to enable that Directive to be implemented, and it is the same Section of the Act that confers power to control the lead content of petrol. Although the prospect of the earlier lead in petrol Directive may have been an additional reason for this power, it was not given as such during parliamentary discussion. Before the power took effect the lead content of petrol had been reduced by voluntary agreement with the oil companies and it is possible that the government would have continued to rely on voluntary agreements in the absence of the Directive. On the other hand, the government may have wanted to introduce legislation even had there been no Directive on the grounds that voluntary agreement might have become more difficult at lower lead levels. Section 75 of the Act cannot therefore with certainty be attributed to both Directive 78/611 as well as to the sulphur in gas oil Directive (see Section 6.1).

The following Regulations concerning lead have been made under Section 75 of the Act:

SI 1976 No 1866	The Motor Fuel (Lead Content of Petrol) Regulations 1976.
SI 1979 No 1	The Motor Fuel (Lead content of petrol) (Amendment) Regulations 1979 – reduction to 0.40 g/l by 1.1.81.
SI 1981 No 1523	The Motor Fuel (Lead content of petrol) Regulations 1981 – reduction to 0.15 g/l by 31 December 1985.
SI 1985 No 1728	The Motor Fuel (Lead content of petrol) Regulations 1985.

The 1979 Regulations were made specifically to implement Directive 78/611. The 1985 Regulations implement Article 7 of the Directive by permitting the sale of unleaded petrol conforming to a new British Standard in the UK from 1 January 1986. Consultation was initiated in October 1985 on how to implement other Articles notably the Article requiring the availability and balanced distribution of unleaded petrol from 1 October 1989. On 20 June 1986, the Minister (William Waldegrave) announced in Parliament:

> We intend that there should be at least a minimal network of petrol stations offering unleaded petrol in 1987, building up to a wide availability of the fuel by October 1989. I hope that

this can be achieved voluntarily by the industry, but the Government does not rule out taking measures to require the provision of unleaded petrol for garages above a particular size.

The Minister confirmed that in the next Budget (in 1987) a tax differential in favour of unleaded petrol would be introduced. He also confirmed that, as soon as the Directive on vehicle emissions was agreed, the government would implement the earliest dates set out in the Directive from which Member States may require new cars to be capable of running on unleaded petrol, namely: 1 October 1988 for new models over two litres; 1 October 1989 for all new model cars; and 1 October 1990 for all new registrations, unless a manufacturer can certify that major re-engineering would be involved.

Effect on UK practice

The reduction of lead in petrol began before Britain joined the Community and the effect of the two Directives in Britain is not straightforward. The earlier Directive may well have exerted an influence, while it was being negotiated, in speeding the rate of reductions although by the time it was agreed it was consistent with government policy. It subsequently acted as a brake on any move to make lead-free petrol obligatory, so that when in 1983 the government decided on a policy of lead-free petrol it had to seek an amendment to the Directive which resulted in Directive 85/210.

The permitted levels of lead in Britain starting at 0.84 g/l in 1970 are shown in Figure 3. Figure 4 indicates a number of the key events which help to explain the shape of the descent.

In 1971 the government received advice from its Chief Medical Officer that air lead levels should not be allowed to increase above the levels then prevailing and accordingly in 1972 the government announced a three-stage reduction to 0.45 g/l in 1976 in line with the increase in car use, although in the event the timescale was prolonged and involved more steps. The first two reductions (to 0.64 and 0.55 g/l) were agreed voluntarily with the petroleum industry, while all subsequent ones were imposed by Regulations. The second reduction (to 0.55 g/l) was postponed from January to December 1974 because of the oil shortage brought on by the Yom Kippur War of 1973. In December 1974 – that is after the earlier Directive had been proposed – the Secretary of State for Energy announced that no further reductions would be made pending a review of the economic and medical implications. This review had been completed by the time of the Commons' debate in March 1976 and as a result the third and fourth reductions were made (to 0.50 and 0.45 g/l). The fifth reduction (to 0.40 g/l) was made specifically to implement Directive 78/611. Even if the Directive did not bring forward the date of the reduction to 0.40 g/l it ensured that there could be no postponement in the event, say, of a falling off of traffic. While it was still a proposal the earlier Directive 78/611 must also have focused the government's mind on the earliest acceptable date for moving to 0.40 g/l and must have provided pressure for an early date.

The sixth reduction (to 0.15 g/l – the lower limit permitted by Directive 78/611) was made on 31 December 1985, as a result of a decision taken in May 1981. This followed a review of two reports. A Working Party on Lead in Petrol (WOPLIP) set up in 1978 by the Department of Transport to assess the feasibility and costs of various options for reducing lead emissions had reported in 1979[3] and another working party, also set up in 1978, by the Department of Health and Social security under the Chairmanship of Professor Lawther to consider the health effects of environmental lead pollution had reported in 1980.[1] The decision taken in May 1981 following these two reports to reduce the lead content of petrol to 0.15 g/l was accompanied by a decision to rule out compulsory lead-free petrol.

This decision was much criticized. The Conservation Society had been campaigning since 1973 for lead-free petrol and in 1977 they formed the Campaign Against Lead in Petrol (CALIP). Following the decision against lead-free petrol, a new campaign was launched in 1982 called the Campaign for Lead-Free Air (CLEAR) which succeeded in placing the issue firmly in the political agenda. It is impossible to say whether the existence of the CLEAR campaign was critical in persuading the government to accept the Royal Commission's recommendation[2] in favour of lead-free petrol, but there is no doubt that the government's quick response was a result of the campaign. CLEAR also mobilized the European Environmental Bureau (EEB) and the Bureau Europeen des Unions des Consommateurs (BEUC) to lobby the EC institutions and in several EC countries.

It was the British government, among others, that had inserted into Directive 78/611 a lower limit of 0.15 g/l and had the British initiative to amend 78/611 not been successful there would have been much resentment. In the event the successful amendment contained in Directive 85/210 repeats the story of the earlier Directive, a story of one Member State taking the initiative to force the pace in others.

Economic effects have always played a large part in the government's considerations. Various figures have been quoted at different times but in answer to parliamentary questions in January 1986 a Minister from the Department of Energy said that the additional capital investments by the UK oil industry to bring about a reduction in the maximum lead content of petrol from 0.4 to 0.15 g/l was of the order of £300 million: that on the basis of a petrol demand of 20.2 million tonnes per year, an additional 3.7m barrels of crude would be required for a reduction from 0.4 to 0.15 g/l and some 4.9 million barrels from 0.15 g/l to unleaded: and that the manufacturing costs would be about 2–3p per gallon for a reduction from 0.4 to 0.15 g/l and a further 2p to 5p per gallon for the subsequent move to unleaded petrol.

The effects on the environment of reductions made so far have been marked. In reply to a parliamentary question on 16 December 1986, the Minister, Mr Waldegrave, said that air lead levels in the first quarter of 1986 had dropped to an average of $0.29 \mu g/m^3$ compared to an average $0.563 \mu g/m^3$ during the same period in 1985. This was said to be a direct consequence of the reduction in the lead content of petrol from 0.4 to 0.15 g/l on 31 December 1985.

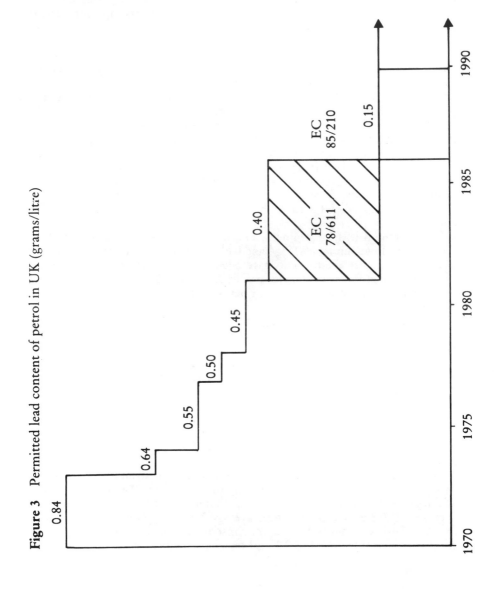

Figure 3   Permitted lead content of petrol in UK (grams/litre)

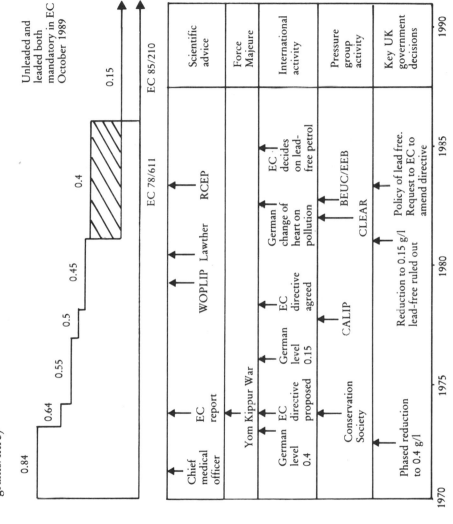

Figure 4   Key events which help to explain reduction in lead levels in petrol (in grams/litre)

Further developments
In March 1987 the Commission proposed an amendment to Directive 85/210 intended to accelerate the introduction of unleaded petrol (COM(87)33 OJ C90 4.4.87). This would enable Member States to prohibit leaded 'regular' petrol from their national market, thus reducing the number of pumps that have to be provided at petrol filling stations.

References
1   Lawther Professor P J (chairman) 1980 *Lead and health: the report of a DHSS working party on lead in the environment.* HMSO.

2   Royal Commission on Environmental Pollution 1983 *Lead in the environment. Ninth Report.* HMSO.

3   Working Party on Lead in Petrol (WOPLIP), Department of Transport 1979 *Lead in petrol: an assessment of the feasibility and costs of further action to limit lead emissions from vehicles.*

6.6 Screening for lead

77/312/EEC (OJ L105 28.4.77) proposed 16.4.75 – COM(75)166	Directive on biological screening of the population for lead.

Binding dates
Notification date	31 March 1977
Formal compliance	31 March 1978
Screening to be concluded	31 March 1982(?)

Purpose of the Directive

Lead can reach individuals by many pathways (air, water, food, pica) and to judge the significance of any one source it is necessary to know the total body burden of lead. The purpose of the Directive is to provide a much more comprehensive and accurate picture than previously existed of blood lead levels in the population as a whole and among critical groups. (The Directive is placed here with the air pollution Directives so that it can sit near the section on lead in petrol and the section on lead in air with which it was associated in its origins.)

Summary of the Directive

Member States are to undertake two screening campaigns, coordinated across the Community, and separated by an interval of two years. This is to be done by sampling the blood of volunteers to determine blood lead levels, though ALAD measurement may be used as a supplementary test. (ALAD, the enzymatic activity of delta-aminolevulinic acid dehydrates, is used as an indicator of the presence of lead.) The whole procedure is to be concluded within four years but it is unclear whether this period is intended to run from the date of the notification of the Directive, or from the start of the first campaign, or from the date for legal compliance. (If the period is supposed to have started with the notification date then it will have been overrun).

During each campaign fifty or more persons per million inhabitants per Member State are to be sampled. Samples in the second campaign need not be taken from the same individuals as in the first campaign. During each campaign, sampling is to be carried out on the following three groups:

1. groups of at least 100 persons in urban areas with more than 500 000 inhabitants;
2. groups of at least 100 persons, in so far as this is feasible, chosen from among people exposed to significant sources of lead pollution;
3. critical groups determined by the competent authorities in the Member States.

In assessing the results of the screening, the following reference levels are to be used:

a maximum of 20 μg of lead per 100 ml of blood for 50 per cent of each group
a maximum of 30 μg of lead per 100 ml of blood for 90 per cent of each group
a maximum of 35 μg of lead per 100 ml of blood for 98 per cent of each group.

Where these reference levels are exceeded, the validity of the results must be checked, and the Member States must then take action to trace the sources responsible and, at their discretion, to take all 'appropriate measures'. The Commission is to be notified of these measures and of the factors presumed to have led to the reference levels being exceeded.

To ensure comparability of results, the Member States are to inform the Commission of the laboratories taking part in the screening programme and the methods of analysis used. The Commission, together with the Member States, is to organize comparison programmes.

A designated competent national authority must provide the Commission with the relevant information about each campaign in agreed form. Complete anonymity of persons sampled is to be preserved. Twice a year the Commission is to convene a meeting of representatives of governments to ensure comparability of the screening programmes and to exchange results.

The Commission is to draw up a collated annual report which is to be forwarded to the Member States, Council and Parliament. At the end of the programme the Commission is to draw up a general report to form the basis for any further proposals.

Development of the Directive

Proposals for two separate Directives were communicated to the Council together in the same document (COM(75)166) and in their early stages were considered together. One of these proposals – concerned with air quality standards of lead – was not agreed until 1982 (see Section 6.4).

The other proposal was amended to become the biological screening Directive, but in its original form it would have set biological standards for lead (which would have had more of a mandatory character than the reference levels of the screening Directive) and would also have required a new screening campaign every two years. The standards would have been mandatory in the sense that if they were exceeded (a) Member States would have had to identify the abnormal sources of exposure and (b) notify the Commission of them. Then within two months (c) the Commission would have had to issue an opinion, after which (d) the Member States would have had to take suitable measures and (e) inform the Commission of these.

The European Parliament welcomed the proposal for mandatory standards in general terms but considered it essential that samples be taken only from volunteers – a point left unclear in the proposal. It also felt that 35 μg per 100 ml could prove too stringent. The Economic and Social Committee reiterated this point by saying that it might prove impossible for 100 per cent of the population to have blood lead levels below 35 μg per 100 ml and suggested a figure of 98 per cent instead – a suggestion that came to be adopted even for the reference levels of the screening Directive.

The British government's view was expressed by the Minister, Denis Howell, in the Commons' debate (4 March 1976) and more fully by the Minister, Baroness Stedman, in the Lords' debate (1 April 1976):

> The Commission's proposals on biological standards for lead
> in blood and air quality standards for lead go, in our view, too
> far...the scientific evidence, despite the effort put in over a
> number of years, is still not such that we can advance to the
> point where we should lay down, in legislation, precise stan-
> dards. Such a step would imply in law that every individual
> exceeding the blood lead limit and everybody in an area in
> which the air quality standard was exceeded would be in
> danger. We would not dissent from the view that the sort of
> figures for the standards proposed are reasonably reliable
> indicators of where investigation of the sources of lead should
> be initiated and action taken. We are, however, opposed to the
> rigidity and overemphasis on particular figures which would
> be consequent on enshrining them in legislation and which
> would carry with them the absolute obligation that they
> should not be exceeded.

The debate in the Lords had followed a report from the Lords' Scrutiny Committee which had criticized the proposal for biological standards as being a wasteful
deployment of money and skilled manpower. The Committee agreed that high
priority should be given to research on the effects of intermediate lead levels but
did not feel that emergency Community legislation along the lines set out was
justified. This opinion was largely based on the evidence of Sir Richard Doll, the
epidemiologist, who said that the monitoring proposed was worth doing once,
but was hardly worth doing every two years:

> . . .I really do not know what the frequency distribution of
> blood lead levels throughout the country is. I think it would
> help our thinking a lot if we had some really firm figures for
> the country as a whole and for special areas, but I see no reason
> to suppose there is any change from one year to another.
> Repeat it again in ten years' time, yes.

Sir Richard Doll had begun his evidence by saying that:

> . . .together with many people, I am disturbed by the fact that
> blood levels of lead in this country are getting – or perhaps I
> should say are, rather than are getting – uncomfortably close
> to what is generally recognized as a toxic level. They are closer
> to a toxic level than blood levels of any other element or toxic
> substance. . .

He went on to refer to the figures proposed:

> My understanding is that the sort of figures which are given
> here would be perfectly reasonable figures to aim at but that at
> the present moment we would find considerable embarrass-
> ment in applying them. Maybe it would be good that we
> should be embarrassed but we should find considerable
> embarrassment because there would be many areas of the
> country where these figures might be exceeded.

H

In the debate the Minister, Baroness Stedman, welcomed the support for the government's views expressed by the Lords' Scrutiny Committee and said:

> We have good reason to believe that a number of other Member States share our views on the Directive and we look forward to arriving at an agreed form of Community document which will meet the real needs of the Community in this matter.

In the form finally agreed mandatory biological standards were abandoned as was the commitment to regular screening. What remained was a substantially different Directive concerned with only two screening campaigns designed to collect information but using certain reference levels: if these were exceeded it would be for the Member States themselves to decide on what measures to take and it would not be for the Commission to express an opinion.

Formal compliance in the UK

The life of this Directive is limited in time. This is in contrast with most other Directives which continue indefinitely until an amending Directive is issued by the Council on a proposal from the Commission.

The Directive only makes two formal, as opposed to practical, requirements:

Member States are to designate a competent authority (Article 9);
'Member States shall take the necessary measures to enable the procedure laid down by this Directive to enter into force within 12 months following its notification and shall immediately inform the Commission thereof' (Article 12).

The government fulfilled the Article 9 requirement by creating an *ad hoc* Steering Group of Implementation of the Directive on Biological Screening of the Population for Lead, but apparently never informed the Commission in writing of the 'necessary measures' under Article 12, nor was the Commission apparently concerned by this omission. In fact, no new legislation was introduced and the government relied on the Public Health Act 1936, Section 91 of which places a duty on local authorities to inspect their districts from time to time for the detection of statutory nuisances. Section 92 includes among statutory nuisances 'dust or effluvia' caused by any trade if they are 'prejudicial to the health of, or a nuisance to, the inhabitants of the neighbourhood'. The government has no powers to compel local authorities to conduct the screening required by the Directive and the local authorities taking part in the two campaigns did so of their own volition. Two local authorities which took part in the first campaign presumably satisfied themselves that there was no nuisance in their areas and consequently felt unable to participate in the second campaign.

Local authorities also have powers under the Control of Pollution Act 1974 (Section 79) to undertake research on air pollution.

None of the people sampled in the first group (people in urban areas with more than 500 000 inhabitants) were children because, as was explained in evidence to the Lords' Scrutiny Committee, a blood sample taken from a child, even with the parents' consent, could constitute an assault unless it was taken for the benefit of the child. To take a sample for the benefit of the public generally is a different matter, and only where the child is exposed to significant sources of lead pollution can it be argued that the sampling is also for the child's benefit.

Effect on UK practice

As the main purpose of the Directive has been to provide information rather than immediately to change practice that is how it should primarily be judged. The work done by the Commission in preparing the Directive involved a survey by R L Zielhuis[1,2] of all available literature reporting blood levels and this enabled him to propose the reference values set out in the Directive. Before the Zielhuis literature survey there was no coherent view of either the normal or the safe distribution of blood lead levels in the population as a whole. The final results of the screening campaign throughout Europe have not yet been analysed and published but it is already clear that some deficiencies in the reference levels have been revealed and that there is now a better data base for proposing new reference levels.

Reports of the two British campaigns carried out in the spring of 1979 and 1981 have been published[3,4] and have been summarized by M J Quinn[5] a DoE official, from which the following description has largely been taken with the author's permission.

The screening in Britain was coordinated by the DoE in cooperation with the Department of Health and Social Security, the Welsh Office and the Scottish Home and Health Department. No surveys were undertaken in Northern Ireland. Sampling was carried out by the local authority with advice from its Medical Officer of Environmental Health, or by the Area Health Authority.

In the 1979 campaign there were thirty-nine surveys in Britain in which nearly 5000 samples were collected. Two thousand randomly selected adults took part in the inner and outer areas of Birmingham, Leeds, Liverpool, London, Manchester and Sheffield; there was one citywide survey in Glasgow. Two thousand children, either children of leadworkers or living near a leadworks, were sampled in nine locations. Three hundred adults and 500 children living near major roads were sampled in London and Leeds. In Glasgow, in addition to the random surveys of adults, blood concentrations of mothers and their three-month old infants were measured as part of a study of dietary intakes of lead. These infants were the only ones in Britain forming a 'critical group' (see Summary of Directive). There were no random samples of children for the legal reason given above.

In the 1981 campaign there were thirty-five surveys in which about 3500 people took part. As the results of the 1979 campaign had shown that the blood lead concentrations in the random surveys of adults were generally well below the reference levels, the emphasis was placed upon specific sources of exposure and groups were selected of people either living in predominantly older housing, or near major roads. About 1700 adults were sampled in the same major cities as before, plus Bristol. The surveys of children exposed to leadworks were repeated, except at three places where it was generally agreed that the position was satisfactory. In addition, there was a survey of mothers with young children at Ayr in Scotland where the water was known to dissolve lead from pipes, and a survey of Bangladeshi infants in the London Borough of Tower Hamlets.

In 1979 thirty-three of the thirty-nine groups studied met all three reference levels generally by comfortable margins. All groups met the 20 μg/100 ml reference level; only the group of infants in Glasgow breached the second reference level of 30 μg/100 ml, and six groups exceeded the upper reference level of 35 μg/100 ml including all three surveys in Glasgow and children of leadworkers at Chester or living near the leadworks. When the results of the 1979 campaign became known the water authority in Glasgow increased the lime dosing of the water supply to reduce its acidity and substantial reductions of lead concentrations in water have been achieved. In Chester the leadworks is to close.

In 1981 three of the thirty-five surveys did not meet the reference levels. The group of mothers of young children in Ayr exposed to high levels of lead in water, was the only survey in the whole of the British campaign which breached all three reference levels. As a result for a time a lead free supply of drinking water was provided for young children, and the acidity of the water supply has been reduced. The randomly selected adults living near the Archway Road in Islington, while otherwise showing fairly typical results for inner city areas, nevertheless revealed three men exceeding the 35 μg/100 ml level. Two were found to have been stripping old lead paint and the third had been burning cables containing lead. All groups where breaches of the reference levels were found in the 1979 campaign were sampled again in 1981 and met the reference levels.

Blood lead levels were already being measured in more than twenty-five different places in Britain before the Directive was agreed, but these were all population groups at risk. Without the Directive, samples would probably not have been taken from the first group mentioned in the Directive (people in urban areas with more than 500 000 population) and so a broader picture of blood lead levels in the population at large has now been provided. The Directive has also ensured that screening in Britain is now carried out in a more coordinated way, both in time and in the methods used. In addition to its main aim of producing information it is also evident that the Directive has resulted in some practical action.

The expenditure incurred by local authorities and central government is estimated at not much more than £60 000 for the first campaign and £50 000 for the second campaign. This represents actual payments and not the salaries of officials.

A summary of the results of the first screening campaign in all Member States was published by the Commission in March 1981[6] and is discussed in the paper by Quinn.[5] Blood lead levels in Britain were about in the middle of the range of other countries, with those in Italy and Belgium being generally higher and those in Germany, Denmark and the Netherlands being generally lower. A summary report of the second campaign has not been published. (It should be noted that the Directive requires the Commission to publish annual reports – it has not done so.) Some countries, it is believed, have published reports of their own results; comparisons would be difficult.

A circular letter sent to the local authorities in September 1982 (DoE Circular 22/82) noted that a Department of Health and Social Security working party had reported in 1980[7] that there was no convincing evidence of adverse health effects at blood lead levels below 35 μg/100 ml and noted that less than 1 per cent of the groups sampled as a result of the screening carried out under the Directive were over this level even though the groups were deliberately sampled to overrepresent those exposed to high levels of lead. However, the Circular went on to say that as a result of more recent scientific work the Department of

Health and Social Security is now recommending that where a person – particularly a child – is confirmed as having a level over 25 µg/100 ml his or her environment should be investigated for sources of lead. The Circular said that it is now government policy:

> to tackle local environmental 'hot spots' where exposure to one source or several is likely to give rise to blood lead levels over 25 µg/100 ml; and
> to seek to reduce exposure generally as far as is reasonably practicable.

The report[4] of the 1981 campaign shows that a small number of people in most groups studied had blood lead levels exceeding 25 µg/100 ml – in Ayr 32 per cent exceeded this level.

The Department of the Environment has subsequently put in hand a large monitoring programme to measure blood lead levels annually over the period 1984 to 1987 with the object of assessing the effect of the reduction in the lead content of petrol to 0.15 g/l from 1 January 1986. The surveys are on a different basis to those in the Directive and include children as well as adults. The results of the 1984 survey have been published[8]. They show that average blood lead levels in both children and adults were generally low and in line with expectations. They also confirm the conclusions of the 1979 and 1981 surveys under this Directive that blood lead levels were related to a range of personal, social and environmental factors including age, sex and smoking and drinking habits.

References

1   Zielhuis R L 1974 Biological quality guide for inorganic lead. *International Archives of Occupational Health* **32**, p 103–27.

2   Zielhuis R L 1975 Dose-response relationships for inorganic lead. *International Archives of Occupational Health* **35** p 1–18 and 19–35, Issue 1.

3   Department of the Environment, CDEP 1981 *European Community screening programme for lead: United Kingdom results for 1979–80.* (Pollution Report No 10).

4   Department of the Environment CDEP 1983. *European Community screening programme for lead: United Kingdom results for 1981.* (Pollution Report No 18).

5   Quinn M J 1982 *The findings of the EC blood lead survey.* Paper given to the 49th Annual Conference of the National Society for Clean Air, October.

6   Commission of the European Communities March 1981 *Progress report on the implementation of the Directive 77/312 – COM(81)88.*

7   Lawther Professor P J Lawther (chairman) 1980 *Lead and health: the report of a DHSS working party on lead in the environment.* HMSO.

8   Department of the Environment 1986 *UK blood lead monitoring programme 1984–87*, Results for 1984. HMSO. No 22. (Pollution Report).

6.7 Emibionsions from vehicles

A series of Directives deals with emissions from vehicles under three classes:

Positive ignition engines (ie petrol engines)

1. 70/220/EEC (OJ L76 6.4.70) proposed 1969 – COM(69)939	Directive on the approximation of the laws of the Member States relating to measures to be taken against air pollution by gas from positive ignition engines of motor vehicles.
2. 74/290/EEC (OJ L159 15.6.74)	(Amendment – Council Directive).
3. 77/102/EEC (OJ L32 3.2.77)	(Amendment – Commission Directive).
4. 78/665/EEC (OJ L223 14.8.78)	(Amendment – Commission Directive).
5. 83/351/EEC (OJ L197 20.7.83) proposed 5.4.82 – COM(82)170	(Amendment – Council Directive).

Diesel engines

6. 72/306/EEC (OJ L190 20.8.72) proposed 1971 – COM(71)1484	Directive on the approximation of the laws of the Member States relating to the measures to be taken against the emission of pollutants from diesel engines for use in vehicles.

Diesel engines for tractors

7. 77/537/EEC (OJ L220 29.8.77) proposed 1975 – COM(75)621	Directive on the approximation of the laws of the Member States relating to the measures to be taken against the emission of pollutants from diesel engines for use in wheeled agricultural or forestry tractors

Purpose of the Directives

Air pollution from vehicles can be regulated either by specifying the composition of the fuel or by specifying the construction of the vehicle itself. Some Directives regulate the content of sulphur and lead in fuels (see Sections 6.1 and 6.5) and the seven Directives listed above regulate the characteristics of the vehicle. The parent Directive under each of the three above headings was introduced primarily to prevent the Member States creating barriers to trade by setting more stringent standards than those specified, but some of the Directives have subsequently been amended to permit more stringent standards.

Summary of the Directives

The Directives are of the kind known as 'permissive' or 'optional' or as providing 'optional harmonization' that is to say, Member States are not obliged to make mandatory the standards in the Directives but they may not refuse national or EEC type approval of a vehicle on grounds relating to air pollution if the requirements of the Directive are met. ('Type approval' shows that a vehicle type conforms with certain standards of design and construction.)

70/220 set limit values for emissions of carbon monoxide (CO) and unburnt hydrocarbons (HC) from petrol-engined vehicles other than tractors and public works vehicles. 74/290 reduced these limits. 77/102 added limits for nitrogen oxides (NO_x). 78/665 reduced the limits for all three pollutants. 83/351 further reduced the limits and, in comparison with those in 78/665, reduced the limits of CO by 23 per cent and of HC and NO_x by 20 to 30 per cent. It also provides for limits on these pollutants from diesel engines.

72/306 sets numerical limits on the opacity of emissions from diesel-engined vehicles except tractors and public works vehicles. It also prescribes an opacimeter for use in measuring emissions. 77/537 sets limits on the opacity of emissions from diesel-engined tractors.

Development of the Directives

The United Nations' Economic Commission for Europe (ECE) has a working group to develop regulations on emissions to air from motor vehicle engines which can then be observed by all countries in Europe. An ECE regulation is not binding but any amendment can only be made by unanimity between those countries that have adopted the original regulation. The Directives have so far all followed ECE regulations and, in order to prevent barriers to trade, ensure that Member States do not set more stringent limits than those laid down in the ECE regulations.

Formal compliance in UK

Quantitative limits on vehicle emissions were first set in Britain in 1973 under the Road Traffic Act 1972 by the Motor Vehicles (Construction and Use) Regulations 1973 (SI 1973 No 1347). These made mandatory the standards of Directive 70/220. The following Construction and Use Regulations introduced the standards of the subsequent Directives:

    SI 1975 No   641 – Directive 74/290 (petrol engines)
    SI 1977 No 1401 – Directive 77/102 (petrol engines)
    SI 1980 No   139 – Directive 78/665 (petrol engines)
    SI 1982 No 1040 – Directive 83/351 (petrol engines)
    SI 1974 No   64 – Directive 72/306 (diesel engines)
    SI 1979 No   843 – Directive 77/357 (tractors)

All these Regulations have been replaced by The Road Vehicles (Construction and Use) Regulations 1986 SI 1078. Since the Directives are of the 'optional' kind, there is no obligation to set limits equal to those in the Directives and any delay in doing so would not constitute a breach of the Directives. The standards of

Directive 72/306 on the opacity of diesel emissions are mandatory in Britain but the standards of Directive 83/351 for emissions from cars are still optional. The standards for cars in force in Britain are those of Directive 78/665.

Effect on UK practice
The main purpose of the Directives is to prevent Member States setting more stringent limits than those specified. When setting its standards Britain has been guided by the ECE regulations which, in each case, preceded the Directive so that the Directives themselves have not provided the occasion for a decision to change the standards in Britain. However, once having agreed a Directive, Britain has not been able to adopt the more stringent standards of the next ECE regulations until they are agreed in an amending Directive. The Directives therefore could have an effect if for some reason in the future there was to be some delay between an ECE regulation and an equivalent Directive.

Further developments
In June 1984 the Commission put forward a proposal (COM(84)226 OJ C178 6.7.84) for further reduction in vehicle emissions linked to another proposal for lead-free petrol that has since been agreed as Directive 85/210 (see Section 6.5). There are two reasons why the proposals were linked. To achieve the emission standards proposed for some vehicles would require the use of catalytic converters, and conventional catalytic converters do not function properly with leaded petrol. Directive 85/210 which makes mandatory the provision of unleaded petrol by October 1989 (and optionally before then) has removed that difficulty. The second reason is that if unleaded petrol is to replace leaded petrol completely it is necessary that all new cars are able to run on unleaded petrol. This is provided for in the proposed vehicle emissions Directive and during negotiations the British government succeeded in bringing the dates forward to 1 October 1988 for new model cars over two litres; 1 October 1989 for all new model cars, and 1 October 1990 for all new registrations unless major new engineering would be involved.

The emission standards originally proposed were fiercely fought over with one of the major battle lines being drawn between countries manufacturing small cars and those manufacturing large cars. The dispute centred on whether the standards should be set so that small and medium-sized cars would have to use catalytic converters or whether the so-called 'lean burn' technology could be used. Eventually a compromise was accepted by all countries except Denmark and Greece. Denmark is insisting on more stringent standards (surprisingly since it had not by early 1987 yet made mandatory the standards of Directive 83/351). The Directive has therefore not been agreed, although it seems likely that motor car manufacturers will work to the new standards. In a debate in the House of Commons on 14 January 1986 the Minister (William Waldegrave) said the government had ruled out the compulsory use of threeway catalysts and was undecided on whether it would introduce emission standards that would require the use of oxidation catalysts that reduce hydrocarbon emissions alone. The standards that have been agreed by all countries except Denmark and Greece are as shown in Table 11.

Table 11   Vehicle emission standards (grams/test)

Class of vehicle	Implementation dates*	CO	$(HC+NO_x)$	NO_x
> 2 litres	1988/89	25	6.5	3.5
1.4–2 litres	1991/93	30	8.0	no separate limit
<1.4 litres				
Stage 1	1990/91	45	15	6.0
Stage 2	1992/93	to be decided in 1987		

* The first date refers to new models; the second refers to all new cars

In June 1986 the Commission proposed two new Directives. The first (COM(86)261 OJ C174 12.7.86) deals with particulate emissions from diesel-powered cars. The second (COM(86)273 OJ C193 31.7.86) deals with emissions from diesel-powered commercial vehicles.

6.8 Emissions from industrial plants

84/360/EEC (OJ L188 16.7.84) proposed 8.4.83 – COM(83)173	Directive on combatting of air pollution from industrial plants.

Binding dates
Notification date	2 July 1984
Formal compliance	30 June 1987

Purpose of the Directive

This Directive is the first significant Community response to the problem of acid deposition and the death of forests. Operation of certain industrial plants is to be authorized in advance in order to prevent or reduce air pollution. This is also a framework Directive in that it foresees subsequent Directives setting emission limit values. Such limits have been set in a subsequent Directive on asbestos (see Section 7.9) which also sets limits on discharges to water.

Summary of the Directive

The Directive requires Member States to ensure that the operation of plants specified in an Annex are given prior authorization. Such authorization must be considered at the design stage; authorization is also required in the case of substantial alteration. Before issuing an authorization the competent authority has to be satisfied that the following conditions are met:

all appropriate preventive measures against air pollution must be taken (this includes applying the best available technology provided this does not entail excessive costs);
emissions, particularly those listed in a second Annex, must not cause significant air pollution;
emission limit values must not be exceeded and air quality limit values must be taken into account.

Applications for authorization and the decisions of the competent authorities are to be made available to the public.

The Directive provides for the Council to fix emission limit values based on the best available technology not entailing excessive costs and to lay down measurement and assessment techniques and methods. Other articles require information on applications for authorization to be made available to the public in accordance with national laws and to other Member States. Member States are also to make known to each other and the Commission information on prevention and reduction of air pollution.

Member States are required to keep up to date with progress on best available technology and to impose conditions accordingly. They are also required to adapt existing plants gradually to the best available technology. Particularly polluted areas and areas to be specially protected may be defined within which more stringent emission limit values may be fixed.

The categories of plants listed in the first Annex fall into the following main divisions: energy industry; metal production and processing; non-metallic mineral product manufacture (eg cement and asbestos production); chemical industry; waste disposal; and paper pulp manufacture. The second Annex lists eight categories of the most important polluting substances including sulphur dioxide, nitrogen oxides, asbestos and fluorine.

Development of the Directive

The pressure for this Directive came from the Federal Republic of Germany. Concern over the effect of air pollution on forests in Germany led the Republic to submit a memorandum to the Council in June 1982 asking for greater priority to be given to a basic Directive on air pollution prevention, and asking that a proposal from the Commission should be submitted before the end of 1982. The subject was discussed at Environment Councils in June and December of that year. June 1982 also saw the Stockholm Ministerial Conference on the acidification of the environment, which emphasized the seriousness of the problem of air pollution and defined guidelines for action nationally and internationally.

The Commission responded to the German memorandum with a proposal in April 1983. The main elements of this were the requirement for Member States to give prior authorizations to plants likely to cause air pollution and particularly those in a specified list covering the most polluting types of plants. Certain conditions were to be met before authorizations were given. One of these was to require all appropriate measures to be taken 'in accordance with the state of the art'.

Further pressure for early action on the proposal came from the unprecedented inclusion in the European Council held at Stuttgart in June 1983 of an item on the environment. In the conclusions reference was made to 'the acute danger threatening the European forests area' and immediate action to avoid an irreversible situation was called for.

The UK government's reaction to the proposal was to acknowledge that the system prescribed was broadly in line with UK practice except for the provision for Communitywide fixed emission limits. There was concern that these limits might prove unduly inflexible. New powers might also be needed to cover certain industries specified in the proposal which, under existing controls, were the responsibility of local authorities and not of the Industrial Air Pollution Inspectorates.

During the course of negotiations in the Council machinery, the Commission issued a Communication to the Council (COM(83)721 of 25 November 1983) concerning environmental policy in the field of combatting air pollution. This reviewed the current concern about air pollution problems, particularly those connected with acid deposition and described the proposed Community programme of work. First among these was the framework Directive proposal followed by a proposal for a Directive dealing with emissions of sulphur dioxides, nitrogen oxides and particulates from large combustion plants (see below – Further developments). Other areas for action included review of the existing Directive on the sulphur content of gas oil (see Section 6.1) and a proposal to limit the emission of pollutants from the burning of used oils.

The Directive as agreed followed the main lines of the proposal. The principal changes were the replacement of the phrase 'state of the art' by 'the best available technology not entailing excessive costs'; the fixing of emission limits to be agreed unanimously instead of by qualified majority; the requirement that such limits should take account of the nature, quantities and harmfulness of the emissions, in addition to being based on the best available technology not entailing excessive costs; and the omission of five categories of food processing plants. The implementing date was also postponed by three years to 30 June 1987.

Formal compliance in the UK

Emissions to air from the works listed in a schedule to the Health and Safety (Emissions into the Atmosphere) Regulations 1983 (SI 1983 No 943) are controlled in Britain under the provisions of the Alkali etc Works Regulation Act 1906 and the Health and Safety at Work etc Act 1974. However, not all the plants listed in the Directive are covered.

In the consultation paper *Air Pollution Control in Great Britain – Review and Proposals* issued by the government in December 1986 (see Relevant British legislation), it is proposed to introduce a new two-part schedule of processes in the proposed new clean air legislation. Part A would specify processes to be subject to control by the national inspectorates and Part B those to be subject to control by local authorities. The schedule would include categories of plants referred to in this framework Directive. This would provide powers to give prior approval to those processes which are not at present subject to control by national inspectorates and thus enable the Directive to be implemented. The consultation paper acknowledges the need to replace quickly the existing schedule of process in order to ensure compliance with the Directive. Powers would also be proposed to set air quality standards and emission limits.

Effect on UK practice

It is clear that the need to comply with this Directive is influencing the form of proposed legislation in that more processes will be subject to prior authorization, and powers are being introduced to set emission limits nationally by means of Regulations. However, the use of best practicable means (bpm) may well continue as the basis of the industrial air pollution control system. Any binding emission limits would be incorporated into 'bpm' notes prepared by the Air Pollution Inspectorate.

Further developments

In the context of concern about acid rain, the proposal for the first daughter Directive entirely eclipses its parent. In December 1983 the Commission proposed a Directive concerned with large combustion plants (COM(83)704 OJ C49 21.2.84) which can be considered a daughter as it would set emission limits for sulphur dioxide, nitrogen oxides and dust. However, it would go much further by setting limits on the amount of total emissions from large combustion plants in each country. Using 1980 as a base, Member States would have, by 1995, to reduce total emissions of sulphur dioxide by 60 per cent, and total emissions of dust and nitrogen oxides by 40 per cent. Three years later the proposal has still not been agreed and it is clear that it will never be agreed in its original form. During 1986 both the Dutch and British, who in turn held the Presidency of the Council, put forward modified proposals which would set different targets for different countries. Britain was seen as a leading opponent of the proposal because until the middle of 1986 it had no national plans to fit flue gas desulphurization (fgd) equipment to existing power stations, but in its original form the proposed Directive exerted little pressure on Britain since it was perfectly clear that it was not acceptable to many other countries. The proposal by the Central Electricity Generating Board in 1986 to fit fgd equipment to three existing power stations would not by itself enable the UK to achieve anything like a 60 per cent reduction in sulphur dioxide emissions by 1993.

6.9 Monitoring of forest damage

3528/86 (OJ L326 21.11.86) proposed 14.6.83 – COM(83)375 and 13.7.84 – COM(84)418	Regulation on the protection of the Community's forests against atmospheric pollution.
526/87 (OJ L53 21.2.87)	Commission Regulation laying down rules for implementation of Regulation 3528/86.
1696/87 (OJ L161 22.6.87)	Commission Regulation laying down rules for implementation of Regulation 3528/86.
1697/87 (OJ L161 22.6.87)	Commission Regulation laying down rules for implementation of Regulation 3528/86
Binding dates Formal compliance Periodic reports	24 November 1986 annually, by 1 November.

Purpose of the Regulations

The stated purpose is to establish a scheme to protect forests against atmospheric pollution but the aim is more accurately set out as helping Member States to establish a periodic inventory of damage and a network of observation points.

Summary of the Regulations

Detailed rules for establishing an inventory of forest damage and a monitoring network are to be decided by a procedure using a Committee on Forest Protection with a chairman from the Commission and not more than two officials from each Member State. Voting on proposals from the Commission will be by weighted majority. When proposals are in accordance with the Committee's opinion, the Commission will adopt the proposal. Alternatively when the Committee does not support the proposal the Commission will submit the proposal to the Council who will decide within three months by a qualified majority. Each Member State is to draw up a periodic forest health report with reference to atmospheric pollution in accordance with rules established through the Forest Protection Committee procedure.

The scheme is also aimed at encouraging experiments to improve understanding of atmospheric pollution in forests and its effects and carrying out of projects to improve observation methods and damage measurement. Each year before 1 November, Member States are to submit to the Commission details of such experiments and projects.

The scheme is to last for five years from 1 January 1987. Finance is to be in accordance with the Community budget; the estimated cost is 10 million ECU for the five-year period. A maximum of 30 per cent of expenditure approved by the Commission will be found from Community funds.

The Commission is to submit an annual report to the European Parliament and Council.

The Council will review the Regulation before 1 January 1992 acting on a proposal from the Commission.

Development of the Regulations

The original proposal from the Commission covered both action against forest fires and acid rain. The appropriations thought necessary were for 100 million ECUs over a five-year period with three-quarters going to fire protection. The case for action was based on the incidence of forest fires largely in the Mediterranean region and the damage to forests in Germany through atmospheric pollution.

The proposal would have required observation posts to be located by the Commission acting on proposals from Member States. It would also have required the setting up in each Member State of a multidisciplinary team of scientists to draw reports and define approaches to combatting the effects of acid deposition. The teams would be supervised by the Commission.

Amendments resulting from the European Parliament's opinion were largely confined to requiring the Commission to define high risk zones and to adding programmes for developing technologies to prevent atmospheric pollution and for research into the causes of acid rain. The proposals concerning forest fire protection were adopted under a separate Regulation (3529/86 OJ L326 21.11.86).

Formal compliance in UK

The Regulation is directly applicable but Member States are required to adopt the necessary measures to ensure that the operations financed by the Community are properly carried out. Member States were waiting for the Committee to establish the rules for the inventory and monitoring network.

Effect on UK practice

There are a number of points at issue; for example, the UK has a much wider variety of trees in its forests compared with Germany and a very different variety of trees from those in Mediterranean regions. A harmonized inventory may be hard to draw up because of the different effects of air pollution on different species. The Forestry Commission has a basic monitoring service and the extent to which additions will be needed will depend on the rules to be established. They also have existing schemes for observing effects of pollution. The Forestry Commission would welcome Community funds for these schemes and others which may be justified but there are problems over 'attribution' which under present Treasury rules would prevent their receiving any benefit.

6.10 Exchange of information – air

82/459/EEC (OJ L210 19.7.82) proposed 14.7.81 – COM(81)361	Decision establishing a reciprocal exchange of information and data from networks and individual stations measuring air pollution.
Binding dates Notification date Exchange of information	June 1982 annually from various dates from 1 January 1979 to 1 October 1982 according to pollutant for a period up to June 1989. -

Purpose of the Decision

The Decision provides for setting up an exchange of information on a number of substances causing air pollution. An earlier Decision 75/441 (OJ L194 25.7.75), which was concerned only with sulphur dioxide and smoke, was repealed by Decision 82/459.

Summary of the Decisions

Decision 75/441 set up a system for exchange of data on sulphur dioxide and smoke (suspended particulates). Sampling or monitoring stations were to be designated according to demographic, geographic and pollution level parameters. Thus each Member State was to specify a maximum of five sites in each of five categories of urban population:

in the first four population categories both residential and industrial areas were to be considered;
in the same four population categories three stations were to be specified for each of the two zones (residential and industrial) according to pollution levels (maximum, minimum and average);
for the fifth category only maximum and average pollution levels were to be considered;
outside urban areas, smaller countries were to nominate up to five sites, larger up to fifteen.

The data (daily average concentrations) were to be sent monthly to the Commission within six months of measurements. The Commission was required to submit an annual report to Member States.

Decision 82/459 replaced 75/441 and in addition to sulphur dioxide and smoke requires data on suspended particulates of heavy metals (cadmium, lead, etc) nitrogen oxides, carbon monoxide and ozone. The data are to be sent annually to the Commission in a specified form within six months of the end of the annual measurement period. The dates by which the new system came into effect varied according to pollutants with those for sulphur dioxide and smoke going back to 1 January 1979 to ensure continuity. In addition to the stations selected under the earlier Decision, Member States are required to select additional stations to be representative of the conditions for the pollutant concerned. An annual report will continue to be prepared by the Commission and distributed to Member States. The Decision ceases to apply in June 1989.

Development of the Decisions

The first Decision 75/441 was essentially a three-year pilot study. As a result of experience the replacement Decision 82/459 was extended to include other air pollutants for which it was possible to get data. The annual reports for the years 1976, 1977 and 1978 have been published and for 1981 and 1982 are in press. A summary report covering 1976 to 1982 is also being prepared to include a commentary on trends and comparisons. Criticism of the operation of the scheme and the reports until now has concentrated on the difficulties of comparison.

Effect on UK practice

The UK had little difficulty in providing the information required for some eighty urban and rural sites for the first study. The number of stations for sulphur dioxide and smoke for the second were reduced by sixty-two to twenty-two but seven sites were added for other pollutants: for heavy metals there are two sites, in London and Leeds; for nitrogen oxides and carbon monoxide there are two sites, in London and Warren Spring Laboratory, Stevenage; for ozone there are three sites, in London, at Warren Spring Laboratory and at Sibton in East Anglia.

CHAPTER 7

Chemicals

7.0 Relevant British legislation

There are at least three quite separate Acts of Parliament administered by three separate government departments controlling the manufacture or use or sale of chemical substances. These are the Health and Safety at Work etc Act 1974 (HSWA) concerned primarily but not exclusively with the workplace; the Control of Pollution Act 1974 (COPA) concerned with effects on the environment; and the Consumer Safety Act concerned with protection of the consumer. Since chemical substances are both so numerous and so widespread in their applications there are also likely to be many other items of legislation controlling particular subject areas not considered here (eg pharmaceuticals, the transport of substances). Broad emergency powers prohibiting activities such as farming, fishing and food preparation in the event of the escape of a substance likely to create a hazard to human health through human consumption of food are contained in the Food and Environment Protection Act 1985.

Although the HSWA and COPA were enacted in the same year they had different origins. Nevertheless there was a common concern among those involved with issues of safety at work and those involved with the environment that new chemicals were a potential source of danger unless effectively controlled. Thus the Royal Commission on Environmental Pollution's second report[1] of 1972 referred to the impact of new products on the environment as one of three topics that had frequently arisen during their enquiries following their first report. The Robens Report[2] of the same year dealing with safety and health at work recommended (para 484) that:

> there should be comprehensive powers of control over toxic substances allied to a general statutory obligation on manufacturers to ensure adequate safety testing of new substances before marketing them for industrial use. Anyone marketing a new chemical or other potentially harmful substance for industrial or commercial use should be required to supply basic information to the Authority for consideration by a standing Advisory Committee on Toxic Substances.

Manufacture and use of chemicals
The HSWA accordingly places a duty on any person manufacturing, importing or supplying any substance for use at work (a) to ensure that the substance is safe, (b) to have the substance tested as may be necessary and (c) to ensure adequate information about such tests. Regulations supplementing these general duties and defining a workable system were made in 1982 to implement Directive 79/831

(Section 7.1) often known as the 'sixth amendment'. COPA contains powers to prohibit or restrict the importation and use of injurious substances, and the Consumer Safety Act contains wide powers to ensure that goods are safe and to prohibit goods that are not safe.

Major accidents involving chemicals

HSWA also places a general duty on employers to secure the health, safety and welfare of persons at work and to provide for the protection of the public from work activities. Regulations supplementing these general duties have been made for the purposes of implementing Directive 82/501 known as the Seveso Directive (Section 7.3) on major accident hazards including fires, explosions and massive emissions of dangerous substances when an activity gets out of control.

Pesticides

The range of Community legislation in the field of pesticides is growing (see Sections 7.5 and 7.6) while in Britian there has been a major development in recent years with the replacement of the nonstatutory Pesticides Safety Precautions Scheme by a statutory scheme under the Food and Environment Protection Act 1985. Under the wider powers made available by this Act, new statutory controls are being introduced over the period 1986–89.

References

1   Royal Commission on Environmental Pollution, 1972 *Three issues in industrial pollution Second Report*. HMSO.

2   Lord Robens (chairman) 1972 *Safety and Health at Work*. HMSO.

7.1 Preventing risks by testing (the sixth amendment)

79/831/EEC (OJ L259 15.10.79) proposed 8.9.76 – COM(76)433	Directive amending for the sixth time Directive 67/548/EEC on the approximation of the laws, regulations and administrative provisions relating to the classification, packaging and labelling of dangerous substances. (See Table 12 for list of seventeen related Directives.)

Binding dates

Notification date	19 September 1979
Formal compliance	18 September 1981
All dangerous substances to be appropriately packaged and labelled before marketing	18 September 1983
Principles of good laboratory practice to be in effect	30 June 1988

Purpose of the Directives

The 'sixth amendment' is a significant departure from its parent Directive 67/548 and the first five amendments. The earlier Directives are fairly described by their titles and set out a procedure for classifying dangerous substances according to the degree of hazard and the nature of the risks entailed as well as provisions for packaging and labelling, the purpose being to protect man, particularly in the workplace. The sixth amendment goes much further by adding a new classification of 'dangerous for the environment' and, more importantly, a scheme of prior notification involving tests for potential hazards before a substance is marketed. Not only does the scheme seek to anticipate effects on man and the environment but it also serves the purpose of the common market in chemicals by ensuring a unified system throughout the Community. Restrictions on the use of chemicals are covered by a separate series of Directives (see Section 7.2).

Summary of the Directives

The whole of the substantive parts of the parent Directive 67/548 and the first five amending Directives are replaced by the sixth amending Directive 79/831 with the exception of the formal articles concerned with the introduction of national laws, regulations and administrative provisions. This means that the parent and the first five amendments remain formally in existence but need not be referred to in order to understand the present scope of the legislation.

The parent Directive had four Annexes, the fourth amendment added Annex V, and the sixth amendment replaced Annex V by new Annexes V to IX. The Annexes have been subsequently adapted and their current state is to be found in Commission Directives 76/907, 79/370, 81/957, 82/232, 83/467, 84/449 and 86/431, as well as in the sixth amendment and Directive 87/17.

Table 12

The seventeen Directives concerned with testing new chemical substances and with classification, packaging and labelling

The parent Directive has been 'amended' six times by Council Directives and the Annexes have been 'adapted' seven times by Commission Directives (and once by a Council Directive following Greek accession); in addition there are separate Directives on good laboratory practice and on the protection of animals used for testing.

Coun 67/548	OJL196 16.08.67		
Coun 69/81	L 68 19.03.69	1st Amendment	– Annex I amended
Coun 70/189	L 59 14.03.70	2nd Amendment	– Time limits changed
Coun 71/144	L 74 29.03.71	3rd Amendment	– Time limits changed
Coun 73/146	L167 25.06.73	4th Amendment	– Annexes I to IV replaced, Annex V added, articles amended
Coun 75/409	L183 14.07.75	5th Amendment	– Articles amended
Comm 76/907	L360 30.12.76	1st Adaptation	– Annexes I, III & IV replaced
Comm 79/370	L 88 07.04.79	2nd Adaptation	– Annexes amended
Coun 79/831	L259 15.10.79	6th Amendment	– Articles amended, Annexes VI to IX added
Coun 80/1189	L366 31.12.80	Greek language	Annexes I to IV added
Comm 81/957	L351 07.12.81	3rd Adaptation	– Annex I amended
Comm 82/232	L106 21.04.82	4th Adaptation	– Annex I amended
Comm 83/467	L257 16.09.83	5th Adaptation	– Annexes I–IV, VI amended or replaced
Comm 84/449	L251 19.09.84	6th Adaptation	– Annex V replaced
Comm 86/431	L247 01.09.86	7th Adaptation	– Annexes I–IV, VI amended
Coun 86/609	L358 18.12.86		– Animal protection
Coun 87/18	L 15 17.01.87		– Good laboratory practice

The sixth amendment repeats in an expanded form the provisions of the parent Directive dealing with classification, packaging and labelling of dangerous substances but adds a procedure for testing and notification of new chemicals. Notification is now a prerequisite for the classification procedure. Packaging and labelling follow from notification and classification.

Certain substances are excluded from the scope of the Directive including medicinal products, narcotics, radioactive substances, foodstuffs and feedingstuffs, and waste covered by Directives 75/442 and 78/319 (see Sections 5.1 and 5.2).

Notification
The Member States are to ensure that before being placed on the market substances are notified to the competent authority of the Member State in which the substance is first manufactured or imported. Exceptions are made for categories of substances 'which shall be considered as having been notified within the

meaning of this Directive'. These include: most polymers; substances marketed for research and analysis purposes if they are placed on the market to determine their properties in accordance with the Directive; substances placed on the market for research and analysis under certain specified conditions; and any substances placed on the market in quantities of less than one tonne per year per manufacturer provided the manufacturer announces their identity, labelling, date and quantity to the appropriate competent authority and complies with conditions which may be imposed. Furthermore, a general exception from notification is made for substances already on the market before 18 September 1981. The Commission is to prepare an inventory of such substances and until the inventory is in existence (see below) in effect the manufacturer's declaration and evidence that a substance was already on the market by 18 September 1981 will suffice: thereafter the inventory will be the last word.

At least forty-five days prior to marketing the manufacturer must provide the competent authority with the following information as part of the notification:

a technical dossier containing the information and the results of tests and studies defined in Annex VII or justification for their omission (known as the 'base set');
a declaration concerning the unfavourable effects of the substance in terms of the various uses envisaged;
the proposed classification and labelling;
proposals for recommended precautions for safe use.

Manufacturers may acquire the right to use data submitted by others in prior notifications but they cannot be freed from their obligations to provide the technical dossier unless the substance falls outside the scope of the Directive or was originally notified ten years previously. They must still provide a basic notification including information on proposed use and production. Finally, notifiers remain responsible for informing the competent authority about changes in annual or total quantities placed on the market, new knowledge about the substance, new uses or any change in properties due to a change in composition.

Testing
The testing methods for determining the physicochemical, toxicological and ecotoxicological properties listed in Annexes VII and VIII are set out in Annex V. The methods are based on those recognized or recommended by competent international bodies (OECD in particular). Annex VII defines the 'base set' of information required with every notification (which are essentially identical to the Minimum Pre-Market Set of Data sufficient for an initial hazard assessment set out in an OECD Council Decision of December 1982). Annex VIII defines two further levels or steps (hence the term step sequence testing). The first additional level (Level 1) beyond the base set must be considered once 100 tonnes per year or 500 tonnes in all of a substance have been marketed, but competent authorities may already require these tests at one tenth this amount. Level 2 is reached when 1000 tonnes per year are marketed (or 5000 tonnes total) and then a further programme of tests must be drawn up by the competent authority as set

out. These tests concern primarily long-term health and environmental effects (eg toxicity to aquatic species) and their predictive ability and cost increase with each level.

Good laboratory practice

Directive 87/17 requires that for the tests specified in Directive 67/548 (as amended) Member States ensure that laboratories apply the principles of good laboratory practice as specified in a Decision of the Council of the Organization for Economic Cooperation and Development (OECD). Laboratories must certify that tests have been carried out in accordance with these principles when submitting test results to authorities (see also Further developments below).

Role of competent authority

Member States are to appoint the competent authority responsible for receiving the notification and examining its conformity with the Directive, in particular the findings on any risks, classification and labelling, and recommended precautions. The competent authority may ask for further information, carry out sampling or take measures relating to safe use of a substance pending the introduction of Community measures (this is a reference to Directive 76/769 – see Section 7.2).

Following notification the Commission must be sent a copy of the dossier or a summary together with any relevant comments. If only a summary is sent the Commission and the other competent authorities nevertheless have assured access to the dossier as well as to any further information obtained. The Commission must then forward this information to the other Member States. The competent authority of any Member State may consult the authority which received the original notification or the Commission on specific details and suggest further tests.

The inventory (EINECS) and the list of notified substances

The Directive requires the Commission to draw up an inventory of substances that were on the Community market before 18 September 1981. Commission Decision 81/437 (OJ L167 24.6.81) explained how the inventory, known as EINECS (European Inventory of Existing Commercial Chemical Substances), is to be drawn up. It is composed of a core inventory known as ECOIN (European Core Inventory) drawn up by the Commission from the data at its disposal – published in May 1982 – and a list of substances made the subject of subsequent declarations by the chemical manufacturers and communicated to the Commission by the Member States. These declarations were to have been made by 31 December 1982; they numbered over 130 000. The procedure for making these declarations was set out in an explanatory document published by the Commission entitled 'Reports for the EINECS inventory'. EINECS exists on magnetic tapes but has not yet been printed.

In addition to the inventory (EINECS) of substances on the market before 18 September 1981 the Commission is to keep a list of all new substances notified under the Directive. Commission Decision 85/71 (OJ L30 2.2.85) sets out what the list is to contain. In addition a list is to be kept of substances that are classified as dangerous under various categories (see below). The Directive thus requires three lists.

Confidentiality

The notifier may indicate the information he 'considers to be commercially sensitive and disclosure of which might harm him industrially or commercially' and must provide adequate justification, but it is the competent authority that decides on its own responsibility that the information is to be treated as confidential. Certain items including the name of the substance and the interpretation of tests may not be claimed as confidential under any circumstances.

Classification

The Directive sets out fourteen danger categories including the category 'dangerous for the environment' (which did not appear in the parent Directive). The general principles of the classification requirements are set out in Annex VI. Annex I contains the list of dangerous substances under their classification categories to which new substances will be added as they are classified following notification.

Packaging and labelling

Member States must ensure that substances are not placed on the market unless they are packaged and labelled according to the quite specific requirements laid down in the Directive. A novel feature of the sixth amendment is that all dangerous substances and not just those on Annex I are to be subject to the packaging and labelling requirements as from 18 September 1983.

Committee for adaptation

A committee is established with power to adapt to technical progress the Directives concerning the elimination of technical barriers to trade in dangerous substances and preparations (including those concerned with restrictions on marketing and use – see Sections 7.2 and 7.6). It may take decisions by qualified majority. Annex VI (Part I) and the essential Annexes VII and VIII are excluded from this procedure.

Access to the market

Member States may not introduce their own notification scheme or otherwise impede access to their market for reasons of classification, packaging or labelling of a substance complying with the Directive unless it has 'detailed evidence' that a substance constitutes a hazard to man and the environment in which case it may take provisional measures. (The provisions for Community restrictions are set out in Directive 76/769, see Section 7.2). In other words, notification in one Member State provides assured access to the entire Community market after forty-five days.

Development of the Directive

The first action programme on the environment of 1973 specifically charged the Commission 'to investigate the measures still required to harmonize and strengthen control by public authorities over chemicals before they are marketed'. This had become an issue in several Member States and in the United States and indeed the development of the Directive would have been quite ·different if it had not been for the legislative activity in the USA and international discussions within OECD.

In Britain, the concept of an 'early warning system' was put forward in 1972 both in the Robens Report on Safety and Health at Work[1] and by the Royal Commission on Environmental Pollution. The Royal Commission included the impact of new products on the environment in their second report[2] as one of three topics which had 'frequently arisen' during the Commission's inquiries following their first report and which it believed 'need to be aired in public'. The Royal Commission already identified scale of production and projected use as two key criteria for pinpointing substances requiring testing as well as the need to provide exceptions for 'laboratory curiosities'. The origin of the public debate in Britain thus coincided with the drafting process of the Community's first action programme in late 1972.

For several years some confusion appears to have reigned, both in Britain and in the Community, about the most appropriate point of departure: in Britain, a control scheme for new chemicals was seen as a responsibility of Health and Safety Executive (HSE) – provision for it was made in the Health and Safety at Work etc Act 1974 – and was also being developed within DoE. Within the Commission, debate centred on whether to amend yet again the existing Directive 67/548 on packaging and labelling (arising out of the internal market harmonization policies) or to develop an entirely new draft. At times, two independent draft proposals appear to have existed prepared by different departments with a power struggle between them.

In November 1974 the OECD adopted a Recommendation on the assessment of the potential environmental effects of chemicals and the preparation of this Recommendation and subsequent work on it provided a forum for technical discussion involving representatives from the USA and Canada as well as all Member States with the lead for Britain being taken by DoE.

In June 1975 draft French legislation on a scheme of premarket testing for new chemicals (which had existed for some months) was communicated to the Commission under the information agreement and served to provide impetus and focus to these discussions. The fact that this draft law was notified by the French environmental authorities to the Commission's environment service may have helped ultimately to strike a distribution of roles rather more favourable to environmental concerns than might otherwise have been achieved in the Community and in several Member States, including Britain.

A working group was established by the Commission and this had the immediate effect of linking discussions which were going on in several Member States at a time when these had reached tentative conclusions only in France. From this time on there was formal liaison in Britain between the HSE and DoE. Development of the sixth amendment can thus be considered as an example of the ideal situation where an issue requiring Community action can be taken up at Community level before sometimes conflicting legal constraints have been created in several Member States. Clearly the absence of any prior legislation on premarket testing of chemicals was an important factor in facilitating agreement on a very complex and potentially divisive topic. On the basis of the French communication and the consultations in the working group, the Commission was able to prepare a proposal for a Directive within just fifteen months.

In 1976 the Toxic Substances Control Act was passed in the USA but the full effect of this began to emerge only in 1977 following publication of implementation rules by the US Environmental Protection Agency (EPA). Thereafter the US legislation became an increasingly important factor in the negotiations in Brussels mainly as a precedent for some of the problems that arose during negotiations and as an argument for strengthening environmental aspects of the Directive.

The basic structure of the Directive as adopted can already be discerned in the proposal. But if one considers the very numerous changes of detail including the requirement for an inventory of existing substances, the ultimately adopted Directive must be considered as having been fundamentally changed. The Economic and Social Committee was favourably inclined to the proposal. The European Parliament was concerned only about a technical issue of labelling and wanted to see the use of national languages on labels an absolute requirement. The point was not taken up in Council.

The House of Commons debated the proposal rather summarily (11 July 1977) because it was linked with four proposals dealing with pesticides. A junior minister from the Ministry of Agriculture simply outlined the proposal and expressed concern about maintaining confidentiality of commercially valuable information and the provision (subsequently deleted) to control the use of substances by majority voting. The opposition generally welcomed the proposal but speakers expressed concern about the need to avoid excessive bureaucracy and costs to industry.

The House of Lords' Scrutiny Committee published its report on 26 April 1977 and a debate took place on 15 November 1977. The report and most of the subsequent debate were concerned primarily with the labelling provisions and their relationship to UN schemes for labelling in transport and with the general practicability of testing. The Lords' report recognized the need for some further limitation of the testing requirement beyond that provided in the draft for 'research, development or analysis' but had doubts about tonnage limits. Only the reply of the Minister, Lord Wallace, to the debate placed what were to be the central issues of the following two years clearly on the table: the definition of appropriate exclusions, and control of use. In the first instance, the difficulties of both an approach through categories ('research', 'development', 'analysis') and of volume were recognized, with British preference indicated for a tonnage cut-off. The ultimately adopted scheme involving both categorical and tonnage cut-offs therefore appears to have been a solution to these difficulties developed at Community level. The British point of view that use should not be controlled under the sixth amendment but under the existing Directive on the control of marketing and use of dangerous substances (see Section 7.2) ultimately prevailed in Council – but apparently only at the very last minute. Not mentioned at all in the Lords' debate was the issue of step sequence testing which was to prove vital in allaying some of industry's fears. Apparently this aspect was new within the British context, even though it is accurate to say, as several speakers emphasized in the House of Lords, that the thrust of the draft was entirely in keeping with British discussions on the issue.

In general, it must be said that both the Economic and Social Committee and the European Parliament failed to appreciate the significance of the draft Directive or even to reflect what were to become the major issues of subsequent concern. In Britain only the House of Lords gave substantial attention to the draft, and even so only covered part of the major problems.

In May 1977 the Health and Safety Commission (HSC) published a discussion document 'Proposed scheme for notification of the toxic properties of substances'.[3] A comparison made in 1981 by HSC[4] of this 1977 discussion document with the Directive gives a clear indication of the impact in the following years of Community deliberations on the British position. Seven points of difference were noted.

1. The Directive requires the notification at least forty-five days before the substance is placed on the market whereas the HSC favoured a period of thirty days.
2. The Directive requires the announcement of a limited amount of information mainly related to identity particulars and the quantity produced in respect of new substances placed on the market in quantities of less than one tonne per annum. The HSC proposals made no provision for such substances on the grounds that it was important to concentrate available scarce resources on substances where the quantity produced suggested a potentially greater degree of hazard.
3. The Directive excludes from the full testing and notification procedure substances which are subject to similar testing and notification requirements under existing Directives. The HSC proposals were designed to include such substances even though they were subject to notification under existing UK schemes (eg pharmaceuticals, pesticides and food additives) because those schemes related only to the areas of specific use.
4. The Directive does not require the notification of isolated intermediate compounds as was envisaged in the HSC scheme.
5. A more specific provision is made in the Directive than proposed by HSC for the carrying out of further tests and the provision of additional information (step sequence testing).
6. The Directive requires an inventory of existing substances unlike the HSC proposal.
7. The Directive extends to the protection of the natural environment whereas the HSC proposals were designed principally to assess the potential of a substance to cause harm to people both in the workplace and outside where they may be affected by the work activity.

The Directive as finally adopted reflects very long, detailed and complex consideration in the Council working group. The nature of changes incorporated sometimes involving subtle shifts from Article to Article are a clear indication of the difficulties which were encountered. It is consequently one of the most difficult of Directives to understand.

A particular contribution made by Britain was the 'base set' of information that has to be submitted with every notification of the proposal to market a new substance. The Robens Report[1] had recommended in 1972 that 'basic information' should be notified and the HSE then developed what this should include. These ideas – later published in outline in the 1977 discussion document[3] – were incorporated with some modification by the Commission into the proposed Directive.

The most important change after the Directive was proposed was the introduction of step sequence testing at the initiative of the German government which was being prodded by its chemical industry. In actual fact, no public allusion to step sequence testing – let alone any text setting out its principles and provisions – can be found in any official document prior to publication of the

Directive in the *Official Journal*. But quite apart from this major omission, by late 1977 it was already increasingly evident that the Directive as finally adopted would differ significantly from the proposal, making the sixth amendment one of the most obvious cases where lack of intermediate public information makes the Community legislative process so difficult to reconstruct.

Formal compliance in the UK

The provisions dealing with the notification of new substances have been implemented separately from those dealing with classification, packaging and labelling.

Notification

The Health and Safety at Work etc Act 1974 places a duty on any person who manufactures, imports or supplies any substance for use at work (a) to ensure that the substance is safe and without risks to health when properly used, (b) to have the substance tested as may be necessary and (c) to ensure adequate information about such tests and about conditions of use. In addition the Act empowers inspectors to serve 'improvement notices' and 'prohibition notices' to secure enforcement of those general duties. These general provisions, which do not extend to protection of the environment, have been supplemented by the Notification of New Substances Regulations 1982 (SI 1982 No 1496) made under both the Health and Safety at Work etc Act 1974 and the European Communities Act 1972. Separate Regulations have been made for Northern Ireland.

The Regulations came into operation on 26 November 1982, over one year after the date set in the Directive, and the Commission was formally sent a copy in January 1983 together with copies of a guidance booklet[5] that had been issued and four Approved Codes of Practice relating to test methods and procedures. The failure to implement the Directive on time was a result of a dispute between the Health and Safety Commission (HSC) and the chemical industry (see below). In February 1981 the HSC had proposed draft Regulations[4] which would have gone further than the Directive in some respects but these were resisted by the industry. In the event the views of industry prevailed and the draft Regulations had to be modified.

The competent authority for the purposes of the Directive is the Health and Safety Executive (HSE) and the DoE acting jointly (the Scottish Development Department and Welsh Office have agreed that the DoE will act on their behalf) and the Regulations require manufacturers to supply information about new substances to the HSE who in turn must forward the information to the DoE. It is because the Regulations give the DoE powers to require information about environmental effects of substances which are outside the powers conferred on HSE by the Health and Safety at Work etc Act that they have also had to be made under the European Communities Act 1972.

On 17 September 1981 (the day before the Directive came into effect) the HSC issued a press statement describing the administrative arrangements that would apply pending the Regulations. Manufacturers and importers intending to market new substances were invited to submit notifications as set out in the Directive and these would be accepted as having been made under the Regulations when they took effect.

The four Approved Codes of Practice sent to the Commission deal with the principles of good laboratory practice and methods for determining toxicity, ecotoxicity and physicochemical properties. They are issued by HSE and are largely based on methods agreed within OECD. They will be modified slightly as a result of Directive 84/449.

An amendment (SI 890) to SI 1982 No 1496 came into force on 18 June 1986. It made minor amendments to the existing provisions on testing and notification to ensure that UK regulations were in full compliance with the Directive and its requirement that manufacturers notify national authorities of the results of toxicity and other tests at least forty-five days before being placed on the market. In July 1985 the Commission sent a formal notice of failure to implement the sixth amendment.

Classification, packaging and labelling
The following Regulations also made both under the European Communities Act 1972 and the Health and Safety at Work etc Act 1974 are concerned with classification, packaging and labelling:

SI 1978 No 209	The Packaging and Labelling of Dangerous Substances Regulations 1978
SI 1981 No 792	(Amendment) 1981
SI 1983 No 17	(Amendment) 1983
SI 1984 No 1244	The Classification, Packaging and Labelling of Dangerous Substances Regulations 1984
SI 1986 No 1922	(Amendment) 1986

SI No 209 implemented Directive 67/548 as amended the first five times and as adapted the first time by Directive 76/907. SI No 792 implemented the second adaptation made by Directive 79/370. SI No 17 implemented the third and fourth adaptations made respectively by Directive 81/957 and Directive 82/232.

SI No 1244 revoked and re-enacted with minor changes SI 209 as amended with effect from 12 September 1984. It implemented several Directives concerning classification, packaging and labelling in addition to the sixth amendment (eg pesticides, solvents, paints and varnishes) as well as labelling provisions of the Directive on toxic wastes. An 'Approved List' providing information on classification of dangerous substances was published in July 1984 enabling manufacturers and others to refer to the list to decide whether substances fall within the provisions of the Regulations. A first revision to the list was published in October 1986. SI No 1922 covers amendments made necessary by the changes to the 'Approved List' of October 1986.

Britain must have been in breach of the parent Directive and its various amendments until the 1978 Regulations were made, and the 1981 Regulations were also late in implementing Directive 79/370 so that the Commission issued a Reasoned Opinion to the effect that there was a failure to implement. The explanation appears to be a desire to await the further adaptation that after delay became Directive 81/957 and that introduced significant changes to Directive 79/370. This is a recurring problem when a Directive is being continually amended because implementation then becomes an attempt to hit a moving target. With the 1983 Regulations the packaging and labelling requirements of nearly 1000 chemicals were specified.

Effect on UK practice

This Directive is possibly the most important of all the environmental Directives agreed so far. The subject matter is important. The costs incurred for industry were originally estimated at about £40 000 for fully testing one new substance with an expected 200 to 400 new substances to be notified in the Community each year. The administrative arrangements necessary for making the system workable are extensive and require trained manpower in both the public and private sectors. Novel relationships between the competent authorities in the Member States have been established. Above all, the Directive is a significant attempt to make concrete the principle enunciated in the first action programme that prevention is better than cure. A yet further aspect of the Directive is that it has enabled the Community to speak with one voice in discussions within the OECD and with the United States and other countries and has strengthened its position in ensuring that the operation of the US Toxic Substances Control Act does not create obstacles to the European chemical industry. The sixth amendment and the US Act have similar goals and eventually some arrangement may be reached to ensure that chemicals notified in USA can be marketed in Europe and vice versa. The ability of the Commission – which can speak for a larger market than that of the USA – to enter into discussions with the USA has been greatly enhanced by the Directive and it is unlikely that each European country on its own could do so as effectively. These discussions are still continuing.

The effect of the Directive on Britain is therefore extremely difficult to assess because it must take into account all these disparate and uncertain matters. It is evident that had there been no Directive some comparable system for prenotification would have been introduced in Britain. We have already noted above some of the differences between the system proposed by the HSC in 1977 with that of the Directive but it would be a mistake to assume that what was proposed in Britain in 1977 would necessarily have been adopted in precisely that form, so a comparison is not particularly helpful in establishing the effect of the Directive even on the detailed form of the British procedure.

One effect of the Directive is similar to an effect of the Seveso Directive (see Section 7.3). There is nothing in either Directive to prevent Member States including more substances within the scope of national regulations than are required by the respective Directives. The scheme proposed by HSC in 1977 involved notification of 'isolated' intermediate compounds, that is to say compounds which are not to be marketed but which are produced or are used to arrive at the marketable product. Some intermediate compounds are transitory compounds produced in a reaction while others are stored and transported and may require labelling (referred to as isolated intermediate compounds). Given the emphasis of the Health and Safety at Work etc Act it was natural that the British proposals would seek to ensure that intermediate compounds that could affect the workforce would be brought within the scheme, but because of the bias of the Directive toward substances placed on the market, and the problems of definition, intermediate compounds were left out of the Directive. Nevertheless, the HSC in the draft Regulations issued for consultation in 1981 proposed to go further than the Directive by bringing such intermediate compounds within the scope of the Regulations. This was resisted by the chemical industry represented by the Chemical Industries Association (CIA) on the grounds that these were already controlled by industry and assessed by the Factory Inspectorate so that the proposals 'would substitute an efficient and cost-effective means of direct discussion with the enforcing authorities by a cumbersome bureaucratic mechanism for centralising information'.[6] The CIA argued – as they did with the Seveso Directive – that the proposed Regulations should not impose greater burdens on

British industry than the Directive placed on its competitors. The CIA view prevailed thus ensuring that in this field Community legislation is coming to set both the maximum as well as the minimum standard for domestic legislation.

A further important effect of the Directive has already been noted. The British scheme proposed in 1977 would have been made under the Health and Safety at Work etc Act and would not have been concerned with effects on the environment. Because the Directive was proposed by the Commission as an environmental Directive and specifically refers to environmental effects which are beyond the responsibilities of the HSE, the DoE has had to be involved and the HSE and DoE jointly act as the competent authority. Without the Directive a liaison in quite this form would not have been achieved. HSE and DoE were both involved in negotiating the Directive and continue to be involved jointly in the further discussions that are still proceeding.

The HSE has established a new inspectorate[7] to ensure that test data for notifications has been generated in accordance with the principles of good laboratory practice originally agreed within OECD.

Finally there is the effect on classification and packaging that can be easily overlooked in concentrating on notification. Britain had no provisions similar to those in the parent Directive and the early amendments and, although a comparable system could well have been introduced and indeed is provided for in the Health and Safety at Work etc Act, the Directive has ensured that this has happened and has prescribed the form.

The full effects of the Directive will not be felt for some time. In November 1985 it was reported that only 100 new substances had been notified within the Community, whereas some 200 a year had been expected according to figures provided by the chemical industry. ICI instead of the expected twenty new substances to test each year had had an average of only five per year. Industry placed the blame on the prohibitive cost of testing. Fears were also expressed about unfair competition with new products appearing in the USA and Japan which did not require disclosure of chemical identities.

By the end of February 1987, 63 notifications had been received in the UK, including some renotifications from other countries. Within the Community the total number of full notifications was 214, of which 116 were notified for the first time. In addition there had been 777 limited announcements, ie of less than one tonne.

The competent authorities from the different Member States meet regularly with the Commission to review the working of the Directive, and their developing relations may yet be creating something entirely new: a Community 'agent' that implements Community policy. The HSE guidance booklet[5] has gone so far as to say that 'a notification made to the (British) competent authority is made to the European Community as a whole, the competent authority in effect acting on behalf of the Community'.

Further developments

The Commission published in December 1986 (COM(86)698) a further proposal for a Council Directive complementing Directive 87/18 on good laboratory practice by specifying a uniform system of inspection and verification of laboratories under government approval. It follows OECD guidelines.

References

1 Lord Robens (chairman) 1972 *Safety and health at work*. HMSO.

2 Royal Commission on Environmental Pollution 1972 *Second Report: Three issues in industrial pollution*. HMSO.

3 Health and Safety Commission 1977 *Discussion document: proposed scheme for the notification of the toxic properties of substances*. HMSO.

4 Health and Safety Commission 1981 *Consultative document: notification of new substances: draft regulations and approved codes of practice*. HMSO.

5 Health and Safety Executive 1982 *A guide to the notification of new substances regulations 1982.* HMSO.

6 Chemical Industries Association 1981 *Notification of new substances: Vol 1 comments and recommendations on the regulations.*

7 Health and Safety Executive 1983 *Establishment of a good laboratory practice compliance programme.*

7.2 Restrictions on marketing and use

76/769/EEC (OJ L262 27.9.76) proposed 25.7.74-COM(74)1189 and 29.4.75 – COM(75)186	Directive relating to restrictions on the marketing and use of certain dangerous substances and preparations (initially PCBs, PCTs and monomer vinyl chloride).
79/663/EEC (OJ L197 3.8.79) proposed 2.3.79-COM(79)84 and 19.3.79 – COM(79)123	(First amendment) (ornamental objects etc)
82/806/EEC (OJ L339 1.12.82) proposed 10.10.80 – COM(80)570	(Second amendment) (benzene in toys)
82/828/EEC (OJ L350 10.12.82) proposed 11.1.80 – COM(79)792	(Third amendment) (PCTs)
83/264/EEC (OJ L147 6.6.83) proposed 1981 – COM(81)573	(Fourth amendment) (fire retardants and novelties)
83/478/EEC (OJ L263 24.9.83) proposed 7.3.80 – COM(79)419	(Fifth amendment) (asbestos)
85/467/EEC (OJ L269 11.10.85) proposed 12.9.84 – COM(84)513 and 17.6.85 – COM(85)302	(Sixth amendment) (PCBs and PCTs)
85/610/EEC (OJ L375 31.12.85) proposed 7.3.80 – COM(79)419 and 10.9.82 – COM(82)498	(Seventh amendment) (asbestos)

Binding dates

Formal compliance 76/769	3 February 1978
Formal compliance 79/663	26 July 1980
Formal compliance 82/806	25 November 1983
Formal compliance 82/828	10 December 1982 (where appropriate)
Formal compliance 83/264	19 November 1984
Formal compliance 83/478	21 March 1986
Formal compliance 85/467	30 June 1986
Formal compliance 85/610	31 December 1987

Purpose of the Directives

Certain other Directives restrict the use of specific substances in specific products, for example lead in petrol and sulphur in gas oil (see Chapter 6). Another Directive (Section 7.1) requires new substances to be tested and notified to the authorities before being marketed and then appropriately packaged and labelled. The first of the present series of Directives goes further by creating a general framework for bans or restrictions on the marketing and use of dangerous substances. Restrictions are set out in an Annex and subsequent Directives have extended the Annex. A separate Directive restricts the marketing and use of pesticides (see Section 7.5).

Summary of the Directives

76/769 – Member States are to take all necessary measures to ensure that the dangerous substances and preparations listed in an Annex are only placed on the market or used subject to the conditions specified in the Annex. The restrictions do not apply to marketing or use for the purposes of Research and Development or analysis. The Directive does not apply to:

the carriage of dangerous substances;
substances exported to non-member countries;
substances in transit and subject to customs inspection.

The Annex lists polychlorinated biphenyls and terphenyls (PCBs, PCTs) and monomer vinylchloride. PCBs and PCTs may only be used in closed system electrical equipment, large condensers and for certain other specified applications. Monomer vinyl chloride may not be used as an aerosol propellant.

79/663 adds to the Annex of 76/769. Trichloroethylene, tetrachloroethylene and carbon tetrachloride may not be used in ornamental objects intended to produce light or colour effects by means of different phases, for example in ornamental lamps and ashtrays. (The substances are defined by reference to Directive 67/548 – see Section 7.1). Tris (2,3 – dibromopropyl) phosphate, commonly known as Tris, and used as a fire retardant, is not to be used in textile articles intended to come into contact with the skin.

82/806 adds benzene to the Annex and bans its use in toys where the concentration of benzene is in excess of 5 mg/kg of the weight of the toy. **82/828** relaxes the Annex of 76/769 by allowing PCTs to be used until 31 December 1984 in re-usable thermoplastic tooling compounds in the manufacture or maintenance of certain products including: gas turbines; nuclear reactors; ship and aircraft frames; semiconductor devices; and high-precision lenses. **83/264** adds to the Annex two substances used as fire retardants and three used in sneezing powders and in novelties, jokes and hoaxes.

83/478 adds asbestos to the Annex. Restrictions on use are defined by type of asbestos. The marketing and use of crocidolite fibres and products containing them is prohibited, but products manufactured before 1 January 1986 may be allowed to be marketed by Member States until 30 June 1988. Their use may also be exempt if manufactured, placed on the market or used before 1 January 1986. Member States may also exclude from the prohibition fibres and semifinished products essential to the manufacture of asbestos-cement pipes, various types of seals and gaskets, and torque convertors. All products containing asbestos, including crocidolite, may be marketed and used only if they bear a label in accordance with the provisions of Annex II of the Directive (the original Annex becomes Annex I).

85/467 bans all new applications of PCBs and PCTs and terminates with effect from 30 June 1986 the exemptions from a general ban on marketing and use of PCBs and PCTs permitted by 76/769. Also banned from the same date is the marketing of second-hand equipment containing PCBs and PCTs and of fluids. Any material containing more than 0.01 per cent by weight of PCB or PCT (previously 0.1 per cent) is covered by the provisions. Discretionary clauses allow Member States to withdraw existing equipment and their labelling with maintenance, use and disposal instructions. Topping up liquid levels in existing equipment is also permitted where no substitute products exist. The use of PCBs and PCTs as primary and intermediate products is allowed to be continued indefinitely provided the Commission is informed and there are no deleterious effects.

85/610 revises the asbestos provisions by adding a further list of products which are not permitted if they contain asbestos fibres other than crocidolite. The list includes toys, items for smoking, catalytic filters and paints and varnishes.

Development of the Directives

Although the parent Directive sets out a general scheme for restrictions on marketing and use of products, its origin is to be found in a draft French law introduced to implement the decision by the Council for the Organization for Economic Cooperation and Development (OECD) restricting one particular group of substances – PCBs (described more fully in Section 5.4). The Commission, however, saw the need for a general measure on the grounds that some Member States were already restricting some substances and that Community measures were needed to prevent barriers to trade. The Commission's explanatory memorandum, for example, quotes a British restriction on benzene in toys as the origin of directive 82/806. The Commission had originally envisaged the Directive establishing a Committee empowered to add other substances by qualified majority vote but this was resisted by Britain, and doubtless other Member States, and in the event extra substances have to be added to the Annex by the Council in separate Directives.

There was some discussion whether the power to restrict marketing and use should form part of the Directives requiring notification and testing of substances before marketing (see Section 7.1) but the power has been kept separate although the two groups of Directives are clearly linked.

Directive 82/828 which relaxes the restriction on PCTs for certain applications for a certain period seems to have arisen because it was found in Britain (and in other Member States though their authorities were unaware of the fact) that PCTs were in use despite the restrictions of Directive 76/769. The deadline for eliminating use of PCTs is intended to stimulate research for a substitute material.

The proposal on asbestos (Directive 83/478) took over three years to be agreed and discussions became linked with negotiations on the Directive on worker protection from asbestos exposure (see Section 7.7 and Directive 83/477). Significant changes were made in the course of negotiations. The difficulties were to reconcile existing practices and differing views on the dangers from asbestos. In particular some continental countries made much use of asbestos-cement pipes manufactured from crocidolite. The result was a relaxation of the original proposal: though marketing and use of products containing crocidolite is prohibited after 30 June 1988, Member States may nevertheless exempt certain types of products (including asbestos-cement pipes) and the requirement to prevent harmful release of fibres was dropped. For other types of asbestos the proposed prohibition of use for thermal and acoustic insulation, air filtering and roadway surfacing and for decorative purposes was replaced by the simple requirement to label the product. The relaxations represent concessions to the powerful lobby of continental manufacturers.

Directive 85/467 seems to have caused few problems though one major change in the proposal came about. The use of PCBs and PCTs as primary and intermediate products which the Commission sought to ban by the end of 1989 was allowed to continue indefinitely.

Directive 85/610 appears according to the preamble to have been a second bite at completing restrictions on asbestos to take account of differences in regulations in Member States. Though the Directive refers only to the original proposal from the Commission (COM(79)419), it does appear to incorporate products first listed in the amendments to that proposal which were not included in Directive 83/478. Those amendments appear to have been influenced by the European Parliament's recommendations and were put forward in September 1982 (COM(82)498). It is not clear why there should have been a three-year delay and a gap of over two years between the fifth and seventh amendment. But the then Minister for Employment (Mr Gummer) gave an assurance in the House of Commons in November 1983 that the UK would seek to persuade other Member States to adopt the tougher asbestos standards to be introduced into the UK in the following year. Discussions had already reopened by then in Brussels on banning products containing asbestos other than crocidolite.

Formal compliance in UK

Section 100 of the Control of Pollution Act 1974 gives the Secretary of State powers to make regulations prohibiting or restricting the import, use in connection with trade, or supply for any purpose, of certain substances for the purpose of preventing damage to man or the environment. The Consumer Safety Act 1978 also gives the Secretary of State wide powers to ensure that goods are safe and to make orders prohibiting goods that are not safe.

The Control of Pollution (Supply and Use of Injurious Substances) Regulations 1980 (SI 1980 No 638) made under the Control of Pollution Act restrict the use of PCBs and PCTs in the manner specified in Directive 76/769 as amended by Directive 82/828. The Regulations came into operation some two and a half years after the date for compliance with Directive 76/769 but eighteen months before Directive 82/828 was even agreed. The reason for not immediately complying with Directive 76/769 was the discovery that there was no readily available substitute for PCTs for the purposes exempted by Directive 82/828. Until Directive 82/828 was agreed Britain was therefore technically in breach of Directive 76/769 although there was a voluntary restriction on its use.

Regulations implementing Directive 85/467 came into effect on 30 June 1986 (SI 1986 No 902, The Control of Pollution (Supply and Use of Injurious Substances) Regulations 1986). The exemptions previously permitted were withdrawn and a ban imposed on the sale of second-hand plant and equipment containing PCBs and PCTs. The regulations also reduced the threshold concentration at which a material is to be regarded as a PCB or PCT from 0.1 per cent to 0.01 per cent by weight. The ban does not apply to certain plant or fluids in use before 30 June 1986 and which have not yet reached the end of their service lives. Another discretionary clause in the Directive was not implemented; it permitted Member States to order such equipment to be labelled with maintenance, use and disposal instructions.

The Dangerous Substances and Preparations (Safety) Regulations 1980 (SI 1980 No 136) made under the Consumer Safety Act 1978 implement Directive 76/769 as respects vinyl chloride monomer (chloroethylene) in aerosols, and also implement Directive 79/663 for ornamental objects and Tris in certain textile products.

The Novelties (Safety) Regulations 1980 (SI 1980 No 958) preceded Directive 82/806 and deal with the only novelty containing benzene then on the British market. In the meantime, a consumer protection proposal for a Directive covering toys generally has been under consideration and is near agreement. Once adopted, regulations will be laid which will implement this Directive and will also cover the requirements of Directive 82/806.

The Asbestos Product (Safety) Regulations 1985 (SI 2042) which came into effect on 1 January 1986 implement Directive 83/478. It permits the continued supply of crocidolite in torque convertors and until 30 June 1988, if manufactured before 1 January 1986 in intermediate brake bands, provided in both cases they are used for-motor vehicle repair. No advantage was taken of the other exemptions allowed for crocidolite. The regulations go beyond the Directive's requirements in banning the supply of products containing amosite. They also require manufacturers of products containing other forms of asbestos to label them in accordance with the requirements of the Directive. This replaces the previous voluntary labelling scheme introduced in 1976.

These regulations complement the Asbestos (Prohibitions) Regulations 1985 (SI 1985 No 910) which also took effect on 1 January 1986. They ban imports of crocidolite and amosite and their supply for use at work, together with asbestos spraying and insulation.

Effect on UK practice

The first two Directives dealing with PCBs can have had little effect in Britain because according to a DoE Waste Management Paper[1] the sole British manufacturer had since 1971 voluntarily operated a more stringent restriction than that now made mandatory by the Directives. That this cannot have been entirely the case is illustrated by the need to relax Directive 76/769 to allow the use of PCT in tooling compounds. This illustrates the problem in control of hazardous chemicals. The product was manufactured in a Community country exported to the USA and incorporated in the tooling compound for re-export but with no indication of its components. The presence of PCT was only discovered through a major firm using the product doing its own analysis and informing the relevant government department.

The effect nevertheless of these measures and the general attitude to PCBs was to stimulate adequate substitutes. So the effect of 85/467 virtually banning all uses of PCBs and PCTs can only have been very slight.

There had been no ban on monomer vinyl chloride in aerosols in Britain before Directive 76/769 but it was not in use in Britain. There had also been no ban on the use of the substances listed in Directive 79/663 in ornamental objects before that Directive. The Directive arose as a result of accidental deaths in other Member States and a precautionary measure taken in one Member State has now resulted in precautionary measures in all. The Community ban on Tris-treated nightwear was in fact prompted by a British ban made under the Consumer Safety Act by the Nightwear (Safety) Order 1978 which has since been superseded by SI 1980 No 136.

In the event the UK has not had to weaken its control of asbestos though this could have been the effect if some proposals had gone through. It will be noted that the UK has imposed more stringent regulations.

The major effect of this series of Directives is to provide a mechanism whereby precautionary measures adopted in one Member State are quickly and uniformly applied across the Community. It is also foreseen that the Annexes will be extended to take account of hazards notified to the authorities under Directive 79/831 (see Section 7.1). One notable effect in the UK of this set of Directives has been the move away from voluntary schemes to regulatory measures (PCBs and asbestos are examples). Another point to note is that in many cases the UK had already taken action to curb the use of the substances concerned and was able to press for equally stringent measures to be applied within the Community.

References
1   Department of the Environment 1976 *Polychlorinated biphenyl (PCB) waste*. HMSO, No 6. (Waste Management Paper).

7.3 Major accident hazards (the 'Seveso' Directive)

82/501/EEC (OJ L230 5.8.82) proposed 16.7.79 – COM(79)384	Directive on the major accident hazards of certain industrial activities.
87/216/EEC(OJ L85 28.3.87) proposed 5.11.85 – COM(85)572	Amendment.

Binding dates

Notification date	8 July 1982
Formal compliance	8 January 1984
Initial declarations for existing industrial activities	8 January 1985
Annexes I,II,III to be reviewed	8 January 1986
Commission to publish report	8 July 1987
Supplementary declarations for existing industrial activities (unless waiver granted)	8 July 1989

Purpose of the Directive

The risks for man and the environment arising from any industrial activity are of two kinds: routine risks in normal operating conditions, and exceptional risks such as fires, explosions and massive emissions of dangerous substances when an activity gets out of control. The Directive is concerned with the second kind of risk and requires steps to be taken to prevent major accidents and to limit the consequences of those that do occur. These steps include preparing safety reports and emergency plans for industries using specified dangerous substances, and informing the public of the correct behaviour to adopt in the event of an accident. The Directive is often called the 'Seveso' or 'post-Seveso Directive' since it was the notorious accident in Italy in 1976 that prompted the Community to legislate.

Summary of the Directive

The essential elements of this apparently complicated Directive are these:

a **general duty** is placed on manufacturers using a wide range of processes to prevent major accidents and to limit their consequences for man and the environment (Articles 3 and 4); there is also a general duty to report major accidents;

four **specific duties** then apply when a manufacturer uses any of a list of 178 substances in quantities above specified threshold levels or stores nine of them. These duties are:

the manufacturer must produce a **safety report** (Article 5);

the manufacturer must produce an **on-site emergency plan** (which may form part of the safety report (also Article 5);

a competent authority must produce an **off-site emergency plan** (Articles 5 and 7);

the **public must be informed** of safety measures and of the correct behaviour to adopt in the event of an accident (Article 8).

In greater detail the elements are as follows.

Definitions

Industrial activity is defined firstly by reference to a list of process installations (Annex I) involving dangerous substances and including transport and associated storage within the establishment and secondly isolated storage as set out in an Annex II. Dangerous substances are defined in terms of substances fulfilling the criteria set out in an Annex IV. Various activities are excluded from the Directive, such as nuclear installations, munitions manufacture, mining and military installations. The definition of 'major accident' is not precise and refers to 'an occurrence such as a major emission, fire or explosion. . .'.

General duty

A general duty is placed on Member States to adopt provisions necessary to ensure that the person in charge of industrial activities is obliged to take all measures necessary to prevent major accidents and to limit their consequences for man and the environment.

Member States must ensure that all manufacturers are required to prove to the competent authority at any time that they have identified major accident hazards, have adopted the appropriate safety measures, and have provided people working on the site with information, training and equipment in order to ensure their safety.

Safety report and on-site emergency plan

Manufacturers must notify the competent authorities if an industrial activity involves any of the 178 dangerous substances listed in an Annex III in certain quantities, or if the nine dangerous substances listed in an Annex II are stored in certain quantities. The notification is to contain information (sometimes called a 'safety report' – although that phrase does not occur in the Directive) relating to:

the substances in Annexes II and III including the data specified in an Annex V;

the installation including a description of where the hazards could arise and the measures to prevent and control them (known as a 'safety case' in Britain);

possible major accident hazard situations including on-site emergency plans ('off-site' emergency plans are to be prepared by the competent authority – see below).

For new installations the notification must reach the competent authority a reasonable length of time before the industrial activity commences. New activities are to include any modification to an existing activity likely to have important implications for major accident hazards. The notification is to be updated periodically to take account of new technical knowledge. When an industrial activity is modified, the manufacturer must revise the accident prevention measures and must inform the competent authority in advance if it affects the notification.

For the purposes of notification a manufacturer with a group of installations close together must aggregate the quantities of a substance listed in Annex II or III.

Existing industrial activities
Extra time is allowed for submitting the notification relating to existing activities but by 8 January 1985 manufacturers must have submitted in a declaration to the competent authority a part of the notification, including information about the types of industrial activity and of the substances involved. A supplementary declaration completing the notification and containing a safety report and on-site emergency plan must be provided by 8 July 1989 unless this requirement is waived by the Member State. In the event of a waiver the supplementary declaration must be submitted if requested by the competent authority.

Duties of competent authorities and off-site emergency plan
Member States must appoint the competent authorities who are to receive the notification (see above) and examine the information provided and who are to ensure that an emergency plan is drawn up for action outside the establishment housing a notified industrial activity (that is an 'off-site' emergency plan in contrast with the 'on-site' emergency plan which has to be prepared by the manufacturer as part of the notification).

The competent authority must if necessary request supplementary information and must ascertain that the manufacturer takes the most appropriate measures to prevent accidents and to limit the consequences. It must also organize inspections.

Information for the public
Member States must ensure that persons liable to be affected by a major accident at a notified industrial activity are informed of the safety measures and of the correct behaviour to adopt in the case of an accident. Member States must also make available to other Member States concerned, as a basis for all necessary consultation within the framework of their bilateral relations, the same information as that which is disseminated to their own nationals.

Action following accident
As soon as a major accident occurs the manufacturer must:

   inform the competent authority;

provide the authority with information on the circumstances of the accident, the dangerous substances involved, the data available for assessing the effects, the emergency measures taken;
inform the authority of the steps envisaged to alleviate the medium and long-term effects of the accident and to prevent recurrence.

The competent authorities must ensure that any emergency and medium and long-term measures which may prove necessary are taken, and must collect where possible the information necessary for a full analysis of the accident.

Member States must inform the Commission as soon as possible of major accidents and must provide the details of the accident set out in an Annex VI.

Community information system
Member States must inform the Commission of the organization with relevant information on major accidents able to advise the competent authorities of other Member States. Member States may notify the Commission of any substance which in their view should be added to Annexes II and III and of any measures they may have taken concerning such substances. The Commission must forward this to the other Member States.

The Commission must maintain at the disposal of the Member States a register containing a summary of major accidents including an analysis of the causes, experience gained and measures taken.

Restrictions are placed on the use of information obtained by the competent authorities and the Commission, some of which may not be used for any purpose other than that for which it was requested. This is not to preclude publication by the Commission of general statistical data. The Member States and the Commission are to exchange information on experience of preventing and limiting major accidents. By July 1987 the Commission must send to the Council and the Parliament a report on the working of the Directive based on this exchange of information.

Review and amendment
By 8 January 1986 the Council is to review Annexes I, II and III. (A proposed amendment has been made (COM(85)572 OJ C305 26.11.85.) A procedure for adapting Annex V to technical progress is laid down.

More stringent measures
The Directive allows Member States to apply more stringent measures than those in the Directive.

Development of the Directive
The Directive was proposed in response to pressure from the European Parliament following a disaster in 1976 when toxic dust – dioxin – escaped from a factory at Seveso near Milan in Italy and spread over the surrounding countryside. Other major accidents at Flixborough, UK (1974), Beek, Netherlands

(1975) and Velbert, FRG (1979) all showed that existing control systems were not satisfactory. The Commission's explanatory memorandum accompanying the proposal recorded that the Netherlands, UK and Italy had all informed the Commission of proposed legislation in the field and the Directive was therefore also an attempt to ensure comparable procedures in all Member States.

Within a year of the Directive being first discussed in the Council machinery the broad outlines of a draft had been generally approved by the Member States except for the issue of transfrontier responsibilities. The proposals on this point were not acceptable to France and took a further 18 months to resolve.

The Department of Employment submitted two explanatory memoranda to Parliament, the first on 8th October 1979 and the second, on 18th June 1980, accompanied by an Appendix giving the latest available version of the text of the proposal then to have emerged from the Council machinery – one of the rare occasions when such a document has been rendered public. Between the dates of these two memoranda the proposal had changed in a number of respects and was to change again.

In Britain the Health and Safety at Work etc Act 1974 had been enacted just before the Flixborough explosion in which 28 people were killed. This Act established the Health and Safety Commission (HSC) with broad responsibilities. Following the Flixborough explosion in 1974 the HSC set up an Advisory Committee on Major Hazards. The Committee published a first report[1] in September 1976 recommending legislation similar to the Directive in providing both for notification of installations handling dangerous substances and the preparation of hazard surveys. These were published in 1978 in a consultative document[2] as draft Hazardous Installations (Notification and Survey) Regulations. A second report[3] of the Committee was published in 1979 just before the Directive was proposed. In a debate in the House of Commons (23 June 1980) the Minister, Patrick Mayhew, said that the government had from the outset supported the principle of the Directive and went on to say:

> The European Commission's proposal has adopted some features of our own proposed regulations, which is satisfactory. There are however considerable difficulties involved in any attempt to produce a Directive which is satisfactory to all Member States. Many countries do not possess such broadly based legislation as our own Health and Safety at Work etc Act 1974. Under that Act, all employers are already required to conduct their operations with full regard for the safety of workers and the public. This foundation of general obligations readily permits the introduction of additional requirements, which can be concentrated on activities which present exceptional risks to public safety.

The Scrutiny Committee of the House of Lords had earlier published a report criticizing the Commission's original proposal for trying to apply across a wide and uncertain spectrum the stringent controls appropriate for the most hazardous installations. It recommended that the Directive be limited in its scope and made more precise in its drafting to specify exactly those areas where Member States should focus their efforts. In this it should, said the report, be brought closer to the regulations proposed in 1978 by the Health and Safety Commission.

To some extent this happened. The Minister explained in the Commons' debate how the more general part of the Directive had been restricted in two ways: the obligation on manufacturers to draw up a safety report had been curtailed and changed to a requirement to demonstrate to the competent authority that provision had been made for identifying major accident hazards and the appropriate measures taken. Secondly, 'industrial activity' was more precisely defined by references to Annexes.

The more specific part of the Directive had also been changed. All the dangerous substances to which the notification requirement applied were listed and quantified in Annexes – somewhat longer than the proposed British list although applying to fewer substances in isolated storage than under the proposed British Regulations. The notification scheme was also simplified, and the degree of reporting was made comparable with the level required for a hazard survey under the proposed British Regulations.

The Minister summed up the changes:

> There is no doubt that implementation of the original draft Directive would have greatly increased the commitment of resources by both industry and the HSE. Under the revised proposals this increase in commitment will be far less than originally expected and the more selective nature of the proposals should make for greater uniformity of enforcement by Member States.

The Minister also explained that the government was troubled by the use of the word environment and believed that the Directive should be confined to substances directly affecting man. As will be seen below, the retention of the word environment may well come to have a considerable effect on British administration.

A significant change to the Directive made after the House of Commons' debate at the insistence of the German government gives to Member States the right to waive the requirement that manufacturers must submit a hazard survey for existing plant. Another significant change to the original proposal is that manufacturers do not have to inform people working at the installation and people outside of potential risks but only of safety measures and of the behaviour to adopt in the event of an accident.

The original proposal made no mention of the transfrontier responsibilities of the Member States and it seems that the provision to be found in the version submitted to the House of Commons in June 1980 was inserted at the insistence of the Benelux countries. In that version the provision reads as follows:

> Where a Member State considers that there is a major accident hazard due to an industrial activity carried out within its territory and notified in accordance with this Directive, affecting persons and/or the environment in one or more Member States, it shall forward to the latter all appropriate information.

> The Member States concerned shall consult on the measures required to prevent major accidents and to limit their effects on man and the environment.

A new article in broadly similar terms was published by the Commission as a formal amendment to the original proposal five months later (COM(80)747) in response to the Resolution of the European Parliament (OJ C175 14.7.80). It is possible that without the pressure of the Parliament the proposed article would not have survived at all since it was not acceptable to the French government. The formula eventually agreed after a long delay requires information to be made available between Member States 'within the framework of their bilateral relations' and means that the Commission does not have the same right to insist on implementation as it would have had otherwise. It also means that other Member States have no rights at all.

Formal compliance in the UK

The letter of formal compliance was not sent to the Commission until 6 August 1985, some seventeen months after the due date. As a result of this delay, the Commission commenced proceedings in February 1985 for failure to incorporate the Directive into national law within the allotted time span. Reasons for this delay included a late input to the Regulations by the Secretary of State for Employment, to the effect that the manufacturer should bear the costs of the public information aspect of the Regulations, together with delays concerning the provision of separate Regulations to cover Northern Ireland. However, by the end of 1984, Regulations implementing the Directive had been made and laid before Parliament, and the Control of Industrial Major Accident Hazards Regulations (SI 1984 No 1902) known as the CIMAH Regulations came into operation on 8 January 1985 for Regulations 6–10, and on 1 April 1985 for all other purposes.

UK compliance with the Directive, although building on a foundation of existing law, effectively rests on a single document, the CIMAH Regulations, which largely derive from powers contained in the Health and Safety at Work etc Act (HSWA) 1974. As discussed above, HSWA forms the bedrock of modern health and safety legislation, laying down basic duties on the part of employers and employees with regard to securing the welfare of those at work, and controlling the use and storage of dangerous substances. HSWA provides the enforcement mechanisms for ensuring that the provisions contained in CIMAH are carried out. The CIMAH Regulations were also made under the European Communities Act 1972 as HSWA, being mainly concerned with man's health and safety, does not specifically cater for environmental protection. This is an interesting development, as the Health and Safety Executive (HSE) – the competent authority for the Regulations – was not originally intended to deal with environmental matters. Nevertheless, despite the increasingly environmental orientation of the Directive, the HSE is happy to oversee the UK Regulations because, they argue, measures taken to protect man will also protect the environment.

Other legislation in the major hazards field includes the Notification of Installations Handling Hazardous Substances Regulations 1982 (SI 1982 No 1357), known as the NIHHS Regulations. Although the NIHHS Regulations have a separate purpose from the CIMAH Regulations, they did help the HSE to locate likely sites falling within the provisions of CIMAH (as all CIMAH sites are also NIHHS sites) and had involved the planning authorities in aspects of major hazards. The CIMAH Regulations apply to Great Britain, and similar, but separate Regulations apply to Northern Ireland (SR 1985 No 175). Further interpretation on the law has been provided by the HSE in the form of guidance notes.[4,5]

The CIMAH Regulations are closely modelled on the Directive and fall into two parts: the first part (Regulations 4 and 5) creates a general duty to operate safely, and a duty to notify the HSE of any major accidents; and a second more specific part (Regulations 7–12) concerning the production of safety reports, emergency plans and information to the public. The specific requirements of CIMAH follow the Directive closely and apply only to those manufacturers using one or more of 178 scheduled substances at higher than specified threshold levels. There are presently approximately 250 such sites in the UK. The main Regulations covering the specific requirements of CIMAH are as follows.

Regulation 7 (reports on industrial activities) requires the manufacturer to submit a safety report (often known as a 'safety case'), which is essentially an abstract of relevant technical information justifying the activity as being carried out safely. This is probably the single most important aspect of CIMAH as it focuses the manufacturer's attention on the hazardous aspects of his activity. Safety cases have to be submitted to area offices of the HSE by 8 July 1989.

Regulation 10 (preparation of on-site emergency plans) requires the manufacturer to produce an emergency plan for use within the installation. Such plans should have been in place since 1 April 1985, and must be kept in an operational state. The availability of a safety case (Regulation 7) is not a prerequisite for an on-site emergency plan although they should be compatible.

Regulation 11 (preparation of off-site emergency plans) requires the local authority (usually the County Council) to produce an emergency plan for use outside the installation in the event of an accident. Such plans, which should have been in place by 1 October 1985, are to be based on information supplied by the manufacturer as to the nature, extent and likely effects of a possible accident. Regulation 15 allows the local authority to charge the manufacturer for any reasonable costs incurred in the production of such plans.

Regulation 12 (information to be given to persons liable to be affected by a major accident) requires the manufacturer to enter into an agreement with the local authority (usually the District Council) to inform the public living near a hazardous site of the fact that the site has been notified; of the nature of the hazard; and of the safety measures and correct behaviour to adopt in the event of an accident. This is typically accomplished by letter from the manufacturer to those persons residing in an area delineated by the HSE.

Effect on UK practice

In the absence of the Directive the process set in train following the explosion at Flixborough and described above, resulted in draft Regulations[2] being proposed in 1978 which would have come into effect some time in 1980 when hazard surveys would have become mandatory. Because of the Directive these were abandoned and the CIMAH Regulations did not come into effect until 1985. Furthermore, the main component of CIMAH, the safety report, need not be submitted until July 1989, a full fifteen years after the Flixborough explosion. Paradoxically, therefore, one effect of the Directive has been to delay the preparation of safety reports. British industry was able to argue that they should not be pressed harder than the Directive presses its competitors abroad, despite the fact that in some countries (for example, Netherlands and the Federal Republic of Germany) safety reports are being prepared well in advance of the 1989 deadline. Nevertheless, by voluntary agreement some manufacturers have submitted safety cases before the deadline.

One broad effect of the Directive is that the duty for manufacturers to operate safely (which is implicitly covered by Sections 2 and 3 of HSWA) has been extended in two ways: by requiring that proof be made available 'at any time'; and by removing the HSWA proviso 'so far as is reasonably practicable'. In this way a qualified duty has been turned into an absolute duty.

The heart of the Directive is the safety report, or safety case as it is more generally referred to in Britain. Before the Directive the HSWA required a safety policy document, but it would not have been as detailed as the safety case. However, had the Regulations proposed in 1978 been adopted, a 'hazard survey' would have been required of around 300–500 sites with a more detailed assessment at about 250 sites – not dissimilar to the requirement for safety cases under the CIMAH Regulations. The requirements of the Directive for safety reports has therefore not added to what would have been required in Britain.

Similarly all sites subject to CIMAH will have had a form of on-site emergency planning as part of the safety policy document. However, the Directives' more detailed requirements as to on-site emergency planning are very similar to the requirements proposed by HSE in 1978 so the Directive cannot be said to have had a major effect. Most CIMAH sites had on-site emergency plans by 1 April 1986, and all had by the end of 1986.

An effect of the Directive is that controls are applied to a greater number of substances than was originally intended in Britain. However, this difference is more apparent than real since many of the substances are not used in Britain and indeed the majority of sites subject to the CIMAH Regulations are accounted for by only two substances: chlorine and LNG/LPG.

Another effect of the Directive on UK practice has been the requirement for Member States to distinguish between 'isolated storage' (storage of certain substances not involved in a manufacturing operation) and 'process activities'. The official British view is that there is no need to distinguish between materials in process and those in storage and such a distinction would not have been made in the absence of the Directive, with the result that more isolated storage sites would have been covered.

The Directive has also led to an intensification of the involvement of local authorities in major hazards. Before the Directive, local authorities were sometimes involved in drawing up non-mandatory off-site emergency plans, and local planners would have been in contact with the HSE concerning hazardous installations. As a result of the Directive, County Councils are now responsible for drawing up off-site emergency plans and this is having an important impact on UK practice. By 1 October 1985 about 80 per cent of CIMAH sites had off-site emergency plans. Similarly, District Councils are also now more involved, as it is the responsibility of the manufacturer to enter into agreement with the District Council as to how the public are to be informed of the correct behaviour to adopt in the event of a major accident. Although Section 3.3 of HSWA makes provision for imparting information to the public on the subject of hazards, the section was never made operational and consequently the Directive has meant major changes for manufacturers, District Councils and the HSE alike on this subject of public information. By the end of 1986 nearly all manufacturers had taken steps to inform the public. The lack of information as to the correct behaviour for the public to adopt had been one of the principle problems at Seveso and led to this provision in the Directive which is not to be found in the draft British Regulations proposed in 1978.

A greater degree of cooperation than previously existed has been needed between all the parties concerned – industrialists, HSE, and local authorities – to satisfy the requirements of the Directive. This cooperation has been necessary because for the CIMAH Regulations to be truly effective the emergency plans must refer to one another, and to the safety case. Similarly, the parties have had to cooperate on issues such as informing the public. Although the CIMAH Regulations are still new, these relationships are, in general, good, so that the Directive has gone some way towards establishing a framework in which the measures necessary to limit the consequences of those accidents that do occur can be taken effectively.

Possibly the most fundamental effect of the Directive has been to extend the powers and duties of the HSE to consider effects on the environment. Indeed, one of the four major accidents reported to the Commission by the HSE by the end of 1986 concerned the discharge of toluene into a river. The Flixborough explosion resulted in the loss of many lives, and the proposals for British legislation developed as a result were clearly concerned with the safety of man. The Seveso accident, however, was clearly an environmental disaster – it killed nobody immediately but resulted in many animals having to be slaughtered and land being sterilized. The accident at the Sandoz plant at Basle in 1986 which resulted in extensive pollution of the Rhine has served to heighten awareness of the possible environmental effects of major accidents.

The Directive has thus helped to bring together considerations of effects on man and the environment. The new duty on the HSE to consider environmental effects is only one possible response to this need. In the Netherlands, for example, the Labour Inspectorate is not having its duties extended, as in Britain, but instead manufacturers will be required to submit a separate safety report dealing with possible environmental effects to the environmental authorities. It will be some time before the relative merits of these different approaches can be assessed.

Further developments

Following the disaster at Bhopal in India where a leak of methyl isocyanate from the Union Carbide plant manufacturing pesticides caused the deaths of thousands, the Commission proposed an amendment to the Directive (COM(85)572 OJ C305 26.11.85) adding substances and lowering the thresholds for others (including phosgene, chlorine, methyl isocyanate, sulphur trioxide and liquid oxygen). This was agreed by the Council in June 1986 but could not be formally adopted until the European Parliament had given its opinion. The Parliament did so in February 1987 and simultaneously proposed more extensive revision of the Directive following the accident at the Sandoz plant at Basle. The Commission has responded by promising a wide-ranging review of the Directive. The amending Directive 87/216 was published in March 1987 (OJ L85 28.3.87).

References

1   Health and Safety Commission 1976 *Advisory committee on major hazards: first report*. HMSO.

2   Health and Safety Commission 1978 *Consultative document – hazardous installations (notification and survey) regulations 1978*. HMSO.

3   Health and Safety Commission 1979 *Advisory committee on major hazards: second report*. HMSO.

4   Health and Safety Executive 1985 *A guide to the control of industrial major accident hazards regulations 1984*. HMSO (booklet HS(R)21).

5   Health and Safety Executive 1985 *The control of industrial major accident hazards regulations 1984 (CIMAH): further guidance on emergency plans*. HMSO. (Booklet HS(G) 25).

7.4 Chlorofluorocarbons (the ozone layer)

80/372/EEC (OJ L90 3.4.80) proposed 1979 – COM (79) 242	Decision concerning chlorofluorocarbons in the environment.
82/795/EEC (OJ L329 25.11.82) proposed 8.10.81 – COM(81)558	Decision on the consolidation of precautionary measures concerning chlorofluorocarbons in the environment.

Binding dates
Notification date – 80/372	31 March 1980
Notification date – 82/795	19 November 1982
30 per cent reduction in aerosol use compared with 1976	31 December 1981

Purpose of the Decisions

Chlorofluorocarbons (CFCs) are relatively nontoxic and nonflammable gases used as propellants in aerosol spray cans, in refrigeration and air conditioning plants, as solvents, and in the manufacture of polyurethane foam. Research suggests that the release of CFCs could result in the destruction of ozone in the stratosphere thus increasing ultraviolet radiation reaching the earth. If this is so, it could result in an increase in the incidence of skin cancer and could also affect vegetation and ecosystems, for example oceanic plankton which forms a fundamental part of the food chain. CFCs also contribute to the 'greenhouse effect'. As a precautionary measure the Decisions seek to limit the production of CFCs and reduce their use in aerosols.

Summary of the Decisions

Decision 80/372 places a duty on Member States to take all appropriate measures to ensure that industry situated in their territories does not increase production capacity of two types of CFCs known as F-11 and F-12. In addition, Member States were to ensure that by 31 December 1981 industry situated in their territories achieved a 30 per cent reduction in the use of CFCs in aerosol cans as compared with 1976 levels.

The measures taken were to be reexamined in 1980 in the light of the scientific and economic data available and Member States were to provide the Commission with the results of any study or research available to them. The Council was to adopt such further measures as were necessary by 30 June 1981.

Decision 82/795 was the result of this reexamination. It repeats the obligation of Decision 80/372 not to increase production capacity but adds a definition of production capacity and a reference figure of Community CFC production capacity (480 000 tonnes per year of F-11 and F-12 by the ten producers in the Community at March 1980).

Member States are to facilitate the periodic collection by the Commission of statistical information and are to cooperate with the Commission in action aimed at reducing CFC losses and developing the best practicable technologies in order to limit emissions in the synthetic foam, refrigeration and solvent sectors.

There is to be a further reexamination not later than 30 June 1983 and the Council is to adopt such further measures as may be necessary not later than 31 December 1983.

Development of the first Decision

The hypothesis was first advanced in 1974 that the release of CFCs could result in depletion of the ozone layer.[1] Theoretical studies then suggested that the continual release of CFCs at 1973 rates would result in ozone destruction until a steady state would eventually be reached in more than fifty years' time with a predicted reduction of between 6 per cent and 18 per cent.[2]

In October 1976 the USA began to place a ban on nonessential uses of CFCs as aerosol propellants, the ban becoming fully effective in 1979. In August 1977 the Commission proposed a Recommendation, and in May 1978 the Council adopted it as a Resolution (C133 7.6.78) calling for a limitation on production. This was then followed by an intergovernmental meeting held in Munich in December 1978 which recommended precautionary measures to reduce global releases of CFCs.

It was thus against a background of international concern that a proposal for a Decision was made in 1979. There was a heated debate in the European Parliament since the report of its Committee on the Environment, Public Health and Consumer Protection had argued for a reduction of 50 per cent (instead of the 30 per cent proposed by the Commission) in aerosol use by December 1981 and a total ban (except for essential medical purposes) by December 1983. In the result the Parliament endorsed the Commission's proposal and turned down the more stringent proposals of its own Committee.

The House of Commons' Scrutiny Committee noted that in Britain an agreement not to increase production of CFCs already existed and that their use in aerosols was already declining. It also recorded that British industry appeared generally to accept the proposal while maintaining that the scientific evidence was not sufficient to justify large changes. The DoE in an explanatory memorandum to the Scrutiny Committee said that before agreement could be reached on the proposal they needed to be satisfied that any scheme for reporting data should preserve the commercial confidentiality of manufacturers. This may explain the deletion from the proposal of a requirement that Member States should supply the Commission with data on aerosol use. (To overcome this difficulty an arrangement has now been made – see COM(81)261 below.)

The Decision also differed from the proposal in being restricted to the two types of CFCs known as F-11 and F-12.

Development of the second Decision

Between the first and second Decisions the Commission submitted a total of five communications to the Council: two in fulfilment of the obligation to reexamine the measures taken in the light of the scientific and economic data available; one proposing the second Decision; one proposing that the Commission should participate in the negotiations for a global convention on protection of the ozone layer; and a further one reporting progress.

The first communication (COM(80)339 16.6.80) reviewed the scientific work carried out in USA and UK and concluded that uncertainty still remained. It also reported a 6.8 per cent drop in Community production of CFCs between 1976 and 1979, a 22.8 per cent drop in sales for aerosols, but a 32.3 per cent increase for foam plastic. The UK was reported to be the largest producer in the Community of aerosol units having actually increased output between 1975 and 1978. In 1974 68 per cent of UK aerosol units were filled with CFCs and 30 per cent with hydrocarbons. The Communication also reviewed CFC substitution and pointed to the substantial capital investment entailed in converting to hydrocarbons because of the extensive safety precautions required. It also concluded that a reduction in aerosol use much beyond 30 per cent would be likely to cause socio-economic problems because of existing overcapacity in the industry.

The second communication (COM(81)261 26.5.81) made four recommendations for action at Community level:

maintaining and consolidating the precautionary measures of the first Decision;
an improvement in the collection of scientific, technical and economic data;
engagement in projects together with the industry concerned designed to decrease CFC emission in other sectors than aerosol filling;
measures at an international level.

The communication revealed that there were about 400 commercial concerns engaged in filling aerosol cans in the Community with 70 of these accounting for 80 per cent of all fillings. Half of these locations were not equipped to handle flammable propellants and 80 per cent of these were not suitable for conversion.

To improve the collection of statistics on CFC production and use the Commission proposed to formalize a system that was already operating under which producers supplied data to an independent auditor (a UK firm of chartered accountants) who aggregated them while keeping confidential the figures for individual producers.

The third communication (COM(81)558 8.10.81) proposed the second Decision and recorded that the Council meeting of 11 June 1981 had endorsed the four recommendations of COM(81)261.

The fourth communication (COM(81)734 30.11.81) proposed a Council Decision authorizing the Commission to participate in the negotiations for a global convention on the protection of the ozone layer being drafted under the auspices of UNEP (United Nations' Environment Programme).

The fifth communication (COM(82)307 7.6.82) was a general progress report. The scientific uncertainties were said to remain and no change in the precautionary policy was recommended. It recorded that total Community CFC production between 1976 and 1981 was down 8.1 per cent and that the 30 per cent target reduction in CFCs in aerosols has been achieved for the Community as a whole – though without giving percentage reductions for individual Member

States. It noted a significant increase in use of CFC in sectors other than aerosol fillings. It outlined an action programme in the sectors of refrigeration, foam plastics and solvents. It also recorded that a decision of the Council on 19 January 1982 authorized the Commission to participate on behalf of the Community in the negotiations on the global convention.

The second Decision differed from the proposal by omitting a requirement that Member States should ensure that industries did not increase CFC use for aerosols above the 1981 levels. Press reports[3] have suggested that this deletion was made because it would have penalized those industries that had cut back most.

Formal compliance in the UK

Unlike most Directives a Decision does not require Member States to report to the Commission on the laws or other measures used to implement it formally. The CFCs Decision leaves to Member States how the duties placed on them are to be carried out and in Britain (as in most Member States apparently) the targets have been reached by voluntary agreement with the industry.

Effect on UK practice

Since hydrocarbons are cheaper than CFCs there are commercial reasons for aerosol manufacturers to use the cheaper propellant, but pulling in the other direction is the better spray produced by CFCs and the reduced risk of fire which entails less expensive safety equipment in the factory. Even before the possible threat to the ozone layer was considered, hydrocarbons were widely used in aerosols particularly for water-based household products, with CFCs being used for alcohol-based cosmetic, medical and industrial products. Some manufacturers blended CFCs with hydrocarbons.

The worldwide concern about the ozone layer in the 1970s – which the EEC Decision reflected – prompted manufacturers to look at alternatives to safeguard their operations and many of the larger aerosol can manufacturers then invested in the safety equipment required for hydrocarbons. In some cases this investment paid off quickly. By and large the medium-sized and smaller manufacturers did not make the switch.

The result was that the 30 per cent reduction of the Decisions was achieved by 1981, but it is difficult to say that the reduction was achieved because of the Decisions. The Decisions reflected the scientific concern, and simultaneous concern in the industry about the possibility of compulsion had already stimu-lated the industry to take certain measures. In fact there is reason to believe that the figure of 30 per cent was chosen because it was known that it could be achieved without creating too much difficulty for the industry. Nevertheless, the Community legislation was a formalized response to the scientific concern and provided a definite percentage reduction and a date by which it had to be achieved. It made action obligatory and has prevented any backsliding.

The Decisions provide the first example in Britain of a limit on the total emission of a particular substance achieved, in this instance, by a limit on total production. A limit to the total emissions of lead from motor car exhausts had been agreed earlier in Britain (see Section 6.5) but that did not cover other sources of air pollution by lead.

Further developments

The Commission has issued a number of progress reports: in May 1983 (COM(83)284), in November 1985 (COM(85)644), and in November 1986 (COM(86)602). The most recent shows that CFC use in aerosols has remained steady between 1981 and 1985 but that other uses, in particular in foam plastics, has been increasing. Total Community production, while increasing, is still well within the production capacity of 480 000 tonnes. COM(86)602 also contained a proposal for a Council Decision authorizing the Commission to participate in the negotiations to the Protocol to the Convention.

Three codes of practice have been published by the Commission concerning the reduction of emissions of CFCs: in the manufacture of rigid polyurethane foam for the construction industry (EUR 9508); in refrigeration and air conditioning applications (EUR 9509); and for the design, construction and operation of CFC 13 solvent cleaning equipment.

On 22 March 1985 the Community signed the Vienna Convention for the protection of the ozone layer along with seven other Member States (see Chapter 11). The negotiations leading to the Convention saw a dispute between two groups of countries – the Community and the so-called Toronto Group (Canada, USA, Finland, Norway, Sweden). The Convention includes only general requirements but foresees subsequent protocols which would impose more precise obligations on the parties. The dispute was the result of the two groups of countries proposing that the first protocol to cover CFCs should embody the policies already adopted in their own countries. The Toronto Group's proposal was for a worldwide extension of a ban on nonessential uses of CFCs as aerosol propellants but involved no limit on other uses of CFCs. The Community, not surprisingly, proposed a production capacity limit for the protocol. The Community's insistence on a production limit is a tenable position since it is the total CFC emitted and not its particular source that effects the ozone layer. The Toronto Group's proposal had the merit of producing an immediate reduction, but did nothing to deal with growing non-aerosol uses. As a result of the dispute no protocol was agreed in 1985.

In late 1986 the US government changed its position by dropping the proposed aerosol ban and proposing instead a freeze on CFC production by all countries followed by reductions leading to a ban. Effectively the USA conceded the correctness of the EC position of a production limit approach, but then made it considerably more stringent. At a Council meeting on 19 March 1987 the Community agreed guidelines for the Commission to negotiate the protocol. These included a freeze at 1986 levels on entry into force of the protocol followed by a 20 per cent reduction four years later. The EC by accepting the US proposal for a freeze thus agreed to lower its previous production capacity limit (which was much larger than actual production) to a limit equal to the 1986 production levels and to add a further reduction later.

At a meeting in Geneva in April 1987 to prepare for the protocol it became clear that many countries favoured a further reduction totalling 50 per cent and that the USA would not accept anything much less. It remains to be seen whether the Community can agree to this and whether a protocol can be agreed on this basis in 1987. The UK, possibly under pressure from ICI – thought to be the largest CFC producer in the Community – was believed by many to be an opponent of significant reductions.

References
1   Molina M J and Rowland F S Stratospheric sink for chlorofluormethanes, chlorine atom-catalysed destruction of ozone *Nature* **249**, 810–812.

2   Department of the Environment 1979 *Chlorofluorocarbons and their effect on stratospheric ozone.* HMSO, No 15. (Pollution Paper).

3   *Environmental Data Services Ltd (ENDS) Report* No 95, December 1982.

7.5 Pesticide residues

76/895/EEC (OJ L340 19.12.76)	Directive relating to the fixing of maximum levels for pesticide residues in and on fruit and vegetables.
80/428/EEC (OJ L1O2 19.4.80)	(Amendment)
81/36/EEC (OJ L46 19.2.81)	(Amendment)
82/528/EEC (OJ L234 9.8.82)	(Amendment)
86/362/EEC (OJ L221 7.8.86) proposed 6.3.80	Directive on the fixing of maximum levels for pesticide residues in and on cereals.
86/363/EEC (OJ L221 7.8.86) proposed 6.3.80	Directive on the fixing of maximum levels for pesticide residues in and on foodstuffs of animal origin.

Purpose of the Directives

The Directives are not primarily intended to protect the environment but to protect consumers by setting limits on the amounts of pesticides on food. The limits can be achieved either by limiting the application of pesticides or ensuring that the pesticides have broken down sufficiently before the food is sold. Separate Directives restrict the use of pesticides (see Section 7.6).

Summary of the Directives

Pesticide residues – fruit and vegetables
Maximum residue limits are laid down for particular pesticides for certain specified fruit and vegetables. Member States may not prohibit the marketing of fruit and vegetables on the grounds that they contain pesticides if these do not exceed the specified limits. However, the residue limits do not have to be enforced.

Pesticide residues – cereals and food of animal origin
Maximum residue limits are laid down for specified pesticides applying to cereals and a broad range of food of animal origin, including meat, meat products, eggs and dairy products. Most of the limits are for organochlorine or organophosphorous pesticides. Member States may not prohibit or impede the 'putting into circulation' of products on the grounds that they contain pesticide residues if the residues are below these limits. Member States must apply the limits set out in Annex II of each Directive by 30 June 1988 (with certain

exceptions) and 'shall take all necessary measures to ensure, at least by check sampling, compliance with the maximum levels laid down. . .'.

However, a derogation from this obligation is available, reportedly at the request of the UK. This allows the limits not to be prescribed provided that the Member State meets two conditions. One is that it continues to apply a residue monitoring system which, together with other measures, ensures the attainment of 'an effect equivalent to the levels of pesticide residues laid down in Annex II'. The other is that it must assess the total dietary exposure of the population to these residues, undertaking regular representative surveys of residues in typical diets for this purpose. This derogation does not apply to products imported from outside the Community or to-products intended for export to other Member States and both the Commission and other Member States must be notified when it is utilized. Furthermore, there is an Article which requires the Directives to be reexamined by 30 June 1991 at the latest which suggests that the derogation may have a limited life.

There is a proposal for another Directive in this series, to cover animal feeding stuffs.

Compliance in the UK

Until 1985 pesticides were controlled in Britain mainly by the nonstatutory Pesticides Safety Precautions Scheme formally agreed between the British government and the agrochemical industry and it was under this scheme that Directives concerned with pesticides were largely implemented. However, this scheme has been replaced by a statutory scheme established under Part III of the Food and Environment Protection Act 1985.

This major change in pesticide policy was precipitated, at least in part, by pressure from the Community. Continuation of the voluntary Pesticides Safety Precautions Scheme became increasingly difficult following a letter of intent dated 23 February 1983 from the Commission to the British Agrochemical Association saying that their code of practice – which formed an important part of the Scheme – infringed Article 85 of the Treaty of Rome concerned with the rules of competition. The new statutory scheme that is being developed brings the UK more into line with other EC countries. One of the key measures concerned, the Control of Pesticides Regulations 1986 (SI 1986/1510), is coming into force over the period 1986-89. Further regulations are also being considered.

When the first EC Directive on residues in fruit and vegetables came into force the UK took advantage of the option not to introduce mandatory regulations. Less direct forms of control have been preferred instead. The recommendations for the use of pesticides, and the harvesting intervals, of the voluntary Pesticides Safety Precautions Scheme were designed to ensure that residue levels did not create a risk to human health. The supply and use of pesticides is now controlled by the Control of Pesticide Regulations 1986, which has similar functions. Food quality in Britain is controlled under a variety of different items of legislation, including Sections 1 and 2 of the Food Act 1984 and is backed up by a system of monitoring and surveillance.

The UK's established preference for optional controls has, however, begun to be reversed in recent years. Since the passage of the Food and Environment Protection Act 1985, ministers have powers of regulation to 'specify how much pesticide or pesticide residue may be left in any crop, food or feedingstuff'

(Section 16(2)(k)). The preference in the Community as a whole for a mandatory system of controls is reflected in the two most recent Directives on cereals and food of animal origin.

The new powers contained in the 1985 Act were not used at first and statutory control over residues was confined to the rather general requirements laid down in the Food Act, 1984, the Imported Food Regulations 1984 and similar legislation. In October 1986, however, a Consultative Document was circulated by MAFF, the DHSS and Welsh Office Agriculture Department, setting out the principles of a possible statutory system of pesticide residue controls. Three sets of reasons are given for contemplating a statutory system at this juncture, one of which is based on the fact that 'the UK is almost alone in having no statutory residue limits and this undermines its position in the Community on enforcement'. Several options are outlined, one of which is to apply the mandatory EC maximum residue limits to all domestic and traded production and, where these have not been fixed, to apply new UK limits, based on good agricultural practice and an assessment of human health issues. Discussion of these proposals with representative organizations was expected to be concluded by the end of March 1987.

7.6 Pesticides: use restrictions and labelling

79/117/EEC (OJ L33 8.2.79)	Directive prohibiting the placing on the market and use of plant protection products containing certain active substances.
83/131/EEC (OJ L 91 9.4.83)	(Amendment)
85/298/EEC (OJ L154 13.6.85)	(Amendment)
86/214/EEC (OJ L152 6.6.86)	(Amendment)
86/355/EEC (OJ L212 2.8.86)	(Amendment)
87/181/EEC (OJ L 71 14.3.87)	(Amendment)
78/631/EEC (OJ L206 29.7.78)	Directive on the approximation of the laws of the Member States relating to the classification, packaging and labelling of dangerous preparations (pesticides).
81/187/EEC (OJ L88 2.4.81)	(Amendment)
84/291/EEC (OJ L144 30.5.84)	(Amendment)

Purpose of the Directives

The use of certain pesticides is banned or restricted. Those that are marketed are to be appropriately classified, packaged and labelled. Separate Directives (see Section 7.5) limit pesticide residues on food for sale.

Summary of the Directives

79/117 – prohibition on use

Member States are to ensure that the plant protection products (including products intended to destroy undesired plants) containing the substances listed in an Annex may not be marketed or used. The Annex lists five mercury compounds and eight persistent organochlorine compounds (DDT, aldrin, dieldrin, endrin, chlordane, HCH, heptachlor, hexachlorobenzene). This Annex has subsequently been amended, most recently to add nitrofen, 1,2 dibromoethane and 1,2 dichloroethane to the list. However by way of derogation Member States may permit the use of the products in certain cases specified in the Annex, but in such cases they must inform the other Member States and the Commission.

No exceptions are made from the ban on chlordane in the Directive but in reply to a European parliamentary question (OJ C225 3.8.82) the Commissioner explained that preparations containing chlordane used for the control of earth-worms responsible for depositing casts on the surface of high-quality turf are not plant protection products within the meaning of the Directive. They are presumably protecting grass in the sense of a lawn and not grass in the sense of a plant.

In June 1982 the Commission issued a Communication to the Council (OJ C170 8.7.82) which concluded that on the basis of existing scientific evidence a Community-wide ban on the marketing and use of 2, 4, 5-T herbicides in the context of Directive 79/117 would not be justified. The Commission recommended instead various precautionary measures.

78/631 – classification, packaging and labelling
Pesticides in the form in which they are supplied to the user are to be classified as 'very toxic', 'toxic', or 'harmful'. Packaging and labelling requirements are specified. Pesticides are not to be marketed unless they comply with the Directive. Member States may not prohibit the marketing of pesticides on the grounds of classification, packaging and labelling if they satisfy the requirements of the Directive. The Directive refers to Directive 67/548 now amended by 79/831 and 83/467 (see Section 7.1).

Compliance in the UK
Directive 78/631 is now implemented by the Control of Pesticides Regulations 1986 (see Section 7.5) and the Classification, Labelling and Packaging of Dangerous Substances Regulations 1984, which are the responsibility of the Health and Safety Executive. Directive 79/117 is now implemented by the Control of Pesticide Regulations 1986 under the new arrangements described in Section 7.5.

Further developments
In response to widespread concern about the effects of exports of hazardous substances, particularly pesticides, on importing countries in the Third World, the Commission has proposed a Council Regulation concerning export from and import into the Community of certain dangerous chemicals (COM(86)362 final OJ C177 15.7.86). This would require what is often referred to as the 'prior informed consent' of the receiving country before pesticides are exported. There has been extensive discussion of the issue in the European Parliament and elsewhere but it may not be easy to reach agreement on some of the most controversial elements of the proposal.

7.7 Worker protection

Framework Directive

80/1107/EEC (OJ L327 3.12.80)	Directive on the protection of workers from the risks related to exposure to chemical, physical and biological agents at work.

Lead – first daughter Directive

82/605/EEC (OJ L247 23.8.82) proposed 10.12.79 – COM(79)699	Directive on the protection of workers from the risks related to exposure to metallic lead and its ionic compounds at work.

Asbestos – second daughter Directive

83/477/EEC (OJ L263 24.9.83) proposed 26.9.80 – COM(80)518 and 28.10.82 – COM(82)685	Directive on the protection of workers from the risks related to exposure to asbestos at work.

Note: the third daughter Directive on noise in the workplace is described in Chapter 9 Noise in the workplace.

Binding dates

Notification date	– framework	4 December 1980
	– lead	12 August 1982
	– asbestos	21 September 1983
Formal compliance	– framework	4 December 1983
	– lead	1 January 1986
	– asbestos	1 January 1987 (1 January 1990 in the case of asbestos mining)

Purpose of the Directives

The Directives provide for a list of measures to be taken to ensure that exposure to harmful agents in the workplace is kept as low as reasonably practicable. The framework Directive (80/1107) sets out a list of measures for the generality of agents; daughter Directives (eg lead (82/605) and asbestos (83/477)) cover or will cover specific substances. A daughter Directive on noise in the workplace is dealt with in Chapter 9 on Noise.

Summary of the Directives

Framework – 80/1107
The Directive sets out a list of measures to be taken by Member States when adopting provisions for the protection of workers from harmful agents. These include such measures as limitations on the use of the agent and on numbers of workers exposed, establishing limit values and sampling procedures, and protec-

tion and hygiene measures. In the case of certain specified substances listed (which also form the list for individual daughter Directives) additional measures such as medical surveillance, information on exposure and tests are to be taken. Member States will, however, determine the extent to which, if any, each of these measures will apply. Where Member States provide medical surveillance in the case of lead and asbestos and access to information on the dangers of asbestos, lead, arsenic, cadmium and mercury, they need not apply the full list of measures first described. The usual technical adaptation committee is set up limited to certain technical aspects.

Lead – 82/605

The Directive specifies the types of activities to which its provisions apply. It sets out the various measures required to be taken if assessments show that certain exposures to lead in air concentrations have occurred or if certain blood lead levels have been exceeded. It requires workers to be subject to medical surveillance and specifies details of such monitoring. It also specifies limit values for lead in air (150 μg/m^3) and blood lead levels (70 μg/100 ml) and the action to be taken if lower limits are exceeded.

Asbestos – 83/477

The Directive specifies the types of asbestos to which it applies (actinolite, amosite, anthrophyllite, chrysolite, crocidolite and hemolite) and sets out measures to be taken. Where certain limits are not exceeded not all measures need be taken. Spraying of asbestos is prohibited. Limit values to be applied are specified (1.0 f/cm^3 for all fibres other than crocidolite, 0.5 f/cm^3 for crocidolite) and the measures to be taken if these are exceeded are laid down. Details of medical surveillance and provision of information and record-keeping including a register of workers and of recognized cases of asbestosis and mesothelioma are other requirements specified.

Development of the Directives

Framework – 80/1107

The final version allowed considerably greater latitude in the degree and nature of the protection accorded to workers than was the case with the original proposal. Member States are able to determine the extent to which measures will apply.

Lead – 82/605

Considerable changes to the proposal were made in the course of negotiations. Limit values originally proposed as guidelines until more stringent limits came into force were retained but no mention is made of tighter limits at a later stage. More particularly the lower limits proposed for workers of child-bearing capacity were dropped. The issue was one of particular concern to the European

Parliament environment Committee, some of whose members felt that specifying different levels amounted to sexual discrimination.

Asbestos – 83/477

Three years of negotiations were needed to agree this Directive, which also became involved with the Directive on asbestos marketing and use (see Section 7.2 and Directive 83/478). The changes from the original proposal have been described as representing a significant victory for asbestos manufacturing interests on the continent who fought off tight controls on blue asbestos (crocidolite). All reference to limiting the use of crocidolite was dropped and the limit value of 0.2 f/cm³ proposed was raised to 0.5 f/cm³. In addition a two tier action level replaced the single limit values proposed. A new action level was agreed at 0.25 f/cm³. The UK which operated stricter controls argued for lower limits.

Formal compliance in the UK

The Health and Safety at Work Act 1974 provides the legal basis for implementing the framework and daughter Directives. In general existing provisions including regulations made under the Act satisfy the requirements of the Directives; in some cases the provisions are more stringent. In the case of the lead Directive (82/605) most provisions were implemented by the Control of Lead at Work Regulations 1980 and their associated approved code of practice, 'Control of Lead at Work'. A revised code of practice was issued on 7 November 1985 to take effect from 1 January 1986. The revised code was issued to comply with the Directive, in particular with the requirement for an employer to suspend employees from work when their blood lead concentrations reached 70 μg/100 ml instead of the former level of 80 μg/100 ml. In the case of the asbestos Directive (83/477) draft regulations were published in December 1983 implementing recommendations made by the Advisory Committee on Asbestos in 1979. As drafted they would be more stringent than the Directive requires, (eg an action level of 0.1 f/cm³ for crocidolite and amosite). Difficulties have arisen over these drafts and it is unlikely now that they will come into force before the summer of 1987. That part relating to prohibition of asbestos spraying was made effective by the Asbestos (Prohibitions) Regulations 1985 (SI 1985 No 910) which came into force on 1 January 1986. The Regulations also cover the requirements of Directive 83/478 – fifth amendment to marketing and use directive (see Restrictions on marketing and use). The Asbestos (Licensing) Regulations (SI 1983 No 1469) which came into force on 1 August 1984 dealt with licensing of firms undertaking removal of asbestos.

Effect on UK practice

Generally these Directives are unlikely to add much to UK provisions for worker safety which in many cases have been ahead of or more stringent than Community requirements. However, the more stringent lead level has had to be put into effect (see above).

Further developments

Two further proposals have been made by the Commission – a third daughter Directive on benzene (COM(85)669 OJ C349 31.12.85) and an amendment to the framework Directive 80/1107 proposing exposure limits for 100 substances (COM(86)296 OJ C124 25.5.86). The latter proposal contains limits which except in two cases are identical to or less stringent than the 'recommended' limits in the UK but they would be legally binding.

K

7.8 Paints and solvents

80/781/EEC (OJ L229 30.8.80)	Directive amending Directive 73/173 (OJ L189 11.7.73) on the approximation of the laws, regulations and administrative provisions relating to the classification, packaging and labelling of dangerous preparations (solvents).
83/265/EEC (OJ L147 6.6.83)	Directive amending Directive 77/728 (OJ L303 28.11.77) on the approximation of the laws, regulations and administrative provisions relating to the classification, packaging and labelling of paints, varnishes, printing inks, adhesives and similar products.
86/508/EEC (OJ L295 18.10.86)	Commission Directive amending the labelling requirements for lead in paint.

Binding dates
80/781
Notification date   24 July 1980
Formal compliance   24 July 1981

83/265
Notification date   19 May 1983 (lead amendment October 1986
Formal compliance   19 May 1984 (lead amendment, 1 September 1987)

Purpose of the Directives
These are harmonization Directives aimed at setting common rules for the classification, packaging and labelling of paints and solvents which consist of or contain dangerous substances. Earlier Directives covering these fields were found to be inconsistent and amending Directives were adopted to try and remedy the position. It is not the purpose of the Directives to set any limits on the quantity of dangerous substances, but only to provide a warning on products.

Summary of the Directives
Both Directives are in similar form and in both cases the amendments effectively replace in their entirety the previous Directives.

Solvents
The Directive covers those solvents containing substances as defined in an Annex and those containing liquid substances classified as extremely flammable, highly flammable or flammable in Directive 67/548 on classification, packaging and

labelling of dangerous substances (see Section 7.1). There are a number of exclusions including medicines, foodstuffs, the carriage of goods and substances in the form of wastes covered by waste Directives (75/442 and 78/319) (see Sections 5.1 and 5.2).

Criteria are given to establish whether substances should be considered toxic, harmful, corrosive, irritant, extremely flammable, highly flammable or flammable. Solvents which are dangerous substances must not be placed on the market unless they comply with the requirements of the Directive with regard to labelling and the Directive 67/548 (see Section 7.1) with regard to packaging.

Preparations which meet the requirements of the Directive must be freely marketed, but a Member State can prohibit for a period of six months such marketing if it establishes that a substance presents a health or safety risk. There is then provision for the Commission to investigate and if necessary procede to amend the Directive through the technical adaptation committee procedure.

The Commission Directive 82/473 (OJ L213 21.7.82) replaced the original Annex.

Paints etc
The Directive applies to all kinds of paints, varnishes and similar products which are classified as dangerous both under the terms of the basic classification, packaging and labelling Directive 67/548 (see Section 7.1) and of this Directive, including paints containing lead and cyanoacrylate-based glues. Exclusions are similar to those in the solvents Directive. Criteria are given to establish whether substances are toxic, harmful, corrosive, irritant, oxidizing, extremely flammable, highly flammable or flammable. Other requirements follow very much the same lines as the solvents Directive.

Two Annexes list respectively a classification of dangerous substances and labelling provisions for paints and varnishes containing lead and cyanoacrylate-based glues. Commission Directive 86/508 (OJ L295 of 18.10.86) amended Annex II by requiring paints containing more than 0.25 per cent of lead to be labelled, in place of the previous limit of 0.5 per cent.

Development of the Directives
The Directives which covered these substances separately date from 1973 and 1977 and were in addition to the basic Directive 67/548 (see Section 7.1) concerning classification, packaging and labelling of dangerous substances of 1967. Difficulties arose because of inconsistencies between the two Directives with different terms describing the same substance being used in both texts. Though it would have been preferable to have replaced them by a single Directive, it was decided to have amendments replacing the originals almost in their entirety. Opportunity was taken to include other revisions which had taken place to Directive 67/548.

The amendment to labelling of paints containing lead was adopted by majority voting in the adaptation to technical progress procedure. The UK argued for a complete ban on lead in paint, having successfully persuaded the Paintmakers Association in Britain to end the addition of lead to all paints by 1 July 1987.

Formal compliance in the UK

Regulations covering classification, packaging and labelling of dangerous sub-stances came into force on 12 September 1984 (SI 1984 No 1244 The Classification, Packaging and Labelling of Dangerous Substances Regulation 1984). These Regulations covered not only these two Directives but other Directives on labelling including the basic Directive 67/548, pesticides and toxic and dangerous wastes (see also Sections 5.2 and 7.1).

7.9 Asbestos

87/217/EEC OJ L85 28.3.87 proposed 29.11.85 – COM(85)632	Directive on the prevention and reduction of environmental pollution by asbestos

Binding dates
Notification date	March 1987
Formal compliance	31 December 1988
Standards to be met for plants built or authorized before 31.12.88	30 June 1991
Commission to report on monitoring methods	March 1992

Purpose of the Directive

Controls over the pollution of air, water and land by asbestos from all significant point sources are set down in this one Directive. This is an example of the 'substance oriented' approach discussed in the fourth action programme and is the first attempt to set controls over pollution of the three environmental media by one substance in a single Directive. It supplements the following controls over asbestos set in other Directives:

worker protection (see Section 7.7);
discharges to air (see Section 6.8);
waste (see Section 5.2);
restrictions on marketing and use (see Section 7.2).

Summary of the Directive

A general duty is placed on Member States to ensure that asbestos emissions into the air, into water, and solid asbestos waste are, as far as reasonably practicable, reduced at source and prevented. The best available technology not entailing excessive costs (including where appropriate recycling or treatment) is to be employed where asbestos is used. This requirement is qualified, for releases to air by existing plant by some flexible provisions of Directive 84/360 (see Section 6.8 Emissions from industrial plants).

The Directive applies to crocidolite (blue asbestos), actinolite, anthophyllite, chrysotile (white asbestos), amosite (brown asbestos) and tremolite. Activities involving less than 100 kg of raw asbestos per year do not constitute 'use', which otherwise includes production of raw asbestos ore (but not mining of ore), and the manufacture and working of asbestos products.

Discharges to air are not to exceed a limit value of 0.1 mg/m³, but plants emitting less than 5000m³/hour total gaseous discharges may be exempted where the discharge of asbestos does not exceed 0.5 grams per hour. Liquid effluents from asbestos cement and paper and board manufacture must be recycled. However, where this is not economically feasible in the asbestos cement industry, a limit is to be set of 30 grams of total suspended matter per cubic metre of effluent discharged, and a limit set on the total quantity of suspended matter discharged per tonne of product.

The working of asbestos products and the demolition of buildings and structures containing asbestos are not to cause significant environmental pollution by asbestos fibres or dust. In this context, a reference is made to Directive 83/477 (see Section 7.7). In the course of transport and landfill no asbestos fibres or dust are to be released and no liquids containing asbestos fibres are to be spilled. At landfills waste is to be so treated, packaged or covered that the release of asbestos fibres is prevented. In this context a reference is made to Directive 78/319 (see Section 5.2).

Discharges to air and water are to be monitored at regular intervals using methods laid down in an Annex or equivalent methods. The Commission is to review the equivalence of different methods and report to the Council in March 1992. A Committee for adapting the Annex to technical progress is established.

The Commission is periodically to make a comparative assessment of the application of the Directive, but no date is set for this and there is no requirement for it to be made public.

Development of the Directive

The explanatory memorandum, issued by the Commission with its proposal, set out tables showing the consumption of asbestos by country and by use. It also showed that national emission standards existed in France and the Federal Republic of Germany for air, and in France for discharges to water. It was on these standards that the proposal was based.

In an explanatory memorandum submitted to Parliament in February 1986 the DoE explained that there were no national emission standards in Britain but that the Industrial Air Pollution Inspectorate was discussing with the asbestos industry the 'best practicable means' for limiting asbestos discharges to air including 'presumptive limits' (see Section 6.0 for an explanation of this term). It also said that the specific proposals for control of discharges to water were technically unsatisfactory and unnecessary.

The Economic and Social Committee considered that the proposed Directive should be made much more stringent in particular by calling for a complete ban on asbestos and mandatory use of substitutes.

Both the emission limits to air and to water proposed by the Commission were modified before the Directive was agreed. In the case of emissions to air smaller plants were exempted, and in the case of discharges to water the French limit of 0.7 m³ of effluent discharged per tonne of asbestos-cement product was dropped.

Formal compliance in the UK

The DoE's explanatory memorandum of February 1986 said that implementation of the proposed Directive's provisions on emissions to air could be achieved under existing legislation but that the provisions on discharges to water might require primary legislation. Although other Directives have set emission limit values for discharges to water (see Sections 4.11 to 4.14) there has always been the possibility for Member States to adopt the alternative of setting quality objectives in the receiving water. The present Directive therefore sets a precedent. It is probable that other provisions of the Directive can be implemented under existing legislation.

Effect on UK practice

The setting of national emission limits for discharges to water for the first time will be a major change at the policy level. It is possible that the emission limit to air will also influence the Industrial Air Pollution Inspectorate when setting its 'presumptive limits'.

Otherwise the practical effects in Britain are likely to be small. Amosite and crocidolite (blue asbestos) are no longer imported into Britain although they are used elsewhere in the Community. Indeed the DoE's explanatory memorandum suggested that British industry might benefit from the imposition of stricter controls on its competitors. It would, however, have to bear the cost of monitoring.

One of the intended effects of setting standards for more than one environmental medium in the same Directive is to force national authorities concerned with emissions to air to consider the possible consequences of dischargers to water (and vice versa) of the controls they impose. The Directive is therefore a step towards the 'cross-media' approach to pollution control (see Chapter 3).

CHAPTER 8

Wildlife and countryside

8.0 Relevant British legislation

Whereas the Community has made a significant entry into the field of protecting fauna with the Directive on birds (see Section 8.1) and Regulations on whales, seals and endangered species (see Sections 8.2, 8.3 and 8.4) its only connection with the protection of flora is as a consequence of its involvement with certain international Conventions. There is also no legislation forming part of the Community's environmental policy concerned with landscape or countryside protection, although Directive 75/268 (see Section 8.6) and Regulation 797/85 (see Section 8.5) which form part of the agricultural policy include countryside protection among their objectives. Only a small part of British legislation on the subject of wildlife and countryside protection is therefore described here.

The first Act protecting certain species of birds was passed in 1869 and the number of species protected has been extended several times, most recently in the Wildlife and Countryside Act 1981 which has consolidated much previous legislation. The 1981 Act protects certain animals in addition to birds and also protects species of flora. It also provides powers to protect habitats. The relevant aspects of this comprehensive Act are described in connection with the birds Directive (see Section 8.1).

In Britain, unlike some other European countries, a distinction is made in the machinery of government administration between the protection of nature and the protection of landscape. The government agency responsible for nature protection is the Nature Conservancy Council (NCC) which was formed in 1973 under the Nature Conservancy Act out of the former Nature Conservancy. The powers of the Nature Conservancy to declare national nature reserves are contained in the National Parks and Access to the Countryside Act 1949 which also made it possible to declare Sites of Special Scientific Interest (SSSIs) for the purpose of drawing attention to land of 'special interest by virtue of its flora, fauna, or geological or physiological features. . .'. The powers to designate SSSIs are now contained in the Wildlife and Countryside Act 1981 and it is the NCC that carries out this function.

The control of international trade in endangered species is now consolidated in the Endangered Species (Import and Export) Act 1976. This requires a licence for the import and export of almost all wild flora and fauna and although it does not itself ban any trade it is possible for the licensing authority (which is the Department of the Environment) to withhold licences and thus achieve the same effect.

The government agency responsible for landscape conservation and recreation activities is the Countryside Commission (CC) which became a corporate body in 1982 under the Wildlife and Countryside Act 1981. The CC was created under the Countryside Act 1968 and replaced the former National Parks Commission. Among its other functions the CC designates national parks and areas of outstanding natural beauty.

Although most agricultural developments are outside the controls available to local authorities under the Town and Country Planning Act 1971, these controls have historically played an important part in restraining urban development on agricultural land. Recent proposals to relax the planning system may diminish this role.

8.1 Birds and their habitats

79/409/EEC (OJ L103 25.4.79) proposed 20.12.1976 – COM(76)676	Directive on the conservation of wild birds.
85/411 (OJ L233 30.8.85)	Commission Directive replacing Annex I.

Binding dates

Notification date	6 April 1979
Formal compliance	6 April 1981
First annual report on derogations relating to capture and killing	6 April 1982*
First three yearly report	6 April 1984

*This is to assume that the first year starts with the date for compliance rather than the notification date. The Directive is unclear.

Purpose of the Directive

The Directive arose out of public disquiet at the annual slaughter of migratory birds that was common in southern Europe, but goes further in providing a general system of protection for all species of wild birds found in Europe. Not only does it seek to control the hunting and killing of wild birds and to protect their eggs and nests but it also requires the provision of a sufficient diversity and area of habitats so as to maintain the population of all species. Some species found in Europe are said to be in danger of extinction and the populations of others have been falling.

Summary of the Directive

General obligations

A general duty is placed on Member States to maintain the population of all 'species of naturally occurring birds in the wild state' in the European territory 'at a level which corresponds in particular to ecological, scientific and cultural requirements, while taking account of economic and recreational requirements'.

Member States are to preserve, maintain or reestablish a sufficient diversity and area of habitats for birds. This is to be done primarily by creating protected areas, managing habitats both inside and outside protected areas, reestablishing destroyed biotopes and creating new ones.

Member States are to lay down a general system of protection for all species of wild birds although exceptions are made for hunting and for certain other reasons. In particular the following are prohibited:

deliberate killing or capture by any method;
deliberate destruction of, or damage to, their nests and eggs or removal of nests;
taking eggs in the wild and keeping them even if empty;

deliberate disturbance particularly during breeding and rearing;
keeping birds whose hunting and capture is prohibited.

Special measures concerning habitats
Annex I lists particularly vulnerable species which are to be the subject of special
conservation measures concerning their habitat in order to ensure their survival
and reproduction. Originally seventy-four species were listed but a new list of
one hundred and forty-four species was substituted by Directive 85/411. Member States are to classify the most suitable territories (both land and sea) as special
protection areas for the conservation of these species. Similar measures are to be
taken for regularly occurring migratory species not listed in Annex I. Particular
attention is to be paid to the protection of wetlands.

Member States are to send the Commission information about the measures
they have taken so that the Commission can ensure that these form a coherent
whole. Member States are to strive generally to avoid pollution or deterioration
of habitats but in respect of the special protection areas they are to take appropriate steps to avoid pollution or deterioration of habitats or any disturbances
affecting the birds in so far as these are significant to the objectives set out for
habitat protection.

Hunting and killing
The seventy-two species listed in **Annex II** may be hunted under national
legislation, but Member States are to ensure that hunting does not jeopardize
conservation efforts.

Annnex II is in two parts. The twenty-four species in Annex II/1 may be
hunted anywhere but the forty-eight species in Annex II/2 may be hunted only
in the Member States indicated in the Annex.

Member States are to ensure that hunting complies with the principles of
wise use and ecologically balanced control of the species concerned. In particular
Member States are to ensure that birds are not hunted during the rearing season
nor during the various stages of reproduction. Migratory birds are in addition not
to be hunted during their return to their rearing grounds. Member States are to
send the Commission all relevant information on the practical application of their
hunting regulations.

The methods of killing birds, particularly those listed in **Annex IV(a)**, are to
be prohibited. These include snares, explosives, nets, use of blind or mutilated
live birds as decoys, and semiautomatic or automatic weapons with a magazine
capable of using more than two rounds of ammunition. **Annex IV(b)** prohibits
hunting from aircraft, motor vehicles and boats driven at more than five kilometres per hour (an exception to the speed limit can apply in the open sea for
safety reasons).

Member States may derogate from the prohibitions on killing or capture,
where there is no other satisfactory solution, for the following reasons:

in the interest of public health and safety;
in the interests of air safety;

to prevent serious damage to crops, livestock, forests, fisheries and water;
for the protection of flora and fauna;
for the purposes of research and teaching;
for repopulation or reintroduction;
to permit, under strictly supervised conditions and on a selective basis, the
capture, keeping or other judicious use of certain birds in small numbers.

An annual report of these derogations must be submitted to the Commission
who must ensure that they are compatible with the Directive. Derogations must
specify: the species; the authorized methods for killing or capture; the time and
place; the conditions of risk; the authority empowered to declare that the
conditions obtain and to decide what methods may be used, within what limits
and by whom; and the controls which will be carried out.

Restriction on sale

Sale of wild birds (including the transport, keeping or offering, for sale) is to be
prohibited. This prohibition is to extend to live or dead birds and to any
recognizable parts or derivatives of such birds. Sale of the seven species of birds
listed in **Annex III/1** is not prohibited provided the birds have been legally killed
or captured or otherwise legally acquired. A further ten species listed in **Annex
III/2** may also be exempted from this prohibition by Member States who must
first consult the Commission. If the Commission believes that sale of any of these
species will result in it being endangered the Commission is to forward a
reasoned recommendation to the Member State. If the Commission believes
there is no such risk it must say so. The Commission's recommendation is to be
published in the *Official Journal*.

A further nine species listed in **Annex III/3** are to be the subject of further
studies by the Commission with a view to inclusion in Annex III/2.

Other provisions

Every three years Member States are to forward a report on the implementation
of national provisions taken to comply with the Directive. In its turn, the
Commission is to prepare a composite report and the part of the draft report
covering information supplied by a Member State is to be verified by the
authorities in that Member State. The final version of the report is to be sent to the
Member States but it does not have to be sent to the Parliament and thus made
public.

Member States are to encourage research and any work required as a basis for
protection and management of birds. Particular attention is to be paid to research
on the subjects listed in **Annex V**. The Commission is to coordinate research.
Member States are to see that the introduction of species of bird which do not
occur naturally does not prejudice the local flora and fauna. They are to consult
the Commission. Member States may introduce stricter protective measures than
those provided for under the Directive. A committee is established for adapting
Annexes I and V to technical and scientific progress.

The Resolution
On the same day that the Directive was adopted (2 April 1979), the Council also passed a Resolution (OJ C103 25.4.79) calling upon the Member States to notify the Commission within two years of:

the special protection areas which they had classified under the Directive;
the wetlands which they had designated or intended to designate as wetlands of international importance;
any other areas classified according to national legislation for bird protection.

The Commission was to keep an up to date a list of these areas and was to submit proposals regarding the criteria for determining the special protection areas. (A committee is now working on criteria.)

Development of the Directive

The Directive stemmed from the public disquiet at the annual slaughter of migratory birds that has been customary in southern Europe and northern Africa. As early as 1971 questions were being asked in the European Parliament (OJ C119 26.11.71) with suggestions for Community legislation and this disquiet was reflected in the first action programme on the environment of 1973:

Hundreds of millions of migratory birds and songbirds are captured and killed in Europe every year provoking world-wide protests against the countries which allow the trapping of birds.

The action programme proposed a study with a view to possible harmonization of national regulations on the protection of animal species and migratory birds in particular. The programme promised action by the end of 1974.

In the autumn of 1974 the European Parliament received a petition (No 8/74) from national and international animal protection organizations under the title 'Save the Migratory Birds'. This called for an international conference to investigate the problem at a bicontinental (European-African) level and recommended a halt to the hunting of birds until the results of the conference were known. This petition resulted in the adoption of a resolution by the Parliament on 21 February 1975 calling in particular for a general prohibition on the trapping of wild birds with nets but also recommending the preservation of certain species and the creation of suitable breeding grounds.

On 9 February 1976 – already over a year behind the date set in the action programme – the Commission replied to an oral question in the Parliament explaining the guidelines which the draft Directive was to follow: there was to be a general system for the protection of wild birds comprising the prohibition of killing and trapping and of trade in birds both dead and alive, followed by exceptions (eg for game birds).

An early draft of a proposed Directive dated 12 May 1976 became public and was attached to another petition (No 10/76) presented to the Parliament in August 1976. This draft was criticized in a debate (15 October 1976) for allowing hunting of certain species (certain larks, thrushes and finches) – a point that was to cause trouble later – and in reply a Commissioner explained that the published draft was only one document of many and that no definite position had been taken. He stressed that the complexity of the problem and the emotive atmosphere surrounding it obliged the Commission to be scrupulously careful in preparing its proposals.

Meanwhile the Commission had conducted studies and consulted experts and its proposed Directive eventually published in December 1976 turned out to be much more comprehensive than the Parliament had ever suggested. The Parliament debated it on 14 June – one day before the Council was due to discuss the proposal – but it took a further eighteen months for important points of detail and a major point of conflict to be resolved. This conflict was the desire of Italy and France to allow hunting of the skylark (Alauda arvensis) and the ortolan bunting, and before agreement could be secured the Council had to insert the skylark into Annex II/2 – but not the ortolan bunting. Both the Economic and Social Committee and the European Parliament welcomed the Directive. Not all their proposed amendments were reflected in the final Directive.

In Britain the Directive was not considered in the House of Lords but was the subject of two reports from the Scrutiny Committee of the House of Commons leading to a debate. In preparing its first report the Commons' Scrutiny Committee took evidence from the DoE, from organizations representing shooting interests, landowners, the Nature Conservancy Council and the Royal Society for the Protection of Birds (RSPB). The RSPB claimed that the Directive was based to a large extent on British legislation (in the drafting of which they had had a hand in the 1920s although it was not enacted until 1954) and indeed it follows the British pattern of providing general protection for all wild birds, providing extra protection for some, and allowing the killing of others.

The first report of the Scrutiny Committee noted that all organizations consulted were generally in favour of the Directive but said that several matters needed further consideration including the needs of game bird management, the restriction on the sale of dead birds, provision for falconry, and the control of birds for airfield clearance. It drew attention to the undesirability of attempting to impose uniform conditions of bird protection throughout the Community.

In the second report the Scrutiny Committee noted that most of these points had been met by promised amendments. It reported that the DoE held that uniform conditions of bird conservation throughout Europe would be of great benefit but that the derogation procedure had been amended to allow Member States autonomy to take action in the interests of public health and safety, aircraft safety and agricultural pest control.

In the Commons' debate (17 November 1977) the Minister, Kenneth Marks, explained that the government had consistently expressed strong support for the principles of the Directive, while seeking a number of detailed changes in its provisions. He was able to report that having consulted a wide range of interests the government had been able to reach agreement on the amendments that should be sought. He outlined the amendments under discussion and reported that the Directive was likely to emerge in a form even closer to present British legislation so that few amendments would be required to the Protection of Birds Acts. Although the Minister only made the point guardedly other MPs took the opportunity to claim national credit. Peter Mills said:

> I think too that as we in Britain look at the draft Directive we
> can congratulate ourselves as a nation, because most of the
> Directive follows closely the general framework of the

United Kingdom legislation on the protection of birds. . . . I only wish that other countries – I mention Italy as one, and the southern Mediterranean area – had the same concern that we have had over the years. I think that we can pat ourselves on the back for our legislation and for the fact that it is a pattern for the Community.

Peter Hardy made a similar point, touching simultaneously on the question of habitat protection:

I am not always enthusiastic about many of the Directives that we have to consider, but I do believe that this one is especially welcome. That is because it is relevant to the interests of many and is broadly similar to our own legislation. It may – perhaps rightly – put a little more stress on habitat than our own legislation, but by and large it is acceptable. I am delighted that it will not require anything but minor amendment to our own legislation.

Concern about habitat protection had been raised in the Scrutiny Committee when DoE officials gave oral evidence but did not feature in the Scrutiny Committee's report. The Chairman, Peter Mills, put it like this in a question:

Could we turn to the important point about the maintenance of habitats. The agriculturalists and landowners say there is going to be further interference in their use of agricultural land. What is the Department's views on this and what is the possibility of compensation?

In reply the responsible DoE official played down the concern:

I do not see the Directive making a great deal of difference in this respect for this reason. . . We do it through the work of the Nature Conservancy Council which has national nature reserves, sites of special scientific interest, and through the work of voluntary bodies such as the RSPB, the Wildfowl Trust and the WAGBI. They all have nature reserves, so that they are in the business of protecting habitats already. We would not see this Directive as imposing any greater obligation in the UK than we are already doing.

On being pressed further he continued:

Clearly the debate has to go on between agricultural and conservation interests as to how one marries the needs of agriculture with the needs of conservation. What I am saying is that I do not think there is anything in this Directive which tilts the balance. I think as far as this Directive is concerned, what we are doing already in terms of the protection of habitats would more than meet the requirements of what is in here. We shall certainly, though, want to continue to have the debate with the agricultural and other interests as to where the balance should be struck as between nature conservation and certain farming practices.

The Commons' debate hardly touched on habitat protection – which was to cause such dissension during the passage of the Wildlife and Countryside Act 1981 – but otherwise many incisive points were made. Neville Sandelson put his finger on a key aspect of Community environmental policy:

> I stress the extent to which the Directive shows how the Community is often able to achieve internal advances that are beyond the internal capability of individual Governments. No amount of pressure over many years on particular Member States which have been the principal offenders in permitting the indiscriminate slaughter of migratory birds has had any real effect. In spite of the efforts of all the bodies in this country – the Royal Society for the Protection of Birds and others – which have done so much valuable work in bringing these appalling circumstances to public and international attention, there has been very little effect before the Community itself stepped in. We have the culmination now in this very welcome draft Directive.

The Minister, Kenneth Marks, took this point one step further by recognizing the ability of the Community to influence policy not only within Member States but outside the Community too:

> Of course it is desirable to extend the principles beyond the limits of the EEC. We are already involved in discussion in the Council of Europe and with the International Union for the Conservation of Nature about further conventions on this subject. We hope that Spain will take part in the conventions. However, these are some way off, and we cannot yet be sure how effective they will be.

> I am convinced that it is right to start at the Community level. Then we can use the Directive as the basis for these wider discussions, as our own Acts have been used as the basis for this Directive.

Formal compliance in UK

Notwithstanding the influence of the Protection of Birds Acts 1954–67 on the form of the Directive some changes in legislation were necessary both in respect of habitat protection and relating to protection of birds themselves. These were made in the Wildlife and Countryside Act 1981 which received the Royal Assent more than six months after the date (April 1981) for formal compliance with the Directive. In fact the sections dealing with bird protection did not come into effect until September 1982 when the Protection of Birds Acts were repealed. Britain was not alone in being late.

It is possible that the government would have introduced an Act dealing with countryside matters and wildlife habitats had there been no Directive if for no other reason than to implement the obligations of the Berne and Bonn Conventions (Chapter 11) but the Directive ensured that existing bird protection legislation had to be amended. The RSPB were seeking to have the existing Acts amended and the Directive provided the opportunity. In fact rather few changes concerned with protection of species can be directly attributed to the Directive although these include:

controls on taxidermy;
a reduction in the number of species regarded as pests which may be killed at all times under licence;
greater controls on the sale of dead birds;
greater controls on the possession of eggs and birds;
the ban on killing using repeating shotguns, although these were probably not much used in Britain.

The more significant changes brought about by the Act relevant to bird protection concern habitats, and Section 29 of the Act specifically refers to compliance with international obligations as a reason for the making of nature conservation orders. This can be taken as a reference to the Berne and Bonn Conventions (see Chapter 11) and Ramsar Conventions of 1971 concerned with wetlands, as well as to the Directive. The combination of all these international obligations seems to have convinced the government that it would be best to have statutory powers for habitat protection and Section 29 cannot be attributed entirely to the Directive. Indeed a view held within government during negotiation on the Directive was that no extra powers for habitat protection were necessary.

On 31 August 1982, over one year late, the DoE wrote to the Commission in accordance with the Council Resolution of 2 April 1979 notifying it of the steps taken to classify special protection areas under the Directive. This letter explained the types of protected area in Britain (national, local and voluntary nature reserves and sites of special scientific interest – SSSIs) and the power of the Secretary of State to make nature conservation orders. It also referred to the relevant legislation:

National Parks and Access to the Countryside Act 1949.
Countryside Act 1968.
Countryside (Scotland) Act 1967.
Wildlife and Countryside Act 1981.

The letter explained that the government was now notifying as special protection areas those nature reserves which were safeguarded from development to the greatest extent by being owned by the Nature Conservancy Council. Seven areas were listed (by May 1987 the figure was twenty-two). The letter also explained that although a good number of the 4000 SSSIs had been designated because of their importance to birds not all were sufficiently safeguarded to meet the requirements of special protection areas. The government had earlier informed the Commission of nineteen wetlands of international importance which were covered by the Ramsar Convention but these are not necessarily classified as special protection areas for the purposes of the Directive (by May 1987 the figure was thirty-one). The Nature Conservancy Council (NCC) has drawn up a list of more than 180 sites (by May 1987 the figure was over 200) satisfying scientific criteria which enable them to be regarded as internationally important as regards birds and it is apparently the intention of the government to classify at least some more of these as special protection areas under the Directive. (The RSPB regard the number classified so far as quite inadequate.)

On 13 December 1982 the government sent the Commission a statement of how it believed each Article of the Directive was complied with. The habitat protection measures were those already submitted to the Commission, as described above, in accordance with the Council Resolution. All other Articles were said to be covered by the Wildlife and Countryside Act which extends to Scotland as well as England and Wales. The legislation for Northern Ireland – The Wildlife (Northern Ireland) Order 1985 and the Nature Conservation and Amenity Lands (Northern Ireland) Order 1985 – did not come into operation until April 1985 and the long delay prompted the Commission to start infringement proceedings by issuing a Reasoned Opinion.

The British legislation appears generally to fulfil the obligations of the Directive with doubt about its adequacy in only the two respects discussed below: the habitat protection measures and the derogations from prohibitions on killing or capture. On these points much will turn on how the British legislation is applied in practice.

The obligations as to habitat protection in the Directive are very general but certain principles are laid down: special conservation measures are to be taken to ensure the survival of the species in Annex I taking certain factors into account and Member States 'must classify in particular the most suitable territories in number and size as special protection areas for the conservation of these species'. The British legislation to implement the obligation is complicated and for its effectiveness relies upon the goodwill of the landowning and farming community, their willingness to enter into management agreements with the NCC and the amount of money made available to the NCC.

Although the Secretary of State is given the new power by Section 29 of the Wildlife and Countryside Act to make nature conservation orders in respect of land and to specify operations which may cause damage, the NCC is not furnished with the power to prohibit such operations, but must first offer to enter a management agreement which may entitle the owner to compensation. The NCC has the ultimate power of compulsory purchase – a power which it has had since 1949 and has only used twice. Both management agreements and compulsory purchase cost money and the NCC's funds are limited. Thus, although the Act in theory provides adequate legal powers to implement the obligations in the Directive – since the NCC could compulsorily purchase many sites if it had the resources – much will turn on how the powers are actually used.

The issue over the power to derogate from the prohibitions on killing and capture is also complicated. The Directive is clear about what the derogations must specify and the purposes for which they may be given while Section 16(5) of the Wildlife and Countryside Act enables 'general' as well as 'specific' licences to be given to people to kill birds. Such general licences could be, for example, to control grey geese in all of central and eastern Scotland and could allow licence holders to permit others to kill for sporting purposes. This point was raised in a European parliamentary question (OJ C168 8.7.81) and in reply the Commissioner, referring to the Bill as amended after debate in the House of Lords, expressed the Commission's opinion that clause 16 (now Section 16) was wider than the Directive permits but went on to say that much would depend on the way the powers of licensing under the Bill are in fact exercised. Government officials have discussed this point with Commission officials and it has been agreed that the annual reports on derogations that the government has to submit to the Commission would be the evidence on which the Commission would judge implementation of the Directive. Regular reports are being submitted.

There are three detailed points about the derogations that require comment because all were raised during discussion of the proposed Directive in the House of Commons. Section 4(2) of the Wildlife and Countryside Act specifically allows for 'mercy killing', that is killing a bird so seriously disabled that there is no chance of its recovering, but there is no comparable provision in the Directive. The Berne Convention (see Chapter 11) similarly does not provide for mercy killing but when this was raised by British government officials during negotiations it was generally agreed that mercy killing went without saying. It may therefore be assumed that the Commission and everyone else will overlook this inconsistency between the Act and the Directive.

Falconry may be licensed under Section 16(1) of the Act but is not mentioned as such in the Directive. Derogations for falconry (both the keeping of the falcons and the killing of their prey) appear to fall within the wording of Article 9(c):

> to permit, under strictly supervised conditions and on a selective basis, the capture, keeping or other judicious use of certain birds in small numbers.

Finally, the taking of gulls' eggs for human consumption and their sale is allowed for by Section 16(2) of the Act although not specifically mentioned in the Directive. It is justified by the government as being a derogation under Article 9(a) and 9(c) from the prohibition on the taking of eggs. Article 9(a) allows derogations 'for the purpose of protecting flora and fauna' and the taking of eggs is one way of keeping down the population of gulls that may otherwise displace other birds. The selling of the eggs is regarded as 'judicious use' under Article 9(c) quoted above – though it should be noted that the Directive speaks of the judicious use of birds and not their eggs and also talks of small numbers.

A fuller discussion of compliance with the Directive has been provided by the RSPB[1]. In particular, the RSPB believe that there is a gap in compliance since SSSIs cannot yet be adequately protected for areas below low water mark which are often important for birds.

Effect on UK practice

It is generally recognized that Britain had amongst the most far-reaching bird protection legislation of any European country before the Directive was agreed. Public opinion and that of the farming and landowning community has also in the past been generally favourable to bird protection so it would be surprising indeed if the Directive were to make any significant difference to British practice. If there were to be any effects one would expect them to be small. Nevertheless, some effects can already be discerned and in the long term the Directive could significantly affect habitat protection.

One effect concerns the licences that may be given under Section 16 of the Act to kill or take birds. As we have seen, these licences may be 'general' or 'specific'. The Minister, Hector Munro, in the Committee stage of the Wildlife and Countryside Bill (2 June 1981) tried to play down fears about 'general' licences: 'I want to say this loud and clear. Many people have been concerned that there will be blanket licences for doing this and that. That will not be the case. . .'. The possibility of 'general' licences would remain were it not for Article 9 of the Directive which requires an annual report to the Commission on derogations. The annual reports will therefore provide a check.

The RSPB claim, for example, that barnacle geese are being shot on the island of Islay in Scotland under licence from the Department of Agriculture and Fisheries in Scotland not so as 'to prevent serious damage to crops' and 'where there is no other satisfactory solution' but for sporting purposes. In the absence of the Directive the RSPB would have made representations to the relevant government departments and will continue to do so. But they can now not only refer to the provisions of the Act but also to the provisions of the Directive. They can and do make representations to the Commission too. What used to be a discussion between two parties now becomes a discussion between three.

Possibly the more important and long-term effect of the Directive will concern habitat protection. We have seen that the Act provides some powers for habitat protection but that much will turn on how these are used. There was much heated discussion in Britain during the passage of the Wildlife and Countryside Bill on whether the powers would be adequate and this continues. Only time will tell whether the government's policy of reliance on essentially voluntary rather than statutory action will work, and whether the provisions for compensation to farmers to forgo certain profitable agriculture practices which may be damaging to nature conservation produce the desired result. The Act lacks general principles about bird and habitat protection comparable to those in the Directive so that if those concerned with bird protection feel that habitats are being lost to an unaccepttable extent they are likely to rely on both the general and specific obligations enunciated in the Directive in preference to the Act in arguments with government. If they feel that the government is not honouring the obligation it entered into in agreeing the Directive they will not hesitate to involve the Commission too. This is already happening in the case of Duich Moss where the Directive is creating pressure for a reconsideration of the plans by a whisky distillery to extract peat on the island of Islay. Duich Moss is a potential 'special protection area' but has not yet been officially classified as such. In winter it contains 4–5 per cent of the entire world population of the Greenland white fronted goose. As a result of complaints made by the RSPB and others, who are not satisfied that the conditions attached to the planning consent provide adequate protection, the Commission wrote to the government urging it to classify the site. Since it has not done so, and following a visit to the site by a Commission official, the Commission has said it will start infringement proceedings by issuing a Reasoned Opinion. There has been much discussion and negotiation between government and Commission officials and it is possible that an alternative site for extracting peat can be found.

References

1   Pritchard D E September 1985 *Britain's implementation of the birds' Directive*, paper presented to a conference of the British Association of Nature Conservationists, Cambridge.

8.2 Whales

348/81 (OJ L39 12.2.81) proposed 25.4.80 – COM(80)150	Council Regulation on common rules for imports of whales or other cetacean products.
3786/81 (OJ L377 31.12.81)	Commission Regulation laying down provisions for the implementation of the common rules for imports of whales or other cetacean products.

These two Regulations have not been repealed but have since been subsumed into Regulation 3626/82 on the implementation of the CITES Convention (see Section 8.4).

Binding dates

Commission to be informed of competent authorities	1 July 1981
Ban takes effect	1 January 1982.

Purpose of the Regulations

The objective of conserving whales was advanced by a control on the import into the Community of certain cetacean products from 1 January 1982 by Council Regulation 348/81. This was subsumed and the extent of the controls extended by Council Regulation 3626/82 on the implementation in the Community of the Convention on International Trade in Endangered Species of Wild Fauna and Flora (CITES), which came into force on 31 December 1982 (see Section 8.4).

Summary of Regulation 348/81

From 1 January 1982 the products listed in an Annex can be imported into the Community only upon production of an import licence. Licences may be issued only for such purposes as scientific research and no licence is to be issued for commercial purposes.

The Annex lists a number of cetacean products such as meat, bones, fats, oil, spermaceti but not ambergris (ambergris used commercially is generally not obtained from killed whales but is gathered from beaches); leather treated with oil from cetaceans; and also articles of leather or furskins treated with oil from cetaceans (eg handbags and shoes). The Annex in fact includes about 95 per cent of all secondary whale products, but excludes for instance cosmetics and lubricating oils containing small quantities of whale products.

Member States must notify the Commission of the competent authorities who are to issue licences and the Commission is to inform the other States.

A committee on cetacean products is set up with a Commission representative as chairman and is to give opinions on the application of the Regulation. The Commission has power to make implementing Regulations if the committee, acting on a qualified majority, agrees. The Commission also has power to make implementing Regulations on its own, despite an adverse opinion of the committee, after having submitted the proposal to the Council and in the event of the Council failing to agree within three months. One implementing Commission Regulation No 3786/81 has been issued prescribing the form of the import licence and making minor exceptions from the need for a licence (eg personal luggage of travellers).

At the earliest opportunity the Commission is to submit a report to the Council on whether the list of products in the Annex should be extended. The Council can extend the list acting on a qualified majority. Pending such a decision, Member States may themselves ban products not in the Annex. In reply to a European parliamentary question (OJ C218 23.8.82) the Commission stated that a study had been carried out but that the committee on cetacean products had advised that extension of the Annex should be considered at a later stage after the Regulation had been in operation for longer.

Development of the Regulation

The action programmes made no reference to an import ban on whale products and the origin of the Regulation is to be found in a British initiative of October 1979. The Regulation shows that the Community can, on occasion, move very quickly: the Regulation was formally proposed in April 1980, agreed in principle in June, formally agreed in December and the ban came into effect one year later.

A United Kingdom ban on the import of products from baleen whales had been in existence since 1973 but the ban did not extend to sperm whale oil which was used for treating leather and for certain other purposes. As a result of a national campaign in Britain against the killing of whales whether threatened with extinction or not, the Conservative party, during the election campaign of May 1979, promised to press for a moratorium on commercial whaling for a limited period if it were to be elected. In July 1979 the International Whaling Commission narrowly failed to ban all commercial whaling but agreed to ban commercial whaling by factory ships, except for minke whales. Although this decision reduced the number of sperm whales killed it would not have completely cut the supply of sperm whale oil and because of its election pledge the government was pressed to take unilateral action. In the event it decided not to act unilaterally but to press for a ban at Community level for three reasons: there was doubt whether a unilateral ban would be consistent with the provisions of the Treaty of Rome on the free movement of goods (EEC Regulation No 1917/80 OJ L186 19.7.80); a unilateral ban would have put British leather manufacturers at a commercial disadvantage in comparison with their continental competitors; and a Community ban would be more effective in the objective of protecting whales. (It should be noted that the uncertainty about the legality of a unilateral ban also applied to the existing ban on the products of baleen whales. That ban was introduced at about the time that Britain joined the Community and perhaps for the reason that it did not extend to products of the same commercial importance as sperm whale oil had not been criticized by the Commission).

In October 1979 the Secretary of State for the Environment, Michael Heseltine, accordingly wrote to the President of the Commission, Roy Jenkins, asking for a Community ban on the primary products of all whales and, as a result, the Commission proposed a Regulation embodying a ban in April 1980. This proposed ban went further than the British request by including leather treated with oil from cetaceans, though it did not include leather products.

The European Parliament in November 1980 adopted a lengthy resolution which welcomed the proposal to limit imports of whale products but wanted the limit extended to cover all products that could be shown to derive from cetaceans. The Parliament's resolution also ranged much more widely than an import ban and requested the Commission among other matters to put forward a ban on commercial whaling in European waters.

The House of Commons' Scrutiny Committee in a report dated 25 June 1980 noted the concern of the British Leather Federation that the proposed Regulation would permit the free import into the Community of leather products treated with whale oil while British manufacturers would suffer the disadvantage of not being allowed to import either treated leather or whale oil. The Committee noted that consideration was being given to the inclusion of leather products treated with whale oil in the list of restricted products, and this inclusion was in fact formally made in a proposal from the Commission (COM(80)788) in November 1980.

On 8 December 1980 the House of Commons debated the Commission's proposal on a motion that welcomed 'the Government's initiative for this Regulation'. In the debate the Minister, Marcus Fox, explained that agreement in principle had been secured for the Regulation at the Council meeting on 30 June, but that there had been prolonged debate on three issues: the legal basis for the ban; whether Member States could go beyond the Regulation; and the list of products to be covered by the ban. Two of these issues had been resolved and the only outstanding point was the legal basis: should the Regulation be based on Article 113 of the Treaty concerned with commercial policy or Article 235 giving the Council general powers. Pressed in the debate the minister named Denmark and Germany as the two countries holding out for Article 235 while all other Member States supported the use of Article 113. In the event, Danish and German arguments prevailed.

The government was congratulated on all sides during the debate on its initiative and one MP said of the Regulation: 'There is no doubt that it will be welcomed by thousands, if not millions, in this country who have campaigned for a long time.'

The principle criticism made by some Members of Parliament was that the Regulation did not ban all products, but the Minister explained that 95 per cent of secondary products would be covered, and that to cover the next 5 per cent would multiply by a far greater percentage the number of checks that would have to be made. To enforce a complete ban was said to be difficult, if not impossible. There is nothing in the Regulations to prevent manufacturers using up existing stocks of sperm whale oil and this fact made the ban more acceptable to some Member States. It may be a few years before all existing stocks are used.

Formal compliance in UK

Community Regulations have the force of law in the UK, and are therefore directly applicable without requiring further legal measures to become effective. However, prior to the Regulations coming into effect, imports of certain cetacean products were already controlled under UK domestic legislation, the Endangered Species (Import and Export) Act 1976, which implemented CITES and other conservation controls in the UK.

Effect on UK practice

Although the Regulation covers most primary and secondary whale products, import of these into Britain was already largely banned with the exception of sperm whale oil. The effect of the Regulation in Britain can therefore be considered in terms of this one product but its effect will have been larger in those Member States which did not already have as extensive an existing ban.

Use of sperm whale oil had in fact already been falling in Britain as a result of the cuts in the allowable catch by the International Whaling Commission and the leather industry was also under considerable pressure from environmentalists not to use sperm whale oil. As a result the leather industry had developed alternatives to sperm whale oil and no great difficulty was encountered in finally phasing out its use by the date specified in the Regulation. The Regulation therefore effectively came at the end of a process of change that had been going on for several years.

The Regulation will have ensured that the British leather industry is not at the disadvantage in comparison with its continental competitors that it would have been in the event of a unilateral ban. This is because leather treated with sperm whale oil is, in the opinion of some, superior to the treated with the alternatives available.

Some organizations that campaigned against the killing of whales had criticized the government's decision to seek a Community ban rather than to proceed unilaterally. Their grounds would probably have been, if they were expressed, that Community action would take longer and would be less certain. In the event a Community ban was secured and has denied whale products to a market of 250 million people as opposed to one of 55 million.

8.3 Seals

83/129/EEC (OJ L91 9.4.83) proposed 20.10.82 – COM(82)639 and 85/444/EC (OJ L259 1.10.85)	Directive concerning the importation into Member States of skins of certain seal pups and products derived therefrom.
Binding dates Notification dates Formal compliance Period in force	31 March 1983 and September 1985 1 October 1983 up to 1 October 1985 extended to 1 October 1989

Purpose of the Directive

In response to widespread repugnance at the annual killing of certain seal pups the commercial import into Member States of skins and articles made from them is stopped for a certain period.

Summary of the Directive

Member States are required to take all necessary measures to ensure that skins of harp and hooded seal pups and articles made from them are not commercially imported into their territories. The Directive applied for an initial two-year period with provision for a subsequent decision by qualified majority to revise it. A later Directive amended the period by extending it for a further four years. It does not apply to products resulting from traditional hunting by the Inuit people.

Development of the Directive

On 9 March 1982 a petition with three million signatures calling for measures to protect seals was presented to the European Parliament[1] which responded by adopting a Resolution requesting the Commission amongst other things 'to introduce, by means of a Regulation, a ban on Community imports of all skins and products derived from young hooded and harp seals'. Prior to that there had been, over a number of years, questions by members of the European Parliament calling for Community measures to stop the annual killing of baby seals in Canada and Norway. A number of countries had also already started to take restrictive measures or were proposing to do so. Consultations with the Canadian and Norwegian governments by the Commission had not produced any significant change. The Commission having contracted with the Nature Conservancy Council in the UK for a study on the consequences of current culling practice[1] put forward a proposal for a Regulation in October 1982.

The draft Regulation was based on Article 113, referring to the common commercial policy and the need to take action at Community level on measures restricting international trade on moral grounds. The draft provided for the prohibition of importation of skins of harp and hooded seal pups and/or articles made from them with certain exemptions referring to transit procedures and personal effects.

The Council considered the proposal at its meeting on 3 December 1983 and on 17 December but were unable to agree on the proposal. They did, however, agree a Resolution calling on the Commission to examine further the whole question of the killing of seal pups including talks with the countries concerned and to report back urgently with proposals for any additional measures to be taken thought appropriate in the light of the examination. The Council also agreed in the Resolution to adopt not later than 1 March 1983 all appropriate measures; in addition Member States undertook to pursue measures under the Convention on International Trade in Endangered Species (CITES) (see Section 8.4) for conservation of harp and hooded seals and to take all possible measures to prevent importation of skins and products of pups and these species.

The UK government position was twofold: it took action to discourage imports within its own powers by requiring, since the beginning of 1981, all seal products to be labelled showing the country where they were taken, and by persuading the British Fur Trade Association to impose a ban on imports from 1 March 1983 for one year, to be monitored by Customs. On the Commission proposal difficulties arose in basing the draft Regulation on Article 113. It was argued that action could only be taken under that article on purely commercial grounds; the proposal was based on moral grounds and the Council's legal services as well as the legal advisers of several Member States including the UK Attorney General had advised that these could not serve as a legal basis for the proposal. In addition there were a number of other considerations to be taken into account including the scientific advice on conservation and the actions of the Canadian and Norwegian governments. There was a willingness to take action provided that an appropriate form of Community measure could be found. These arguments were all displayed in a well-attended debate in the House of Commons in the small hours of 16 February 1983. The debate reflected the widespread concern amongst a section of the public. It also illustrates how an emotive subject concerning wildlife conservation in countries outside the Community can arouse far greater interest in this country than proposals for Community action on major pollution problems affecting the Community.

Another point of interest in the UK was the question of which Whitehall department took the lead on this subject. Initially it was the Department of Trade which was held to be primarily responsible. This would follow from the fact that the proposal was based on Article 113. Subsequently, the Department of the Environment assumed primary responsibility because the proposal was a matter for the Council of Environment Ministers and because of the Department's responsibility for policy under CITES.

The Commission duly reported to the Council within two months – COM(83)71. It concluded that the various proposals by the Canadian government would not deal with the immediate problem and that their existing proposal should stand. On 28 February 1983 the Council agreed to adopt a Directive banning imports of seal pup skins and products for two years under Article 235 on conservation grounds. The government claimed that they played a major part in achieving unanimous support for this proposal for which they had pressed at the two previous meetings. The later Directive, extending the two-year period to six years, seems to have been adopted without any difficulty.

Formal compliance in the UK

The Secretary of State for the Environment laid an order – the Endangered Species (Import and Export) Act 1976 (Modification) Order 1983; SI 1609 – which came into force from 26 November 1983. This allowed the UK to restrict trade in skins and products of harp and hooded seals and gave force to the requirements of the Directive for the initial two years. An extension of the period was made in 1985 under SI 1985 No 1502. No expiry date was specified as the threat to the species concerned may have to be monitored after 1989.

Effect on UK practice

The voluntary agreement with the British Fur Trade Association to a ban on imports had been in effect from 1 March 1983. The order which came into effect in November therefore gave legal backing to the voluntary action. Given the existence of the voluntary ban, the introduction of the 1983 SI had no practical affect on imports as there were none recorded (though it was possible that some traders did not observe the ban). However, the SI did ensure that no further imports could be brought in legally.

References

1   von Moltke K 1983. In Macrory R (ed) *Influences on EEC environmental policy* in *Britain, Europe and the environment*. Imperial College, Centre for Environmental Technology.

8.4 Trade in endangered species (CITES)

3626/82 (OJ L384 31.12.78) proposed 21.7.80 – COM(80)413	Regulation on the implementation in the Community of the Convention on international trade in endangered species of wild flora and fauna.

Binding dates
Notification date	31 December 1982
Formal compliance	1 January 1984

There have been three Council Regulations and eight Commission Regulations amending the basic Regulation, mostly resulting from changes to the Convention, but the first Commission amendment provides for a uniform system of documentation within the Community:

Council Regulation	3645/83	OJ L367 28.12.83
	1831/85	OJ L173 03.07.85
Commission Regulation	3418/83	OJ L344 07.12.83
	3646/83	OJ L367 28.12.83
	577/84	OJ L 64 06.03.84
	1451/84	OJ L 64 06.03.84
	1452/84	OJ L140 26.05.84
	2384/85	OJ L231 29.08.85
	2295/86	OJ L201 24.07.86
Council Regulation	1422/87	OJ L136 26.05.87
Commission Regulation	1540/87	OJ L147 06.06.87

Purpose of Regulation

The purpose of the Regulation is primarily to ensure uniform application of the Convention – known as CITES – within the Community.

Summary of Regulation

The Convention, drawn up in March 1973, institutes a system of licensing for the trade in endangered species and prohibits trade in the most endangered species[1]. The Regulation does the same but goes rather further, for example in banning trade in certain species which the Convention does not ban. It requires a system of permits and certificates for imports and exports to be issued by competent authorities in each Member State. The names and addresses of such authorities are to be communicated to the Commission. Provision is made for a Committee to adopt further Regulations (eg for documentation) to enable the Regulation to function.

A number of subsequent EC Regulations (see above) have made minor amendments to the rules governing CITES in the EC, mostly by changes in the Appendices and Annexes listing controlled species.

Formal compliance in the UK

Regulation 3626/82 came into force on 31 December 1982 but Articles 1–17 only applied from 1 January 1984. Detailed procedures for the implementation of the Regulation were laid down in Commission Regulation 3418/83.

The UK is a party to the CITES Convention and prior to 1 January 1984, it was implemented by UK domestic legislation in the Endangered Species (Import and Export) Act 1976, which also controlled certain non-CITES species as well. The EC Regulations are directly applicable law in the UK and take precedence over the 1976 Act which effectively now only applies where the UK has decided to take stricter measures as allowed under Article 15 of Regulation 3626/82. The CITES controls are administered in the UK by the Department of the Environment, Endangered Species Branch, Tollgate House, Houlton Street, Bristol, BS2 9DJ.

Effect on UK practice

The Regulation has had some effects on administration in Britain since it empowers the Commission to prescribe the form of various documents which has been done in Regulation 3418/83. Current British practice is at least as stringent as the requirements of the Regulation, and in some respects more so, and the Regulation ensures that this must remain the case. The major effect of the Regulation will be to compel those Member States that had not ratified the Convention to implement it. One justification for the Regulation was that unequal implementation by different Member States would upset the operation of the common market, but the Regulation does allow Member States to maintain or take stricter measures than those set out.

The CITES Convention requires parties to it to submit annual reports to the secretariat with summaries of trade in specimens of species. One effect of the Regulation is that the United Kingdom is no longer submitting annual reports but instead the EC Commission is submitting EC reports. This has been criticized as it is not now possible to know about trade between EC Member States.

The Commission has asked the Wildlife Trade Monitoring Unit of IUCN to report on implementation of the Regulation in all Member States.

References
1   Lyster S 1985 *International wildlife law*. Grotius, Cambridge.

8.5 Environmentally sensitive areas

797/85 (OJ L93 30.3.85) proposed 1983 – COM(83)559	Regulation on improving the efficiency of agricultural structures.
Binding dates Enters into force Formal compliance Re-examination of detailed rules Estimated life of Regulation Annual report by the Commission to the European Parliament and the Council	1 April 1985 30 September 1985 1 April 1990 until 31 December 1994 by 1 August annually.

Purpose of the Regulation

This Regulation introduces the concept of environmentally sensitive areas into the Common Agricultural Policy (CAP). The CAP is financed by the European Agricultural Guidance and Guarantee Fund (usually known by its French acronym FEOGA). The 'guarantee' part of the fund is concerned with supporting the prices of products, while the 'guidance' part is used to finance the development of farms and food marketing. 'Agricultural structures' is the term usually used for policies concerned with farm development.

There is a considerable history of EC farm structures policies embodied in a whole series of Directives and Regulations including the 'less favoured areas' Directives (see Section 8.6). These have been designed to assist farmers in modernizing their holdings and making them more efficient, with a particular emphasis on investment aids.

The present Regulation introduces a series of financial aid measures aimed at farm development, some of which Member States are obliged to implement, others of which are purely optional. It also sets out rules which Member States must comply with when introducing purely national farm support schemes of certain types. The Regulation represents a significant step in efforts to integrate environmental considerations into agricultural structures policy. As well as containing general references to the need to conserve the environment, the Regulation introduces for the first time a scheme whereby Member States are allowed to give special aid to farmers in 'environmentally sensitive areas'. Only that part of the Regulation relevant to environmental protection will be discussed here.

Summary of the Regulation

The Regulation brings together in one piece of legislation a number of related agricultural support measures intended to alleviate some of the 'structural problems' of Community agriculture. It effectively replaces and amends several earlier measures, including two Directives originally agreed in 1972 (Directives 72/159 on the modernization of farms (OJ L96 23.4.72) and 72/161 on the provision of socioeconomic guidance for and acquisition of occupational skills by persons involved in agriculture (OJ L96 23.4.72)) and Directive 75/268 which is described in Section 8.6. As well as amending previous measures, the Regulation introduces some new forms of aid for farmers and provides the centrepiece for all Community farm structures measures for a decade.

As far as the environment is concerned, the main points of interest are as follows.

1. Article 1 sets out the overall purpose which is 'to improve the efficiency of holdings and to help develop their structures'. However, this statement is then qualified by the words 'while at the same time ensuring the permanent conservation of the natural resources of agriculture'.

2. In several respects the Regulation amends the primary system of investment aids for farmers which was originally established under Directive 72/159. This system, which the Regulation obliges Member States to operate, is designed to assist improvements in farmers' incomes and their living and working conditions. In the first paragraph of Article 3, aid for investments relating to 'the protection and improvement of the environment' are specifically allowed. This, together with other amendments, is representative of a new emphasis in the capital grants system.

3. Several amendments are made to Directive 75/268 on mountain and hill farming and farming in certain less favoured areas (see Section 8.6).

4. Under Article 19, Member States are permitted to introduce their own national aid schemes for the support of appropriate agricultural practices in 'environmentally sensitive areas'. These areas are defined as being 'of recognized importance from an ecological and landscape point of view' and aid may be granted to those who undertake to farm in such a way as to preserve or improve the environment. There is specific mention of farming practices compatible with 'conserving the natural habitat'. In order to qualify for aid, farmers must also agree not to further intensify their production and to set stocking densities and the intensity of production at a level compatible with the specific environmental needs of the area.

Unlike most of the other schemes set out in the Regulation, this one does not attract a contribution from the Community agricultural budget and the cost must be met from national resources. Nonetheless, Article 19 requires Member States to provide the Commission with full details of all prospective schemes and a list of the areas where they are to be applied. The Commission, having consulted the Standing Committee on Agricultural Structures, will then decide whether the schemes proposed are compatible with Articles 92 to 94 of the Treaty, which deal with fair competition. The Commission's role is further enlarged by Article 29 of the Regulation which requires it to produce an annual report on structural measures currently in force, including those under Article 19. This is intended to assist the Council in making an evaluation of these measures.

The Regulation is expected to be in force for about ten years, with an expiry date of 31 December 1994. Under Article 23, the total Community contribution to the cost of implementing the whole Regulation is estimated at 1988 million ECU for the first five years. For most of the measures set out in the Regulation Member States can apply for reimbursement of 25 per cent of their expenditure from the Guidance Sector of FEOGA. This rate rises to 50 per cent for certain schemes in specified parts of the Community, notably the poorer agricultural regions. However, Community reimbursement is not available for aid schemes for environmentally sensitive areas.

Development of Article 19

The UK was instrumental in securing the inclusion within the Regulation of the scheme for environmentally sensitive areas. The original Commission proposal contained no such scheme and the idea was introduced by the UK in the course of the negotiations over the final text. Some of the impetus for this initiative was provided by the House of Lords' Select Committee on the European Communities, which had established a special *ad hoc* subcommittee to hold an inquiry on the draft Regulations with particular reference to the subject of agriculture and the environment. When they reported in June 1984, one of their main conclusions was

> that the draft Regulation is too closely production-orientated, despite its gestures in other directions. MAFF, by their narrow interpretation of the few innovative features it contains, reinforce this backward-looking tendency. What is required instead is greater emphasis on the new elements of the proposal, which would help to diversify rural activity and enhance the environment, and the committee recommend that MAFF should encourage these objectives. The Committee suggest that MAFF should regard this proposal not as a continuation of existing legislation, but as the start of an improved approach to agricultural structural policy.'[1]

A month later the Minister, Lord Belstead, announced that MAFF would be seeking a new title in the Regulation which would 'enable us in environmentally sensitive areas to encourage farming practices which are consonent with conservation'.

At the time this announcement was made there was considerable controversy over the government's role in controlling environmentally damaging farming practices in Halvergate Marshes, a wetland area in East Anglia. It was not altogether clear whether MAFF required new powers to support forms of agriculture compatible with conservation requirements. MAFF faced some opposition from other Member States over the need for a new title in the Regulation, but an amended version of the original proposal survived to form the basis of Article 19.[2]

Effect on the UK

The principal farm capital grant schemes available to farmers in the UK prior to 1985 needed to be amended as a result of the Regulation. From 1 October 1985 the two main existing schemes were phased out and two new amended schemes were brought in. One of these is provided for by the Agriculture Improvement Regulations SI 1985 1266, and the other by the Agriculture Improvement Scheme Regulations SI 1985 1029. While there are two schemes, one requiring the farmer to prepare an improvement plan, the other not, in practice they are both known simply as the Agriculture Improvement Scheme. Compared with their predecessors, these schemes do have a greater emphasis on environmental protection. Most of the items for which a grant is available under the second scheme, where an improvement plan is not required, have an environmental as well as an agricultural value, for example the planting of hedges or installation of waste disposal facilities. The rates of grant available for activities which may be environmentally damaging, such as land drainage, are generally lower than in previous schemes.

New powers were provided in order to implement Article 19 in the UK. Section 9 of the Agriculture Act 1986 now empowers Ministers to designate by order environmentally sensitive areas and within them to enter into agreements with farmers to manage the land in ways set out in the agreement in return for certain payments. The Act requires that the Treasury's consent is obtained before areas are designated and that consultations are held with the Secretary of State for the Environment, the Countryside Commission (or its Scottish equivalent) and the Nature Conservancy Council. Areas can be designated by virtue of their landscape, ecological or historical importance.

In August 1986 it was announced that the first six environmentally sensitive areas (ESAs) had been chosen by MAFF from a short list provided by the Countryside Commission and Nature Conservancy Council. Five of the sites are in England and one in Wales. Two further sites in Scotland were announced in September and one in Northern Ireland in October. All the sites designated at the end of 1986 are listed in Table 13. Initially, a ceiling on annual payments of £6 million prevented any enlargement of this scheme but it was announced in March 1987 that the government was proposing to double this initial allocation of funds and to designate further ESAs beginning in early 1988.[3] This timetable was shortened two months later when a decision was made to designate a further six sites drawn from the earlier shortlist. The scheme will be voluntary, with farmers free to enter agreements if they wish. The detailed management prescriptions and payment scales will vary between sites. The scheme has been welcomed in many quarters as a significant departure from past agricultural practice, but has been criticized by some conservationists as being too restrictive and small scale.[4]

Table 13   Environmentally sensitive areas in the UK – December 1986

England	The Broads
	The Pennine Dales
	The Somerset Levels and Moors
	The eastern half of the South Downs
	West Penwith
Wales	The Cambrian Mountains
Scotland	Breadalbane
	Loch Lomond
Northern Ireland	Mourne

Further developments

In April 1986 the Commission submitted proposals to the Council for a new Regulation significantly amending some aspects of the agricultural structures policy (COM(86)199 OJ C273 29.10.86). In full, the title is 'Proposal for a Council Regulation amending Regulations (EEC) No 797/85, (EEC) No 270/79, (EEC) No 1360/78 and (EEC) No 355/77 as regards agricultural structures, the adjustment of agriculture to the new market situation and the preservation of the countryside'.

According to Mr Andriessen, the Commissioner for Agriculture, the aim of the new proposals was 'to help farmers adapt to the new situation of the markets, to help achieve a better balance between supply and demand, to support farming and to contribute to conservation of the environment and the preservation of the countryside'.[5] Most of the proposals consist of amendments to the various parts of Regulation 797/85, but there are also new ideas including a prepension scheme for farmers aged fifty-five or more who agree to take their land out of production or to hand it over to a younger relative. Another new scheme would involve younger farmers receiving incentives to adopt less intensive forms of production or to switch to the production of crops of a higher quality. The system of compensatory allowances available to farmers in less favoured areas would also be altered so as to make it more flexible while at the same time limiting the cost to the Community budget.

Amendments to Article 19 of Regulation 797/85, as proposed, would have the effect of linking environmentally sensitive areas more explicitly with efforts to reduce agricultural production. However, a contribution of 25 per cent from the Community budget would be available for such areas for the first time, up to a limit of 100 ECU per hectare. These proposals, particularly the prepension scheme, have been subject to some criticism. In the UK a critique was provided by the House of Lords' Select Committee on the European Communities and by several of the bodies giving evidence to it.[6] However, in March 1987 the bulk of the proposals were agreed by the Council, with the notable exception of the prepension scheme. They were finally agreed on 15 June as Regulation 1760/87 OJ L167 26.6.87.

References

1   House of Lords' Select Committee on the European Communities *Agriculture and the Environment*, 20th Report Session 1983–84. HMSO.

2   Baldock D 1985, Farm structures in Europe: the British Initiative. *ECOS* 6(3).

3   Ministry of Agriculture, Fisheries and Food 1987 *Farming UK*. HMSO.

4   Sinclair G 1986 Environmentally sensitive areas or green figleaves? *ECOS* 7(3).

5   EC Commission 1986 *Supplementary proposals in the field of socio-structural policy for the adaptation of farming to the new situation of the markets and for the preservation of the countryside*. Memorandum from Mr Andriessen, mimeo.

6   House of Lords' Select Committee on the European Communities, *Socio-structural policy in agriculture* 20th Report Session 1985–86. HMSO.

8.6 Countryside protection in agriculturally less favoured areas

75/268/EEC (OJ L128 19.5.75) proposed 1973 – COM(73)202	Directive on mountain and hill farming and farming in certain less favoured areas.
76/400/EEC (OJ L108 26.4.76)	(Amendment)
80/666/EEC (OJ L180 14.7.80)	(Amendment)
82/786/EEC (OJ L327 24.11.82)	(Amendment)
797/85 (OJ L93 30.3.85) proposed 1983 – COM(83)559	Regulation on improving the efficiency of agricultural structures (see Environmentally sensitive areas).

In addition to these four Directives and the Regulation, which amended them, a separate Directive for each Member State was issued in 1975 listing the less favoured areas falling within the meaning of Directive 75/268. The one relevant to the UK is Directive 75/276 (OJ L128 19.5.75) but the areas listed were adjusted in Directive 76/685 (OJ L231 21.8.76) in Directive 82/656 (OJ L277 29.9.82) and quite substantially in Directive 84/169 (OJ L82 26.3.84).

Binding dates

Notification date (75/268)	30 April 1975
Formal compliance (75/268)	30 April 1976
Aids may be introduced	1 October 1974
Financial contributions from Community	during 1975 and thereafter

Purpose of the Directives

These Directives are often thought of as environmental measures but this is not strictly correct. Their purpose is stated as 'the continuation of farming thereby maintaining a minimum population level or conserving the countryside' in certain agriculturally less favoured areas. This is to be achieved by selective financial incentives. A reply by the Commission to a European parliamentary question (OJ C287 4.11.82) explained:

> that Directive 75/268 may not be used to encourage con-
> servation *per se* but is to be used for the encouragement of
> farming which, in turn, will (sic) have a positive effect on the
> conservation of the countryside. This does not interfere with
> the Member States' right to introduce additional schemes for
> aid for conservation.

(The use of the word 'will' is perhaps overconfident and 'may' would have been more appropriate.)

The Directives have always been tied in part to other Community farm structures policies. Originally the link was with Directive 72/159 (OJ L96

23.4.72) concerned with the modernization of farms. Since March 1985, however, the link has been with Regulation 797/85, which replaced several earlier structures Directives, including 72/159, and at the same time modified the less favoured areas Directive 75/268. Together these various instruments form part of the common measures within the meaning of Council Regulation No 729/70 (OJ L94 28.4.70) on the financing of the common agricultural policy. Thus, although the Directives exist optionally for environmental purposes they are formally part of the agricultural policy.

The first action programme on the environment of 1973 noted the interconnection between environmental and agricultural policy by mentioning that a Directive on this subject had been proposed and affirming that the Commission would increase: 'its campaign in the future for the protection of the natural environment and particularly within the framework of the agricultural policy'. The need to integrate environmental policy with other Community policies has since been given new emphasis in the third and fourth action programmes on the environment. A full assessment of the effect of these Directives can only be undertaken within the context of an assessment of agricultural policy. The Directives are therefore merely listed here for completeness with only limited analysis.

Summary of the Directives

Member States are authorized to introduce a special system of aids for specified less favoured areas in order to ensure the continuation of farming thereby maintaining a minimum population level or conserving the countryside. The areas are to be proposed by the Member States but have to be agreed by the Council. In practice this has been done in a series of separate Directives. The areas are to fall into one of three categories (all must have adequate infrastructures, eg access roads to farms, electricity and drinking water):

mountain areas handicapped because of high altitude by a short growing season, or at a lower altitude by steep slopes, or by a combination of the two – Article 3(3);

less favoured areas in danger of depopulation: these are areas, regional in character, where the conservation of the countryside is necessary and which exhibit all the following three disadvantages: infertility, poor economic situation and a low or dwindling population dependent on agriculture – Article 3(4);

other less favoured areas affected by specific handicaps: these may be small areas 'in which farming must be continued if necessary subject to certain conditions, in order to ensure the conservation of the environment, to maintain the countryside and to preserve the tourist potential of the area or in order to protect the coastline'. The total extent of such areas in any Member State is not to exceed 4 per cent of the area of the State – Article 3(5).

There has been some uncertainty about the precise nature of 'specific handicaps'. The Commission have stated that they must arise principally from permanent natural conditions which are unfavourable for farming (Reply to European Parliamentary Question No 819/82, C 287 – 4.11.82). Under the original wording, this appeared to mean that handicaps which have been artificially imposed by, for example, conservation legislation, were excluded. However, the wording was changed by Regulation 797/85 to put a stronger emphasis on conservation of the environment and in the preamble to this Regulation there is reference to the need to support agriculture in certain circumstances in nature and national parks.

A map has been published in the *Official Journal* (OJ L128 19.5.75) showing all the areas throughout the Community initially listed. Most Member States have subsequently added further areas. All but one of the listed areas in the UK fall within the category of less favoured areas 'in danger of depopulation and where the conservation of the countryside is necessary' (Article 3(4)). No areas in the UK have been listed as mountain areas (Article 3(3)) and only the Isles of Scilly have been listed under Article 3(5). The proportion of the UK agricultural land area that is listed rose from 42 per cent to 51 per cent following a major extension in 1984. Since this date the original Article 3(4) areas have been categorized as 'severely disadvantaged' by MAFF, while the more recently added areas, which were selected on slightly different criteria, are categorized as 'disadvantaged'. No such distinction is drawn in the text of the Directives, but it is anticipated that the severity of handicap will vary.

Following the revisions made to the Directive by Regulation 797/85, Member States may apply certain types of aid within approved less favoured areas. Reimbursement of 25 per cent (or 50 per cent in certain cases in parts of Italy, Ireland, the French overseas departments and Greece) may be paid from the guidance section of the European Agricultural Guidance and Guarantee Fund. The types of aid permitted are as follows.

Compensatory allowances
Annual allowances to compensate for permanent natural handicaps may be paid in the form of headage payments for beef cattle, sheep, goats and equines at rates decided by the individual Member States but subject to a maximum and minimum of 20.3 and 101 ECU per livestock unit (one cow equals one unit, one sheep or goat 0.15 units). In general, payments may only be made to farmers with at least three hectares of usable agricultural land, although this condition is relaxed to two hectares in some areas, such as the Mezzogiorno. Cows whose milk is intended for marketing are eligible for payments only in certain circumstances. Some forms of non-livestock farming are also eligible for compensation in certain areas where allowances may be paid per hectare and, whatever method of payment is made, the total allowance must not exceed 101 ECU per hectare.

Investment aids to farms
Farms with authorized improvement plans under the terms of Regulation 797/85 may receive higher rates of capital grants in less favoured areas than elsewhere. For investment in fixed assets the ceiling on grants is 45 per cent compared with 35 per cent elsewhere, while for other types of investment the ceiling is 30 per cent, rather than 20 per cent. Equivalent interest rate subsidies are also permitted. In less favoured areas only, investments in tourist and craft industries on farms may be included in improvement plans and are eligible for aid up to a certain limit.

The general conditions of eligibility which are applied to farmers who submit improvement plans are also slightly relaxed in these areas.

Aids for joint investment schemes
Aids may be given for joint investment schemes for fodder production, storage and distribution and for the improvement and equipping of pastures which are farmed jointly. In mountain areas joint schemes may also cover investment in water-points, including water supply and irrigation projects, and pasture access roads.

Effect on the UK
Since in the United Kingdom nearly all the areas have been designated under Article 3(4) they have been identified by the government and approved by the Community as areas 'in danger of depopulation and where the conservation of the countryside is necessary'. The Directive therefore embodies a policy statement of considerable importance for a very large proportion (about 51 per cent) of land in agricultural use in Britain since no comparable statement about conserving the countryside had previously been made. It is by no means certain that the implications of this have been understood either by the relevant Ministries or by the environmental bodies concerned with countryside protection.

In evidence given to the House of Commons' Select Committee on Agriculture[1] the Ministry of Agriculture, Fisheries and Food said that the Directives had provided a means of continuing special aids to the hills and uplands, and also that the UK had been the major beneficiary of Community money. Four reports from the House of Lords' Select Committee on the European Communities[2,3,4,5] have discussed either the original Directive or subsequent amendments. A report published by the Council for National Parks[6] is critical both of the Directives and of the UK farm support system for less favoured areas which it regards as a 'parody of the EEC Directive under which it is supposed to operate, and through which it obtains a quarter of its finance'. Two reports by the Arkleton Trust are of note. One compares the operation of the Directives in six Member States including Britain,[7] the other, by Malcolm Smith, compares France and the UK, with particular emphasis on the conflict between agriculture and nature conservation and makes several recommendations for change.[8]

References
1   House of Commons' Agriculture Committee. 1st Report Session 1981–82. HMSO.

2   House of Lords' Select Committee on the European Communities *Policies for rural areas in the European Community* 27th Report Session 1979–80. HMSO.

3   House of Lords' Select Committee on the European Communities *Socio-structural policy* 2nd Report Session 1982–83. HMSO.

4   House of Lords' Select Committee on the European Communities, *Agriculture and the environment* 20th Report Session 1983–84. HMSO.

5   House of Lords' Select Committee on the European Communities, *Socio-structural policy in agriculture* 20th Report Session 1985–86. HMSO.

6   MacEwan Malcolm and Sinclair Geoffrey 1983 *New life for the hills*. Council for National Parks.

7   The Arkleton Trust 1982 *Schemes of assistance to farmers in less favoured areas of the EEC.*

8   Smith Malcolm 1985 *Agriculture and nature conservation in conflict – the less favoured areas of France and the UK*. The Arkleton Trust.

CHAPTER 9

Noise

9.0 Relevant British legislation

Legislation to control noise in the environment generally – often known as neighbourhood noise – is contained in Part III of the Control of Pollution Act 1974 which replaced and extended the Noise Abatement Act 1960. Before the 1960 Act neighbourhood noise was not a matter for the public authorities but could only be controlled by the courts following a common law action for nuisance. Since all the existing Directives concerned with noise set standards for noise in the workplace or from specific mobile sources – vehicles, aircraft, lawnmowers and construction plant – British legislation on neighbourhood noise is not described here.

Vehicles

Noise standards for cars, lorries, buses, motorcycles and tractors are now all laid down in Regulations made under the Road Traffic Act 1972 although the first such Regulations setting quantitative limits were set in the 1968 Motor Vehicles (Construction and Use) Regulations and came into effect in 1970. Enforcement in service is a police responsibility.

The Road Traffic Act 1974 provides for the operation of a compulsory national type approval scheme under which the manufacturer, before marketing a new type of vehicle, has to produce a sample production vehicle for testing by the Department of Transport. The vehicle has to comply with all relevant safety and environmental standards including noise, and the manufacturer has to demonstrate that he has adequate quality assurance procedures. He then has to certify that every vehicle sold conforms to an approved type and random checks are made that this is so.

National type approval for cars was introduced by Regulations in 1976 and is now governed by the Motor Vehicles (Type Aproval) (Great Britain) Regulations 1984 (SI 1984 No 981). National type approval for lorries was introduced in 1982 and is now governed by the Motor Vehicles (Type Approval for Goods Vehicles) (Great Britain) Regulations 1982 (SI 1982 No 1271). There is no type approval in Britain for motorcycles and although there is limited type approval for tractors it does not extend to external noise.

Aircraft

The Civil Aviation Act 1949 (as amended by the Civil Aviation Act 1968) provides for the prohibition of any aircraft landing or taking off in Britain unless it has a noise certificate and is complying with the certificate's requirements. The scheme is based on international agreements drawn up within the International

Civil Aviation Organization (ICAO). The current Order made under the Act is the Air Navigation (Noise Certification) Order 1986 (SI 1986 No 1304) and this contains in its Schedules the noise emission standards prescribed by ICAO although the Civil Aviation Authority is empowered to relax prohibitions. Any exemptions made are listed in the Authority's official record.

Construction plant
There are two sections of the Control of Pollution Act 1974 dealing with construction plant. Section 60 empowers local authorities to specify the plant that may or may not be used on a construction site, the hours when works may be carried out and the noise levels which may be emitted from the premises. Section 68 creates the power to make Regulations requiring the use of devices or arrangements for reducing the noise caused by plant or machinery, or for limiting the noise of construction plant when in use. The wording of this section – which has not yet been used – is a little unclear and may not cover construction plant as manufactured (as opposed to when in use), a fact which resulted in certain Directives (see Section 9.4) being implemented under the European Communities Act 1972.

Other products
There are no powers in British legislation for setting noise standards for products such as lawnmowers and household appliances although the Wilson Committee on Noise had recommended legislation as long ago as 1963. Directives dealing with noise from such products are therefore having to be implemented under the European Communities Act 1972.

Workplace noise
Workplace noise falls under health and safety legislation and Regulations setting standards can be made under the Health and Safety at Work etc Act 1974.

References
1   Department of the Environment 1976 *Pollution control in Great Britain: how it works*. HMSO. (Pollution Paper No 9).

2   Wilson Sir Alan (chairman) 1963 *Noise: final report* Cmnd 2056. HMSO.

9.1 Cars, buses and lorries

The noise of four-wheeled vehicles (other than tractors) is regulated by three Council Directives and three Commission Directives:

70/157/EEC (OJ L42 23.2.70) proposed 11.7.68 – COM(68)529	Council Directive relating to the permissible sound level and the exhaust systems of motor vehicles.
73/350/EEC (OJ L321 22.11.73)	Commission Directive adapting 70/157 to technical progress.
77/212/EEC (OJ L66 12.3.77) proposed 24.7.74 – COM(11)75	Council Directive amending 70/157.
81/334/EEC (OJ L131 18.5.81)	Commission Directive adapting 70/157 to technical progress.
84/372/EEC (OJ L196 26.7.84	Commission Directive adapting 70/157 to technical progress.
84/424/EEC (OJ L238 6.9.84) proposed 5.7.83 – COM(83)392	Council Directive amending 70/157.

Binding dates
Formal compliance – 84/424	1 January 1985
EEC type approval may only be granted if limits of 77/212 as amended by 84/424 met using measuring system of 81/334 as amended by 84/372	1 October 1985

Purpose of the Directives
The original Directives and the succeeding amendments have two purposes: one, to ensure that noise limits by individual Member States do not create barriers to trade; and two, progressively to reduce noise limits for environmental reasons. These Directives are of the kind known as 'optional' or as providing 'optional harmonization' which means that Member States are not bound to set limits equal to those in the Directive but may not erect trade barriers by setting more stringent limits.

Summary of the Directives
Directive 70/157 defines 'vehicles' to mean four-wheeled road vehicles having a maximum design speed greater than 25 kph but excluding agricultural tractors and public works vehicles. An Annex lists seven categories of cars, buses and lorries and sets a noise limit against each. A noise-measuring method is specified covering both the conditions of measurement and the vehicle operating conditions. The Annex also sets out requirements for exhaust systems (silencers).

No Member State may prohibit the sale or use of a vehicle or may refuse to grant EEC type approval or national type approval of a vehicle on grounds relating to the permissible sound level or the exhaust system if these satisfy the requirements in the Annex. The Directive thus prevents Member States from setting more stringent noise limits than those specified. If one Member State chooses to adopt national limits equal to the limits in the Directive, then manufacturers from other countries interested in selling in that market will be induced to meet the limits of the Directive. It can therefore have a powerful persuasive effect.

The Directive has a provision allowing the Annex to be adapted by the Commission to take account of technical progress but not so as to make changes to the noise limits set against each category of vehicle. That power is reserved to the Council.

Directive 73/350 expands the requirements in the parent Directive relating to silencers. **Directive 77/212** reduced the noise limits set in 70/157 but has been superseded by Directive 84/424 (see below). **Directive 81/334** introduces a new test procedure to reflect the increased range of gears now commonly used. It requires tests using more than one gear rather than one gear only as previously. It also contains provisions to permit replacement silencers for passenger cars and light commercial vehicles to be type approved. From 1 October 1984 type approval may only be granted if the limits of Directive 77/212 are met using the new test method and from 1 October 1985 Member States may prohibit the entry into service of vehicles that have not been tested by the new method. **Directive 84/372** amends further the test procedure amended by 81/334 but leaves unchanged the compliance dates therein.

Directive 84/424 amends the noise limits in 77/212 and also changes the categories of vehicles slightly by putting bus and lorries under 3.5 tonne together and creating three categories of vehicles over 3.5 tonne differentiated by horsepower. The reduced values in dB(A) are given in Table 14 with their equivalents according to the 1977 and 1970 Directives.

Table 14   Reduced noise values for vehicles in dB(A)

	84/424	*77/212*	*70/157*
Cars	77	80	82
Buses over 3.5 tonne			
less than 200 HP	80	82	89
over 200 HP	83	85	91
Buses and goods vehicles			
less than 2 tonne	78 }	81	84
over 2 and under 3.5 tonne	79 }		
Goods vehicles over 3.5 tonnes			
less than 100 HP	81 }		
over 100 and under 200 HP	83 }	86	89
over 200 HP	84	88	91

Note: for cars and buses and goods vehicles of less than 3.5 tonnes with diesel engines the limit values are 1 dB(A) higher.

From 1 October 1985 Member States may not prohibit the sale or use of a vehicle or refuse to grant EEC or national type approval if the requirements of the Directive are met. From 1 October 1988 Member States may refuse to grant national type approval to vehicles which do not meet the requirements of the Directive and from 1 October 1989 may prohibit the entry into service of such vehicles. A further review of the provisions of the directive is to be taken by 31 December 1990.

Development of the Directives

The parent Directive 70/157 was agreed before Britain joined the Community and was the earliest Community legislation concerned with noise. It was closely modelled on the United Nations Economic Commission for Europe's nonmandatory Regulation 9. The explanatory memorandum accompanying the proposal for Directive 77/212 records that on 20 June 1973 and 5 September 1973 the governments of France and the United Kingdom respectively had informed the Commission of their interest in a substantial reduction of the limits set in 70/157. The explanatory memorandum set out a short-term programme aiming at an initial reduction of the existing limits, which resulted in Directive 77/212 – and a longer-term programme to find a new method of noise measurement which would more accurately reflect the actual conditions in which vehicles are used in urban traffic, which resulted in Directive 81/334. It took two and a half years for Directive 77/212 to be adopted and much earlier dates were proposed than were agreed: for example, according to the proposed Directive Member States would have been able to make the limits mandatory from October 1976 rather than October 1982, a difference of six years.

When Directive 77/212 was agreed the Council made a declaration that:

> efforts should be made to achieve a noise level of around 80 dB(A) for all categories of vehicles by 1985. The levels decided on will have to take into account what is technically and economically feasible at the time. Moreover, they will have to be established sufficiently early to give manufacturers an adequate transition period in which to improve their products.

This declaration therefore intended, not that a new Directive should be agreed by 1985, but that a new Directive would have to be agreed in sufficient time for vehicles meeting the limits to be on the road by 1985. This target was not met.

Directive 84/424 introduced new limits effective from 1 January 1985 but limits for buses and vehicles over 3.5 tonnes were generally over 80 dB(A). The proposals for this Directive were based on the global approach to Community legislation on motor vehicles (see Section 6.7 Emissions from vehicles) but were regarded as an intermediate step.

Formal compliance in the UK

Motor vehicle noise was first controlled in Britain in 1970 by the 1968 Motor Vehicles (Construction and Use) Regulations made under the Road Traffic Act. On accession to the Community in 1973 Britain became subject to Directive 70/157 which prescribed slightly different limits: 2 dB(A) more stringent for cars and 2 dB(A) more relaxed for buses and lorries. Since the Directive is 'optional' it was not necessary to tighten the British limits for cars but in order to prevent a barrier to trade the limit for buses and lorries had to be relaxed. This was done by the Motor Vehicles (Construction and Use) Regulations 1973 (SI 1973 No 1347) made under the Road Traffic Act 1972.

Since the new limits were first introduced there have been a number of amendments, which are now consolidated in Regulation 55 of the Road Vehicles (Construction and Use) Regulations 1986 (SI 1986 No 1078). This Regulation applies to vehicles first used on or after 1 October 1983, which must comply with the limits set in Directive 77/212, using either the test procedure in that Directive or the test procedure in Directive 81/334 and 84/372. In practice vehicles are now approved to the later test procedure, which has the general effect of being more stringent by about 2 dB(A). Vehicles first used on or after 1 April 1990 (1991 in the case of heavy lorries and some buses) will have to comply with the limits set by Directive 84/424.

National type approval for cars was introduced by the Motor Vehicles (Type Approval) (Great Britain) Regulations 1976 (SI 1976 No 937) made under the Road Traffic Act 1974 and this set the limits of Directive 70/157 (82 dB(A) for cars). This was amended by Motor Vehicles (Type Approval) (Great Britain) Regulations 1981 (SI 1981 No 1619) to introduce the limits of Directive 77/212. It has been amended again by Motor Vehicles (Type Approval) (Great Britain) Regulations 1984 (SI 1984 No 81) which covers the requirements of Directive 81/334. National type approval for lorries was introduced on 1 October 1982 by the Motor Vehicles (Type Approval) (Great Britain) Regulations 1981 (SI 1981 No 1340). Both sets of type approval Regulations will be amended to make approval to Directive 84/424 compulsory for new vehicle types from 1 October 1988 (1989 in the case of heavy lorries).

Effect on UK practice

When Britain joined the Community in 1973 British noise limits for lorries and buses were more stringent than elsewhere in Europe. The first practical effect of Directive 70/157 was therefore a relaxation of the noise limits for buses and lorries from 89 dB(A) to the 91 dB(A) specified. Unlike the bulk of the other environmental Directives, the noise Directives, reflecting their origins as measures to prevent barriers to trade, prevent Member States from setting more stringent standards than those specified. The British government had in fact been ready just before accession to the Community to reduce noise levels still further and in December 1970 had issued a draft consultation document proposing further reductions. These had to be abandoned upon accession but the frustrated intentions nevertheless created the pressure that led to the British request to the Commission in September 1973 for a substantial noise reduction which led in turn to Directive 77/212. However, any claim that Community legislation has continued as a brake on British efforts to reduce vehicle noise cannot easily be sustained since the British motor industry was not in a position to lower noise levels for all vehicles to meet the limits of Directive 77/212 at the earliest date allowed by the Directive (October 1982) so that these limits were only made obligatory in Britain for new vehicles manufactured after 1 April 1983 and first used from 1 October 1983. This point is explained in a memorandum submitted by the Department of Transport for a House of Lords' report reviewing Community noise policy[1].

The net result of the Directives is that noise limits for new vehicles in dB(A) have been reduced in Britain as follows (see Table 15).

There has thus been an overall reduction of 7 dB(A) for cars and 6 dB(A) for buses in eighteen years but only a 5 dB(A) reduction for lorries. A further effective reduction for some new vehicles of 2 or 3 dB(A) was made in 1984 when the testing method of Directive 81/334 was introduced in Britain although the numerical limits were unchanged. These levels fall a long way short of the target of 80 dB(A) in 1985 set in 1977.

The question whether Britain would have set more stringent limits after the early 1970s if it had not been for Community legislation is difficult to answer. The vehicle market is international and it is difficult for a vehicle manufacturing country interested in the export market to set significantly more stringent limits than its competitors if this entails a cost penalty. Nevertheless, there has been considerable pressure in Britain for a reduction in lorry noise and as a result of public pressure an experimental quiet heavy vehicle (QHV) was developed in government research laboratories during the 1970s[2] which meets the 1977 target of 80 dB(A) using the then test procedure. The Commission admitted, in reply to a European parliamentary question in 1980 (OJ C236 15.9.80), that in no other Member State was there a prototype of the heaviest category of lorry that also met the target. Given the opposition there has been in the British Parliament to an increase in lorry weights for environmental reasons it is quite possible that the government would have been forced to insist on some tighter noise limits for lorries if Community legislation did not preclude this, even if not down to 80 dB(A). A Department of Transport official put it like this in giving evidence to the House of Lords[1]:

> In the early 1970s we had gone out to consultation about more stringent noise levels with the idea of introducing these in 1974 and our entry into the Community did in fact slow that. However I think it must be seen against our longer-term goals, and you probably know that the various Ministers have made known that we are trying to get heavy lorries to around 80 decibels . . . and I think it is open to debate whether our membership of the Community will have moved that target further away. My own personal view is that for that goal it is not retarding it. . . .

Table 15   Reduction in noise limits in dB(A))

	1970	1983	1988/9
Cars	84	80	77
Heaviest buses	89	85	83
Heaviest lorries	89	88	84

References
1   House of Lords' Select Committee on the European Communities 1982
    Noise in the environment 13th Report Session 1981–82. HMSO.

2   Nelson P M and Underwood M C P 1982 *Operational performance of the
    TRRL quiet heavy vehicle*. Transport and Road Research Laboratory, Sup-
    plementary Report 746.

9.2 Motorcycles

78/1015/EEC (OJ L349 13.12.78) proposed 12.12.75 – COM(75)634	Directive on the permissible sound level and exhaust system of motorcycles.
87/56/EEC (OJ L24 27.1.87) proposed 6.9.84 – COM(84)438	Amendment

Binding dates (78/1015)
Notification date	27 November 1978
Formal compliance	1 October 1980
Limits not to take effect until	27 May 1981
Council to decide on further reduction in limits	31 December 1984

Binding dates (87/56)
Formal compliance	1 October 1988
Limits not to take effect until	1 October 1988

Purpose of the Directive

Noise limits for motorcycles are set both for environmental reasons and to prevent national limits creating barriers to trade. Like other vehicle noise Directives (see Section 9.1) these Directives are of the 'optional' kind.

Summary of the Directives

Directive 78/1015
An Annex sets out a measuring method and sets the following noise limits (mopeds, ie motorcycles under 55 cc are not covered by the Directive) (Table 16).

Member States may not refuse national type approval or refuse sale or use of motorcycles which have been officially tested in accordance with the Directive and meet the above limits.

Table 16

Cubic capacity (cc) of motorcycle	dB(A)
Less than 80	78
80–125	80
125–350	83
350–500	85
Over 500	86

Table 17

| Cubic capacity (cc) | dB(A) and date for national type approval | | | |
	first stage		second stage	
less than 80	77	1 Oct 1988	75	1 Oct 1993
80–175	79	1 Oct 1989	77	31 Dec 1994
over 175	82	1 Oct 1988	80	1 Oct 1993

Directive 87/56
The Annex is replaced by a new one which reduces the number of types of motor cycles to three categories and sets lower limits to be reached in two stages as shown in Table 17.

Modifications to the test procedures are introduced to make the conditions of testing more representative of road traffic conditions. Member States may prohibit the initial entry into service of motorcycles which do not comply with these limits two years after the above dates.

Development of the Directive
In January 1974 the French government notified the Commission that it intended to introduce national legislation on motorcycle noise and this led to a proposal for a Directive in 1975. It took over three years for the Directive to be agreed which suggests some resistance from Member States. The UK government considered the amending proposals put forward in 1984 to be not strict enough. In the event they succeeded in achieving a one dB(A) reduction in the limits for motorcycles in the 80–175 cc range – the most common. The House of Lords in a report on the 1984 proposal said that the single most effective measure to reduce noise nuisance from motorcycles would be to control the sale of replacement exhaust systems. The Commission has included that proposal in its draft fourth action programme on the environment.

Formal compliance in UK
The Motor Vehicles (Construction and Use) (Amendment) (No 6) Regulations 1980 (SI 1980 No 1166) made under the Road Traffic Act 1972 specifically refers to Directive 78/1015 and to the test method and noise limits set out in the Directive. The noise limits are to be met by motorcycles manufactured on or after 1 October 1982 and first used on or after 1 April 1983. The 1980 Regulations have been replaced by The Road Vehicles (Construction and Use) Regulations 1986 (SI 1078). There is no type approval procedure for motorcycles in Britain. The government intends to prohibit motorcycles that do not meet the first stage limits of Directive 87/56 two years after the dates in Table 17 (ie 1990 and 1991).

Effect on UK practice
Noise limits for motorcycles were first set in Britain in 1970 by the Motor Vehicles (Construction and Use) Regulations 1968. These set limits of 77 dB(A) for mopeds (less than 50 cc); 82 dB(A) for motorcycles between 50 and 125 cc; and 86 dB(A) for motorcycles of over 125 cc. These noise limits remained

unchanged until modified by the 1980 Regulations mentioned above which introduced the noise limits and measuring method of the Directive from 1 October 1982.

The Directive has therefore had no effect on the numerical noise levels of the most powerful motorcycles (over 500 cc) but the testing method under the Directive differs from that in the previous construction and use Regulations so that in practice there has been a 3 dB(A) reduction in noise levels. For the less powerful categories of motorcycle the numerical noise limits have in all cases been reduced.

In a memorandum to the House of Lords for its review of Community noise policy[1] the Department of Transport noted that:

> there have been statements in the motorcycling press that some manufacturers will be unable to meet the new limits (for 1982) but the Department of Transport have been assured by the manufacturers that they will be able to comply with the Regulations.

Although the point cannot be proved, it seems probable that in the absence of the Directive 78/1015 the limits set in 1970 would have been lowered by now so that whether the Directive has had a positive or negative effect cannot be established. Again, it must be remembered that the market for motorcycles is international and action on noise by one country alone is extremely difficult even in the absence of a Directive. Since the Directive is of the 'optional' kind there was no obligation on the United Kingdom to reduce its limits to meet those in the Directive and the reasons for doing so will have been mainly environmental, but also so that the rather small British motorcycle industry has to meet the same limits for the home market as for export. Directive 87/56 should have some effect, but the problem of faulty silencers or silencers deliberately tampered with remains.

References

1   House of Lords' Select Committee on the European Communities *Noise in the Environment* 13th Report Session 1981–82. HMSO.

9.3 Tractors

74/151/EEC (OJ L84 28.3.74) proposed in April 1966	Directive relating to certain parts and characteristics of wheeled agricultural or forestry tractors.
77/311/EEC (OJ L105 28.4.77) proposed 15.3.74 – COM(74)316	Directive relating to the driver perceived noise level of wheeled agricultural or forestry tractors.
Binding dates Notification date (74/151) Formal compliance (74/151)	7 March 1974 7 September 1975

Purpose of the Directives

Directive 74/151 is concerned with preventing the creation of barriers to trade in tractors. It was introduced as part of an EEC type approval procedure for tractors set out in a separate Directive 74/150 which is not yet in operation. It relates to a number of technical characteristics, such as maximum weight, in addition to noise levels and silencers. **Directive 77/311** sets standards, also as part of the EEC type approval procedure of Directive 74/150, to protect the hearing of agricultural workers driving tractors. As such it is not concerned with environmental protection and will not be further described here. Both Directives are of the 'optional' kind (see Section 9.1).

Summary of Directive 74/151

The Directive is restricted to two-axle agricultural or forestry tractors having pneumatic tyres and a maximum design speed of between 6 and 25 km/h.

No Member State may prohibit the sale or use of tractors or may refuse to grant EEC type approval or national type approval if these satisfy the requirements set out in the Annexes on grounds relating to:

maximum laden weight;
the location of rear registration plates;
fuel tanks;
ballast weight;
audible warning devices;
noise levels and exhaust system (silencer).

Provision is made for adapting the Annexes to technical progress with the exception of the noise limits. The Annexes relate to the various technical requirements listed above and only Annex VI is concerned with noise limits and a method of measuring noise. The noise limits are as follows: unladen weight greater than 1.5 tonne, 89 dB(A); unladen weight less than 1.5 tonne, 85 dB(A).

Development of the Directive
The Directive was proposed well before Britain joined the Community.

Formal compliance in the UK
The Motor Vehicles (Construction and Use) (Amendment) (No 6) Regulations 1980 (SI 1980 No 1166) made under the Road Traffic Act 1972 specifically refer to Directive 74/151 and require the test method set out in the Directive to be used in achieving certain noise limits. These noise limits are not the same as those in the Directive. Thus there is no requirement for tractors with an unladen weight of less than 1.5 tonne to meet a noise limit of 85 dB(A). Instead there is a limit of 89 dB(A) for tractors less than 90 hp and 92 dB(A) for tractors greater than 90 hp. These are to apply for tractors made after 1 October 1982 and first used after 1 April 1983. Since the Directive is of the 'optional' kind it is nevertheless complied with in law. There is limited national type approval of tractors in Britain but it does not extend to external noise.

Effect on UK practice
The Directive has not had any effect in reducing tractor noise limits in Britain as it is of the 'optional' kind. Noise limits for tractors were first set in Britain in 1970 by the Motor Vehicles (Construction and Use) Regulations 1968. These set limits of 89 dB(A) for the vehicle as constructed but noise levels when the vehicle was in use on a road could be 3 dB(A) more, ie 92 dB(A). These noise limits remained unchanged until modified by Regulations made in 1980. When, in October 1979, the Department of Transport issued these Regulations in draft to introduce the measuring method of the Directive it received representations from tractor manufacturers that 92 dB(A) rather than 89 dB(A) should be allowed for tractors fitted with engines of more than 90 hp. According to a memorandum submitted by the Department to a House of Lords' Committee[1] these tractors are made in relatively small numbers and are used almost entirely off the road and because of the use to which they are put the fitting of engine shields to reduce noise was considered impracticable. It seems possible that these tractors were not meeting the previous limits.

References
1   House of Lords' Select Committee on the European Communities *Noise in the Environment* 13th Report Session 1981–82. HMSO.

9.4 Construction plant

84/532/EEC (OJ L300 19.11.84) proposed 14.4.75 – COM(74)2195 (corrigenda OJ L41 12.2.85)	Directive on the approximation of the laws of the Member States relating to common provisions for construction plant and equipment – framework Directive.
79/113/EEC (OJ L33 8.2.79) proposed 20.12.74 – COM(74)2195	Directive relating to the determination of the noise emission of construction plant and equipment.
81/1051/EEC (OJ L376 30.12.81) proposed 1979 – COM(79)573	(Directive amending 79/113)
85/405/EEC (OJ L233 30.8.85)	Commission Directive adapting 79/113 to technical progress.
84/533/EEC (OJ L300 19.11.84) as amended by 85/406/EEC (OJ L233 30.8.85) proposed 19.4.78 – COM(78)121	Directive on permissible sound power level of compressors.
84/534/EEC (OJ L300 19.11.84 corrigendum OJ L41 12.2.85)	Directive on permissible sound power level of tower cranes.
84/535/EEC (OJ L30 19.11.84) as amended by 85/407/EEC (OJ L233 30.8.85) proposed 8.3.76 – COM(75)558	Directive on permissible sound power level of welding generators.
84/536/EEC (OJ L300 19.11.84) as amended by 85/408/EEC (OJ L233 30.8.85) proposed 8.3.76 – COM(75)558	Directive on permissible sound power level of power generators.
84/537/EEC (OJ L300 19.11.84) as amended by 85/409/EEC (OJ L233 30.8.85) proposed 14.4.75 – COM(75)2195	Directive on permissible sound power level of powered handheld concrete breakers and picks.
86/662/EEC (OJ L384 31.12.86) proposed 28.11.80 – COM(80)468	Directive on limitation of noise from hydraulic excavators, rope-operated excavators, dozers, loaders and excavator loaders.

Binding dates

Notification dates

79/113	22 December 1978
81/1051	14 June 1981
84/532–537	26 September 1984
85/405–409	12 July 1985
86/662	29 December 1986

Formal compliance

79/113	22 June 1980
81/1051	14 June 1983
84/532–537	26 March 1986 and 26 September 1989
85/405–409	26 March 1986

86/662   29 December 1988
Noise limits to be met   26 March 1986 and 26 September 1989

Purpose of the Directives

The purpose of this family of Directives is to establish a framework for avoiding barriers to trade in construction plant and equipment by setting up a type approval system. Detailed daughter Directives set noise limits to be met by different types of construction plant and equipment: compressors, tower cranes, welding generators, power generators, and concrete breakers and picks.

Summary of the Directives

The framework **Directive (84/532)** sets out an approval, examination, verification and certification procedure for all types of construction plant and equipment. The daughter Directives listed all deal with noise from such plant and equipment.

Directive 79/113 as amended sets out methods of measuring noise generally. The two Annexes deal respectively with determining noise from machines used outdoors and with noise emitted to the operator's position (see also 86/662 below). The other daughter Directives (**84/533 to 537**) as amended deal with the following different types of plant and equipment: compressors, tower cranes, welding generators, power generators, concrete breakers and picks. In them are set noise level limits to be met in two stages, March 1986 and September 1989. The Council is also to act unanimously within eighteen months of the Commission submitting proposals for further reductions of noise levels. These proposals are to be presented by 1989 at the latest.

Directive 86/662 covers permitted noise levels in the environment and at the operator position of earth moving equipment; it adds to the Annex of 79/113 dealing with noise at the operator's position. Limits are to be observed for a six year period from December 1988 after which more stringent levels will be set by a reduction of about 3 dB(A).

A Committee on the adaptation to technical progress is set up to deal with the determination of noise emission from construction plant and equipment.

Development of the Directives

The first action programme on the environment of 1973 proposed legislation to reduce noise from construction plant but by then the Community had already decided to legislate in the field in order to prevent the creation of trade barriers. Proposals were put to the Council at various dates between 1975 and 1978. Progress was made in agreeing their texts but final approval and adoption was held up pending resolution of what was referred to as the 'third country' question[1].

There are two aspects to the 'third country' question. First, since the Directives would allow a manufacturer to obtain Community wide type approval or certification in any Member State and is then free to sell the product in all Member States, and since it is argued that in certain fields not every Member State has the expertise and facilities to test all equipment, a manufacturer outside the

Community may choose a 'weak' Member State in which to have his product approved and so gain entry to the whole Community market. Secondly, certain Member States believe that if a third country is given access to the Community market there should be some reciprocal agreement by which access is given to the market of that third country. The 'third country' question illustrates how matters quite unrelated to environmental policy may hold up agreement on environmental measures.

The 'third country' question was finally resolved by establishing an elaborate complaints procedure. If a Member State is informed that machinery it has approved is defective it must suspend or withdraw approval. Disputes between Member States are to be resolved with the help of the Commission.

Formal compliance in the UK
The first Directive (79/113) to be adopted was not formally complied with by the date specified due to the delay in adopting the framework Directive and the daughter Directives. Formal compliance with all the Directives listed was achieved by the Construction Plant and Equipment (Harmonization of Noise Emission Standards) Regulations 1985 (SI 1985 No 1968) made under the European Communities Act 1972. These came into force on 26 March 1986. They provide for two sets of limits, the first coming into force in March 1986 with the second, more stringent, standards becoming effective in September 1989. Compliance with the noise limits is to be assured by a certification procedure run for the government by nine consultancies accredited under the National Testing Accreditation Scheme.

Effect on UK practice
The noise limits which came into force in March 1986 were already being met by most manufacturers but the 1989 levels will mean further reductions with the likelihood of another reduction to come at the latest after March 1991, the date by which the Council is due to agree the Commission's further proposals.

Further development
A proposal to amend Directive 84/534 on tower cranes has been submitted to the Council by the Commission (COM(86)491 of 25.9.86 OJ C267 23.10.86). It provides for limits of sound pressure level to be set at the operator position as well as in the environment.

References
1   House of Lords' Select Committee on the European Communities *Noise in the Environment* 13th Report Session 1981–82. HMSO.

9.5 Aircraft

80/51/EEC (OJ L18 24.1.80) proposed 20.4.76 – COM(76)157	Directive on the limitation of noise emissions from subsonic aircraft.
83/206/EEC (OJ L117 4.5.83) proposed 15.9.81 – COM(81)512	(Amendment)

Binding dates

Notification date (80/51)	21 December 1979
Notification date (83/206)	26 April 1983
Formal compliance (80/51)	21 June 1980
Formal compliance (83/206)	26 April 1984
Ban on use of non-noise certificated subsonic jets on registers of Member States	1 January 1987
Ban on use of aircraft registered outside the Community and not meeting standards	1 January 1988

Purpose of the Directives

The Directives ensure that Member States implement the noise standards for subsonic aircraft which have been agreed, but without mandatory force, within the International Civil Aviation Organization (ICAO). They also implement certain recommendations of the European Civil Aviation Conference (ECAC) concerning non-noise certificated aircraft. The Directives differ from the other noise Directives by not precluding the imposition of stricter measures by Member States (see Sections 9.1 to 9.4).

Summary of the Directives

The two Directives taken together require Member States to ensure that the relevant categories of civil aircraft registered in their territories are not used unless certificated in accordance with certain chapters of Volume 1 of Annex 16/5 to the Convention on International Civil Aviation. (Annex 16 only covers certain categories of aircraft.)

Subject to certain exemptions Member States are also to ensure that from January 1980 all civil subsonic jet aeroplanes newly registered in their territories that use aerodromes situated in any Member State are certificated in accordance with requirements at least equal to the applicable standards of Volume 1 of Annex 16/5. From June 1980 the same rule applied to propeller-driven aeroplanes weighing not more than 5700 kg but a Member State may make exceptions if the aeroplanes operate only in their territory or in that of consenting States.

Each Member State is to ensure that as from 1 January 1987 civil subsonic jet aeroplanes registered in its territory may not be used unless granted noise certification in accordance with requirements at least equal to those in Part II,

Chapter 2 of Volume 1 of Annex 16/5. Temporary exceptions may be made in specific circumstances.

As from 1 January 1988 Member States are not to permit the operation of civil subsonic jet aeroplanes which are registered outside the Member States and which do not comply with the noise standards of Part II, Chapter 2 of Volume 1 of Annex 16/5. Temporary exceptions may be made in specific circumstances.

Development of the Directives

The first international standards for aircraft noise were adopted by ICAO in 1971 and have been revised on several occasions since. ICAO's recommendations are not legally binding on its 144 Member States but most of the major aircraft manufacturing countries base their national regulations upon ICAO's work.

The first mention of Community action on aircraft noise is to be found not in the first action programme on the environment of 1973 (although the preamble to the Directive claims erroneously that there is such a mention) but in a written reply in 1973 (No 654/73) by the Council to a European parliamentary question. Given that there were discrepancies between Member States in the implementation of the ICAO standards the Commission decided that the best approach for the Community was not to lay down its own standards but to ensure that the existing standards were applied consistently across the Community.

In the original proposal for a Directive an 'EEC noise limitation certificate' would have been introduced but this idea was abandoned. The proposal was also changed by the introduction in mandatory form of recommendations emanating from the European Civil Aviation Organization (ECAC) concerning non-noise certificated aircraft.

In the House of Commons considerable concern was expressed that acceptance of the Directive might lead to an extension of Community competence into the field of aviation. It was envisaged that the Commission might want to represent the Member States at international meetings such as those of ICAO. However, any fears in the mind of the government were overcome and in a debate (19 June 1979) the Minister, Norman Tebbit, expressed himself satisfied that 'the extension of the Community's authority which the Directive will produce is justified by the extra powers that it will bring to enable us to limit the noise of aircraft from other Member States'. In 1983 the Commission asked for observer status at the ICAO Committee on Aircraft Noise but the request was turned down.

The House of Lords[1] considered the proposal for the amending Directive as a natural extension of the parent Directive and supported its adoption. It brought the parent Directive up to date by incoporating new standards agreed by ICAO in 1979 and also introduced a ban on foreign registered aircraft that do not meet specified standards by 1 January 1988.

Formal compliance in the UK

The Air Navigation (Noise Certification) Order 1979 (SI 1979 No 930) made under Section 19 of the Civil Aviation Act 1968 came into operation on 1 August 1979. This Order, which replaces earlier Orders, contains in its Schedules the noise emission standards prescribed by ICAO in Annex 16 (1978 edition). The

Order prohibits the use of all aircraft which do not conform to the prescribed international standards including some categories which are not yet covered by Annex 16. The scope of the prohibition is then relaxed by the use of exempting powers given to the Civil Aviation Authority by the Secretary of State for Trade under Article 16 of the Order. Exemption is given to all aircraft outside the categories defined in ICAO Annex 16. These exemptions are listed in the Authority's Official Record. The end result is that British legislation gives full effect to the provisions of Directive 80/51 and whilst the Civil Aviation Authority have delegated powers of exemption these can only be used after consultation with the Secretary of State. A further Order was introduced to take account of Directive 83/206 in 1984. However, Air Navigation (Noise Certification) Order 1986 (SI 1986 No 1304) came into effect from 1 August 1986 and replaced both preceding Orders, subsuming their provisions and adding others including noise certification for helicopters in accordance with ICAO requirements. A further Order may come into effect in the summer of 1987.

Effect on UK practice

Directive 80/51 has had no effect on British registered aircraft since the ICAO recommendations and those of ECAC were already applied in Britain. The main effect of the Directive will be to compel those Member States that were not already applying the standards to do so eventually. This was explained in evidence given by the Department of Trade to a House of Lords' Select Committee for its review of Community noise policy[1]. Giving evidence in April 1982, an official said that Italy, Luxembourg and Greece did not have legislation on the subject two years after the due date. To the extent that aircraft registered abroad, which have the right to land in Britain, now have to conform to the standards there will have been a slight improvement to the environment in Britain. The ban from 1988 of aircraft registered outside Member States unless they meet certain standards should also have a beneficial effect.

Further developments

In October 1981 the Commission proposed a Directive limiting helicopter noise (OJ C275 27.10.81 – COM(81)554), but it has been held in abeyance.

References

1   House of Lords' Select Committee on the European Communities. *Noise in the environment* 13th Report Session 1981–82. HMSO.

9.6 Lawnmowers

84/538/EEC (OJ L300 19.11.84) proposed 18.12.78 – COM(78)387	Directive on the approximation of the laws of the Member States relating to the permissible sound power level of lawnmowers.
87/252/EEC (OJ L117 5.5.87)	Commission Directive adapting to technical progress Directive 84/538, amending Annexes I, II and III.

Binding dates
Notification date	29 September 1984
Formal Compliance (84/538)	1 July 1987
(87/252)	1 January 1988

Purpose of the Directives

Noise levels are set for motorized lawnmowers to reduce the nuisance they cause. The Directive is also part of the programme for eliminating barriers to trade. For the time being cylinder mowers (a type commonly used in the UK) are excluded.

Summary of the Directives

The Directive applies to all types of motorized machines used for cutting grass except motorized cylinder mowers, agricultural and forestry equipment, non-independent devices such as drawn cylinders and other devices with motors of over 20 kW power. Noise limits are set according to the cutting width of the mower and range from 96 to 105 dB(A). Machines are to be certificated and to be marked with the name of the manufacturer, the type and the maximum sound power level guaranteed by the manufacturer.

Member States may not limit the sale of mowers which meet the requirements of the Directive. If a mower does not meet the limits a Member State must ensure that further production conforms. Verification of conformity with the requirement of the Directive is to be by spot checks.

An Annex sets out methods for measuring noise from mowers and as amended provides for hover mowers. Other Annexes specify the form of the manufacturer's certificate and the mark for sound power level.

Development of the Directive

The proposal had its origin in a notification of legislation under the 'Information Agreement'. There was much discussion with trade associations before the proposal was submitted. The intention to propose legislation led to some adverse publicity in the UK as an example of the Community getting involved in inappropriate matters (which still continues, though the opposition appears to be based on a misunderstanding of the purpose of the Directive and its trade benefits to the UK). Yet the Wilson Committee's 1963 Report on Noise [1] had recommended that maximum limits be set for lawnmowers. There were, however, real difficulties in achieving harmonization because of different practices arising out of differing ways of life. A rather different housing and garden pattern between the continent and the UK and climatic variations has led to different machines being used, with rotary mowers being preferred on the continent while much more use is made in the UK of the more traditional cylinder mower. Limiting noise levels without reducing efficiency is more difficult for the cylinder mower.

Though agreement was reached on noise levels, it was not possible to arrive at a testing procedure for cylinder mowers which could be agreed. Cylinder mowers were therefore excluded until a satisfactory testing procedure could be found (see below). The Commission's proposal made no exemptions for types of mowers except for agricultural and forestry equipment. The noise limits proposed ranged between 103 and 111 dB(A), as against the range 96 to 105 dB(A) in the Directive.

Formal compliance in UK

The Directive was put into effect by a Regulation under the European Communities Act 1972 (SI 1986/175) the Lawnmowers (Harmonization of Noise Emission Standards) Regulation 1986 which came into effect on 18 November 1986. After 1 July 1987, a lawnmower requires a certificate of conformity to be marketed in Great Britain.

After the Regulations came into effect, some Members of Parliament expressed their concern about them. A debate subsequently took place in the First Committee on Statutory Instruments on 17 December 1986. The concern of MPs appears to have been based on a misunderstanding of the purpose of the Directive and the implementing Regulations and included the fear that members of the public might have their mowers inspected. The Minister for Industry (Mr Giles Shaw) assured the Committee that the Regulations applied to manufacturers and not to individual users of mowers; and that their purpose primarily was to prevent barriers to trade though they also served the environmental need to limit noise. However, the debate did result in eliciting the admission that the Regulations did not specify that checks would be carried out at manufacturers' premises. The Minister stated that, probably by means of a guidance note, this point would be made clear and that the Regulations applied to the manufacturer, agent or importer and not members of the public.

Effect on UK practice

A Commission proposal to amend the Directive to establish a testing method for cylinder mowers was sent to the Council on 10 April 1987 (COM(87)133 OJ C113 24.4.87). Once adopted, cylinder mowers will then cease to be exempt and will be required to conform to the noise levels in the Directive. A Commission proposal covering noise limits at operator level has also been made (COM(86)682 OJ C20 27.1.87). It remains to be seen whether the testing procedure proposed for cylinder mowers meets UK requirements, thus enabling UK manufacturers to meet the noise levels; otherwise, higher costs would result and would affect competition between cylinder and rotary mowers.

References
1   Wilson Sir Alan (chairman) 1963 *Noise: final report* Cmnd 2056. HMSO.

9.7 Noise in the workplace

86/188/EEC (OJ L137 24.5.86) proposed 15.10.82 – COM(82)646 and 26.7.84 – COM(84)426	Directive on the protection of workers from the risks related to exposure to noise at work.

Binding dates
Notification date	15 May 1986
Formal compliance	1 January 1990
Council to reexamine Directive	1 January 1994

Purpose of the Directive

The aim of the Directive is to protect workers from risks to their hearing by setting limits on noise levels at which preventive action is required. The Directive is the third individual Directive to be adopted under Directive 80/1107 (see Section 7.7 Worker protection) which set a framework for Directives on the protection of workers from risks related to chemical, physical and biological agents at work.

Summary of the Directive

The Directive applies to all workers except those in sea and air transport. Employers are required to assess and, where necessary, measure noise levels to identify workers and workplaces to which the Directive applies and to determine the conditions under which its provisions apply. Noise exposures are generally to be reduced to the lowest levels reasonably practicable, taking account of technical progress and the availability of measures to control the noise.

Where noise levels are likely to exceed 85 dB(A), or the peak sound pressure level exceeds 200 pascals, workers must receive adequate information and, where necessary, training on:

potential risks to hearing;
measures to be taken in accordance with the Directive;
obligations under national legislation;
wearing of personal ear protectors;
checks on hearing.

Personal ear protectors must be made available to workers, where levels exceed 85 dB(A). Workers exposed to such levels must also be able to have their hearing checked by a doctor.

Where the daily personal noise exposure exceeds 90 dB(A), or the peak sound pressure level is more than 200 pascals, the reasons for the excess level must be identified and measures taken to reduce the level as far as reasonably practicable. Personal ear protectors must also be worn. Areas where noise exposures exceed these levels must be marked with signs and access restricted.

M

Member States are required to ensure that new plant or substantial changes to existing plants comply with the requirement to reduce noise exposure to the lowest level reasonably practicable. Adequate information must be made available about the noise of new machinery which exceeds the 85 dB(A) or 200 pascal levels.

Derogations may be allowed to these requirements where noise levels vary provided that the average weekly noise exposure is within the limits in the Directive. Other derogations may be granted exceptionally for limited periods where it is not reasonably practicable to meet the limits: they must be reported to the Commission every two years. The Council is to reexamine the Directive before 1 January 1994 with a view to reducing the risks from noise. Annexes provide 'indications' for measuring noise and checking worker's hearing.

Development of the Directive

The proposal was produced by the Commission after consultation through the Advisory Commission on Safety, Hygiene and Health Protection at Work. Its provisions were in line with the recommendations of the International Labour Organization (ILO) and the Intergovernmental Maritime Consultative Organization (IMCO) and took into account work by the World Health Organization (WHO) and other international bodies. The main element of the proposal was to set a limit of 85 dB(A) for exposure to noise for a worker. Derogation from this limit up to 90 dB(A) would be permitted for a temporary period of five years. An audiometric examination was to be required where the limit laid down could not be met and hearing protectors had to be worn.

There were major differences between the Commission's proposal and those for regulations proposed by the Health and Safety Commission in a consultative document published in 1981. The HSC limit was put at 90 dB(A) and audiometry would only be compulsory at 105 dB(A). On the other hand the draft Directive would not require manufacturers, designers and suppliers to reduce levels where reasonably practicable or place duties on employers in relation to persons not in their employ as would the HSC proposals.

The government's point of view was made clear in a debate in the House of Commons on 7 December 1983. While the proposal was welcomed in principle the maximum exposure of 85 dB(A) was not regarded as reasonably practicable for a number of industries. Some compromise between 90 and 85 dB(A) seemed possible. It was also felt that audiometric testing at exposures over 85 dB(A) would not be practicable. The opposition urged acceptance of the 85 dB(A) limit as a long-term goal.

The European Parliament in March 1984 called on the Commission in a Resolution to fix the limit of noise exposure at 90 dB(A) instead of 85 dB(A). The Economic and Social Committee had earlier also advised that the limit would initially be better set at the higher level. The Commission issued amendments in July 1984 which included changing the limit to 90 dB(A). The main differences between the original proposal and the final Directive were the raising of the limit from 85 to 90 dB(A) and the dropping of any reference to audiometric examination. The date of implementation was also deferred from 1984 to 1990.

Formal compliance in UK

The Health and Safety Executive will be issuing a further consultative document as the result of this Directive. This is not likely to appear before autumn 1987. It will probably be another year after that before Regulations are introduced under the Health and Safety at Work etc Act 1974.

Effect on UK practice

It seems likely that levels now agreed will not lead to major changes in present practices. On the other hand, the possibility of further lowering of limits may cause manufacturers to look to improvements.

9.8 Household appliances

86/594/EEC (OJ L344 6.12.86) proposed 12.1.82 – COM(81)811 and 23.11.83 – COM(83)694	Directive on airborne noise emitted by household appliances.

Binding dates	
Notification date	4 December 1986
Formal compliance	4 December 1989

Purpose of the Directive

The principal purpose is to prevent barriers to trade being erected. It will also help the public to be made aware in a uniform way of the noise levels of household appliances and should thus drive manufacturers to produce less noisy models.

Summary of the Directive

The Directive requires informative labelling, if used, to be based on prescribed methods of noise measurement. It thus ensures that no barriers to trade within the Community are created by individual Member States requiring measurements of another kind. The Directive does not itself lay down noise limits. The Directive covers principles on the publication of information on noise from household appliances, the measuring methods and the monitoring arrangements for such noise. It does not apply to machines designed exclusively for industrial or professional purposes or those which form an integral part of buildings.

It is for Member States to decide whether information on noise emissions of appliances should be published. If this course is followed, the level of noise must be determined by the testing methods laid down in the Directive and may be subject to spot checks. The manufacturer or importer is responsible for the accuracy of the information. Where information on labels is already required, for example under Directive 79/530 (OJ L145 13.6.79) which provides for the energy consumption of household appliances to be published, the information on noise should be given on the same label.

Member States may not prevent in any way the marketing of goods which meet the requirements of the Directive. Member States in setting national standards for measurement are expected to use harmonized standards, references to which have been published in the *Official Journal*, except where no such standards exist and national standards and technical regulations are used instead. Details in all cases are to be sent to the Commission who will send them on to other Member States. Member States are required to publish their standards which the Commission will ensure are also published in the *Official Journal*. The harmonized standards are those established by the Comité européen de normalisation (CEN) and the Comité européen de normalisation électrotechnique (CENELEC) recognized as the competent bodies in this field in accordance with Directive 83/189 (OJ L108 26.4.83) laying down a procedure for the provision of information for technical standards and regulations.

Provision is made for referring any differences of opinion on the harmonized standards to the Committee set up for this purpose under Directive 83/189. National standards proposed shall also be considered by this Committee which is empowered to take a decision by majority voting. The Commission will adopt the decision. Where no decision is made, the Commission has to submit a proposal to the Council and if no decision is taken by them within three months the Commission will adopt the measure itself.

Development of the Directive

The original proposal had two objectives, to form part of the action programme on the environment, and to remove barriers to trade formed by differing noise legislation being formulated by France, Germany and the Netherlands. The proposal took the form of a framework Directive which would enable a standardized system of noise measurement indicated on a label to be introduced; the system would be optional but other labelling systems would be forbidden.

Trade and consumer organizations consulted were generally against the proposal as they saw little or no benefit and some expense. The House of Lords[1] reported that no adequate case for noise labelling had been made and considered that it would be preferable to deal with the provision of information to the consumer by means of labelling or other means in a more comprehensive method which also covered performance. In the subsequent debate the government made clear its support if only to prevent the emergence of barriers to trade.

The proposal was amended as a result of the Opinion of the European Parliament by removing the clause by which Member States who found that the noise level was higher than the claimed level could request that the marketing of the appliance be suspended pending the issue of accurate information by the manufacturer or importer. The detailed description of the method of determining noise was replaced by a reference to methods defined in a publication of the International Electrotechnical Commission which had been widely approved internationally. The latter amendment was in line with government policy but the other was thought to remove the point of Member States making checks on the accuracy of the information given.

The main changes in the final version as adopted were to exclude appliances designed for industrial and professional purposes. The replacement of the original Annexes by a reference to international standards established by CEN and CENELEC meant a very much smaller and simpler Directive. At the same time, a separate committee on technical adaptation was found unnecessary.

Formal compliance in UK

The date for formal compliance is not until 4 December 1989. As for similar Directives, reliance may be placed on the European Communities Act 1972.

Effect on UK practice

Noise of household appliances does not appear to have been a matter of great concern to consumers but the introduction of a common system of labelling in the Community is likely to have some effect on informing opinion as well as avoiding the creation of barriers to trade.

References
1   House of Lords' Select Committee on the European Communities 1982
    Noise in the Environment 13th Report Session 1981–82. HMSO.

CHAPTER 10

Assessment, information and finance

10.0 Relevant British legislation

There is no distinct corpus of legislation covering the Directive, Decision and Regulation described in this Chapter. The Directive on environmental assessment of development projects has not yet been formally implemented, but it is already clear that existing town and country planning legislation will not be sufficient and that some extra provisions will have to be introduced.

10.1 Environmental impact assessment

85/337 (OJ L175 5.7.85) proposed 11.6.80 – COM(80)313	Directive on the assessment of the effects of certain public and private projects on the environment.

Binding dates

Notification date	3 July 1985
Formal compliance	3 July 1988
Commission's report on exemptions	annually from 3 July 1989
Commission's report on application and effectiveness	3 July 1990

Purpose of the Directive

The Directive can be thought of as an embodiment of the preventative approach to environmental protection. Before consent is given for certain development projects – mostly large-scale industrial or infrastructure projects – an assessment is to be made of the effects they may have on the environment. To enable the assessment to be made the developer has to supply certain information and the public, and certain authorities, have to be consulted.

Summary of the Directive

General provisions

Projects likely to have significant effects on the environment by virtue *inter alia* of their nature, size or location are to be made subject to an assessment of their effects before consent is given. The projects listed in an Annex I must be made subject to an asessment, while other projects, listed in an Annex II, are to be made subject to an assessment where Member States consider that their characteristics so require.

The effects on the following four factors are to be identified, described and assessed, as appropriate, in the environmental impact assessment:

human beings, fauna and flora;
soil, water, air, climate and the landscape;
the inter-action between the first two groups;
material assets and the cultural heritage.

Information supplied by the developer (see below) and gathered as a result of consultations (see below) must be taken into consideration in the development consent procedure. The public is to be informed of the content of the decision and any conditions attached to it but the authority need not inform the public of the reasons for the decision unless required to by national legislation.

Exemptions
In exceptional cases a project may be exempted from the provisions of the Directive. In that event the Member State must make public its reasons and must consider whether another form of assessment would be appropriate and whether the public should be informed of the information collected. The Member State must also inform the Commission which must immediately inform the other Member States.

Projects whose details are adopted by a specific act of national legislation are exempt from all provisions of the Directive, as are projects serving national defence purposes.

Projects subject to assessment
Projects which must be made subject to an environmental impact assessment, unless exempted, fall under nine headings in Annex 1. In summary they are:

oil refineries;
large thermal power stations and nuclear power stations and reactors;
installations for storage or disposal of radioactive waste;
iron and steel works;
installations for extracting and processing asbestos;
integrated chemical installations;
construction of motorways, express roads, railway lines and airports;
trading ports and inland waterways;
installations for incineration, treatment or landfill of hazardous waste.

Member States are to make the projects in Annex II subject to an assessment if they consider that their characteristics so require, ie if they consider that they have a significant effect on the environment. They may specify certain types of project as being subject to an assessment and may establish criteria or thresholds for deciding when an assessment is necessary. Annex II lists classes of project under twelve headings. Under each heading the class is described in some detail so that the headings below only give a broad indication of the projects for which an assessment may be required:

agriculture;
extractive industry;
energy industry;
processing of metals;
manufacture of glass;
chemical industry;
food industry;
textile, leather, wood and paper industries;
rubber industry;
infrastructure projects;
other projects;
modifications to projects included in Annex I.

Information to be supplied by the developer
The developer is to supply at least the following information:

a description of the project with information on its site, design and size;
measures intended to avoid, reduce or remedy significant adverse effects;
the data required to identify and assess the main environmental effects;
a nontechnical summary of the above three.

An Annex III gives a fuller specification of the information that the developer must supply amplifying these four points. Any authorities with relevant information in their possession are to make it available. The developer is to supply the information only in as much as the Member State considers it relevant to a given stage of the consent procedure; to the particular project; to the environmental features likely to be affected; and that it is reasonable having regard to current knowledge. This specification is set out under seven headings and includes:

production processes, quantity of materials used, expected residues and emissions;
where appropriate, an outline of main alternatives studied by the developer and reasons for his choice;
a description of the aspects of the environment likely to be affected including population, fauna, flora, soil, water, air, climatic factors, architectural and archaeological heritage and landscape;
a description of the likely significant effects on the environment, and of the forecasting methods used to assess these effects;
an indication of any difficulties encountered in compiling the required information.

Consultations
The arrangements for public consultation are to be decided upon by the Member States but any request for development consent and the information supplied by the developer must be made public. The public concerned must also be given the opportunity to express an opinion before the project is initiated.

Authorities with specific environmental responsibilities likely to be concerned by a project must also be given an opportunity to express their opinion. The detailed arrangements for this are a matter for the Member State.

Where a project is likely to have effects in another Member State, the developer's information is to be forwarded to that Member State and should serve as a basis for any consultations between the two Member States.

Experience gained
The Member States and the Commission are to exchange information on experience gained in applying the Directive. The Commission is to submit a report on the application and effectiveness of the Directive to the Council and to the Parliament by July 1990. Its report must be published.

Development of the Directive
The inspiration for this Directive comes, not from the land use planning procedures of any of the Member States, nor from the procedures for authorization of industrial plant that exist in most, but from an item of legislation in the USA – the National Environment Policy Act of 1969 – known as NEPA[1]. This is acknowledged in the second action programme on the environment of 1977 in which the Commission formally announced its intentions of making proposals on 'environmental impact assessment'. The Commission had by then already asked consultants (N Lee and C Wood from Britain among others) to study the subject, and then starting from the consultants' report the Commission between 1977 and 1980 produced twenty internal drafts before formally proposing a Directive in 1980. Even during this gestation period the proposal generated considerable interest to the extent of the House of Lords taking evidence from Commission officials in the summer of 1979 and the European Parliament holding a hearing in January 1980. One of the internal drafts even appeared in the press[2].

The requirements of NEPA are very different from those of the Directive. NEPA applies only to actions by a Federal agency and requires the agency, that is, the promoter of the development, itself to prepare an 'environmental impact statement'. This idea of the developer preparing an assessment is to be found in the Commission's proposal of 1980 which would effectively have required two assessments: a first forming part of the published information provided by the developer, and a second prepared and made public by the competent authority. In the Directive as agreed the developer now only has to supply information including data required to assess the main environmental effects. The Directive now does not say that the 'assessment' has to be published, and the 'assessment' is effectively a procedure involving the provision and publication of information on the part of the developer; the collecting of information from the public and others; and culminating in a mental process on the part of the competent authority in arriving at its decision to grant or withhold consent for development. However, it is quite probable that the developers' written information will come to be known as the 'assessment' or 'environmental impact statement'. If this happens it will be to depart from the wording of the Directive and may yet cause confusion.

The first formal statement of the UK government's views appeared in a letter in September 1980 from the DoE to the House of Lords (published in their report) stating that the government supported the principle of environmental assessment as a key element in the planning process but had serious reservations on the practicability and wisdom of seeking to legislate for such assessments as proposed.

Despite these reservations the Lords' Scrutiny Committee came out firmly in favour of a Directive in February 1981 – the first time that the Committee had positively disagreed with the government on a matter of EC environmental policy. This was all the more remarkable given that, with the exception of environmental bodies, and of consultants who might benefit financially from the Directive, none of the bodies giving evidence to the Lords welcomed the Directive. The Royal Town Planning Institute revealed itself as divided on the issue. In the subsequent debate in the Lords (30 April 1981) the Minister (Lord Bellwin) outlined the government's objections. These were:

the difficulty of defining projects subject to assessment;
delays caused by the need to secure agreement of the Commission for any exemption;
delays caused by the consultation procedures;
the scope for dispute and litigation about which aspects of a development need to be covered in the assessment;
delays occasioned by the competent authority having to make its own published assessment.

In addition the government were unconvinced that the subject was appropriate for the Community although this point of principle was made rather ambiguously, perhaps fortunately since it was later forgotten. Some of these points were reiterated in the debate in a standing committee of the House of Commons (9 June 1981) by the Minister, Giles Shaw. In the Lords' debate all nine speakers, except the Minister, favoured the Directive. In the Commons' debate, where only five people spoke including the opposition spokesman, Gordon Oakes, the mood was strongly against the Directive and a resolution was adopted welcoming 'the Government's policy of encouraging environmental assessment within the general principle of the existing law'. This resolution was presumably designed to prevent the Government agreeing to any Directive that would introduce significant changes.

The fears of the government over the matter of delays and litigation were in part that opponents to a development would be provided with the opportunity to seize on some procedural failure as a ground for challenging a planning decision in the courts. These fears may well have been fuelled by stories of the early days of NEPA in the USA where there had been much litigation, but where the tradition of resolving disputes over policy matters in the courts is well established.

These objections have been largely overcome by amendment. Annex I is much shorter than in the proposal and exemptions can be made without the Commission's agreement being sought. The information in Annex III to be supplied by the developer is to be supplied only to the extent that the Member States consider it relevant, so that whatever regulations implement the Directive can leave a large measure of discretion to the competent authority and therefore reduce substantially the risk of litigation. Thus the developer will now not always have to describe the main alternatives studied or the reasons for his choice. Nor does he need to provide a description of the relationship between the proposed project and existing environmental and land-use plans and standards for the area likely to be affected. Finally, the competent authority no longer has to publish its own statement of assessment.

The UK was not the only country to have reservations but there is no doubt that the UK was the leading opponent of the Directive as proposed. The British reservations were maintained until November 1983 by which time the proposal had been amended in significant ways. However, at that point a Danish objection continued to delay agreement. The Danish Parliament – the *Folketing* – objected in principle to having to submit development projects to the procedures of the Directive when they were being authorized by an Act of Parliament on the grounds that this impinged upon their sovereignty. The Danish government refused to make any concession on this point which was eventually met by the Council agreeing to exempt any project 'the details of which are adopted by a specific act of national legislation'.

The European Parliament delivered an opinion in February 1982. As well as proposing detailed amendments it called on the Commission, as soon as possible, to submit a proposal to extend environmental assessment to public plans and programmes and not just to projects. It also requested the Council to declare the Directive applicable to plans concerning the Community.

The House of Lords' report and debate, which both supported the Directive, played a key role in persuading the British government to withdraw its opposition. It was well known that some government departments were strongly opposed and those within the government who supported a Directive had their hands greatly strengthened. Had the Lords' debate been as hostile as that in the Commons the Directive may well never have been agreed.

Formal compliance in the UK

The resolution adopted in the House of Commons in June 1981 (see above) neatly summarizes the government's policy throughout – that the Directive should not significantly add to existing procedures. In answer to a written parliamentary question on 3 November 1986, the Minister (Mr Tracey) reiterated the government's intention to make full use of existing powers and procedures under planning legislation to implement the Directive, while recognizing that a few new legislative provisions would be required. The government's intention is to introduce these new provisions under powers contained in the European Communities Act 1972.

In 1984, while the Danish objection was still holding up agreement on the Directive, the DoE began considering how to implement it. They established a working party with members drawn from industry, local government, the planning professions, environmental groups and other government departments to consider how best those projects subject to planning control under the Planning Acts were to be implemented. Some of the projects of Annex I, such as power stations and highways, are approved under separate legislation and are being considered by other government departments. In April 1986 the DoE issued a consultation paper based on the discussions in the working group. The consultation paper sought comments by July 1986 on a draft advisory booklet to be published by DoE setting out the procedures to be followed by both developers and authorities, and also on the proposed new statutory provisions. The government is considering the replies to the consultation paper and may issue the statutory provisions, the booklet and a circular during 1987.

An outline of the proposed statutory provisions is contained in an appendix to the DoE's consultation paper. It proposes powers to direct that an assessment is or is not required for a particular development. Obligations will be placed on a developer to provide an 'assessment' with his planning application where relevant. (This use of the word 'assessment' to cover the 'information' required of the developer departs from the wording of the Directive and may cause confusion.) Obligations will also be placed on the planning authority to notify statutory consultees and to place the 'assessment' with the planning application on Part I of the planning register. In considering the planning application the authority will be required to have regard to the information contained in the 'assessment' and to any comments made by the statutory consultees. The decison, including any conditions imposed, will have to be placed on Part II of the planning register.

The question of requiring the procedures of the Directive to be applied to projects of Annex II has been a matter of controversy. The consultation paper said that the government proposed that 'in relation to projects falling outside Annex I the appropriate Secretary of State should have the power to direct that an assessment should be carried out in any particular case'. At that time (April 1986) the government believed it had complete discretion whether or not to require an assessment for a particular Annex II project and the intention was that the power would be used rarely and certainly not for agricultural and forestry developments. Article 4(2) read on its own would appear to support such an interpretation of the Directive. Following representations from the Commission, the DoE now appears to accept that its discretion is not unfettered since Article 4(2) must be read in conjunction with Article 2 which declares that all projects likely to have significant effects on the environment by virtue *inter alia* of their nature, size or location are to be made subject to an assessment. According to this interpretation, if an Annex II project is bound to have 'significant effects' then it must be made subject to an assessment. The Member States' discretion then only lies in deciding whether the characteristics of particular projects are such that they are or are not likely to have significant effects. It therefore seems that unless a decision is made in advance that all Annex II projects will be subjected to an assessment, some kind of screening process must be introduced to decide on particular cases.

If a forestry project or an agricultural drainage scheme (listed in Annex II) has a significant effect on the environment then it should be subject to an assessment. However, whereas other projects listed in Annex II are all subject to planning permission or some other form of authorization, there is no authorization procedure at present in Britain for forestry and agriculture. This suggests that some kind of authorization procedure will have to be introduced to deal with such developments.

Effect on UK practice

The proposal for a Directive was subtly modified in the process of negotiations so that it now accords very closely with existing British development control procedures. In Britain the developer already has to supply certain information; the public already has the chance to comment; the planning authority already goes through a mental process in arriving at a decision which involves considering the information supplied by the developer and others; and when the decision is taken it is published (the reasons for it need only be published if the application is refused). When an application is 'called in' for his own decision by the Secretary of State and subjected to a public inquiry the main procedures of the Directive are also already followed and the published report of the inspector who holds the inquriy provides an account of the 'assessment'. For those developments already subject to authorization it is therefore in the type and quantity of information that will have to be provided, and in the range of environmental effects that will have to be considered, that the Directive will change matters in Britain.

These novel provisions are not insignificant since in effect they will bring within the development-control procedure considerations of pollution control which have hitherto often been considered separately by other authorities. An example is provided by the procedure for authorizing a landfill site for receiving toxic waste. At present there is a two-stage authorization procedure: the planning authority must give planning permission for the use of the land for landfill; and the waste disposal authority must grant a disposal licence (often known as a 'site licence') setting conditions such as what kind of waste is acceptable and how it is to be handled. If planning legislation is being used to implement the Directive then it would seem that the conditions of the site licence will have to be in discussion during the process of obtaining planning permission since the developer will have, in the information he supplies with his planning application, to discuss the pollution matters which have hitherto been controlled by the site licence.

On some estimates the Directive is likely to be applied formally to only about five Annex I projects a year, many of which are likely to be the subject of public inquiries. The full effect of the Directive will therefore very much depend on the way Annex II projects come to be selected for assessment.

References

1   Haigh N 1983 The EEC Directive on environmental assessment of development projects *Journal of Planning and Environment Law* September.

2   *ENDS Report* No 24, 1979.

10.2 Information on state of environment (CORINE)

85/338/EEC (OJ L176 6.7.85) proposed 14.10.83 – COM(83)528	Decision on the adoption of the Commission work programme concerning an experimental project for gathering, coordinating and ensuring the consistency of information on the state of the environment and natural resources in the Community (CORINE).
Binding dates Start of programme	1 January 1985 for four years

Purpose of Decision

The general aim is to assemble basic information on the state of the environment in the Community in a number of specific fields. This Decision sets up an experimental project – known as CORINE – to collate information in four fields of priority concern:

biotopes for conservation;
acid deposition;
protection of the Mediterranean environment;
improvement in comparability and availability of data and methods of analysing data.

CORINE should not be confused with reports on the state of the environment published by the Commission for 1977, 1979 and 1986 and promised for future years although from now on these reports will increasingly depend on the information gathered under the CORINE programme.[1]

Summary of the Decision

A four-year work programme starting from 1 January 1985 is authorized as an experimental project at an estimated cost of 4 million ECUs under which the Commission is to gather, coordinate and ensure the consistency of information on the state of the environment in the Community. The programme covers four priority fields:

biotopes of major importance for nature conservation: the aim is to identify and describe such biotopes in the Community, working closely with the Council of Europe;
acid deposition: the aim is to contribute to the solution of the 'acid rain' problem by gathering consistent information on emissions to air and giving an overall picture of damage at Community level;

protection of the environment in the Mediterranean region: the aim is to gather consistent information on environmental resources most directly affected by development programmes;
improvement in the comparability and availability of data and in the methods of analysing data: work will include organization of exchange of information, setting up an inventory of various kinds of data systems and choice of computer techniques for information management.

The Commission is required to submit a report at the end of the second year and a final report to the European Parliament and the Council.

Development of the Decision
The origin of this decision goes back to June 1974 when the Italian government presented a memorandum to the Council asking for efforts to be made to implement that part of the Community environment programme referring to improvement of the environment. The Council as a result requested the Commission in November 1974 to start on a study of the classification of the Community on the basis of its environmental characteristics so that the required objectives and measures could be identified and determined. Thus began the project which came to be known as 'ecological mapping'.

After an initial study carried out by the Commission, with the help of national experts, of the various methods in use within the Community, to plot environmental information on maps and charts, a four-phase study was proposed and included in the 1977–81 Community environment programme. The initial phase was devoted to devising a pilot method to be used in a number of case studies within Member States. The subsequent phases were dependent on Council approval of the recommended method.

The Commission selected a method devized by Professor Ammer of Munich University which was based on the principle of plotting environmental characteristics by kilometre squares using different colours and shades. Twelve regional case studies were carried out in Member States, the UK study being in South Yorkshire. The report of the UK study contained a fundamental criticism of the method used by challenging its validity[2]. Other studies were carried out on such subjects as remote sensing and computer applications.

By the end of 1982 the Commission was reporting that the studies had revealed that the programme was far too theoretical and would need to be modified. There followed the proposal for a very much reduced effort concentrating initially on certain priority areas. The Decision as adopted showed very little difference in essentials though finance was reduced from 5.8 million to 4 million ECUs and the Council insisted on the project being described as experimental with no specific commitment to further stages.

The UK attitude to the 'ecological mapping' project was throughout one of concern as to the practicality of the method favoured by the Commission. Its belief that the project was overambitious and unworkable seems to have been justified by events. However, the basic concept of a large system covering all aspects presumably remains with the emphasis rather more on computer techniques for information management. The present very much modified and reduced scale of action was put forward as the first stage of such a comprehensive

Community system. The UK though able to accept the reduced scale of the proposal remains sceptical about the justification for an overall system.

The European Parliament has always looked upon the need for collecting environmental information on a Community scale as important and has given its support to the ecological mapping project. On the proposal from the Commission it put forward a number of major amendments and passed a Resolution demonstrating the importance Parliament attached to developing an information system and extending the proposed programme.

Effect on UK practice

Data required in Britain for the purposes of the Decision are to be taken from what is available. The effect on UK practice is therefore negligible. The long-term effect on policy of having more information on the state of the environment in the Community cannot yet be assessed.

In November 1986 it was announced that 351 000 ECUs had been approved by the Commission for a series of actions under this Decision. Work was already under way on harmonization of environmental statistics, the compilation of a register of data sources and of biotopes, and the digitization of basic data on soil, climate, etc. The funds announced were to go to projects on assessment of erosion risk and land resources in the Mediterranean, evaluating risk of soil pollution, a dangerous waste inventory in Portugal, and to help to establish inventories of emissions of air in Spain and Italy.

The draft fourth action programme makes clear that the Commission, on completion of the present phase covered by the Decision, intends to present further proposals which will extend this phase with the aim of ensuring the availability of a wide range of up-to-date and comparable environmental and natural resource data.

References

1   Commission of the European Communities 1987 *The state of the environment in the European Community 1986*. EUR 10633.

2   France J and Briggs D J Environmental mapping of the European Community: A review of the proposed method *Journal of the Operational Research Society* **31** (6).

10.3 Finance (ACE)

1872/84 (OJ L176 3.7.84) proposed 13.1.83 – COM(82)349	Regulation on action by the Community relating to the environment (ACE).

Binding dates	
Effective date	4 July 1984
Duration	three years

Purpose of the Regulation

Community finance is made available for environmental protection in three fields: 'clean technologies'; measuring the quality of the environment; and habitats for endangered species. The scheme is known as 'ACE'.

Summary of the Regulation

Three categories of projects may be supported by ACE up to the limits shown:

demonstration projects to develop new 'clean technologies' as defined in a list (30 per cent);
demonstration projects to develop new technologies for measuring the quality of the natural enviornment (30 per cent);
projects to protect habitats of endangered species (50 per cent).

The list of eligible 'clean technologies' falls under seven headings: surface treatments, leather industry, textile industry, cellulose and paper industries, mining and quarrying, chemical industry, agrifood industry.

The total amount estimated to be required is 13 million ECUs over the three year period in which the Regulation is in force; 6.5 million ECUs for the first two categories and 6.5 million ECUs for the third. A committee consisting of representatives of Member States, chaired by the Commission, is set up to advise the Commission on selection of projects. Decisions are taken by the Commission subject to a Member State referring the matter to the Council within twenty days of being informed; the Council will decide in such a case by qualified majority within forty working days of the referral. Any person or organization may submit projects direct to the Commission in respect of the first two categories; only Member States may submit projects in the third category. Those granted aid are required to submit annual reports or as requested on the progress of the projects. The Commission has to submit an annual report to the European Parliament and Council. The Community may request repayment of any contribution if there is commercial exploitation resulting from the project.

Development of the Regulation

For some years before the Commission had put forward the proposal, there had been much discussion about creating an environnment fund on the lines of other funds such as the regional development fund. Community money was at that time already being made available for environmental purposes from a number of sources but in an uncoordinated way.[1,2] The European Parliament took a leading role in developing pressure for an environment fund and in 1981 they took the initiative of entering in the 1982 budget an article entitled 'Community operations concerning the environment' with a total budget allocation for four new headings within that article of 6.5 million ECUs.[3] The budget signed by the President of the European Parliament contained an allocation of 4 million ECU and although the Council had withheld approval of the budget, the Commission had been spending the money so in effect the environment fund had come into existence. The budget as a whole was in dispute and such spending was on an *ad hoc* basis. Parliament agreed a 3.75 million ECU item for the environment fund for the 1983 budget but the Commission moved to put the environment fund on a proper footing by proposing the draft Regulation (ACE) in January 1983.

This proposal consisted of two elements: support for clean technologies and protection of sensitive areas of Community interest with up to 50 per cent of costs payable by the Community. For 1983 the Commission asked for appropriations of 3 million ECUs for clean technologies and 3.5 million ECUs for nature protection, with substantial increases for 1984 and 1985.

The UK government were at some pains to stress that the proposal should not be considered as an environment fund. Though not opposed to the proposal as such, its aims were to try to limit its duration, to increase Member State's influence on selection of projects and to try to avoid being a net contributor. Some countries were opposed to increasing the budget; but others were enthusiastic in support.

The major change in the proposal was to introduce a third category of project – those concerned with measuring environmental quality. Other changes were: to confine aid to 'demonstration' projects aimed at developing clean technologies; to reduce the proportion of costs for this category to 30 per cent (both these conditions also applied to the new category introduced – measuring environmental quality); to specify the total amount available and its allocation; and to limit the period during which the Regulation would be in force to three years. Opportunity was also taken to simplify the administration while specifying in greater detail the functions of the advisory committee.

Effect on UK practice

Following adoption of the Regulation the Commission published an invitation in the *Official Journal* (OJ C100 20.4.85) to submit proposals in the first two categories. This set out in more detail the requirements to be met, financial conditions and selection criteria.

For the first two categories (clean technologies and measuring and monitoring methods) one Commission Decision has been published (C(86)184 of 25.9.86). It provides for a total of 0.430 million ECUs for three clean technology projects (none in the UK) and 1.922 million ECUs for twenty-six monitoring and measurement projects of which three are in the UK.

For the third category (maintenance or reestablishment of threatened habitats of endangered species) three Decisions by the Commission have been published (C(85)1513 of 26.9.85, C(85)1976 of 23.12.85 and C(86)1286 of 25.7.86). They provide for a total of 4.02 million ECUs in financial support to twenty-eight different projects. Six of those listed are in the UK.

Overall the effect on UK practice is not likely to be very great given the limited amount of money available to twelve countries and the time limit. The funds granted for habitat protection, however, have been greatly welcomed and have made a significant contribution to work undertaken in England and Scotland. The Royal Society for Protection of Birds has reported that of the nearly 800 000 ECUs allocated to the UK, 600 000 has been granted to the Society. This amount has helped with the purchase of land for two reserves – Frampton Marshes on the Wash and Tore Hill in the Scottish Highlands – and with a programme to develop an existing reserve in Essex.

It remains to be seen whether the opportunity is taken by organizations of various kinds to get support for projects in the other two categories (clean technologies and measuring and monitoring methods). Until the introduction of the government's Environmental Protection Technology (EPT) scheme early in 1987 there had not been much government encouragement for clean technologies. There is now up to £2 million available per year under the EPT scheme.

Further developments

The Regulation expires on 4 July 1987. In December 1986 the Commission proposed a new Regulation (OJ C18 24.1.87) extending the areas to be eligible for funds from three to six. The three new areas are:

demonstration projects for recycling waste;
for restoring sites contaminated by hazardous wastes or substances;
for restoring or conserving populations of species in danger of extinction.

The scheme would not be limited in time and the funds available would be entered annually in the Community budget. If such a proposal were to be agreed with an adequate budget an environment fund could truly be said to exist.

References

1   Haigh N and Levy C 1983 *Use of Community funds for environmental purposes*, Institute for European Environmental Policy, January.

2   Levy C 1983 *Towards a European Community environment fund*, Institute for European Environmental Policy, October.

3   Johnson S 1983 *The pollution control policy of the EEC*. Graham and Trotman, London.

CHAPTER 11

International conventions

International conventions (or treaties or agreements) are the means by which sovereign nation states place obligations upon one another. They can be between two nations (bilateral) or several (multilateral). Their negotiation has traditionally been the field of diplomacy and the terms of a treaty or convention have often been negotiated in secrecy before being adopted and opened for signature by the negotiating parties. Since conventions are formally agreements between the sovereigns of nation states, the signing of conventions by Ministers or officials is not, depending on the constitutional practices of individual nations, always sufficient for them to become effective and they usually have to be ratified by the 'sovereign'. The constitutions of some countries require them to be approved by the parliament, and in Britain it has become the practice for them to be laid before Parliament before ratification. Multilateral conventions frequently require ratification by a given number of parties before they take effect.

Conventions are now frequently promoted and drafted by international organizations provided with a permanent staff (eg the Council of Europe; the United Nations' Environment Programme), but some conventions may themselves establish a secretariat or commission to service the convention. The obligations undertaken by a nation state in acceding to a convention are a matter for that nation state itself to implement, and in general conventions have no directly effective enforcement mechanism.

The Community is party or has sought to be a party to a number of international conventions covering a wide field of environmental concerns. Those of relevance to the UK are listed below for reference with only a very brief description of the purpose of the convention. Where the UK is a party in its own right to the convention Community participation will strictly involve no additional obligations. Community participation may nevertheless mean that Member States lose the freedom to negotiate independently additions (in the form of amendments or protocols) to the particular convention. The UK has ratified all the conventions listed below except those covering geographical areas which do not involve Britain, such as the Rhine, Barcelona, and Helsinki conventions. Proposed conventions obviously cannot have been ratified.

The general policy adopted by the Commission is to seek Community participation wherever it can establish Community 'competence'. Competence can be a complex matter, but where the Community has adopted measures which cover the same aspects as those in a convention, or just some of those aspects, there will be competence. The process usually starts by the Commission seeking Council authority to negotiate on behalf of the Community either to become party to an existing convention or to take part on behalf of the Community in the negotiations leading to a new convention. Problems frequently arise over whether the Community has competence, over the extent of that competence when it is agreed it exists, and over the loss of independence resulting from the Community becoming a party to a convention. In addition non-Member States may not always be ready to accept the Community in a convention to which they are a party (eg, the Helsinki Convention on the protection of the Baltic – see below). Thus the situation can arise where the Council has recognized competence and given authority to the Commission to act on behalf of the Community but where signature and ratification by the Community is not achieved and the Community position is left in a sort of limbo. The means by which the Community is understood to ratify a convention is a Council Decision although the actual wording of the Decision is such that it does no more than authorise conclusion.

A further development came about in 1986 with a proposal from the Commission for a Council Decision to negotiate on behalf of the Community in relation to a number of regional agreements concerning river and marine pollution, and in particular the limit values and quality objectives to be observed (COM(86)563, 1.12.1986 OJ C324 17.12.86). This proposal concerns the Barcelona, Paris, and Rhine Conventions and the Bonn Agreement on the North Sea (see below). Where the Community already has measures specifying certain limit values and quality objectives, it is clear that there is an interest in these being as far as possible consistent with measures to be observed in international agreements to which the Community is a party.

Water

Convention on the protection of the Rhine against chemical pollution (Bonn 1976) (usually known as the Rhine Convention)

77/586/EEC (OJ L240 19.9.77)	Decision concluding the Convention by the Community.
82/460/EEC (OJ L210 19.7.82)	Decision on the supplement to Annex IV (limit values for mercury discharges from chloralkali plants).
85/336/EEC (OJ L175 5.7.85)	Decision on the supplement to Annex IV (cadmium).

The Convention was drawn up by the riparian states (Switzerland, France, Federal Republic of Germany, Luxembourg, Netherlands) to protect the Rhine against chemical pollution with the object of improving the standards of water for various uses. The European Community also became a party. The Convention provides for strict control of discharges of substances to the Rhine. Annex I substances are to be controlled in accordance with limit values to be set by the International Commission for the Protection of the Rhine against Pollution. Annex II substances are to be controlled by governments under the supervision of the International Commission. These Annexes are similar but not identical to the lists of Directive 76/464 (see Section 4.8). The work of setting limit values goes hand in hand with the issue of daughter Directives under Directive 76/464. Hence the subsequent Decisions listed above.

Confusion can arise over another Convention concerning the Rhine. This is the Convention on the protection of the Rhine from chloride pollution also adopted at Bonn in 1976 to which the Community is not a party. The members are the riparian states listed above but France and Luxembourg delayed ratification until 1984. There is also a convention on thermal pollution of the Rhine.

Draft European Convention for the Protection of International Watercourses against Pollution (Strasbourg Convention)

COM(74)2029 (OJ C99 2.7.75)	Proposal for a Council Decision approving participation in the Convention.

In May 1969 the Council of Europe started drawing up a convention on the protection of fresh water from pollution. By the time that a draft had been completed the Community's environment programme was under way and the Commission took the view that because of the overlap between the proposals in the draft Convention and the Community's programme of action, the latter might be affected. The Commission was given authority to approach the Council of Europe with a view to amending the draft convention while Member States agreed to reserve their position on the convention. An agreement was reached with the Council of Europe on the lines proposed (see also the section on the development of the Directive on dangerous substances in water, Section 4.8). Though there have been occasional attempts to complete the draft and to get it adopted by the Council of Europe, it has not yet been so adopted and the Commission proposal for approving the convention rests also unadopted.

Convention for the prevention of Marine Pollution from Land-based Sources (Paris Convention)

75/437/EEC (OJ L194 25.7.75)	Decision on conclusion of the Convention.
75/438/EEC (OJ L194 25.7.75)	Decision on participation in the Interim Commission.
85/613/EEC (OJ L375 31.12.85)	Decision on adoption of programmes and measures on mercury and cadmium discharges.
87/57/EEC (OJ L24 27.1.87)	Decision concluding the Protocol extending the scope of the Convention to cover atmospheric inputs.

The Convention was drawn up in 1974 to prevent pollution of the North East Atlantic including the North Sea from land-based sources. Other conventions cover dumping and oil pollution at sea (see Oslo Convention below and Section 4.16 on oil pollution at sea). The initial signatories were those whose coasts bordered the area concerned. The Commission took part as an observer initially in the preliminary meetings in 1973 and was subsequently authorized to negotiate the participation of the Community. The Council took Decisions as listed above to conclude the Convention and subsequent instruments. The Commission represents the Community in accordance with such instructions as given by the Council. The Convention provides for elimination of pollution from substances listed in Part I of an Annex and to limit strictly pollution from substances listed in Part II (see also Section 4.8 on dangerous substances in water). The scope of the Convention has been extended to cover atmospheric inputs to the sea.

Agreement for Cooperation in dealing with Pollution of the North Sea by Oil (Bonn Agreement)

84/358/EEC (OJ L188 16.7.84)	Decision on conclusion of the Agreement.

The Agreement drawn up in 1969 between states with coasts on the North Sea was to ensure cooperation in providing manpower, supplies, equipment and scientific advice at short notice to deal with discharges of oil or other noxious or hazardous substances in the North Sea. The area was divided into national zones in which the country concerned had prime responsibility. It came into force in 1969. The Community was not originally a party but a new Agreement was drawn up in 1983 incorporating provisions for the Community to sign and ratify, and the Community is now a party (see also Section 4.16).

Convention for the Prevention of Marine Pollution by Dumping from Ships and Aircraft (Oslo Convention)

COM(78)744	Proposal for a Decision to negotiate accession of the Community to the Convention.

The Convention was drawn up in 1972 and came into force in 1974. It covers the same area as that in the Paris Convention (North East Atlantic). The signatories were those countries with coasts on the area concerned. They undertook to stop dumping certain materials as listed in Annex I and only allow dumping of materials in Annex II with a specific permit. The Commission sits as an observer but the Community is not a party.

Convention for the Protection of the Mediterranean Sea against Pollution (Barcelona Convention)

77/585/EEC (OJ L240 19.9.77)	Decision on concluding the Convention and Protocol on dumping from ships and aircraft.
81/420/EEC (OJ L162 19.6.81)	Decision on concluding the Protocol on cooperation in combatting pollution from oil and other harmful substances.
83/101/EEC (OJ L67 12.3.83)	Decision concluding the Protocol on pollution from land-based sources.
84/132/EEC (OJ L68 10.3.84)	Decision concluding the Protocol on Specially Protected Areas.

Under the United Nations' Environment Programme countries bordering the Mediterranean met in Barcelona in 1975 to draw up a programme of action to protect the Mediterranean although preparatory work had already been done by other international organisations. The UK is not a party though Gibraltar is located in the region concerned.

Convention for the Protection and Development of the Marine Environment of the Wider Caribbean Region (Cartagena Convention)

COM(83)733 (OJ C5 10.1.84)	Proposal for a Decision signing the Protocol and concluding the Convention.

The Convention was drawn up to take similar measures as for the Barcelona Convention in respect of the wider Caribbean region and was opened for signature in 1983. An associated Protocol deals with oil spills. The Convention has been signed and ratified by three Member States, namely France, Netherlands and UK. The Community signed the Convention but has not yet ratified it.

Convention on the Prevention of Marine Environment of the Baltic Sea Area (Helsinki Convention)

COM(77)48	Proposal for a Decision to negotiate the Convention.

The Convention was adopted by the seven countries bordering the Baltic Sea in 1980. Parties undertook to control and restrict discharge of harmful substances into the area, by preventing pollution from land-based sources, dumping and exploitation of the seabed. Though authority was given to the Commission to enter into negotiations for Community accession, no agreement was reached and the Community is not a party.

Atmosphere

Convention on Long-range Transboundary Air Pollution (Geneva Convention)

81/462/EEC (OJ L171 27.6.81)	Decision concluding the Convention.
86/277/EEC (OJ L181 4.7.86)	Decision concluding the Protocol on financing the programme for monitoring and evaluation (EMEP).

This Convention was drawn up under the auspices of the United Nations' Economic Commission for Europe (ECE) and is open for accession by members of ECE and regional economic integration organizations. Its aim is to protect man and his environment against air pollution and to limit and gradually reduce such pollution including transboundary air pollution. It provides for exchange of information, research and monitoring and development of policies to combat the discharge of air pollutants. It was adopted in 1979 and came into force in 1983.

The Commission represented the Community in accordance with the instructions given by the Council and the Community signed with other Member States of the Community.

A Protocol provides for funding the Monitoring and Evaluation Programme (EMEP) to cover the costs of the international centres taking part in the programme. Another Protocol signed at Helsinki requires parties to reduce their emissions or transboundary fluxes of sulphur dioxide by 30 per cent by 1993 taking 1980 as a base. Parties to the Protocol are known as the '30 per cent club'. The UK is not a party to the Helsinki Protocol but is a party to the EMEP Protocol. The Commission has proposed that the Community should become a party to the Helsinki Protocol (COM(87)67).

Convention for the Protection of the Ozone Layer (Vienna Convention)

COM(85)644	Proposal for a Decision concluding the Convention.

The Convention was opened for signature in 1985 and was signed by the Commission on behalf of the Community on 22 March 1985. It is the first global Convention concerned with the atmosphere. A Protocol is now being negotiated to reduce emission of chlorofluorocarbons (see Section 7.4).

Wildlife and Countryside

Convention on Wetlands of International Importances especially as Waterfowl Habitat (Ramsar Convention)

75/66/EEC (OJ L21 28.1.75)	Commission Recommendation that Member States accede to the Convention.

The Convention aims to stem the progressive encroachment on and loss of wetlands. Parties undertake to designate at least one national wetland and to establish wetland reserves. The Convention was adopted in 1971 and came into force in 1975. The UK ratified in 1976. The Community is not a party.

Convention on International Trade in Endangered Species (Washington Convention) (usually known as CITES)

Regulation 3626/82 (OJ L384 13.12.82)	Regulation on implementation in the Community of the Convention.

The Community is not a party although an amendment to the Convention has been agreed which, when ratified by the necessary number of parties, will enable the Community to become a party. See Section 8.4 for a discussion of this Regulation.

Convention on the Conservation of Antarctic Marine Living Resources (Canberra Convention)

81/691/EEC (OJ L252 5.9.81)	Decision on conclusion of the Convention.

The Convention was drawn up in May 1980 and seeks to control the harvesting of marine living resources in the Antarctic, particularly krill.

Convention on the Conservation of European Wildlife and Natural Habitats (Berne Convention)

82/72/EEC (OJ L38 10.2.82)	Decision on conclusion of the Convention.

The Convention – drawn up by the Council of Europe in September 1979 – seeks to conserve wild flora and fauna in their natural habitats, particularly endangered species, especially when conservation requires the cooperation of several states.

Convention on the Conservation of Migratory Species of Wild Animals (Bonn Convention)

82/461/EEC (OJ L210 19.7.82)	Decision on conclusion of the Convention.

The underlying principle of this Convention, drawn up in June 1979, is that states within whose borders there are threatened populations of migratory species should take concerted action to ensure appropriate conservation and management.

References

1   United Nations Environment Programme, May 1985 *Register of international treaties and other agreements in the field of the environment.* Nairobi.

2   Burhenne W (ed) 1974 *International environmental law – multi-lateral treaties* (four volumes, loose leaf) (Beitrage zur Umweltgestaltung B7) Erich Schmidt Verlag, Berlin.

3   Lyster S 1985 *International wildlife law.* Grotius Publications.

POSTSCRIPT – AUGUST 1990

The Single European Act amending the Treaty of Rome came into effect on 1st July 1987. As well as setting the target date of the end of 1992 for the completion of the EC's internal market it has altered the EC's decision making process so that more decisions can be taken by majority voting in the Council. This increases the likelihood that barriers to the internal market will indeed be removed. Among other matters, the Act has provided a firm legal base for the EC's environmental policy.

The heightened interest in the EC generated by '1992' and the Act, coupled with increasing attention to the environment shown not least by world leaders as a result of concern over acid rain, the ozone layer and global warming, has greatly increased the importance of EC environmental policy. Fortunately this has co-incided with some successes for the EC. The adoption of a Directive to deal with the acid rain issue after five years of heated argument, and the role the EC has played in dealing with the ozone layer, have created confidence in the EC's ability to contribute solutions to the major environmental issues that confront Europe. The test will now be whether it can contribute to countering global warming.

'1992' will bring its own problems for the environment, not least in the poorer regions of the EC, and these have been discussed elsewhere[1]. In dealing with these, the principle enshrined in the Single European Act that 'environmental protection requirements shall be a component of the Community's other policies' will be of the greatest importance.

The changes in the EC decision making procedure have already been used with startling results in the environmental field. The European Parliament, with the support of the Commission, used the so called 'cooperation procedure' to overrule the Council so that small cars will now have to be fitted with catalytic converters (see Section 6.7 below). The many other new items of EC legislation are discussed below.

In Britain environmental protection has also advanced up the agenda of politicians and a long overdue reform of legislation is under way, often under the influence of EC legislation. The Water Act 1989 and the Environmental Protection Bill currently before Parliament will together make the following significant changes among others:

- The hand of central government is strengthened by giving Ministers powers to set standards for emissions, environmental quality and drinking water in Regulations and to make binding plans for achieving improvements. EC legislation has provided a major pressure for this.
- Previously the water authorities were both dischargers and regulators, and county councils both managed waste disposal sites and regulated them. Regulators and regulated are now being separated.
- National environmental agencies are being created and strengthened. The National Rivers Authority (NRA) is new, and the powers of Her Majesty's Inspectorate of Pollution (HMIP) are being extended and defined more precisely.
- A duty of care to take reasonable measures in connection with waste is

being placed on producers, importers, carriers and persons who treat waste. Breach of the duty will be an offence.

–   Controls over the generation and discharge of wastes from the most polluting plants are to be subject to 'integrated pollution control'. HMIP will now grant a single written authorisation covering discharges to air and water and concerning the generation of waste with the objective of minimising impact on the environment overall. Integrated pollution control (IPC) should concentrate the minds of industrialists on waste minimisation. The development of IPC has been described elsewhere[2].

–   More information on the environment and on drinking water will be publicly available in registers.

A government White Paper outlining further policies for the environment is expected in the autumn of 1990.

The addendum to Appendix I lists the items of EC environmental legislation adopted since the manuscript of this second edition was completed three years ago. In addition, a number of specific steps have been taken in Britain to implement EC legislation. The following brief summary covers only the most important developments under the existing chapter headings. EC proposals that have not been agreed are not discussed.

Chapter 4   Water

4.0   *Relevant British legislation*
The Water Act 1989 allowed privatisation of the drinking water supply and sewerage functions of the ten regional water authorities in England and Wales and created a National Rivers Authority (NRA) to be responsible for pollution control. The Act for the first time gives the Secretary of State powers to make Regulations setting water quality standards and these are now being used to implement EC Directives. A Drinking Water Inspectorate has been established under the Act and the Secretary of State has made Regulations prescribing the quality of drinking water.

The NRA is now the competent authority for authorising all discharges to water. However, discharges from the most polluting plants – which include those which discharge the most dangerous substances to water – will be prescribed for the purposes of integrated pollution control under the Environmental Protection Bill. The Bill will require discharges from these plants to all environmental media to be authorised by HM Inspectorate of Pollution (HMIP), although their authorisations will include any conditions required by the NRA to safeguard the water environment. Authorisations under IPC will be based on best available techniques not entailing excessive cost. The Secretary of State will have powers to give directions to HMIP on particular authorisations and to set emission standards in Regulations.

4.2   *Surface water for drinking*
The Surface Waters (Classification) Regulations (SI 1989 No 1148) now prescribe a classification system in accordance with the Directive.

4.4   *Drinking water*

The Water Act has entirely changed the way this Directive has been formally implemented. The Water Supply (Water Quality) Regulations (SI 1989 No 1147 as amended by SI 1989 1384) set statutory limits for the first time in the UK. They also reflect the government's acceptance in late 1987 of the Commission's interpretation that the Maximum Admissible Concentrations (MACs) set in the Directive are absolute and that every sample has to meet them rather than an average of samples over time. As a result, the costs of complying with the Directive have been raised substantially.

DoE Circular 20/89 gives advice to local authorities on their responsibilities for private water supplies among other matters. The DoE has also published a booklet called *Guidance on Safeguarding the Quality of Public Water Supplies* which will be used as a reference by the Drinking Water Inspectorate.

In October 1989 the Commission began an action in the European Court against the UK referring to 29 supply zones in England where the MAC for nitrates is exceeded and 17 zones in Scotland where the MAC for lead is exceeded.

4.7   *Bathing water*

There are now 440 identified bathing waters, of which 76 per cent met the EC standards in 1989. In October 1989 the government announced an investment programme of £1.4 billion to achieve 95 per cent compliance by the mid 1990s and full compliance within ten years. This was to involve the construction of long sea outfalls. In March 1990 the government announced a further investment programme of £1.5 billion so that all significant discharges should be treated at sewage works before discharge. The Commission has nevertheless started infringement proceedings relating to the failure of certain waters to meet the standards.

4.8 and 4.10 to 4.14   *Dangerous substances*

Directive 88/347 is another 'daughter' of Directive 76/464. It sets standards for the 'drins' pesticides, chloroform, HCB, and HCBD.

DoE Circular 18/85 has been replaced by DoE Circular 7/89. The Surface Waters (Dangerous Substances) (Classification) Regulations (SI 1989 No 2286) set quality standards which reflect the standards in the Directives. The Trade Effluents (Prescribed Processes and Substances) Regulations (SI 1989 No 1156 as amended by SI 1990 No 1629) enable the Secretary of State to control discharges to sewers of the dangerous substances in these Directives.

4.9   *Groundwater*

Following a complaint about leachate migration from a waste disposal site, the Commission alleged that the UK was failing to comply with this Directive. As a result the DoE is proposing to supplement Circular 4/82 with a new circular. The DoE proposes a more specific procedure for determining which substances belong to List I and List II. This may result in significant changes in the substances allowed to be disposed in landfill sites or discharged through soakaways.

4.15   *Titanium dioxide*

The 'harmonising' Directive 89/428 was adopted by the Council unanimously, although the Commission has now taken the Council to the Court on the grounds that the Directive should have been adopted by majority vote under Article 100A. The government abandoned its opposition to the uniform discharge reduction approach and discharges are to be reduced significantly.

Chapter 5   Waste

5.0   *Relevant British legislation*

At present waste disposal authorities (usually county councils) not only manage waste disposal sites but also regulate them by granting and policing waste disposal licences. The Environmental Protection Bill will separate these functions. Waste regulation authorities will be responsible for regulation, waste disposal authorities will arrange for disposal, but disposal can only be done by arrangement with other persons. Waste disposal licences are now to be known as waste management licences, and the Secretary of State will have powers to specify or prohibit licence conditions. A duty of care to take reasonable measures in connection with waste will be placed on producers, importers, holders, carriers and persons who treat waste, and breach of the duty will be an offence. Waste collection authorities will have to draw up waste recycling plans and waste disposal authorities will be able to make arrangements for the production of heat and electricity from waste.

The Control of Pollution (Amendment) Act 1989, introduced as a Private Member's Bill, will require waste carriers to be registered with a Waste Disposal Authority.

Resolution on waste strategy

In May 1990 the Council adopted a Resolution (OJ C 122, 18.05.90) on waste policy referring to a waste management strategy drafted by the Commission. The Resolution supports waste minimisation through the use of clean technology and clean products and the maximum possible use of recycling. For unavoidable waste arisings, it calls for pre-treatment and high environmental standards for final disposal. The Resolution also refers to the desirability of the EC, and the Member States individually, aiming for self-sufficiency in waste disposal and calls for an adequate network of disposal facilities.

5.1   *Waste – framework Directive*

The Council adopted a common position on an amending Directive in June 1990 (not yet published). It places greater emphasis on recycling and the development of clean technologies and encourages Member States to become self-sufficient in waste handling facilities.

In Britain 15 waste disposal authorities failed to meet a government deadline of October 1989 for preparing waste disposal plans. The Environmental Protection Bill will give the Secretary of State power to prescribe the timing and content of waste disposal plans.

In September 1989 the Commission published a report – SEC(89)1455 – on the formal implementation in the Member States of four waste Directives (see Sections 5.1, 5.2, 5.3 and 5.4) which concluded that all Member States except Belgium had adopted the key provisions of the four Directives – a view not consistent with that expressed in this book at least in respect of the waste oil Directive.

5.3   *Transfrontier shipment of toxic waste*

The long overdue Transfrontier Shipment of Hazardous Waste Regulations (SI 1988 No 1562) came into effect in 1988 and the DoE published a Circular 16/89 giving advice.

Policy on transfrontier shipment will change as a result of the Basle Convention to control the transport and disposal of hazardous waste that was agreed in March 1989. The UK is a signatory but the Member States, and the EC, cannot ratify the Convention until the transfrontier shipment Directive is amended. The Commission is preparing a proposal for a Regulation to do this.

5.7   Sewage sludge
The Sludge (Use in Agriculture) Regulations (SI 1989 No 1263 as amended by SI 1990 No 880) now implement the Directive. The DoE in 1989 published a *Code of Practice for Agricultural Use of Sewage Sludge* recommending action going beyond the Regulations.

Chapter 6   Air

6.0   *Relevant British legislation*
The Environmental Protection Bill will introduce the most radical overhaul of British air pollution legislation since 1874. The Secretary of State will be able to prescribe processes as subject to central or local control, and these will require written authorisation. About 5000 of the most polluting plants in England and Wales will be subject to central control and about 27 000 subject to local control. For processes subject to central control a single authorisation will be given by HMIP covering emission to air and water and the generation of waste with the objective of minimising the pollution of the environment taken as a whole. This is called integrated pollution control. The old phrase 'best practicable means' is replaced by the phrase taken from an EC Directive (see Section 6.8) 'best available technology not entailing excessive cost' (BATNEEC). The Secretary of State is given powers to give directions to HMIP, to set emission limits and environmental quality standards, and to make plans setting limits on the total amount of any substance which may be released.

Local authorities will for the first time give prior written authorisation for the prescribed plants under their control.

6.1   *Sulphur content of gas oil*
The Oil Fuel (Sulphur Content of Gas Oil) Regulations (SI 1990 No 1096) and the Motor Fuel (Sulphur Content of Gas Oil) Regulations (SI 1990 No 1097) replace the earlier Regulations and limit the sulphur content to 0.3 per cent.

6.2   *Air quality – smoke and sulphur dioxide*
The Air Quality Standards Regulations (SI 1989 No 317) make mandatory the air quality standards for smoke and sulphur dioxide, nitrogen dioxide and lead set in the three Directives (see also Sections 6.3 and 6.4). The discussion as to whether any of these Directives were previously adequately implemented by administrative means has now become of academic interest only.

Seven areas exceeded the limit values in 1987/88, including one area – Easington – for which a derogation had not been given, but only three areas breached the limits in 1988/89. In May 1989 the Commission announced its intention to begin infringement proceedings because of slow progress with improvement measures in Sunderland.

Directive 89/427 amends the measurement provisions for the gravimetric method used in Germany, Italy and Denmark.

6.3   Air quality – nitrogen dioxide

SI 1989 No 317 (see Section 6.2 above) made the standards mandatory.

The question of kerbside levels has attracted attention. A survey by London Scientific Services showed that 18 out of 65 sites monitored in 1988 recorded levels above the limit value, all close to busy roads. The two Directive monitoring sites in London recorded levels above the guide value but below the limit value. The Minister, William Waldegrave, stated in April 1987 that kerbside areas were 'not considered relevant for monitoring with regard to the Directive' as the general public spend only a limited amount of time there. The Commission is examining the issue of monitoring sites in accordance with Annex III of the Directive, following a complaint.

6.4   Air quality – lead

SI 1989 No 317 (see Section 6.2 above) made the standards mandatory. An area around the Walsall works had a derogation from the limit value until December 1989.

The Commission's first report on implementation appeared in January 1990 and concluded that there were few problems in meeting the directive's limit values except in some traffic and industrial 'hot spots'.

6.5   Lead in petrol

Sales of unleaded petrol increased following the introduction of a tax differential. Unleaded petrol became available at more than 80 per cent of petrol stations during 1989. No legislation was introduced for the purpose of banning leaded 'regular' petrol under Directive 87/416, but a tax differential introduced in the 1989 Budget made it more expensive and caused its withdrawal from the market.

6.7   Emissions from vehicles

Directive 88/76 was agreed with the standards set out in Table 11 (page 223). It is the first environmental Directive to have been agreed by majority voting under the provisions of the Single European Act. The second stage standards for small cars proved contentious and the outcome was dramatically influenced by the Parliament's use of the 'cooperation procedure' introduced by the Single European Act. The Council in 1988 had adopted a 'common position' on standards which would not have made catalytic converters obligatory. In April 1989 the Parliament amended the proposal at 'second reading' and, based on this amendment, the Commission revised its proposal effectively to make three way catalytic converters obligatory. This could only be changed back to the 'common position' by unanimity in Council, which was not forthcoming, and in June the Council adopted the more stringent standards (19 g/test for CO, 5 g/test for HC and NO_x) in Directive 89/458.

Directive 89/491 made minor amendments to Directive 70/220 and others with regard to the composition of fuel and to take account of the requirements of unleaded petrol. Directives 88/77 and 88/436 set standards for diesel vehicles.

The Road Vehicles (Construction and Use) (Amendment No 2) Regulations (SI 1990 No 1131) now implement many of the Directives.

6.8   *Emissions from industrial plant*

Long overdue interim Regulations have been made to implement this Directive which will be replaced when the Environmental Protection Bill is in force. These are the Health and Safety (Emissions into the Atmosphere) (Amendment) Regulations (SI 1989 No 319) and the Control of Industrial Air Pollution (Registration of Works) Regulations (SI 1989 No 318).

Large combustion plant

A substantial EC response to the acid rain problem was made when Directive 88/609 was finally adopted in November 1988. New plant must meet the emission limits laid down for sulphur dioxide, nitrogen oxides and dust based on best available technology not entailing excessive cost (BATNEEC). Emissions from existing plant must be reduced in three stages amounting to an overall EC reduction of sulphur dioxide of 58 per cent by the year 2003 compared to 1980. Different reductions have been agreed for different countries and the British reductions of SO_2 are 20 per cent, 40 per cent and 60 per cent by 1993, 1998 and 2003 respectively.

Member States are to draw up national plans showing how these reductions are to be met. The British plans will be published under powers contained in the Environmental Protection Bill.

Municipal waste incinerators

Emission standards for new and existing municipal waste incinerators are set in Directives 89/369 and 89/429. New incinerators are those authorised after 1st December 1990. Existing incinerators with a capacity of more than six tonnes per hour are to meet the standards for new incinerators by 1st December 1996. Others are to meet specified standards by 1st December 1995.

Chapter 7   Chemicals

7.1   *Preventing risks by testing*

Directive 87/42 (eighth adaptation) amends Annex I and was implemented by SI 1989 No 2208 which amended the previous Classification, Packaging and Labelling of Dangerous Substances Regulations. Directives 88/302 (ninth adaptation) and 88/490 (tenth adaptation) amend Annexes I, V and VI. The *European Inventory of Existing Chemical Substances* (EINECS) was published in June 1990 listing over 100 000 chemicals.

Directive 88/320 lays down procedures for a uniform system of inspection of laboratories carrying out tests on chemicals and Directive 90/18 amended it to refer to an OECD decision on the subject.

Dangerous preparations

Directive 88/379 complements the sixth amendment (see Section 7.1) by introducing testing, marketing and labelling requirements for preparations ie combinations of substances. Minor amendments on packaging and labelling were introduced by Commission Directives 89/178 and 90/35.

7.2   Restrictions on marketing and use

Directive 89/677 (eighth amendment) adds several substances to the Annex. Lead carbons and lead sulphates in paints are banned, although their use may be authorised for the restoration of works of art and historic buildings. The use of arsenic and mercury compounds in anti-fouling, wood preservative and biocidal preparations is banned, as too are organotin compounds used on boats of less than 25 metres in length. Other substances are also restricted. Directive 89/678 provides for adaptation of the annex of 76/769 to technical progress to be made by the Commission in consultation with the expert committee established by Directive 67/548 (see Section 7.1).

7.3   Major accident hazards (the 'Seveso' Directive)

Following the spill into the Rhine from the Sandoz plant at Basle a second amending Directive 88/610 was adopted. It increases the number of warehouses ('isolated storage') subject to the Directive and increases and clarifies the information to be made available to the public.

CIMAH (Amendment) Regulation (SI 1988 No 146) now implements the first amending Directive 87/216 and new Regulations have been proposed to implement Directive 88/610.

7.4   Chlorofluorocarbons (the ozone layer)

A protocol to the Vienna Convention adopted in Montreal in September 1987 was ratified by the EC in December 1988. Regulation 3322/88 implements the Montreal protocol throughout the EC by requiring manufacturers to cut production of CFCs by 50 per cent by the end of the century. Without this Regulation many Member States could not have ratified the Protocol in time. Commission Decisions 89/419 and 90/349 allocate import quotas to importers of CFCs and halons into the EC.

In June 1990 in London the parties to the Protocol adopted an amendment which, among other matters, will require a complete phase out of CFCs by the year 2000. The EC is expected to bring this date forward to 1997.

7.5   Pesticide residues

The first statutory maximum residue levels were introduced in the UK by the Pesticides (Maximum Residue Levels in Food) Regulation (SI 1988 No 1378) to implement Directives 86/362 and 86/363. Minor amendments to the annexes of Directives 86/362 and 76/895 were made by Directives 88/298 and 89/186.

7.6   Pesticides: use restrictions and labelling

Directive 89/365 extended the expiry of the derogation for two uses of ethylene oxide by one year. The Preservatives in Food Regulations (SI 1989 No 533) were amended accordingly by SI 1989 No 2287. Some of the derogations were deleted from the annex to Directive 79/117 by Commission Directives 87/477 and 90/335.

7.7   Worker protection

Directive 88/642 amends Directive 80/1107 by allowing substances to be added to the Annexes. Directive 88/364 bans four substances. Directive 90/394 deals with carcinogens.

7.8   *Paints and solvents*
The threshold above which paints and varnish containing lead are required to carry labelling warnings was lowered from 0.25 per cent to 0.15 per cent lead by weight by Directive 89/451.

7.9   *Asbestos*
The Control of Asbestos in the Air Regulations (SI 1990 No 556) require the prevention of 'significant environmental pollution' and set the 0.1 mg/m³ limit for emissions to air. The Directive's provisions for water are replicated in DoE Circular 7/89 (see Section 4.8). The Trade Effluents (Prescribed Processes and Substances) Regulations (SI 1989 No 1156) require consents for discharges to sewer to be referred to HMIP. Other provisions, including those on the packaging and labelling of asbestos waste, are contained in the Control of Asbestos at Work Regulations (SI 1987 No 2115).

Export of chemicals
Trade in dangerous chemicals into and out of the EC is controlled by Regulation 1734/88. Before any of a list of 21 chemicals is exported the authority in the country of import is to be informed. This is a weakened version of the proposal for 'prior informed consent' put forward by the Commission. Use of all the 21 chemicals listed is already restricted within the EC by the Directives described in Sections 7.2 and 7.6.

Genetically modified organisms
Directive 90/220 controls the deliberate release into the environment of genetically modified organisms (GMOs). It requires Member States to take measures 'to avoid adverse effects on human health and the environment' and establishes a notification and consent system for releases. Directive 90/219 applies similar requirements to the contained use of GMOs, imposing stricter conditions for more potentially dangerous GMOs and for larger-scale, commercial uses.

The Genetic Manipulation Regulations (SI 1989 No 1810) require notifications to be made to the HSE but the main provisions of the Directives are likely to be implemented under Part VI of the Environmental Protection Bill.

Chapter 8   Wildlife and countryside

8.3   *Seals*
Directive 89/370 has made the import ban permanent.

8.4   *Trade in endangered species (CITES)*
Regulation 197/90 incorporates the amendments to the Appendices to the CITES agreed at a conference in Lausanne in 1989 including a ban on the import of raw and worked ivory from the African elephant previously introduced in Regulation 2496/89. The Appendices are also amended by four other Regulations.

Agriculture – set-aside
Regulation 1094/88 requires Member States to introduce schemes to encourage farmers to set aside at least 20 per cent of their arable land. Land set aside must be left fallow, wooded or used for non-agricultural purposes. The British scheme began in September 1988 and in the first two years farmers agreed to withdraw about 110 000 hectares from production.

Forestry action programme
A large number of Regulations have been adopted to form a Community Forestry Action Programme 1989–92.

Chapter 9   Noise

9.2   *Motorcycles*
The Road Vehicles (Construction and Use) (Amendment) (No 3) Regulations (SI 1989 No 1865) made compulsory the first stage reductions set in Directive 87/56. Directive 89/235 amends Directive 78/1015 and enables Member States to ban the marketing and use of replacement silencers. It was influenced by the Motor Cycle Noise Act 1987.

9.5   *Aircraft*
Directive 89/629 further tightens the standards for aircraft noise.

9.7   *Noise in the workplace*
The Noise at Work Regulations (SI 1989 No 1790) now implement Directive 86/188.

9.8   *Household appliances*
The Household Appliances (Noise Emissions) Regulations (SI 1990 No 161) implement Directive 86/594.

Chapter 10   Assessment, information and finance

10.1   *Environmental impact assessment*
A whole series of Regulations have been made to implement the Directive. The Town and Country Planning (Assessment of Environmental Effects) Regulations (SI 1988 No 1199) deal with developments requiring planning permission and DoE Circular 15/88 explains them. An advisory booklet produced in November 1989 by DoE called *Environmental Assessment: A guide to the proce-*

dures lists all the Regulations that had then been introduced. In the first year that the Directive was implemented, over 100 environmental statements were submitted by developers. These were of uneven quality.

10.2   *Information on the state of the environment (CORINE)*
The Commission submitted a half term report to the Council and Parliament in July 1988 – COM(88)420. By Decision 90/150 the four year work programme was extended to six years and the cost increased from 4 to 10.5 million ECU. CORINE is now to be subsumed in the tasks of the European Environment Agency (see below).

10.3   *Finance (ACE)*
The embryonic 'environment fund' known as ACE expired in 1987 but has been continued and extended in scope by Regulation 2242/87. A sum of 24 million ECU is now available for six categories of projects over four years. The Commission published a report in July 1990 – COM(90)342.

European Environment Agency
'The European Environment Agency and the European environment information and observation network' is established by Regulation 1210/90 to provide the EC and Member States with 'objective, reliable and comparable information at European level' as a basis for environmental protection measures, to assess the results of such measures, and 'to ensure that the public is properly informed about the state of the environment'. It is not intended to be an enforcement agency. The Regulation comes into force when the seat of the Agency has been decided.

Freedom of access to information on the environment
Directive 90/313 will oblige all public authorities holding information on the environment to make it available on request, subject to certain exclusions. Member States are also to provide 'general information to the public on the state of environment by such means as the periodic publication of descriptive reports'.

References
1   Haigh N and Baldock D 1989 *Environmental Policy and 1992*. Institute for European Environmental Policy.
2   Irwin F and Haigh N (eds) 1990 *Integrated Pollution Control in Europe and North America*. The Conservation Foundation and Institute for European Environmental Policy.

APPENDIX I

Chronological list of Directives, Decisions and Regulations

All items mentioned in this book are listed below even when they have been repealed and even when they are referred to only incidentally and are not the main subject of the relevant section. All items are Directives unless marked with an R (Regulation) or D (Decision).

No		Official Journal Ref.		Section	Section Heading
1967					
67/548	L196	16.08.67		7.1	Preventing risks by testing
1969					
69/81	L 68	19.3.69		7.1	Preventing risks by testing
1970					
70/157	L 42	23.02.70		9.1	Cars, buses and lorries (noise)
70/189	L 59	14.03.70		7.1	Preventing risks by testing
70/220	L 76	06.04.70		6.7	Emissions from vehicles
R729/70	L 94	28.04.70		8.6	Countryside protection in agriculturally less favoured areas
1971					
71/144	L 74	29.03.71		7.1	Preventing risks by testing
1972					
72/159	L 96	23.04.72		8.5	Environmentally sensitive areas
72/161	L 96	23.04.72		8.5	Environmentally sensitive areas
72/306	L190	20.08.72		6.7	Emissions from vehicles
1973					
73/146	L167	25.06.73		7.1	Preventing risks by testing
73/173	L189	11.07.73		7.8	Paints and solvents
73/350	L321	22.11.73		9.1	Cars, buses and lorries (noise)
73/404	L347	17.12.73		4.1	Detergents
73/405	L347	17.12.73		4.1	Detergents
1974					
74/63	L 38	11.02.74		3	Approaches to pollution control
74/151	L 84	28.03.74		9.3	Tractors (noise)
74/290	L159	15.06.74		6.7	Emissions from vehicles

No		Official Journal Ref.	Section	Section Heading

1975

75/268	L128	19.05.75	8.6	Countryside protection in agriculturally less favoured areas
75/276	L128	19.05.75	8.6	Countryside protection in agriculturally less favoured areas
75/409	L183	14.07.75	7.1	Preventing risks by testing
D75/437	L194	25.07.75	11	International Conventions
D75/438	L194	25.07.75	11	International Conventions
75/439	L194	25.07.75	5.5	Waste oils
75/440	L194	25.07.75	4.2	Surface water for drinking
D75/441	L194	25.07.75	6.10	Exchange of information – air
75/442	L194	25.07.75	5.1	Waste – framework Directive
75/716	L307	27.11.75	6.1	Sulphur content of gas oil

1976

76/160	L 31	05.02.76	4.7	Bathing water
76/400	L108	26.04.76	8.6	Countryside protection in agriculturally less favoured areas
76/403	L108	26.04.76	5.4	Disposal of PCBs
76/464	L129	18.05.76	4.8	Dangerous substances in water
76/685	L231	21.08.76	8.6	Countryside protection in agriculturally less favoured areas
76/769	L262	27.09.76	7.2	Restrictions on marketing and use
76/895	L340	19.12.76	7.5	Pesticide residues
76/907	L360	30.12.76	7.1	Preventing risks by testing

1977

77/102	L 32	03.02.77	6.7	Emissions from vehicles
77/212	L 66	12.03.77	9.1	Cars, buses and lorries (noise)
77/311	L105	28.04.77	9.3	Tractors (noise)
77/312	L105	28.04.77	6.6	Screening for lead
77/537	L220	29.08.77	6.7	Emissions from vehicles
D77/585	L240	19.09.77	11	International Conventions
D77/586	L240	19.09.77	11	International Conventions
D77/651	L267	19.10.77	5.7	Sewage sludge
77/728	L303	28.11.77	7.8	Paints and solvents
D77/795	L334	24.12.77	4.17	Exchange of information – water

1978

78/176	L 54	25.02.78	4.15	Titanium dioxide
78/319	L 84	31.03.78	5.2	Toxic waste
78/611	L197	22.07.78	6.5	Lead in petrol
78/631	L206	29.07.78	7.6	Pesticides: use restrictions and labelling
78/659	L222	14.08.78	4.5	Water standards for freshwater fish

No	Official Journal Ref.		Section	Section Heading
78/665	L223	14.08.78	6.7	Emissions from vehicles
78/1015	L349	13.12.78	9.2	Motorcycles (noise)

1979

No	Official Journal Ref.		Section	Section Heading
79/113	L 33	08.02.79	9.4	Construction plant (noise)
79/117	L 33	08.02.79	7.6	Pesticides: use restrictions and labelling
73/370	L 88	07.04.79	7.1	Preventing risks by testing
79/409	L103	25.04.79	8.1	Birds and their habitats
79/530	L145	13.06.79	9.8	Household appliances (noise)
79/663	L197	03.08.79	7.2	Restrictions on marketing and use
79/831	L259	15.10.79	7.1	Preventing risks by testing
79/869	L271	29.10.79	4.3	Sampling surface water for drinking
79/923	L281	10.11.79	4.6	Shellfish waters

1980

No	Official Journal Ref.		Section	Section Heading
80/51	L 18	24.01.80	9.5	Aircraft (noise)
80/68	L 20	26.01.80	4.9	Groundwater
D80/372	L 90	03.04.80	7.4	Chlorofluorocarbons
80/428	L102	19.04.80	7.5	Pesticide residues
80/666	L180	14.07.80	8.6	Countryside protection in agriculturally less favoured areas
R1917/80	L186	19.07.80	8.2	Whales
D80/686	L188	22.07.80	4.16	Oil pollution at sea
80/777	L229	30.08.80	4.4	Drinking water
80/778	L229	30.08.80	4.4	Drinking water
80/779	L229	30.08.80	6.2	Air quality – smoke and sulphur dioxide
80/781	L229	30.08.80	7.8	Paints and solvents
80/1107	L327	03.12.80	7.7	Worker protection
80/1189	L366	31.12.80	7.1	Preventing risks by testing

1981

No	Official Journal Ref.		Section	Section Heading
R348/81	L 39	12.02.81	8.2	Whales
81/36	L 46	19.02.81	7.5	Pesticide residues
81/187	L 88	02.04.81	7.6	Pesticides: use restrictions and labelling
81/334	L131	18.05.81	9.1	Cars, buses and lorries (noise)
D81/420	L162	19.06.81	11	International Conventions
D81/437	L167	24.06.81	7.1	Preventing risks by testing
D81/462	L171	27.06.81	11	International Conventions
D81/691	L252	05.09.81	11	International Conventions
81/957	L351	07.12.81	7.1	Preventing risks by testing
D81/981	L355	10.12.81	4.16	Oil pollution at sea
81/1051	L376	30.12.81	9.4	Construction plant (noise)
R3786/81	L377	31.12.81	8.2	Whales

No	Official Journal Ref.		Section	Section Heading
1982				
D82/72	L 38	10.02.82	11	International Conventions
82/176	L 81	27.03.82	4.10	Mercury from chloralkali industry
82/232	L106	21.04.82	7.1	Preventing risks by testing
82/242	L109	22.04.82	4.1	Detergents
82/243	L109	22.04.82	4.1	Detergents
D82/459	L210	19.07.82	6.10	Exchange of information – air
D82/460	L210	19.07.82	11	International Conventions
D82/461	L210	19.07.82	11	International Conventions
82/473	L213	21.07.82	7.8	Paints and solvents
82/501	L230	05.08.82	7.3	Major accident hazards (Seveso)
82/528	L234	09.08.82	7.5	Pesticide residues
82/605	L247	23.08.82	7.7	Worker protection
82/656	L277	29.09.82	8.6	Countryside protection in agriculturally less favoured areas
82/786	L327	24.11.82	8.6	Countryside protection in agriculturally less favoured areas
D82/795	L329	25.11.82	7.4	Chlorofluorocarbons
82/806	L339	01.12.82	7.2	Restrictions on marketing and use
82/828	L350	10.12.82	7.2	Restrictions on marketing and use
82/883	L378	31.12.82	4.15	Titanium dioxide
82/884	L378	31.12.82	6.4	Air quality – lead
R3626/82	L384	31.12.82	8.4	Trade in endangered species
1983				
83/29	L 32	03.02.83	4.15	Titanium dioxide
D83/101	L 67	12.03.83	11	International Conventions
83/129	L 91	09.04.83	8.3	Seals
83/131	L 91	09.04.83	7.6	Pesticides: use restrictions and labelling
83/189	L109	26.04.83	9.8	Household appliances (noise)
83/206	L117	04.05.83	9.5	Aircraft (noise)
83/264	L147	06.06.83	7.2	Restrictions on marketing and use
83/265	L147	06.06.83	7.8	Paints and solvents
83/351	L197	20.07.83	6.7	Emissions from vehicles
83/467	L257	16.09.83	7.1	Preventing risks by testing
83/477	L263	24.09.83	7.7	Worker protection
83/478	L263	24.09.83	7.1	Restrictions on marketing and use
83/513	L291	24.10.83	4.12	Cadmium
R3418/83	L344	07.12.83	8.4	Trade in endangered species
R3645/83	L367	28.12.83	8.4	Trade in endangered species
R3646/83	L367	28.12.83	8.4	Trade in endangered species

No	Official Journal Ref.		Section	Section Heading

1984

R577/84	L 64	06.03.84	8.4	Trade in endangered species
D84/132	L 68	10.03.84	11	International Conventions
84/156	L 74	17.03.84	4.11	Mercury from other sources
84/169	L 82	26.03.84	8.6	Countryside protection in agriculturally less favoured areas
R1451/84	L140	26.05.84	8.4	Trade in endangered species
R1452/84	L140	26.05.84	8.4	Trade in endangered species
84/291	L144	30.05.84	7.6	Pesticides: use restrictions and labelling
R1872/84	L176	03.07.84	10.3	Finance (ACE)
D84/358	L188	16.07.84	11	International Conventions
84/360	L188	16.07.84	6.8	Emissions from industrial plants
84/372	L196	26.07.84	9.1	Cars, buses and lorries (noise)
84/422	L237	05.09.84	4.17	Exchange of information – water
84/424	L238	06.09.84	9.1	Cars, buses and lorries (noise)
84/449	L251	19.09.84	7.1	Preventing risks by testing
84/491	L274	17.10.84	4.13	Lindane
84/532	L300	19.11.84	9.4	Construction plant (noise)
84/533	L300	19.11.84	9.4	Construction plant (noise)
84/534	L300	19.11.84	9.4	Construction plant (noise)
84/535	L300	19.11.84	9.4	Construction plant (noise)
84/536	L300	19.11.84	9.4	Construction plant (noise)
84/537	L300	19.11.84	9.4	Construction plant (noise)
84/538	L300	19.11.84	9.6	Lawnmowers (noise)
84/631	L326	13.12.84	5.3	Transfrontier shipment of toxic waste

1985

D85/71	L 30	02.02.85	7.1	Preventing risks by testing
85/203	L 87	27.03.85	6.3	Air quality – nitrogen dioxide
D85/208	L 89	29.03.85	4.16	Oil pollution at sea
R797/85	L 93	30.03.85	8.5	Environmentally sensitive areas
85/210	L 96	03.04.85	6.5	Lead in petrol
85/298	L154	13.06.85	7.6	Pesticides: use restrictions and labelling
R1831/85	L173	03.07.85	8.4	Trade in endangered species
D85/336	L175	05.07.85	11	International Conventions
85/337	L175	05.07.85	10.1	Environmental impact assessment
D85/338	L176	05.07.85	10.2	Information on state of environment (CORINE)
85/339	L176	06.07.85	5.6	Containers for liquids
R2384/85	L231	29.08.85	8.4	Trade in endangered species
85/405	L233	30.08.85	9.4	Construction plant (noise)
85/406	L233	30.08.85	9.4	Construction plant (noise)
85/407	L233	30.08.85	9.4	Construction plant (noise)
85/408	L233	30.08.85	9.4	Construction plant (noise)

No	Official Journal Ref.		Section	Section Heading
85/409	L233	30.08.85	9.4	Construction plant (noise)
85/411	L233	30.08.85	8.1	Birds and their habitats
85/444	L259	01.10.85	8.3	Seals
85/467	L269	11.10.85	7.2	Restrictions on marketing and use
85/469	L272	12.10.85	5.3	Transfrontier shipment of toxic waste
85/536	L334	12.12.85	6.5	Lead in petrol
85/610	L375	31.12.85	7.2	Restrictions on marketing and use
D85/613	L375	31.12.85	4.12	Cadmium

1986

No	Official Journal Ref.		Section	Section Heading
D86/85	L 77	22.02.86	4.16	Oil pollution at sea
86/94	L 80	25.03.86	4.1	Detergents
86/188	L137	24.05.86	9.7	Noise in the workplace
86/214	L152	06.06.86	7.6	Pesticides: use restrictions and labelling
D86/277	L181	04.07.86	11	International Conventions
86/278	L181	04.07.86	5.7	Sewage sludge
86/279	L181	04.07.86	5.3	Transfrontier shipment of toxic waste
86/280	L181	04.07.86	4.14	DDT, carbon tetrachloride and pentachlorophenol
R2295/86	L201	24.07.86	8.4	Trade in endangered species
86/355	L212	02.08.86	7.6	Pesticides: use restrictions and labelling
86/362	L221	07.08.86	7.5	Pesticide residues
86/363	L221	07.08.86	7.5	Pesticide residues
86/431	L247	01.09.86	7.1	Preventing risks by testing
86/508	L295	18.10.86	7.8	Paints and solvents
R3528/86	L326	21.11.86	6.9	Monitoring of forest damage
R3529/86	L326	21.11.86	6.9	Monitoring of forest damage
D86/574	L335	28.11.86	4.17	Exchange of information – water
86/594	L344	06.12.86	9.8	Household appliances (noise)
86/609	L358	18.12.86	7.1	Preventing risks by testing
86/662	L384	31.12.86	9.4	Construction plant (noise)

1987 (to 30 June)

No	Official Journal Ref.		Section	Section Heading
87/18	L 15	17.01.87	7.1	Preventing risks by testing
87/56	L 24	27.01.87	9.2	Motorcycles (noise)
D87/57	L 24	27.01.87	11	International Conventions
87/101	L 42	12.02.87	5.5	Waste oils
87/112	L 48	17.02.87	5.3	Transfrontier shipment of toxic waste
R526/87	L 53	21.02.87	6.9	Monitoring of forest damage
D87/144	L 57	27.02.87	4.16	Oil pollution at sea

No	Official Journal Ref.		Section	Section Heading
87/181	L 71	14.03.87	7.6	Pesticides: use restrictions and labelling
87/216	L 85	28.03.87	7.3	Major accident hazards (Seveso)
87/217	L 85	28.03.87	7.9	Asbestos
87/219	L 91	03.04.87	6.1	Sulphur content of gas oil
87/252	L117	05.05.87	9.6	Lawnmowers (noise)
R1422/87	L136	26.05.87	8.4	Trade in endangered species
R1540/87	L147	06.06.87	8.4	Trade in endangered species
R1696/87	L161	22.06.87	6.9	Monitoring of forest damage
R1697/87	L161	22.06.87	6.9	Monitoring of forest damage
R1760/87	L167	26.06.87	8.5	Environmentally sensitive areas

ADDENDUM

1987 (July to 31 December)

R2242/87	L207	29.07.87	10.3	Finance (ACE)
87/405	L220	08.08.87	9.4	Construction plant (noise)
87/416	L225	13.08.87	6.5	Lead in petrol
87/432	L239	21.08.87	7.1	Preventing risks by testing
87/477	L273	26.09.87	7.6	Pesticides: use restrictions and labelling
R3143/87	L299	22.10.87	8.4	Trade in endangered species

1988

88/76	L 36	09.02.88	6.7	Emissions from vehicles
88/77	L 36	09.02.88	6.7	Emissions from vehicles
88/180	L 81	26.03.88	9.6	Lawnmowers (noise)
88/181	L 81	26.03.88	9.6	Lawnmowers (noise)
R869/88	L 87	31.03.88	8.4	Trade in endangered species
R1094/88	L106	27.04.88	8	Agriculture 'set-aside'
R1272/88	L121	11.05.88	8	Agriculture 'set-aside'
R1273/88	L121	11.05.88	8	Agriculture 'set-aside'
88/298	L126	20.05.88	7.5	Pesticide residues
88/302	L133	30.05.88	7.1	Preventing risks by testing
88/320	L145	11.06.88	7.1	Preventing risks by testing
R1734/88	L155	22.06.88	7	Export of chemicals
D88/346	L158	25.06.88	4.16	Oil pollution at sea
88/347	L158	25.06.88	4.14	Dangerous substances in water
88/364	L179	09.07.88	7.7	Worker protection
88/379	L187	16.07.88	7	Dangerous preparations
D88/381	L183	14.07.88	11	International Conventions
D88/382	L183	14.07.88	11	International Conventions
88/436	L214	06.08.88	6.7	Emissions from vehicles
88/490	L259	19.09.88	7.1	Preventing risks by testing
R3188/88	L285	19.10.88	8.4	Trade in endangered species
R3322/88	L297	31.10.88	7.4	Chlorofluorocarbons
D88/540	L297	31.10.88	11	International Conventions
88/609	L336	07.12.88	6.8	Large combustion plants
88/610	L336	07.12.88	7.3	Major accident hazards (Seveso)

No	Official Journal Ref.		Section	Section Heading
88/642	L356	24.12.88	7.7	Worker protection

1989

89/178	L 64	08.03.89	7	Dangerous preparations
R610/89	L 66	10.03.89	8.4	Trade in endangered species
89/186	L 66	10.03.89	7.5	Pesticide residues
89/235	L 98	11.04.89	9.2	Motorcycles (noise)
89/365	L159	10.06.89	7.6	Pesticides: use restrictions and labelling
89/369	L163	14.06.89	6	New municipal waste incinerators
89/370	L163	14.06.89	8.3	Seals
R1609/89–1615/89	L165	15.06.89	8	Forestry Action Programme
D89/419	L192	07.07.89	7.4	CFCs (import quotas)
89/427	L201	14.07.89	6.2	Air quality – smoke and sulphur dioxide
89/428	L201	14.07.89	4.15	Titanium dioxide
89/429	L203	15.07.89	6	Existing municipal waste incinerators
89/451	L216	27.07.89	7.8	Paints and solvents
89/458	L226	03.08.89	6.7	Vehicle emissions (small cars)
89/491	L238	15.08.89	6.7	Vehicle emissions
R2496/89	L240	17.08.89	8.4	Ivory imports
89/514	L253	30.08.89	9.4	Noise – construction plant
R2995/89	L287	05.10.89	6.9	Monitoring of forest damage
D89/569	L315	28.10.89	7.1	Good laboratory practice
89/629	L363	13.12.89	9.5	Aircraft (noise)
R3981/89	L380	29.12.89	8	Agriculture 'set-aside'
89/677	L398	30.12.89	7.2	Restrictions on marketing and use
89/678	L398	30.12.89	7.2	Restrictions on marketing and use

1990 (1 January to 31 August)

D90/2	L 1	04.01.90	4.17	Exchange of information – water
90/18	L 11	13.01.90	7.1	Preventing risks by testing
90/35	L 19	24.01.90	7	Dangerous preparations
R197/90	L 29	31.01.90	8.4	Trade in endangered species
D90/150	L 81	28.03.90	10.2	Information on state of environment (CORINE)
R752/90	L 83	30.03.90	8	Agriculture 'set-aside'
90/219	L117	08.05.90	7	Genetically modified organisms – contained use
90/220	L117	08.05.90	7	Genetically modified organisms – deliberate release
R1210/90	L120	11.05.90	10	European Environment Agency

No	Official Journal Ref.		Section	Section Heading
90/313	L158	23.06.90	10	Freedom of access to information
90/335	L162	28.06.90	7.6	Pesticides: use restrictions and labelling
D90/349	L171	04.07.90	7.4	CFCs (import quotas)
90/394	L196	26.07.90	7.7	Worker protection – carcinogens
90/415	L219	14.08.90	4	Dangerous substances in water
D90/420	L222	17.08.90	7.1	Preventing risks by testing